MEDIA ETHICS

Cases & Moral Reasoning

Fourth Edition

Clifford G. Christians
University of Illinois

Mark Fackler
Wheaton College

Kim B. Rotzoll
University of Illinois

Longman *Publishers USA*

Media Ethics: Cases and Moral Reasoning, Fourth Edition

Copyright © 1995 by Longman Publishers USA.
All rights reserved.
No part of this publication may be reproduced,
stored in a retrieval system, or transmitted
in any form or by any means, electronic, mechanical,
photocopying, recording, or otherwise,
without the prior permission of the publisher.

Longman, 10 Bank Street, White Plains, N.Y. 10606

Associated companies:
Longman Group Ltd., London
Longman Cheshire Pty., Melbourne
Longman Paul Pty., Auckland
Copp Clark Longman Ltd., Toronto

Executive editor: Pamela Gordon
Production editor: Linda Moser
Cover design: Lisa Delgado, Delgado Design
Production supervisor: Richard Bretan

Library of Congress Cataloging-in-Publication Data
Christians, Clifford G.
    Media ethics : cases and moral reasoning / Clifford Christians,
Mark Fackler, Kim Rotzoll.—4th ed.
        p. cm.
    Includes bibliographical references and index.
    ISBN 0-8013-1186-1
    1. Mass media—Moral and ethical aspects. I. Fackler, Mark.
II. Rotzoll, Kim, B.   III. Title.
P94.C45 1994
    170—dc20
                                                                94-26625
                                                                CIP

2 3 4 5 6 7 8 9 10-MA-98979695

Contents

CHAPTER 7 **WHAT TO ADVERTISE** 159

CHAPTER 8 **HOW TO SAY IT** 173

CHAPTER 9 **MEDIA CONSIDERATIONS** 191

CHAPTER 10 **MACRO ISSUES** 205

PART III   PERSUASION AND PUBLIC RELATIONS   223

CHAPTER 11 **CORPORATE PUBLIC RELATIONS** 225

Preface

Media ethics has been traveling a rough road at the junction of theory and practice. Occasionally textbooks will include an ethics chapter at the beginning but will not integrate it with the workaday problems that follow. Principle and practice do not merge well in such endeavors, nor in our daily actions. The rush of events forces us to make ethical decisions by reflex more than by reflection, like drivers wheeling around potholes, mindful that a blowout sends them into a courtroom at one ditch and into public scorn at the other.

Two different mindsets are involved; thus, it makes fusion difficult. The study of ethics requires deliberation, careful distinctions, and extended discussion. The newsroom tends to emphasize other virtues: toughness and the ability to make quick decisions in the face of daily crises. Advertising and public relations professionals are expected to be competitive and enterprising. Entertainment writers and producers value skepticism, confident independence, and hot blood. For the teaching of ethics to be worthwhile, the critical capacity must emerge; reasoning processes need to remain paramount. Yet executives of media firms value people of action, those who produce in a high-pressure environment. If media ethics is to gain recognition, the gap between daily media practice and the serious consideration of ethics must be bridged creatively.

Like the previous editions, this revision attempts to integrate ethics and media situations through case studies and commentaries. Communication is a practice-oriented field. Reporters for daily newspapers tend to work with episodes, typically pursuing one story after another as they happen. Advertisers ordinarily deal with accounts and design campaigns for specific products. Public relations professionals advocate a specific cause. Actors and writers move from program to program. Because communication is case oriented, media ethics would be uninteresting and abstract, unless it addressed practical experiences. However, media ethics ought to be more than a description of professional ethics. Therefore, in this book we will analyze cases and connect them with the ethical guidelines set forth in the Introduction. The reader will be prodded and stimulated to think ethically. Considering situations from a systematic framework advances our problem-solving capacity, which prevents us from treating each case independently or having to reinvent the wheel. The commentaries pinpoint some crucial issues and introduce enough salient material to aid in resolving the case responsibly. Much of the book's inspiration originally came from Robert Veatch's award-winning *Case Studies in Medical Ethics,* published in 1977 by the Harvard University Press. Veatch mixed his commentaries, and we have followed suit—raising questions for further reflection in some, introducing relevant ethical theories in others, and pushing toward closure where doing so seems appropriate.

All the cases are taken from actual experiences. In order to ensure anonymity and increase clarity, names and places are changed in many of them. Though our adjustments do not make these cases timeless, they help prevent them from becoming prematurely dated and shopworn. We attempted to find ongoing issues that occur often in ordinary media practice and did not select only exotic, once-in-a-lifetime encounters. In situations based on court records, or in a few instances of historic significance where real names aid in the analysis, the cases have not been modified.

As the integration of theory and practice in ethics is important, so is the integration of news with other aspects of the information system. The three sections of this book reflect the three major media functions: reporting, persuading, and entertaining. Since we want readers to do ethics rather than puzzle over their immediate experience, we have chosen a broad range of media situations. Many times when similar issues are encountered in several phases of the communication process, new insights can be gained and sharper perspectives result. As the cases-by-issue list in the Appendix indicates, deception, economic temptation, and sensationalism, for example, are common in reporting, advertising, public relations, and entertainment. The issue of how violence is handled can be explored in reporting as well as in entertainment. Stereotyping is deep seated and pervasive in every form of public communication; cases dealing with this issue occur in all three sections. Moreover, the wider spectrum of this book allows specialists in one medium—television, newspapers, or magazines, for example—to investigate that medium across all its uses. The cases-by-medium list in the Appendix organizes the cases according to the major division of media. Often practitioners of journalism, advertising, public relations, and entertainment are part of the same corporation and encounter other media areas indirectly in their work. As a matter of fact, the Supreme Court has specifically included all three media functions—information, persuasion, and entertainment—under First Amendment protection. The distinctions among them will continue to blur as convergent technologies and integration of the industry accelerate toward the twenty-first century.

The Potter Box is included in the Introduction as a technique for uncovering the important steps in moral reasoning. It is a model of social ethics, in harmony with our overall concern in this volume for social responsibility. It can be used for analyzing each case and reaching responsible conclusions. This book is intended for use as a classroom text or in workshops for professionals. We are especially eager to have communication educators and practitioners read and think their way through the book on their own. Whether using this volume as a text or for personal reading, the Introduction can be employed flexibly. Under normal circumstances we recommend that the Potter Box be studied first and the theoretical foundation given in the Introduction be considered thoroughly before readers proceed to the cases. However, readers can fruitfully start elsewhere in the book with a chapter of their choosing and return later to the Introduction for the theoretical perspective.

Whether used in an instructional setting or not, the book has two primary goals. First, it seeks to develop analytical skills. Ethical appraisals are often disputed; further training and study can improve the debate and help weaken rationalizations. Advancement in media ethics requires more attention to evidence, more skill in valid argument, and more patience with complexity. Without explicit procedures, as Edward R. Murrow reportedly complained: "What is called thinking is often merely a rearranging of our prejudices."

Second, this book aims to improve ethical awareness. Often the ethical dimension goes unrecognized. The authors are not content merely to exercise the intellect; they believe that the moral imagination must be stimulated until real human beings and their welfare become central. Surprising as it may seem, improving ethical awareness is in many ways more elusive than honing analytical skills. In stark cases, such as the Janet Cooke affair, we realize instantly the cheating and deception involved.* But often the ethical issues escape our notice. What about the abortion clinics in Case 7? The legal questions regarding entrapment are relatively clear, but what is unethical about using undercover strategies? Or naming a shoplifter, printing photographs of grieving parents whose children just died in a fire, writing about the sexual escapades of a senator, exposing a prominent right-to-lifer concealing an abortion, or revealing secret information about government policy that contradicts public statements? The ethical issues here are not always self-evident; thus actual and hypothetical cases become a primary tool for firing the moral imagination.

Improving analytical skills and raising moral sensitivity are lifelong endeavors that involve many facets of human behavior. Studied conscientiously, the terms, arguments, and principles introduced in these chapters may also improve the quality of discourse in the larger area of applied ethics. We trust that using the Potter Box model for the 78 cases in this volume will aid in building a conceptual apparatus that facilitates the growth of media ethics over time.

We are fully aware of the criticism from various areas of radical social science that ethics is a euphemism for playing mental games while the status quo remains intact. That criticism warrants more discussion than this preface permits, but it

---

* For a thoughtful analysis of this historic case, see Lewis H. Lapham, "Gilding the News," *Harper's,* July 1981, pp. 31–39.

should be noted that we find this charge too indiscriminate. Much of the current work in professional ethics is largely a matter of semantics and isolated incidents, but this volume does not belong to that class. The social ethics we advocate challenges the organizational structures. Many of the commentaries—and even entire chapters—probe directly into significant institutional issues. Certainly that is the cumulative effect also. Reading the volume through in its entirety brings into focus substantive questions about economics, management and bureaucracy, allocation of resources, the press's *raison d'être,* and distributive justice. We have employed the case and commentary format for its instructional benefits—it allows us to separate issues into their understandable dimensions without slipping into small problems of no consequence on the one hand, yet not encouraging a complete dissolution of the democratic order on the other.

We recognize also that today's crusading relativism is a formidable challenge to such efforts. Moral commitments are crumbling beneath our feet. Cultural diversity has hoodwinked us into ethical relativity. Divine command theories and metaphysical foundations for norms are problematic in a secular age on the far side of Darwin, Freud, and Einstein. Many academics believe truth claims are impossible after Jacques Derrida and Michel Foucault. In a world of sliding signifiers and normlessness, ethical principles seem to carry little resonance. Though this textbook is not an appropriate place for coming to grips with the complexities of relativism, we believe the idea of normative principles can be successfully defended in contemporary terms. For example, Chapter 6 of *Good News: Social Ethics and the Press* by Clifford Christians, John Ferré, and Mark Fackler (Oxford University Press, 1993) develops such a defense. Two other recent books construct normative models also: Edmund Lambeth's *Committed Journalism: An Ethic for the Profession* (Indiana University Press, 2d ed., 1992), and John C. Merrill's *The Dialectic in Journalism* (Louisiana State University Press, 1989). Deni Elliott has demonstrated in empirical terms that without shared values the practice of everyday journalism is impossible. In other words, while reporters and editors are pluralists, they are not relativists.[*]

Serious students will recognize that we maintain the traditional distinction between ethics and morality. Ethics we understand as the liberal arts discipline that appraises voluntary human conduct insofar as it can be judged right or wrong in reference to determinative principles. The original meaning of *eethos* (Greek) was "sent," "haunt," "abode," "accustomed dwelling place," that is, the place from which we start out, the "home base." From *eethos* is derived *eethikos*, meaning "of or for morals." In the Greek philosophical tradition this word came to stand for the systematic study of the principles that ought to underlie behavior.

On the other hand, morality is of Latin origin. The Latin noun *mos* (pl. *mores*) and the adjective *moralis* signify a way, manner, or customary behavior. The Romans had no word that is the exact equivalent of the Greek *eethos*. Unlike the Greeks, they paid less attention to the inner disposition, the hidden roots of

---

[*] Deni Elliott, "All Is Not Relative: Essential Shared Values and the Press," *Journal of Mass Media Ethics* 3:1 (1988), pp. 28-32.

conduct, the basic principles of behavior, than they did to its external pattern. This perspective is in accord with the Roman genius for order, arrangement, and organization and with its generally unphilosophical bent of mind. The Romans looked to the outside more than to the inside. The Latin *mores* has come into the English language without modification (meaning folkways, how people behave). However, in English usage, the ethics of a people are not the same as their morality. Morality refers to practice and ethics to a basic system of principles.

We incurred many debts while preparing this volume. The McCormick Foundation generously supported our research into ethical dilemmas among media professionals; many of the cases and the questions surrounding them emerged from this research. Ralph Potter encouraged our adaptation of his social ethics model. Louis Hodges wrote the initial drafts for the commentaries in Cases 2, 12, 18, 20, and 21 and read earlier editions of the Introduction and Part I. Richard Streckfuss prepared the first draft of Cases 2, 12, 14, 18, 20, and 21. David Craig wrote Case and commentary number 5, as David Protess did for number 7. Eve Munson wrote the initial drafts for numbers 4, 8, and 60, and gathered material for several more. Richard Craig wrote Case 23 and secured the original materials for the commentary. Robert Reid provided a detailed response to a previous version of the manuscript and spared us several inadequacies. James Haefner wrote the first draft of Cases 50–53 and 55–57. Dick Christian and Jim Fish appraised many of the advertising cases from the wealth of their practical experience, and many advertising practitioners, in a limited survey in 1989, provided insights into current ethical confrontations. Vinita Hampton compiled material for the entertainment cases. Christopher Hudson and Diane Kusemark assisted in editing the fourth edition. Jay Van Hook and John Ferré edited the Introduction along with other chapters. Diane Weddington recommended the Potter Box as the organizing idea and wrote the original draft applying it to communications. Several teachers, students, and professionals who have used the first three editions provided worthwhile suggestions that we have incorporated into this revision. The following individuals reviewed the manuscript and provided helpful suggestions.

Mary Helen Brown, Auburn University

Tim Gleason, University of Oregon

Margaret Haefner, Illinois State University

Larry Leslie, University of South Florida

Shawn W. Murphy, Oklahoma Panhandle State University

Richard Alan Nelson, Louisiana State University

Jon Rosenraad, University of Florida

Harold Shaver, Marshall University

Mindy S. Trossman, Northwestern University

Patrick Washburn, Ohio University

K. Tim Wulfemeyer, San Diego State University

The growing interest in public relations required that we expand our two chapters on that subject this time. We absolve these friends of all responsibility for the weaknesses that remain.

Clifford G. Christians

Mark Fackler

Kim B. Rotzoll

Introduction: Ethical Foundations and Perspectives

The true story out of Liverpool, England, was beyond belief. Two ten-year-old boys skipped school last February 12, went to a shopping mall, and spent the day stealing candy and soft drinks. They hung around a video store and shoplifted cans of modeling paint. In the autumn term Robert Thompson had missed 49 days of school and Jan Venables 40 days. February 12 was routine for them, until they carved out their diabolical plan. They lured a two-year-old child away from his mother, dragged and kicked him along a two-and-one-half-mile journey, stoned him with bricks, and smashed his head with a 22-pound iron bar. Police found Jason Bulger's half-naked body two days later. Thompson and Venables had tied the battered corpse to a railroad track, and a passing train had cut it in two. Forty-two injuries were identified; one of the accused's shoes had left a sole print on Jason's cheek.

Already at age 10 children can face criminal charges in Britain, but defendants must be found to have recognized that what they were doing was seriously wrong. Under British law, reporting on the family background and revealing the children's names are prohibited until their trial is completed. Jan and Robert were 11 as their trial began before a 12-member jury in Preston.[1]

Imagine a London television station honoring British law and only reporting on the court proceedings by reference to Child A and Child B. In contrast, imagine a U.S. newspaper revealing the defendants' names and providing detailed information on their personal histories. As the trial progressed, the question of motive was most troubling. What could drive ten-year-old boys to commit a vicious murder? Are there telltale signs other parents might recognize in their children? As it turned out, both boys were from broken homes, lived in poverty, and were prone to stealing and outbursts of anger. Jan Venables was easily led. A neighbor testified that if anyone told Jan to throw stones at someone, he would do it. When

1

Robert was six, his father ran off with another woman, leaving his twenty-nine-year-old mother to raise seven sons on her own.

Both the London and the U.S. news teams had a rationale for their decisions—the London station feeling constrained by the law and a foreign newspaper responding to intense reader interest. Is the legal standard the only possible one here? If so, is this domestic standard compelling on the international scene? What if no such legal restrictions existed once the trial was underway and the news directors wanted to act in a morally appropriate manner?

When a case such as this is presented to a media ethics seminar for discussion, the students usually argue passionately without making much headway. Analysis degenerates into inchoate pleas that eleven-year-old boys deserve mercy or into grandiose appeals to the privilege of the press. Judgments are made on what Henry Aiken calls the evocative, expressive level—that is, with no justifying reasons.[2]

Too often communication ethics follows such a pattern, retreating finally to the law as the only reliable guide. Students and practitioners argue about individual sensational incidents, make case-by-case decisions, and never stop to examine their method of moral reasoning. Instead, a pattern of ethical deliberation should be explicitly outlined in which the relevant considerations can be isolated and given appropriate weight. Those who care about ethics in the media can learn to analyze the stages of decision making, focus on the real levels of conflict, and make defensible ethical decisions. This test case can illustrate how competent moral justification takes place. Moral thinking is a systematic process: A judgment is made and action taken. The London television station concludes that the juvenile defendants ought to be protected and withholds names. What steps are used to reach this decision? How does a paper decide that an action should be taken because it is right or should be avoided because it is wrong? The newspaper in the United States considers it unnecessary to withhold news from its readers and prints the names.

Any single decision involves a host of values that must be sorted out. These values reflect our presuppositions about social life and human nature. To value something means to consider it desirable. Expressions such as "her value system" and "American values" refer to what a woman and a majority of Americans, respectively, estimate or evaluate as worthwhile. We may judge something according to esthetic values (harmonious, pleasing), professional values (innovative, prompt), logical values (consistent, competent), sociocultural values (thrift, hard work), and moral values (honesty, nonviolence). We often find both positive and negative values underlying our choices, pervading all areas of our behavior and motivating us to react in certain directions.[3]

Newspeople hold several values regarding professional reporting; for example, they prize immediacy, skepticism, and their own independence. In the case of the Liverpool murder, readers, family members, and reporters all value juvenile rights in varying ways. Taken in combination with ethical principles, these values yield a guideline for the television news desk, such as, in the case of the juveniles, protect their privacy at all costs. The good end, in this instance, is deemed to be guarding a person's right to a fair trial. The means for accomplishing this end is withholding information about the defendants.

Likewise, the U.S. newspaper came to a conclusion rooted in values, and based an action on that conclusion. The public has a right to know public news, the newspaper decided; we will print the names and background details. What values prompted this decision? This paper strongly values the professional rule that important information should be distributed without hesitation, that everyone ought to be told the truth. But professional values may be stated in positive or negative terms. In fact, in debates about values, an ethical principle might be invoked to help determine which values are preferable. In the newspaper's case, the moral rule "tell the truth under all conditions" is particularly relevant.

If we do this kind of analysis, we can begin to see how moral reasoning works. We understand better why there can be disagreement over whether or not to publicize presonal details in this case. Is it more important to tell the truth, we ask ourselves, or to preserve privacy? Is there some universal goal that we can all appreciate, such as truthtelling, or do we choose to protect some persons, suppressing the truth in the process? We do ethical analysis by looking for guidelines, and we quickly learn to create an interconnected model: We size up the circumstances, we ask what values motivated the decision, we appeal to a principle, and we choose loyalty to one social group instead of another. Soon we can engage in conflicts over the crucial junctures of the moral reasoning process, rather than argue personal differences over the merits of actual decisions. One disagreement that appears to be at stake here is a conflict between the norm of truthtelling and the norm of protecting the privacy of juvenile defendants. But differing values and loyalties can be identified too.

THE POTTER BOX MODEL OF REASONING

Creative ethical analysis involves several explicit steps. Dr. Ralph Potter of the Harvard Divinity School formulated the model of moral reasoning introduced in our analysis of the London murder. By using a diagram adapted from Professor Potter (the "Potter Box"), we can dissect this case further (see Figure I.1). The Potter Box introduces four dimensions of moral analysis to aid us in locating those places where most misunderstandings occur.[4] Along these lines we can construct action guides.

Note how this box has been used in our analysis: (1) We gave a definition of the situation, citing legal constraints, details of the abduction and murder, and events from the trial. One news outlet printed the names and biographical material when the court case was completed; the other waited until the trial began, but then decided it was free to make news available to its readers that was already available to it. In this case, they chose differently. (2) We then asked: Why? We have described the values that might have been the most important. The London station valued legal orderliness. For the U.S. newspaper, the

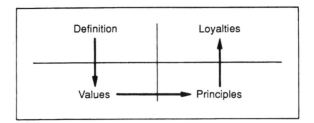

FIGURE I.1 The Potter Box

Permission to reprint was granted by Ralph Potter, Center for Population Studies, Harvard University.

professional value operative was not to suppress news. Its London correspondent had received anonymous information on the assailants shortly after Jason Bulger was killed. Presumably the victim's family and supporters wanted it known that Thompson and Venables were conniving, mean-spirited, and ruthless—not mentally deranged. The newspaper completed its investigation by the time the trial began and followed the newsroom value of publishing without delay. But these overriding values may not exhaust all the possibilities. We could have stressed that public persons—in this case, the juvenile defendants—must be reported consistently in news dissemination or readers and viewers will not trust the media's integrity in other situations. American newspaper readers may not make fair trials a supreme value or see any relevance in the fact the murderers were ten years old. A professional value regarding the news flow may be interpreted as less than humane. Each value influences our discourse and reasoning on moral questions. (3) We named at least two ethical principles, and we could have listed more. The TV station concluded that the principle of other-regarding care meant protecting the victim's right to privacy. The newspaper invoked truthtelling as an ethical imperative. But other principles could have been summoned: Do the greatest good for the greatest number, even if innocent people such as the murderers' families might be harmed. The television station did not broadcast the names, even at the risk of losing some credibility. The news hungry may conclude that it is not competent enough to obtain these details. (4) From the outset a conflict of loyalties is evident. The station claimed to act sympathetically toward the juvenile offenders. The newspaper insisted it was acting out of sympathy to its readership in general.

Moving from one quadrant to the next, we finally construct our action guides. But the problems can be examined in more depth: Conceive of the box as a circle and go one step further. This time concentrate on the ethical principles. Next time in the cycle, focus on the definition of loyalties. If the major source of disagreement is over professional values, for example, concentrate on that area the second time around. Often we value certain things without thinking about them; debating them with those who are not easily convinced will make us more critical of ourselves in the positive sense. The newspaper valued release of information and properly so. But was that an absolute, overriding all other considerations? Our professional values are often honestly held, but having them periodically challenged leads to maturity. In such a process of clarification and redefinition, each element can be addressed in greater detail and then the deeper insight can be connected to the other quadrants.

The matter of choosing loyalties usually needs the closest scrutiny. The Potter Box is a model for social ethics and consequently forces us to articulate precisely where our loyalties lie as we make a final judgment or adopt a particular policy. And in this domain we tend to beguile ourselves very quickly.

Examine the station's decision once again: Protect juveniles in court, publish no names or background data. Who was the staff thinking about when they made that decision? Perhaps they were considering only themselves. They say they did not wish to increase the suffering of the accused and the grief of their families. They claim they did not want to inflict pain. They contend they did not want to lead people to label the defendants or to become overly involved in the motivations for their behavior. They seem to be saying that they could not live with their conscience if they were to broadcast the news. But on additional reflection their loyalties may actually be different. Is the news team really protecting the juveniles, or protecting themselves? Certainly, not reporting names is a means to an end, but the end could be their private comfort. The staff members appear to be interested in a gain for society. They appear to protect the trial process, maximizing the defendants' privacy and minimizing scandalous gossip. But the crucial question must be faced once more: For whom did they do all this? If we do not return to the top right-hand quadrant of the diagram and inquire more deeply where their allegiances lie—for whom they did it—we have not used the Potter Box adequately.

Consider the newspaper's decision in the same manner. Tell the truth; print the names, it was decided. If the paper does not withhold juvenile names in a domestic trial, why should it make an exception this time? Will exceptions be necessary again and again until the paper's credibility is ended? The newspaper's readers have certain expectations; the staff seems to be asking if such expecta-tions should be met. But in responding to a short-term expectation, could its decision undermine the paper's overall credibility? Has the newspaper's long-range ability to contribute to society been damaged? What is more important: the welfare of the readers or the welfare of those involved in the crime?

In the initial analysis, the newspaper did not seem to be concerned for the juvenile offenders. Its imperative was to tell the truth or lose the trust of advertisers, readers, and employees. But maybe this newspaper's loyalties to its readers can actually benefit both the victim's and criminals' families. In time those dealing directly with the tragedy could become more than objects of curiosity. The truth of this devastating event may finally outweigh idle speculation about Venables and Thompson, and cool the gossip about a mother not watching her two-year-old closely enough or mall security guards inattentive to detail. Important issues such as these are encountered and clarified when the loyalty quadrant is considered thoroughly, either in the first round of decision making or later in more intensive analysis.

Choosing loyalties is an extremely significant step in the process of making moral decisions. As the preceding paragraphs indicate, taking this quadrant seriously does not in itself eliminate disagreements. In this arena, honest disputes may occur over who should benefit from a decision. For media personnel who are sincere about serving society, choices must be made among various segments of that society: subscribers and viewers, sources of information, politicians, ethnic minorities, children, law enforcement personnel, judges and lawyers, and so forth. Our calculations need to consider that flesh-and-blood people known by name ought not be sacrificed for euphemisms and abstractions such as the public, clients, audience, or market. In any case, the Potter Box is an exercise in social ethics that does not permit the luxury of merely playing mental games. Conclusions must be worked out in the rough and tumble of social realities. As developed in the next section, ethical principles are crucial in the overall process of reaching a justified conclusion. However, in the pursuit of socially responsible media, clarity regarding ultimate loyalties is of paramount importance.

In addition to considering each step carefully, the Potter Box must be seen as a circle, an organic whole (see Figure I.2). It is not merely a random set of isolated questions, but a linked system. We have moved from first impressions to explaining various aspects of what happened in this case. Each news outlet declared its loyalties. The Potter Box gives us a mechanism to further assess the values and principles in this case. But the Potter Box can also be used to adopt policy guidelines that will govern future behavior in similar circumstances. On the basis of this episode, the station or the newspaper might decide to alter their policy regarding names and background data. At least the editorial staffs could be made aware that there is a system for reaching a comprehensive policy regarding similar events. Through the four steps, media institutions can establish or strengthen their policy regarding anonymous sources, suicide coverage, confidentiality, trial coverage, deception in advertising, and so forth.

FIGURE I.2

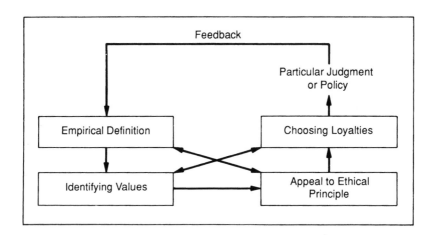

But we are still left with the initial question: Which news team made the right decision? This returns us to a central inquiry raised by this exercise: Is there a universal ground for making ethical decisions, an overarching theory from which we can choose among competing alternatives? Or is ethical decision making a process of adjusting to the mores and commitments of a given community? Potter's circular model, with its potential for continual expansion, takes both aspects seriously (see Figure I.3). Community mores are accounted for when we elaborate in step two on the values people hold and when we identify our loyalties before making a final choice. But these sociological matters are tempered in the Potter Box by an appeal to an explicit ethical principle. Without such an appeal, a conclusion is not considered morally justified. Unfortunately, under the

FIGURE I.3

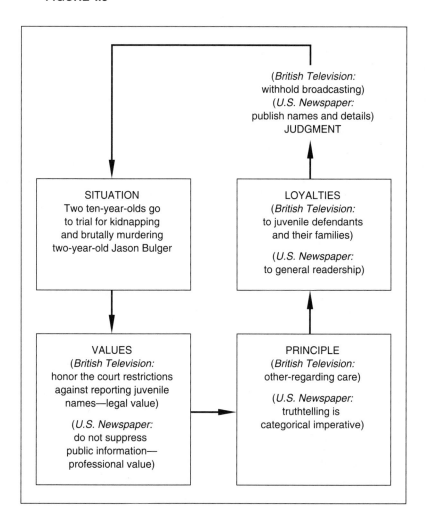

(*British Television:*
withhold broadcasting)
(*U.S. Newspaper:*
publish names and details)
JUDGMENT

SITUATION
Two ten-year-olds go
to trial for kidnapping
and brutally murdering
two-year-old Jason Bulger

LOYALTIES
(*British Television:*
to juvenile defendants
and their families)

(*U.S. Newspaper:*
to general readership)

VALUES
(*British Television:*
honor the court restrictions
against reporting juvenile
names—legal value)

(*U.S. Newspaper:*
do not suppress
public information—
professional value)

PRINCIPLE
(*British Television:*
other-regarding care)

(*U.S. Newspaper:*
truthtelling is
categorical imperative)

press of circumstances, the media tend to move directly into action from quadrant two, ignoring three and four.

In this situation, both the station and the newspaper make a defensible decision in terms of their newsroom values. In this particular case, both values can be defended; neither is outrageous. Both news staffs aim toward a social value that is widely held in Western society. Often one media company will adopt a morally enlightened option and the other will choose to break promises, cheat, and deceive. Such immoral behavior cannot be justified through the Potter Box cycle. Fortunately, there are situations in which different values are themselves credible. In such instances one professional value can compete legitimately with another using the Potter Box process. Then the values can be resolved in quadrant three or four.

When competing values all seem appropriate in quadrant two, resolution usually occurs in step three while working on ethical theory. Typically one news operation appeals to an explicit ethical principle and the other has made a decision based on a professional value after step two. But in this case two different ethical theories are relevant. The agape principle of other-regarding care insists on protecting the juvenile offenders by withholding personal information until they are convicted by a jury. Telling the truth is a categorical imperative with Kant, and in this case the newspaper has made every reasonable effort to verify the facts. When two different ethical theories both appear to be relevant, as in this situation, conflicts can be addressed in terms of the adequacy of the theories themselves, and through metaphysics or theology.[5]

In resolving this case, the appropriate ethical choice does not appear until quadrant four. A news bureau seeking an ethically sound conclusion cannot merely appeal to a professional value and argue for an ethical theory that corresponds to that value. Although most cases come to a head over ethical principles in step three, the loyalty issue is the deciding factor here. Loyalty to the innocent victims of tragedy is paramount in this instance. How can the news bureaus demonstrate their total commitment to the Bulger family? The newspaper appears to be taking advantage of this family's tragic circumstances for its own gain—it busily publishes all the gory details. Should one be loyal to oneself—that is, to a newspaper's credibility or competence or inquisitive readership—at the expense of the suffering few? Under conditions of innocence, should the suffering family be able to control information about itself through publically certified legal procedures, rather than surrender those prerogatives to others ruled by their own agenda?

For our purposes, the process by which choices are made is of the greatest importance. Media professions are demanding, filled with ambiguous situations and conflicting loyalties. The practitioner must make decisions quickly and without much time for reflection. Knowing the elements in moral analysis sharpens our vocabulary and thereby enhances our debates in media ethics. By understanding the logic of social ethics, we improve the quality of our conceptual work and thereby the validity of the choices actually made in media practice over the long term. The four dimensions introduced with the Potter Box instruct media practitioners and students in developing normative ethics rather than leaving situations trapped in a crisis or confusion.

USING ETHICAL PRINCIPLES

The Potter Box can help guide us through the various cases presented in this book. In the Liverpool murder case, the relevant empirical matters are complicated but not impossible to sort out. There may be some dispute over the circumstances in the mall and which of the two ten-year-olds was the most vicious. But the body was found in two days and the suspects arrested 24 hours later. The essential details are fairly easy to list, and the Potter Box insists that we always treat the specifics very carefully.

Our disagreements often result from our seeing the actual events differently. For example, when a newspaper purchases a building secretly, sets up a bar, and records city officials on camera, a host of details must be clear before a conclusion can be reached, before we can decide whether the paper is guilty of entrapment, invasion of privacy, or deception. Or, when debating a television station's responsibility to children, much of the disagreement involves the station's profits and how much free programming of high quality it can contribute without going broke. The question of controlling advertising is usually divided over the effect we consider advertising to have on buyer behavior. Often we debate whether we must overthrow the present media system or work within it. Actually these quarrels are usually not genuine moral disagreements. Regarding the need to destroy the system or work within it, for example, both sides may appeal to a utilitarian principle that institutions must promote the greatest amount of good possible. The debate might simply be over facts and details, over conflicting assessments of which strategy is more effective, and so forth.[6]

Also, our values need to be isolated and accounted for. Several values usually enter and shape the decision-making process. No exhaustive list of the values held by participants is ever possible, but attention to values helps prevent us from basing our decisions on personal biases or unexamined prejudices.

Our values constitute the frame of reference in which theories, decisions, and situations make sense to us. Sometimes our moral values correspond favorably to carefully articulated ethical theories. We may value gentleness and compassion so highly, for example, that our attitudes and language mesh with a stringently systematic ethics of pacifism. It is more likely, however, that stepping into quadrant three to examine principles will critique the values that may cloud our judgment. For example, journalists sometimes defend the "smoking-out" process—making public an accusation about a politician under the assumption that guilt or innocence will emerge once the story gets played out fully in public. This professional value is usually contradicted by ethical principles regarding truth and protecting privacy.

Values motivate human action. Values are a distinctive mark of the human species. But our values are never pure. We tend to become defensive about them and typically rationalize our behavior when we violate them. Professional values are inscribed in power.[7] Professions such as journalism or law or engineering are very influential; generally they operate in their own interests. Often our professional values are high-minded. Film producers may be strongly committed to aesthetic values and advertisers to hard work, for example. But no values are innocent. In institutions, values are a complicated mixture of ideas that often need to be checked, questioned, or corrected. Steps three and four in the Potter Box (naming the principles and loyalties) help us think critically about the conflicting or inappropriate signals we receive from quadrant two (naming the values).

The format in this book of citing cases and giving commentaries attempts to clarify the first two quadrants in the Potter Box. Case studies, by design, give the relevant details and suggest the alternatives that were considered in each situation. The cases themselves, and the commentaries particularly, explicate the values held by the principal figures in the decision-making process. Usually in conversations, speeches, memos, and animated defenses of one's behavior, a person's important values become clear. Ethicists examine rhetoric very carefully in order to determine what material is relevant for quadrant two. The manager of an advertising agency, for example, may value innovation so highly that other dimensions of the creative process are ignored. Efficiency may be so prized in a film company that only subordinate values survive. A reporter's commitment to the adversary relationship may distort her interpretation of a politician's behavior.

Occasionally the commentaries extend even further and offer ethical principles by which the decision can be defended—yet, on the whole, these norms or principles must be introduced by readers themselves. To aid this process, the following pages summarize five major options. As the Potter Box demonstrates, appealing to ethical principles that illuminate the issues is a significant phase of the moral reasoning process. Often one observes newspapers and broadcasters short-circuiting the Potter Box procedures. They typically act on the basis of professional values, in effect deciding in quadrant two what their action will be. For example, in the Pentagon Papers (Case 12) the *New York Times* decided to publish the story because it valued First Amendment privileges so strongly that no other considerations seemed important. However, on the basis of the Potter Box we insist that no conclusion can be morally justified without a clear demonstration that an ethical principle shaped the final decision. The two quadrants on the left side, including values, explicate what actually happens. The two on the right side, including ethical principles, concern what ought to happen. The left half of the box is descriptive and the right half normative.

We will follow the standard definitions that locate the act of valuing deep within the human will and emotions, whereas ethics involves critical reasoning about moral questions. As Sigmund Freud argued in *Totem and Taboo*, all societies, as far as we know, raise up certain ideals to emulate—but they also separate themselves from other cultures by establishing boundaries or taboos. A totem pole may indicate that a tribe supremely values the strength of a lion or the craftiness of a weasel. Rituals are maintained to pronounce a curse on behaviors considered totally unacceptable. In other words, valuing occurs as an aspect of our human condition as moral beings; it automatically comes to expression in everyday circumstances.[8] Values pervade all dimensions of human experience; even scientific experiments are saturated with value components. On the other hand, ethics involves an understanding of theology and philosophy as well as debates in the history of ideas over justice, virtue, the good, and so forth. Ethics emphasizes reasoning ability and adequate justification.

Sometimes a working journalist will comment "Why worry about principles? We know what we should do!" Such a comment often reflects a professional impatience with the idea of a moral dilemma, but it sounds a note that many moral philosophers are also asking: "Why principles? What principles? Whose principles?" The philosophical mind and social critics today tend to challenge the practice of searching for moral norms.[9] Yet norms rightly understood are foundational for moral commitment. Charles Taylor has written: "A framework is that in which we make sense of our lives spiritually. Not to have a framework is to fall into a life which is spiritually senseless."[10]

However, while the morally appropriate options can be outlined, the imposing of ethical principles by teachers and authors is normally counterproductive in that it undercuts the analytical process. The purpose of sound ethical reasoning is to draw responsible conclusions that yield justifiable actions. For this purpose, several ethical norms are introduced below. In analyzing the cases, these principles can be incorporated wherever appropriate and beneficial to given situations. Historically, ethicists have established many ethical principles.[11] The five ethical guidelines we will consider have achieved significance in the Western tradition, and together they represent a reasonably wide scope of time-tested alternatives. By working with these theories, students learn how they apply in situations close to their own experience. Readers acquainted with other theories from across the globe and with moral issues in other cultures are encouraged to substitute them instead.

These master theories are not canonical; that is, they are not a body of self-evident truths without contradiction. Such a celebration is too glib and ignores the cultural power that dominant theories represent. The Greek *Kanon* means measuring stick, a taxation table, or a blueprint. Canons do grant privilege to certain texts on the grounds that without boundaries, there is only chaos, dissipated energies, "a babble of . . . complaints rather than a settled critique." Diversity arises out of unity; without a buffer zone, struggle is impossible. The canon "depends on who is teaching it how; . . . living in the same place does not mean living with the same history." The French philosopher Maurice Merlean-Ponty once wrote: "What is original about Machiavelli is that having laid down the source of struggle, he goes beyond it without ever forgetting it." Socrates makes the same point in the *Crito*—recognizing that the fact that he criticizes, what he criticizes, and how he criticizes is made possible by the very city he is criticizing. Throughout this text, theorists provide a common language not as abstract authority, but in order that we can think on our own—rebelliously or amiably, as circumstances demand it.[12]

FIVE ETHICAL GUIDELINES

1. *Aristotle's Golden Mean: "Moral virtue is the appropriate location between two extremes."*

The golden mean is a middle-level principle that emerged at the earliest beginnings of Western philosophy, in fourth-century BC Greece. An ethical norm of enduring quality, the theory of the mean—more exactly rendered as "Equilibrium and Harmony"—was developed before Aristotle by the grandson of Confucius in fifth-century BC China.

By his "Principle of the Mean" Aristotle meant that moral virtue is a mean between two extremes, the one involving excess and the other deficiency.[13] From Aristotle's predecessor, Plato, the Greeks inherited the four cardinal virtues: temperance, justice, courage, and wisdom. When doing his ethics, Aristotle emphasized moderation or temperance and sharpened it. Just as wisdom is reasoning well, moderation is living well. In moral virtue, excellence is regarded as a mean between excess and defect. Courage is a mean between cowardice and temerity; a generous person follows a mean between stinginess and wastefulness; modesty is a mean between shamelessness and bashfulness; righteous indignation stands between envy and spite. Propriety is stressed rather than sheer duty or love. As a biologist, Aristotle noted that both too much food and too little spoil health. Whereas many ethical theories focus on behavior, Aristotle emphasizes character rather than conduct per se. Outer behavior, in his view, reflects our inner disposition. Virtuous persons have developed habits in terms of temperance; in order for them to flourish as human beings, the path they walk is the golden mean.

One begins operating with this principle by identifying extremes—doing nothing versus exposing everything, for example, in a question of how to report some event. In Case 2 (Civic Duties in Lewiston) two competing obligations can be resolved through the golden mean. The newspaper rejects both extremes: the excess of excluding all outside involvements and the defect of paying no attention to external affiliations. In this situation, the application of Aristotle's principle enables the newspaper to publish a financial disclosure of the publisher's holdings, withdraw from potential conflicts of interest such as local industry boards, report all staff connections, and so forth, while allowing other civic involvements. The basic idea is prominent in several diverse areas. In journalism, the sensational is derided and the virtues of balance, fairness, and equal time are recognized. When faced with a decision of whether to prohibit all raising of tobacco or to allow unregulated promotion, the Federal Trade Commission took the golden mean—they banned cigarette ads from television and placed warning labels on cigarette packages. In Case 32, recommendations about liquor advertising fall in between the extremes of not advertising at all and no restrictions on it whatsoever. A classic political example is nuclear arms reduction. Those who favor an arms buildup without restrictions on the one hand and those who favor total dismantling of nuclear weapons on the other both stymie a summit meeting. The legitimate claims of two legally appropriate entities must be negotiated, Aristotle would contend. The golden mean is the most fair and reasonable option for honorably resolving disputes between labor and management, between school board and striking teachers, and between Palestinians and Israelis after Rabin and Arafat shake hands. Generally speaking, in extremely complicated situations with layers of ambiguity and uncertainty, Aristotle's principle has the most intelligent appeal. This is the path William Raspberry recommends, for example, in the Charles Stuart murder case (Case 16).

The point for ethics is that virtue stands between two vices. That such vices are not always easy to locate is true enough, though some persons possess the virtue and character to discern them with precision. In considering action regarding a hostile editor, a reporter cannot say, "The two extremes are to murder him or burn down his house, so I will take the mean and merely pummel him senseless in a back alley." Bank robbers cannot justify themselves by operating at night so customers will not be hurt, and by taking only $10,000 instead of $100,000. Finding excess and defect involves honesty and imagination before the mean—that is, responsible behavior—becomes clear. Moreover, some issues are not amenable to a center. A balanced diet positioned between famine and gluttony is undoubtedly wise, but occasionally our health requires drastic surgery also. There were slaves in Greece; Aristotle opted for treating them well and fairly but not for the radical change of releasing them altogether.

However, it bears repeating that Aristotle was not advocating a bland, weak-minded consensus or the proverbial middle-of-the-road compromise. The mean is not isolated action reduced to political wheeling-and-dealing or bureaucratic fixing. We say of an artistic masterpiece, "nothing can be added or subtracted without spoiling it," and this is Aristotle's intent with the golden mean as well. Although the word *mean* has a mathematical flavor, a sense of average, a precise equal distance from two extremes is not intended. Aristotle speaks of the "mean relative to us," that is, to the individual's status, particular situation, and strong and weak points.[14] Thus, if we are generally prone to one extreme, we ought to lean toward another this time. Affirmative action programs can be justified as appropriate in that they help correct a prior imbalance in hiring. The mean is not only the right quantity, but it occurs at the right time, toward the right people, for the right reason, and in the right manner. The distance depends on the nature of the agents as determined by the weight of the moral case before them. Consider the Greek love of aesthetic proportion in sculpture. The mean in throwing a javelin is four-fifths of the distance to the end, in hammering a nail nine-tenths from the end.

2. *Kant's Categorical Imperative: "Act on that maxim which you will to become a universal law."*

Immanuel Kant, born in 1724 in Konigsberg, Germany, influenced eighteenth-century philosophy more than any other Western thinker. His writings established a permanent contribution to epistemology and ethics. Kant's *Groundwork of the Metaphysic of Morals* (1785) and *Critique of Practical Reason* (1788) are important books for every serious student of ethics.

Kant gave intellectual substance to the golden rule by his categorical imperative, which implies that what is right for one is right for all. As a guide for measuring the morality of our action, Kant declared: "Act only on that maxim whereby you can at the same time will that it should become a universal law."[15] In other words, check the underlying principle of your decision, and see whether you want it applied universally. The test of a genuine moral obligation is that it can be universalized. The decision to perform an act must be based on a moral law no less binding than such laws of nature as gravity. "Categorical" here means unconditional, without any question of extenuating circumstances, without any exceptions. Right is right and must be done even under the most extreme conditions. What is morally right we ought to do even if the sky should fall, that is, despite whatever consequences may follow.

Kant believed there were higher truths (which he called *noumena*) superior to our limited reason and transcending the physical universe. Conscience is inborn in every person, and it must be obeyed. The categorical imperatives, inherent in human beings, are apprehended not by reason but through conscience. By the conscience one comes under moral obligation; it informs us when we ought to choose right and shun evil. To violate one's conscience—no matter how feeble and uninformed—brings about feelings of guilt. Through the conscience, moral law is embedded in the texture of human nature.

The moral law is unconditionally binding on all rational beings. Someone breaks a promise, for example, because it seems to be in his or her own interest, but if all people broke their promises when it suited them, promises would cease to have meaning and societies would deteriorate into terror. Certain actions, therefore, are always wrong: cheating, stealing, and dishonesty, for example. Benevolence and truthtelling are always and universally right. These moral duties are not abrogated by the passage of time nor superseded by such achievements as the Bill of Rights. Even if one could save another's life by telling a lie, it would still be wrong. Deception by the press to get a good story or by advertisers to sell products cannot be excused or overlooked in the Kantian view. Violent pornography in entertainment is not just one variable among many; it is too complex an issue to be explained away by an appeal to the First Amendment.

Kant's contribution is called *deontological ethics* (*deon* from the Greek word for duty). The good will "shine like a jewel," he wrote, and the obligation of the good conscience is to do its duty for the sake of duty.[16] Ethics for Kant was largely reducible to reverence for duty, and his work is like a hymn on its behalf. For Kant, categorical imperatives must be obeyed even to the sacrifice of all natural inclinations and socially accepted standards. Kant's ethics have an austere quality, but they are generally regarded as having greater motivating power than subjective approaches that are easily rationalized on the basis of temporary moods. His categorical imperative encourages obedience and faithful practice.

3. *Mill's Principle of Utility: "Seek the greatest happiness for the greatest number."*

Utilitarianism is an ethical view widespread in American society and a notion well developed in philosophy. There are many different varieties, but they all hold in one way or another that we are to determine what is right or wrong by considering what will yield the best consequences for the welfare of human beings. The morally right alternative produces the greatest balance of good over evil. All that matters ultimately in determining the right and wrong choice is the amount of good promoted and evil restrained.

Modern utilitarianism originated with the British philosophers Jeremy Bentham (1748-1832) and John Stuart Mill (1806-1873). Their traditional version was hedonistic, holding that the good end is happiness or pleasure. The quantity of pleasure depends on each situation; it can be equal, Bentham would say, for a child's game of kickball as for writing poetry.[17] Mill contended that happiness was the sole end of human action, and the test by which all conduct ought to be judged.[18] Preventing pain and promoting the pleasurable were for Bentham and Mill the only desirable ends.

Later utilitarians, however, have expanded on the notion of happiness. They have noted that if pleasure is upheld as the one object of desire (in the sense of "wine, women, and song"), then all people do not desire it (Puritans did not) and therefore it cannot be the only desired goal. Thus, these utilitarians argue that other values besides pure happiness possess intrinsic worth—values such as friendship, knowledge, health, and symmetry. For these pluralistic utilitarians, rightness or wrongness is to be assessed in terms of the total amount of value ultimately produced. For example, the press's role in Watergate did not yield a high amount of pleasure for anyone except enemies of Richard Nixon. Yet for utilitarians, the overall consequences were valuable enough so that most people considered the actions of the press proper, even though pain was inflicted on a few.

Worked out along these lines, utilitarianism provides a definite guideline for aiding our ethical choices. It suggests that we first calculate in the most conscientious manner possible the consequences of the various options open to us. We would ask how much benefit and how much harm would result in the lives of everyone affected, including ourselves. Once we have completed these computations for all relevant courses of action, we are morally obligated to choose the alternative that maximizes value or minimizes loss. To perform any other action knowingly would result in our taking an unethical course.

The norm of utility actually becomes a double principle. It instructs us (1) to produce the greatest possible balance of good over evil and (2) to distribute this as widely as possible. Hence, utilitarianism is often defined as promoting the greatest good for the greatest number. In this sense, the principle directs us to distribute a good consequence to more people rather than to fewer, whenever we have a choice.[19]

Two kinds of utility are typically distinguished: act and rule utilitarianism. For act utilitarians the basic question always involves the greatest good in a specific case. One must ask whether a particular action in a particular situation will result in a balance of good over evil. Rule utilitarians, also attributing their view to Mill, construct moral rules on the basis of promoting the greatest general welfare. The question is not which action yields the greatest utility, but which general rule does. The principle of utility is still the standard—but at the level of rules rather than specific judgments. The act utilitarian may conclude that in one specific situation civil disobedience obtains a balance of good over evil, whereas rule utility would seek to generate a broadly applicable moral rule such as "civil disobedience is permitted except when physically violent."[20]

Although happiness is an end few would wish to contradict, utilitarianism does present difficulties. It depends on our making accurate measurements of the consequences, when in everyday affairs the result of our choices is often blurred vision, at least in the long term. For instance, who can possibly calculate the social changes that we will face in future decades in the wake of converging media technologies? Moreover, the principle of the greatest public benefit applies only to societies in which certain nonutilitarian standards of decency prevail. In a society of ten people, nine sadists cannot justly persecute the tenth person even though it yields the greatest happiness. In addition, utilitarians view society as a collection of individuals, each with his or her own desires and goals; the public good is the sum total of private goods. These ambiguities, although troublesome and objectionable, do not by themselves destroy the utilitarian perspective, at least for an intellectually sophisticated audience. For our purposes in examining media ethics, no moral norms can be considered free of all uncertainties, and the obvious difficulties with utilitarianism can be addressed in round two or three when circulating through the Potter Box for specificity and clarification.[21] Occasionally in resolving the cases in the following pages, utility is the most productive principle to include in the lower right-hand quadrant. In the classic case of Robin Hood accosting the rich in order to provide for the poor, act utilitarianism appropriately condones his behavior as morally justified.

4. *Rawls's Veil of Ignorance: "Justice emerges when negotiating without social differentiations."*

John Rawls's book, *A Theory of Justice* (1971), is widely quoted in contemporary work on ethics, and from his perspective fairness is the fundamental idea in the concept of justice.[22] He represents a return to an older tradition of substantive moral philosophy and thereby establishes an alternative to utilitarianism. He articulates an egalitarian perspective that carries the familiar social contract theory of Hobbes, Locke, and Rousseau to a more fundamental level.

In easy cases, fairness means quantity. Everybody in the same union doing similar work would all fairly receive a 10-percent raise. Teachers should give the same letter grade to everyone who had three wrong on a particular test. At a birthday party, each child should get two cookies. Eliminating arbitrary distinctions expresses fairness in its basic sense. However, Rawls struggles more with inherent inequalities. For example, players in a baseball game do not protest the fact that pitchers handle the ball more times than outfielders do. We sense that graduated income taxes are just, though teachers pay only 22 percent and editors, advertisers, public relations staff, and film producers perhaps find themselves in the 50-percent bracket.

When situations necessitating social contracts are inherently unequal, blind averages are unfair and intuitional judgments are too prone to error. Therefore, Rawls recommends his now classic "veil of ignorance," asking that all parties step back from real circumstances into an "original position" behind a barrier where roles and social differentiations are eliminated.[23] Participants are abstracted from individual features such as race, class, gender, group interests, and other real conditions, and are considered equal members of society as a whole. They are men and women with ordinary tastes and ambitions, but each suspends these personality features and regains them only after a contract is in place. Behind the veil, no one knows how he or she will fare when stepping out into real life.

The participants may be male or female, 10 years old or 90, a Russian or a Pole, rookie or veteran, black or white, advertising vice-president or sales representative for a weekly. As we negotiate social agreements in the situation of imagined equality behind the veil of ignorance, Rawls argues, we inevitably seek to protect the weaker party and to minimize risks. In the event that I emerge from the veil as a beginning reporter rather than a big-time publisher, I will opt for fair treatment for the former. The most vulnerable party receives priority in these cases and the result, Rawls would contend, is a just resolution.

Because negotiation and discussion occur, the veil of ignorance does not rely merely on intuition. Such individual decisions too easily become self-serving and morally blind. Nor is the veil another name for utility, with decisions based on what is best for the majority. Again, the issue is morally appropriate action, not simply action that benefits the most people. In fact, Rawls's strategy stands against the tendency in democratic societies to rally around the interests of the majority and give only lip service to the minority.

Two principles emerge from the hypothetical social contract formulated behind the veil. These, Rawls declares, will be the inevitable and prudent choices of rational women and men acting in their own self-interest. The first principle calls for a maximal system of equal basic liberty. Every person must have the largest political liberty compatible with a like liberty for all. Liberty has priority in that it can never be traded away for economic and social advantages. Thus, the first principle permanently conditions the second. The second principle involves all social goods other than liberty and allows inequalities in the distribution of these goods only if they act to benefit the least advantaged party. The inequalities in power, wealth, and income upon which we agree must benefit the members of society who are worse off.[24]

Consider press coverage in the well-known case of William Kennedy Smith for the alleged rape of a woman at the Kennedy Palm Beach compound. The extensive media coverage has been justified on the basis of Senator Edward Kennedy's role at the bar earlier in the evening, and public interest in the Kennedy family. Given conventional news values, the public's right to know supersedes the Kennedy family's right to privacy. But what if we go beyond values to ethical theory? Put Ted Kennedy and a newsperson behind the veil of ignorance, not knowing who will be who when they emerge. Undoubtedly they would agree that reporting on the public acts of public officials is permissible, but that publicizing the alleged rape incident itself, now several years later, would be undue harassment in the absence of any new material. Rawls's principle precludes reporters from using their power to pester without end those who are caught in a news story.

On a broader level, place politicians and journalists behind the veil and attempt to establish a working relationship agreeable to all after the veil is parted and space/time resumes. All stark adversary notions would disappear. There would be no agreement that elected officials as a class should be called the enemy or liars since those who emerge as politicians would resent such labels. Independence, some toughness, and persistence seem reasonable for media professionals, but a basic respect for all humans would replace an unmitigated and cynical abrasiveness among those wielding instruments of power.

5. *Judeo-Christian Persons as Ends: "Love your neighbor as yourself."*[25]

Ethical norms of nearly all kinds emerge from various religious traditions. The highest good in the Bhagavad-Gita, for example, is enlightenment. Of all the options, however, the Judeo-Christian tradition has dominated American culture to the greatest extent, and its theological ethics have been the most influential. By studying a prominent religious perspective in terms of the issues and cases in this book, students should be inspired to take other religious ethics seriously as well. The intention here is pedagogical—to learn a system of ethical reasoning and ethical concepts within a familiar context. On that foundation, other frameworks can be added and dilemmas in different cultural contexts can be addressed responsibly. Islam and Confucianism, for example, have developed sophisticated ethical traditions.[26]

The ethics of love is not exclusively a Judeo-Christian notion. Already in the fourth century BC, the Chinese thinker Mo Tzu spoke in similar terms: "What is the Will of Heaven like? The answer is—To love all men everywhere alike."[27] Feminist theory in the last decade has given more precise development and higher status to cognate terms: nurturing, caring, affection, empathy, and inclusiveness.[28] Nor are all Judeo-Christian ethics a pure morality of love; some ethicists in that tradition make obedience or justice or peace supreme.[29] But the classic contribution of this religious perspective, in its mainline form, contends that ultimately humans stand under only one moral command or virtue: to love God and humankind. All other obligations, though connected to this central one, are considered derivative.

"Love your neighbor" is normative, and uniquely so in this tradition, because love characterizes the very heart of the universe. Augustine is typical in declaring that the supreme good is divine love.[30] The inexhaustible, self-generating nature of God Himself is love. Therefore, human love has its inspiration, motive, and ground in the highest reaches of eternity. Humans are made in the image of God; the more loving they are, the more like God they are. At this very point the Judeo-Christian norm differs from other ethical formulations. Love is not only a raw principle, stern and unconditional, as in Kant's categorical imperative. Regard for others is not based on just a contract motivated by self-interest, as in John Rawls's theory. It remains personal at its very roots, and while rigorously dutiful, it is never purely legalistic. As Heinrich Emil Brunner noted in summarizing the biblical exhortations:

> "Live in love." Or, still more plainly: "Remain in love." . . . It is the summons to remain in the giving of God, to return to Him again and again as the origin of all power to be good and to do good. There are not "other virtues" alongside the life of love. . . . Each virtue, one might say, is a particular way in which the person who lives in love takes the other into account, and "realizes" him as "Thou."[31]

The Old Testament already spoke of loving kindness, but the Christian tradition introduced the more dramatic term *agape*—unselfish; other-regarding care and other-directed love; distinct from friendship, charity, benevolence, and other weaker notions. In the tradition of agape, to love a human being is to accept that person's existence as it is given; to love him or her as is.[32] Thus, human beings have unconditional value apart from shifting circumstances. The commitment is unalterable; loyalty to others is permanent, indefectible, in sickness and in health. It is unloving, in this view, to give others only instrumental value and to use them merely as a means to our own ends. Especially in those areas that do not coincide with a person's own desires, love is not contradicted. In this perspective, we ought to love our neighbors with the same zeal and consistency with which we love ourselves.

Agape as the center of meaning in Judeo-Christian ethics raises significant issues that ethicists in this tradition continue to examine: the regular failure of its adherents to practice this principle; the relationship of love and justice, of the personal and institutional; the role of reason as distinguished from discernment; and whether agape is a universal claim or, if not, what its continuity is with other alternatives.[33]

However, all agree that loving one's neighbor in this tradition is far from sentimental utopianism. In fact, agape is strong enough to serve as the most appropriate norm in chapters 4, 5, and 13. Moreover, it is thoroughly practical, issuing specific help to those who need it—"neighbor" designated the weak, poor, orphans, widows, aliens, and disenfranchised in the Old Testament. Even enemies are included. This love is not discriminatory: no black or white, no learned or simple, no friend or foe. Although agape does not deny the distinctions that characterize creaturely existence, it stays uniquely blind to them. Love does not estimate rights or claims and then determine whether the person merits attention. The norm here is giving and forgiving with uncalculating spontaneity and spending oneself to fulfill a neighbor's well-being. Because of its long attention to understanding the character of humanness, the agape principle has been especially powerful in its treatment of social injustice, invasion of privacy, violence, and pornography.

TO WHOM IS MORAL DUTY OWED?

The Potter Box forces us to get the empirical data straight, investigate our values, and articulate an appropriate principle. Once these steps are accomplished, we face the question of our ultimate loyalties. Many times, in the consideration of ethics, direct conflicts arise between the rights of one person or group and those of others. Policies and actions inevitably must favor some to the exclusion of others. Often our most agonizing dilemmas revolve around our primary obligation to a person or social group. Or we ask ourselves, is my first loyalty to my company or to a particular client?

To reach a responsible decision, we must clarify which parties will be influenced by our decision and which ones we feel especially obligated to support. When analyzing the cases in this book, we will usually investigate five categories of obligation:

1. Duty to ourselves. Maintaining our integrity and following our conscience may be the best alternative in many situations. However, careerism is a serious professional problem and often tempts us to act out of our own self-interest while we claim to be following our conscience.

2. Duty to clients/subscribers/supporters. If they pay the bills and if we sign contracts to work for them, do we not carry a special obligation to them? Even in the more amorphous matter of a viewing audience that pays no service fee for a broadcast signal, our duty to them must be addressed when we are deciding which course of action is the most appropriate.

3. Duty to our organization or firm. Often company policy is followed much too blindly, yet loyalty to an employer can be a moral good. Whistle blowing, that is, exposing procedures or persons who are harming the company's reputation, is also morally relevant here. Reporters might even defy court orders and refuse to relinquish records in whistle-blowing cases, under the thesis that ultimately the sources on which media companies depend will dry up. Thus, duty to one's firm might conceivably take priority over duty to an individual or to a court.

4. Duty to professional colleagues. A practitioner's strongest obligation is often to colleagues doing similar work. Understandably, reporters tend to prize, most of all, their commitments to fellow reporters and their mutual standards of good reporting. Some even maintain an adversary posture against editors and publishers, just short of violating the standards of accepted etiquette. Film artists presume a primary obligation to their professional counterparts, and account executives to theirs. However, these professional loyalties, almost intuitively held, must also be examined when we are determining what action is most appropriate.

5. Duty to society. This is an increasingly important dimension of applied ethics and has been highlighted for the media under the term *social responsibility*. Questions of privacy and confidentiality, for example, nearly always encounter claims about society's welfare over that of a particular person. The "public's right to know" has become a journalistic slogan. Advertising agencies cannot resolve questions of tobacco ads, political commercials, and nutritionless products without taking the public good fully into the equation. When some Tylenol bottles were laced with cyanide, the public relations staff of Johnson and Johnson had its foremost obligation to the public. Violence and pornography in

media entertainment are clearly social issues. In such cases, to benefit the company or oneself primarily is not morally defensible. In these situations, our loyalty to society warrants preeminence.

Throughout this volume the media practitioner's moral obligation to society is stressed as critically important. Admittedly the meaning of that responsibility is often ill-defined and subject to debate. For example, when justifying one's decision, particular social segments must be specified: the welfare of children, the rights of a minority, or the needs of senior citizens. We have emphasized that, in spite of the difficulties, precisely such debate must be at the forefront when we are considering the loyalty quadrant in the Potter Box. No longer do the media operate with a crass "public be damned" philosophy. Increasingly the customer is king, and belligerent appeals to owner privilege have been lessened. However, these gains are only the beginning. They need to be propelled forward, so that a sincere sense of social responsibility and a genuine concern for the citizenry become characteristic marks of all contemporary media operations in news, advertising, public relations, and entertainment.

The version of the Potter Box described in this introduction furthers the book's overall preoccupation with social responsibility. Consider the upper tier of the Potter Box (empirical definition and ultimate loyalties), which stresses the social context and social order. As was noted earlier, the Potter Box as a schematic design is not just an eclectic, random gathering of several elements for justifying a decision or policy. The lower half (values and ethical principles) deals more with analytical matters than it does with sociological ones in everyday experience. But the lower tier feeds into the higher. Also the two levels are integrated at crucial junctures so that social situations initiate the process and the choice of cultural loyalties forces one toward the final decision. Thus, the loyalty component especially provides a pivotal juncture in moral discourse and indicates that conceptual analysis can hardly be appraised until one sees the implications for institutional arrangements and the relevant social groups. Nel Noddings strongly urges that caring—a notion of relatedness between people—take a central role in decision making. From her perspective, mere subscription to principle without concentrating on the people involved has caused much needless wrong.[34]

The line of decision making that we follow, then, has its final meaning in the social context. Certainly precision is necessary when we are dealing with ethical principles, and their relation must always be drawn to the values held and empirical definition described. But the meaning becomes clear when the choice is made for a particular social context or a specific set of institutional arrangements. Considered judgments, in this view, do not derive directly from normative principles but are woven into a set of obligations one assumes toward certain segments of society. In this scheme, debate over institutional questions is fundamental and ethical thinking is not completed until social applications and implications have been designated. In social ethics of this kind, the task is not just one of definition but an elaboration of the perplexities regarding social justice, power, bureaucracies, and cultural forms. Social theory is central to the task, not peripheral.[35]

WHO OUGHT TO DECIDE?

During each phase of ethical reasoning, some actor or group of actors is directly involved in deciding, determining values, selecting moral norms, and choosing loyalties. The cases in this book cannot be read or discussed fruitfully without constant attention to the question of who is making the decision. At every step applied ethics always considers seriously the issue of who should be held accountable.

There are usually numerous decision makers involved. In simple cases, it is an organizational matter where an editor or executive decides rather than a reporter or sales representative. In more complicated areas, can producers of entertainment dismiss their responsibility for quality programming by arguing that they merely give the public what it wants? Are parents to be held solely accountable for the television programs that children watch or do advertisers and networks carry responsibility also? If advertisers and networks carry responsibility, in what proportions? Does the person with the greatest technical expertise have the greatest moral obligation? We must be wary of paternalism in which consumers and informal social networks are removed from the decision-making process. When is the state, through the courts, the final decision maker? Giving absolute authority or responsibility to any person or group can be morally disastrous. Requiring accountability across the board helps to curb the human penchant for evading one's own liability.

For all the emphasis in this book on social ethics, individual practitioners ought not become lost. The individual is the authentic moral agent. A firm or institution, when infused and animated by a single spirit and organized into a single institution, is more than a mere sum of discrete entities—it has a personality of its own. It is also true that such institutions can in a sense be held accountable for their deeds and become the object of moral approval or disapproval. But only in a limited sense. Such institutions are real enough, but they lack concreteness. It is the individual who reasons morally that we consider the responsible agent. These individuals alone can be praised or blamed.[36]

Certainly corporate obligation is a meaningful notion. When individuals join an organization, and for as long as they remain members, they are co-responsible for the actions taken by that organization. What is most important, however, is that ultimate responsibility finally rests upon individuals. It should be obvious that this is not a plea for a heavy-handed individualism; that would stand directly at odds with the social ethics of the Potter Box model. The point is that responsibility, to be meaningfully assigned and focused, must be distributed among the individuals constituting the corporation. Individuals are not wholly discrete, unrelated, atomistic entities; they always stand in a social context with which they are morally involved. But individuals they nevertheless remain. And it is with each person that ethics is fundamentally concerned. Gross attacks and broad generalizations about entire media systems usually obscure more than they enlighten. On most occasions, such assessments are not normative ethics but hot-tempered moralism. The cases and commentaries that follow, filtered through the

Potter Box model, steer media practitioners toward socially responsible decisions that are justified ethically.

NOTES

1. For details, see AP wire copy, 12 February and 26 November 1993. See also Ray Moseley, "What Made Toddler's Killers Tick?" *Chicago Tribune*, 26 November 1993, sec. 1, p. 1.
2. Henry D. Aiken, *Reason and Conduct* (New York: Alfred A. Knopf, 1962), pp. 65-87.
3. For helpful background, see Richard L. Morrill, "Values as Standards of Action," in his *Teaching Values in College* (San Francisco: Jossey-Bass Publishers, 1980); David Boeyink, "What Do We Mean by Newspaper Values," unpublished paper, 8 February 1988, Southern Newspaper Publishers Association, St. Petersburg, Florida. For values among artists, see Horace Newcomb and Robert Alley, *The Producer's Medium: Conversations with Creators of American TV* (New York: Oxford University Press, 1983).
4. Dr. Karen Lebacqz of the Pacific School of Religion named the model "Potter Box" after the original version described in Ralph B. Potter, "The Structure of Certain American Christian Responses to the Nuclear Dilemma, 1958-63" (Ph.D. diss., Harvard University, 1965). See also Ralph B. Potter, "The Logic of Moral Argument," in *Toward a Discipline of Social Ethics*, ed. Paul Deats (Boston: Boston University Press, 1972), pp. 93-114.
5. Potter himself labeled it the "ground of meaning" level. As he describes it in his dissertation, "Even when ethical categories have been explicated with philosophical exactitude it is possible for one to ask, 'Why ought I to be moral?' or 'Why ought I to consider your expressions of ethical judgment and your pattern of ethical reasoning to be convincing?'" Further inquiry "drives men ultimately to reflect on their more fundamental ideas concerning God, man, history, and whatever is behind and beyond history." Potter, "The Structure of Certain American Christian Responses," pp. 404-405.
6. While taking the empirical dimension seriously, this does not imply a commitment to neutral facts and what is called "abstracted empiricism" in C. Wright Mills, *The Sociological Imagination* (New York: Oxford University Press, 1959), pp. 50-75. W. I. Thomas's "definition of the situation" is actually a more sophisticated way of explicating the empirical dimension of moral questions; see W. I. Thomas, *Primitive Behavior: An Introduction to the Social Sciences* (New York: McGraw-Hill, 1937), p. 8. For a comprehensive introduction to this strategy, see *Handbook of Qualitative Research*, eds. Norman K. Denzin and Yvonna S. Lincoln (Newbury Park, CA: Sage Publications, 1994).
7. See Karen Lebacqz, *Professional Ethics: Power and Paradox* (Nashville, TN: Abingdon Press, 1985).
8. Obviously the anatomy of values and their relation to beliefs and attitudes is a complex question both in psychology and axiology. In terms of the Potter Box model, our concern is to identify the values invoked in various cases and to ensure that they are understood as only one phase of the decision-making process. In that sense, instead of the values-clarification approach of Louis Rath, Sidney Simon, and Merrill Harmin, we insist on the critical normative reflection represented in quadrant three.
9. Richard Rorty, *Contingency, Irony, Solidarity* (New York: Cambridge University Press, 1989).

10. Charles Taylor, *Sources of the Self* (Cambridge, MA: Harvard University Press, 1989), p. 18; see also his *Ethics of Authenticity* (Cambridge, MA: Harvard University Press, 1991).

11. Ethical egoism has not been included in the list despite its immense popularity. The authors stand with those who doubt its adequacy and coherence as an ethical theory. Furthermore, the view that everyone ought to promote his or her own self-interests does not agree with the emphasis on social responsibility in the Potter Box model. However, there are several formulations of ethical egoism, and students interested in pursuing this option should see Edward Regis's significant attempt to present a conception that overcomes the standard objections. Edward Regis, "What Is Ethical Egoism?" *Ethics* 91 (October 1980): 50-62. For a history of the debates in this area, see Tibor R. Machan, "Recent Work in Ethical Egoism," *American Philosophical Quarterly* 16 (1979): 1-15.

12. Peter Euben, "The Debate Over the Canon," *The Civic Acts Review* 7:1 (Winter 1994): 4-15. Euben gives a comprehensive overview of the canonicity issue in this article. The ideas in this paragraph and the cited material are taken from Euben's essay.

13. For example, see *Nicomachean Ethics*, in his *Introduction to Aristotle*, ed. Richard McKeon (New York: Modern Library, 1947); (1104a) p. 333; (1106a) p. 340; (1107a) p. 341; (1138b) p. 423.

14. Ibid. (1107a) p. 340.

15. Immanuel Kant, *Groundwork of the Metaphysic of Morals*, trans. H. J. Paton (New York: Harper Torchbooks, 1964), pp. 69-71, 82-89.

16. Ibid., p. 62.

17. Bentham suggested a scheme for measuring the quantity of pleasure in human acts in Jeremy Bentham, *An Introduction to the Principles of Morals and Legislation* (New York: Hafner, 1948), chs. 3-7.

18. John Stuart Mill reached this conclusion in the last chapter of *A System of Logic* (London: J. W. Parker, 1843). He attempted 18 years later to expand and defend this conviction. See John Stuart Mill, *Utilitarianism* (London: J. M. Dent & Sons, 1861), esp. ch. 2.

19. For a significant discussion of these and related issues, see *Utilitarianism: Text and Critical Essays,* ed. Samuel Gorovitz (Indianapolis: Bobbs Merrill, 1971), pp. 59-401.

20. The Potter Box can function without this distinction, but a working knowledge of act and rule utility increases the Potter Box's sophistication. Students are therefore encouraged to read additional descriptions of these two forms of utilitarianism, such as William Frankena, *Ethics* (Englewood Cliffs, NJ: Prentice-Hall, 1962), pp. 29-35; C. E. Harris, Jr., *Applying Moral Theories*, 2d ed. (Belmont, CA: Wadsworth, 1992), pp. 123-154; and Robert L. Holmes, *Basic Moral Philosophy* (Belmont, CA: Wadsworth, 1993), pp. 154-174. A twentieth-century act utility is presented in George E. Moore, *Principia Ethica* (Cambridge, England: Cambridge University Press, 1954), ch. 5. Richard Brandt and J. O. Urmson are prominent rule utilitarians. See Richard Brandt, "Toward a Credible Form of Utilitarianism," in *Morality and the Language of Conduct*, ed. H. N. Casteneda and G. Nakhnikian (Detroit: Wayne State University Press, 1963), pp. 107-143; and J. O. Urmson, "The Interpretation of the Moral Philosophy of J. S. Mill," *The Philosophical Quarterly* 3 (1953): 33-39.

21. For an exceptional analysis of utilitarianism for beginners, see Arthur J. Dyck, *On Human Care: An Introduction to Ethics* (Nashville, TN: Abingdon Press, 1977), pp. 57-71.

22. John Rawls, *A Theory of Justice* (Cambridge, MA: Harvard University Belknap Press, 1971), pp. 3-53.

23. Ibid., pp. 118-192.

24. For a critique and elaboration of the two principles, see *Reading Rawls: Critical Studies of A Theory of Justice,* ed. Norman Daniels (New York: Basic Books, 1976), pp. 169-281. For an effective classroom strategy to teach Rawls's theory, see Ronald M. Green, "The Rawls' Game: An Introduction to Ethical Theory," *Teaching Philosophy* 9:1 (March 1986): 51-60.

25. A rationalized and secularized account of this principle was developed by Kant, who contended that we ought to treat all rational beings as ends in themselves and never as means only. The Judeo-Christian version is included here because of its vast influence on the popular level. William Frankena judged Judeo-Christian ethics to be even more important to Western society than utilitarianism.

26. For an introduction to the central concepts and relevant literature, see Part IV, "East Asia," in *Beyond the Western Tradition: Readings in Moral and Political Philosophy,* eds. Daniel Bonevac, William Boon, and Stephen Phillips (Mountain View, CA: Mayfield Publishing Co., 1992); and Hamid Mowlana, "Communication Ethics and the Islamic Tradition," in *Communication Ethics and Global Change,* eds. Thomas W. Cooper et al. (New York: Longman, 1990), pp. 137-146. The best historical background for Confucianism is Kai-wing Chow, *Ethics, Classics, and Lineage Discourse: The Rise of Confucian Ritualism in Late Imperial China, 1600-1830* (Stanford, CA: Stanford University Press, 1993). A comprehensive list of the relevant material is included in *Bibliography of Comparative Religious Ethics,* eds. John Carmen and Mark Jürgensmeyer (New York: Cambridge University Press, 1991).

27. See E. R. Hughes, *Chinese Philosophy in Classical Times* (London: J. M. Dent and Sons, 1942), p. 48.

28. For an assessment of the relevant literature on media ethics, see Linda Steiner, "Feminist Theorizing and Communication Ethics," *Communication* 12:3 (1991): 157-174. Of particular interest to students of communication is Virginia Held's *Feminist Morality: Transforming Culture, Society, and Politics* (Chicago: University of Chicago Press, 1993). For a general overview of the current theorists, see Rosemarie Tong, *Feminine and Feminist Ethics* (Belmont, CA: Wadsworth, 1993).

29. Pedro Gilberto Gomes, *Direto de ser: A ética da Comunicácáo na Americana Latina (The Right to Be: An Ethics of Communication in Latin America)* (Sao Paulo, Brazil: Ediciones Paulinas, 1989).

30. Augustine, *The Confessions,* trans. J. G. Pilkington (New York: Liveright Publishing Corp., 1943); (2.2) p. 40; (4.10-4.13) pp. 71-75; (7.12) p. 150; (9.1) p. 188; (10.1) p. 218; (10.29) p. 249; (13.1-13.4) pp. 340-343. God's love is a basic theme throughout Augustine's writings. For a summary, see Frederick Copleston, "St. Augustine: Moral Theory," in his *A History of Philosophy,* vol. 2 (Westminster, MD: Newman Press, 1960), pp. 81-86.

31. Heinrich Emil Brunner, *The Divine Imperative,* trans. Olive Wyon (Philadelphia: Westminster Press, 1947), pp. 165 and 167.

32. For a comprehensive review of this concept, see Gene Outka, *Agape: An Ethical Analysis* (New Haven, CT: Yale University Press, 1972); pages 7-16 are particularly helpful in understanding the meaning of agape.

33. For the best available introduction to the historical and contemporary issues in Christian ethics, see Edward LeRoy Long, Jr., *A Survey of Christian Ethics* (New York:

Oxford University Press, 1967); and his *A Survey of Recent Christian Ethics* (New York: Oxford University Press, 1982). James M. Gustafson develops a systematic approach to theological ethics in his *Ethics from a Theocentric Perspective* (Chicago: University of Chicago Press, 1981 and 1984).

34. Nel Noddings, *Caring: A Feminine Approach to Ethics and Moral Education* (Berkeley: University of California Press, 1984), p. 3. Noddings goes further than urging that human loyalty mitigate stern application of principles; she rejects outright the "ethics of principle as ambiguous and unstable" (p. 5). We retain principle precisely to avoid the instability of boundless relativism, while insisting with Noddings that human care play a strong role in moral decision making. For an accessible summary and critique, see "Nel Nodding's Relational Ethics," in Rosemarie Tong, *Feminine and Feminist Ethics* (Belmont, CA: Wadsworth, 1993), pp. 108-134.

35. The precise role of philosophical analysis and social theory has been debated even among those who generally follow this decision-making paradigm. Potter himself emphasized philosophical analysis as the primary element in moral deliberation, highlighting, in effect, the third quadrant as the key to a tough-minded social ethics. James Childress follows the spirit of Potter's apparent focus on philosophical ethics in the analytical tradition. See James Childress, "The Identification of Ethical Principles," *Journal of Religious Ethics* 5 (Spring 1977): 39-66.

    The desire for precision threatens the power of a comprehensive method. But the issue is not over the desirability of philosophical rigor versus the benefit of social theory. Both are indispensable forms of knowledge for ethical reflection. The question is which domain galvanizes the total process of reaching a justifiable moral decision. Which particular emphasis achieves a superior disciplinary coherence for applied ethics? Stassen argues for a "focus upon social theory which includes philosophical analysis but extends beyond it" (Glen H. Stassen, "A Social Theory Model for Religious Social Ethics," *The Journal of Religious Ethics* 5 [Spring 1977]: 9). In this volume, we provide a streamlined version of Stassen's adaptation of Potter, a schematic model that seeks to be both useful and rigorous.

36. Henry Stob, *Ethical Reflections: Essays on Moral Themes* (Grand Rapids, MI: Eerdmans, 1978), pp. 3-6. For a distinction between task and collective responsibility, see Clifford G. Christians, "Can the Public Be Held Accountable?" *Journal of Mass Media Ethics* 3:1 (1988): 50-58.

part I

News

Democratic theory gives the press a crucial role. In traditional democracies, education and information are the pillars on which a free society rests. Informed public opinion is typically believed to be a weapon of enormous power—indeed, the cornerstone of legislative government. A free press is central to Jefferson's understanding of politics, for example, and Jefferson characteristically referred to an independent information system as "that liberty which guards our other liberties."[1]

Because of the press's privileged position (commonly called the enlightenment function) outside critics and inside leaders have persistently urged it toward responsible behavior. Thomas Jefferson himself lamented how such a noble enterprise could degrade itself by publishing slander and error. Joseph Pulitzer worried that without high ethical ideals newspapers would fail to serve the public and could even become dangerous. Early in the seventeenth century the French moralist La Bruyère chided newswriters for reporting trivia and demeaning their high obligation: "They lie down at night in great tranquility upon a piece of news . . . which they are obliged to throw away when they awake." A few years earlier John Cleveland cautioned against respecting diurnal makers, "for that would be knighting a Mandrake . . . and giving an engineer's reputation to the maker of mousetraps."[2]

Modern criticisms of journalism seem merely to echo complaints that are centuries old. However, the number of today's cavilers and the bitterness of their attacks set the present decade apart. A free press remains our national glory in a complicated world where expectations of journalistic performance are higher than ever before. Actually, the intense and widespread carping may have yielded a modest dividend: Never before have the media been so aware of the need for responsible behavior.

A self-conscious quality hangs heavily over newsrooms and professional conventions. Aside from the bandits and the pompous who remain untouched by any attacks, some movement is evident. How can journalists fulfill their mission credibly? Should Pulitzer Prizes be given to reporters who use deception to get a story? Why not form an ethics committee? Should journalism schools teach ethics courses or not? Such well-intentioned questions crop up more and more. Like the horsemen of old, one sees a stirring in the mulberry trees. Ezekiel's dry bones are revivifying. Only a little, perhaps, but a splendid little. As always, the smoke means at least a small fire somewhere. The cases in Part I present the primary issues and problems that are currently being debated among those with a heightened awareness of journalism's ethical responsibility.

The fresh interest in ethics and the profit to be gained from working through these cases are threatened by the press's commitment to independence. There is a rhetoric from as far back as Jefferson, who called for a nation "where the press is *free.*" Others have argued: "You cannot chain the watchdog"; "The First Amendment guarantees the news media's independence"; "Allowing controls by anyone makes us a mockery." And in a country where freedom is valued above all, accountability is not often understood clearly. Accountability, properly requested and unreservedly given, is alien territory. Although the belief in a free press is sincere and of critical importance, it often plays tricks on the press's thinking about ethics. Ethical principles concerning obligation and reckoning do not find a natural home within a journalism hewn from the rock of negative freedom. Part I advocates freedom of the press but promotes an accountable news system and attempts to provide content for that notion.

Ethical questions concerning conflict of interest, truthfulness, privacy, social justice, confidentiality, and the other issues we address here must be considered in an environment of stress. The latest Gallup polls reveal press credibility at 13.7 percent, the lowest figure in decades and an alarming one by anyone's measure. For some it represents kicking the chair on which you stubbed your toe. The anxieties experienced in a nation downsizing its world leadership often provoke outbursts against the messenger. Nonetheless, we must continue working on media ethics, even in these hard times. Restrictions tend to make newspersons feel stifled, yet the contemporary cultural climate demands that journalism employ restraint and sobriety.[3] Although the five chapters in this section cannot solve all the problems, the analysis and resolution of the moral dilemmas presented here address matters of high priority on the journalist's agenda.

NOTES

1. Thomas Jefferson, Address to Philadelphia Delegates, 25 May 1808, in *The Writings of Thomas Jefferson,* ed. Andrew J. Lipscomb (Washington, DC: The Thomas Jefferson Memorial Association, 1903), vol. 16, p. 304. For similar highly quoted passages, see his Letter to Marquis De Lafayette, 4 November 1823, and his Letter to Dr. James Currie, 18 January 1786, in *The Writings of Thomas Jefferson,* ed. Paul L. Ford (New York: G. P. Putnam's Sons, 1894), vol. 4, p. 132.

2. La Bruyère and Cleveland are quoted in William Rivers, Wilbur Schramm, and Clifford Christians, *Responsibility in Mass Communication,* 3d ed. (New York: Harper and Row, 1980), p. 2.

3. An important line of recent scholarship accounts for some of these shifts and stresses by understanding news as social narrative. See *Reading the News,* eds. Robert K. Manhoff and Michael Schudson (New York: Pantheon Books, 1986); James W. Carey, "The Press and Public Discourse," *The Center Magazine* (March/April 1987): 4-16; Theodore L. Glasser, "Communication and the Cultivation of Citizenship," *Communication* 12:4 (1991): 235-248. The implications for ethics are outlined in *The Communicative Ethics Controversy,* eds. Seyla Benhabib and Fred Dallmayr (Cambridge, MA: MIT Press, 1990).

chapter 1

Business Pressures

William Peter Hamilton of the *Wall Street Journal* once argued that "A newspaper is private enterprise owing nothing whatever to the public, which grants it no franchise. It is emphatically the property of the owner, who is selling a manufactured product at his own risk."[1] This is an extreme statement, yet over the last two centuries many American publishers and broadcasters have shared this attitude. Based on the principles of classical democracy and traditional capitalism, the individual's right to publish has been a strongly held convention.

This mood may be shifting somewhat, at least in theory. Increasingly, enlightened newspaper owners and executives realize their special obligation precisely because news—and not widgets—is their business. In First Amendment perspective, journalism is in fact a business, but of a particular kind.

Nothing is more difficult in the mass media enterprise than promoting the public good even though the rewards—professionally and financially—are not commensurate with such altruism. In actual practice, it becomes extraordinarily difficult to separate the media's financial interests from the public's legitimate news interests. The Constitution protects the media from government constraint, but the news is under the perpetual risk of corporate control. Granted, a conflict between the public's need for unpolluted information and the stockholders' need for profit is not inevitable. Needing to earn a respectable income and deciding to stop a dead-ended investigation could both be appropriate; moral questions emerge when the two are connected as cause and effect. Without a press pool to help pay expenses for a charter, a minor party candidate could not conduct a modern campaign. One person serving in two potentially conflicting capacities— for example, as executive for Columbia Broadcasting and board member for Columbia University—may indeed be working ethically.[2] Not every owner or executive is automatically suspect.

Nonetheless, ever since mass communications took on the character of big business at the turn of the twentieth century, there have been built-in commercial pressures. The angry critic Upton Sinclair said accusingly in 1920: "The Brass Check is found in your pay envelope each week . . . the price of your shame—you who take the fair body of truth and sell it in the market-place, who betray the virgin hopes of mankind into the loathsome brothel of Big Business."[3] As the ominous trend continues toward concentrated ownership of media properties, cost-conscious publishers threaten to overwhelm the press's noble mission.[4] The five cases that follow demonstrate how media practitioners are often caught in conflicting duties to their employers, to their readers or viewers, and to their own professional conscience. Examples in Part II regarding persuasion (advertising and public relations) and in Part III involving media ownership illustrate some of the conundrums that occur regularly in today's news business. It is no wonder the public remains enormously concerned whether media enterprises spend money honorably.

The first case, "The Time Warner Colossus," illustrates a disturbing trend in cross-media ownership. The pattern toward concentration has been occurring for decades, but it is reaching dangerous levels of integration. Although it may be financially beneficial in this case to combine the strengths of print and visual communications, Time Inc.'s acquisition of Warner raises ethical questions about independent artists and cultural imperialism.

The second case, "Civic Duties in Lewiston," considers potential conflicts between newspaper employment and activity in community affairs. It focuses on the owner's outside commercial affiliations as the most morally problematic.

The third case, "NBC and GM's Pickup," concerns the blurred lines between news and entertainment. Given the profitability of television news magazines, the pressures toward big audiences and cheap production have become virtually unstoppable.

The fourth case, "The Wichita Experiment," deals with *The Wichita Eagle*'s twin commitment to society and to subscribers/investors. The *Eagle* attempts to combine this traditional dichotomy in innovative ways.

The fifth case, "New Times in Los Angeles," revolves around the expanding percentage of ethnic subcultures in American cities. Highminded talk about social welfare and minority hiring clashes directly in this instance with the newspaper's profitability. Agape is the ethical principle by which a weekly supplement for the central city is evaluated.

Since biblical times, sages have warned against serving two masters. Nearly all professions—politics most notably—confront the same problem. Yet the issues cut especially deep in reporting. The conviction of former *Wall Street Journal* reporter R. Foster Winans was a highly publicized reminder that easy cash is always a temptation—for individuals as well as for companies. Leaking advance information from his "Heard on the Street" column to stockbroker Peter Bryant yielded a $30,000 under-the-table payment. Apparently even small amounts of money are occasionally worth more than our integrity as journalists. As some observers have noted, the issues of handling profit responsibly and spurning fattened pockets are not just a chapter in a book; they are the cornerstone of media ethics.

1. THE TIME WARNER COLOSSUS

In June 1989, Time Inc. acquired Warner Communications for $13 billion in cash and securities following a ferocious struggle against Paramount's takeover attempt. Over four months, the dramatic story filled 12,000 pages of sworn depositions about the legal entanglements that accompanied the clashes in the corporate boardrooms. The result was a business deal made in heaven: Time Warner had assets of $25 billion. "It is awesome how impressive this company will become," concluded Dick Munro, one of Time Warner's new chief executive officers.[5]

When Time Inc. was a separate company, its magazines included *Time, Southern Living, Sports Illustrated, Fortune, Life, Money,* and *People.* The magazine division had long been wonderfully profitable, controlling nearly one-fourth of all U.S. magazine advertising revenue. However, in recent years Time's investment bankers could not project more than 6 percent revenue growth annually for the future. The corporate strategy began to focus investment on video programming. But in spite of increasing involvement in video, the company considered itself underdeveloped here, given today's explosion in visual technologies. Since the early 1960s, Time Inc. had diversified into cable and book publishing in order to expand its growth potential. Most of these ventures had become household words: Book of the Month Club, HBO Video, Home Box Office, Time-Life Books, and Scott-Foresman. However, Warner's wildly successful records-and-music division, its film production capabilities, and extensive overseas marketing made the merger an attractive way to prevent an unwelcome buyout from a hostile company such as Paramount. Warner Bros. had long been one of the movie industry's top studios, scoring number one in the box office four of the last five years. It owned 2,200 films—including *Batman* and *Lethal Weapon*—1,500 popular cartoons, and 23,000 TV programs. Management predicted that combining the revenues and sales of Time and Warner would jump-start the new corporation into a growth cycle neither one would experience separately.

Critics have charged that executives from both companies were more interested in padding their income and stock holdings than in serving either stockholders or the public. According to *Fortune,* Steve Ross of Warner orchestrated a compensation package for himself with the new corporation "so abundant in dollars that, should the oilman fail to show this winter, Ross can shovel money into his furnace and have plenty left over in the spring." In addition to a multi-million-dollar salary and pension packages, upon completion of the deal Ross received $193 million in cash and stock-based compensation. In fact, these early warning signals about Ross dogged his career until he died of cancer in December 1992, when the company was in a positive cash flow but still staggering "under $15 billion in debt, and $1.2 billion in annual debt service."[6]

> Henry Luce III of Time Inc.'s Board of Directors, and former editor-in-chief Hedley Donovan objected to the merger on the grounds that Time had been primarily a journalistic enterprise in contrast to Warner's entertainment structure. As a matter of fact, the management staff responsible for the acquisition turned the independence of the news-editorial component into one of Time's problems. Video and print had never been integrated, they said; putting *Sports Illustrated*'s swimsuit issue in video format had been one of Time's few meager attempts to exploit the company's resources. Warner's electronic and visual expertise was seen to overcome that "deficiency" forever.

The Time Warner merger illustrates a disturbing trend of the last decade toward media conglomeration.

> Five years ago (1983) I suggested that sooner or later a handful of corporations would control most of what the average American sees and hears. Today leaders of the media industry are themselves predicting this. . . . And many of them are engaged in trying to make the predictions come true, but none of them talk about the social consequences. . . . The public learns only of the stock market transactions, the building of dazzling empires, and the personalities of corporate leaders.[7]

Ten years ago, 50 firms controlled half the U.S. media whereas 25 firms (including Time Warner) now hold that distinction. Furthermore, the structure is currently in place for those corporations soon to be controlling it all. If the current trends continue, spurred to frenzy by the information highway, the mass media will be owned largely by a dozen major companies before the next century. The unsettling political and economic results are obvious for a nation that prizes diversity of opinion and access to the marketplace. Obviously the independent decision making of practitioners becomes increasingly difficult as corporations expand into impersonal behemoths.

In terms of the agape principle in ethics, two issues arise from the Time Warner's development: (1) the rights of independent producers and (2) the problem of cultural imperialism.

In spite of the profitability of Time Inc. and its general corporate luster, its top executives were complaining that it did not own any important copyrights in the video sector of its business. Time's cable operations gave the company a distribution system, but software had to be purchased in the open market where prices continued to climb. Time concluded that "In the media and entertainment business of the future, the winners will own the copyrights to creative products, as well as avenues of distribution. We intend to increase our ownership of both."[8]

In order to own copyrights without violating the law, Time needed to own more creative talent. Thus, with the merger it expanded its copyright capabilities a hundredfold. In the process Time Warner was no longer motivated to draw on the resources of independent writers and producers. Time Warner solved its copyright problem by cutting itself off from the world's pool of ideas in favor of a creative staff that generally conforms to the values of the mainstream media. This is "repression by the bottom line"; enhancing a corporation's business position ironically diminishes the quality, flexibility, independence, and variety of the very programming it is designed to market.[9]

In addition to putting a squeeze on the creative sector, Time Warner viewed the international audience in an ethically inappropriate manner according to the agape principle. At a time when so-called foreign markets offered the greatest growth opportunities, only 10 percent of Time Inc.'s revenues were from overseas. Warner Communications, however, was a stunning financial success worldwide, with 40 percent of its profits coming from outside the United States.

In the media business, Warner's concept is called "synergy"; that is, an article can be spun off as a book, movie, or TV show domestically and then sold abroad through an international distribution network. Warner's prowess in spinning off *Batman*, *Superman*, and *Wonder Woman* set the standard by which the merged corporation would now compete with Sony of Japan, Bertelsmann of West Germany, Pearson PLC of England, and the handful of communications companies that control the world's media. Whenever the merger talks were threatened, global international media competition became the trump card to move them forward.

The ethical problem is that throughout the planning and execution of the merger, the international audience has been seen exclusively as a paying market, as an exploitable resource. No attention has been given to indigenous programming and enhancing local talent. It is this notion of a one-way information flow that carries over the colonial and paternalistic spirit no longer acceptable in politics or even in international economics. Since World War II, seeking to dominate another's culture is becoming increasingly as reprehensible as dominating another's government or business out of exploitative self-interest.

2. CIVIC DUTIES IN LEWISTON

The *Lewiston* (Idaho) *Morning Tribune* recently took a look at the community interests of its staff. Staff member Cassandra Tate summarized the issue in the newspaper article that resulted: "Should the journalist exercise the rights and responsibilities of citizenship by participating in civic and political affairs? Or should he/she remain above the fray, a neutral observer? There is a danger of conflict in the first course, the potential for social isolation and sterility in the second."[10]

As would be expected, the *Morning Tribune*'s publisher had the lengthiest list of civic involvements. A. L. "Butch" Alford, Jr., was president of the Idaho Board of Education and a director of the Lewiston Roundup Association, the Lewis-Clark Boys Club, the Nez Perce National Historical Park Advisory Committee, and the Twin County United Way. He also served on the St. Joseph's Hospital Lay Advisory Board, the Bonneville Power Regional Advisory Council, and Potlatch Corporation's Foundation for Higher Education. He was active in the Lewiston Chamber of Commerce and was a director of the Idaho First National Bank and of the University of Idaho Foundation.

The newspaper's editorial-page editor, Bill Hall, had recently returned to the paper after 16 months as press secretary for Idaho Senator Frank Church. Night managing editor Perry Swisher was serving on the Governor's Blue Ribbon Committee on Taxation, the Idaho Manpower Board, and the Idaho Advisory Committee to the United States Commission on Civil Rights. He was also advisor to the Lewiston Downtown Beautification Committee and the Public Safety Building Committee. Executive editor James E. Shelley had held a position five years earlier as campaign coordinator for a Democratic Senate candidate. Reporter Thomas W. Campbell was chair of the Lewiston Historic Preservation Commission, a Democratic precinct committee member, and a member of the Civic Theater Board. Part-time writer Diane Pettis was a member of the County Planning and Zoning Commission. Business writer Sylvia Harrell chaired the Lewiston Planning and Zoning Commission. Harrell's husband worked for Potlatch, the area's largest industry and a frequent subject of pollution stories.

A similar list could be drawn up for the staffs on most newspapers, particularly the smaller ones. The *Morning Tribune* follows standard policy: Staff members do not report on their own activities. But, of course, those who draw the assignments are aware they are reporting on the performance of their friend and co-worker or, in cases where editors or publishers are participants, on the performance of their bosses. For example, Gary Sharpe, a young reporter uninvolved in the community, encountered difficulties in covering the Roundup, Lewiston's annual rodeo, because the publisher served on its board. Said Sharpe, "I don't know how many times I've been confronted by a person aware of Butch's membership on the board who says, 'I think Butch would like to see this in the paper.'"

As one concrete result of the *Tribune*'s study, reporter Campbell was told he could no longer write about politics if he did not resign as a Democratic precinct committee member. Campbell took exception: "They're saying I won't give a fair interview to the Republicans because I'm a Democratic precinct committeeman. I'm saying that doesn't make one bit of difference."

Publisher Alford commented on the story about external involvements of his staff: "It's the first time in my association with the paper that we've thought to look at ourselves. . . . I hope as a result of our editorial coverage of ourselves we can see the weaknesses in our own process."[11] Alford's newspaper departed from tradition in publishing an open examination of its own operation. Alford also broke another tradition. Copies of his complete income tax return were filed with the newsroom secretary to be examined by anyone interested.

Most of the problems in this case come from potential role conflicts. The journalist's role as practitioner may at times contradict the journalist's role as citizen. The good a journalist can achieve is the publication of news as free from bias as possible. The good a citizen can achieve, on the other hand, is the social service that comes from responsible citizenship. The question, in part, is whether journalists should sacrifice their role as contributing citizens in order to be journalists, or whether the conflicts in this case are more apparent than real. For example, publisher William Branen of the *Burlington* (Wisconsin) *Standard Press* calls it a "terrible mistake" when journalists refuse to become involved in their communities. "That's why many large newspapers are going down the drain," he says. "They've lost contact with their readers."[12]

It can be reasonably argued that organizational memberships themselves are not a significant source of biased journalism. In the present case, it is likely that a reporter who is a Democratic precinct committee member could not be entirely fair in an interview with a Republican candidate. That bias, however, would not be the consequence of committee membership. The reporter might show bias whether on the committee or not. Hence, resignation from that job would be essentially cosmetic, since the reporter would surely remain a Democrat with perhaps strong political views.

On the other hand, it is possible that the reporter with active political interests is much more likely to be well informed about political matters than a politically disinterested reporter. It may be that even with a Democratic bias, reporter Campbell would do a better job interviewing either Democrats or Republicans than would someone who had no political interests. Thus, it does not seem possible that a human being can "remain above the fray, a neutral observer." Since humans are valuing creatures, neutrality is not possible. The moral obligation, then, cannot be to produce value-free journalism. The objective, as the Potter Box suggests, is to make clear at all times what values are operating.

Since bias-free reporting is not possible, another distinction becomes necessary. Note, for example, Alford's membership in United Way. A bias in favor of the ideals for which an institution stands must be distinguished from a bias toward the organization itself. Bias in favor of charitable giving is a proclivity that can be tolerated, but favoritism toward the United Way organization, its directors, and its paid employees cannot. Corruption or misuse of public funds by that organization should be reported vigorously and, indeed, can be if the journalist's bias is simply toward charitable giving and not in favor of the United Way as an institution. Moreover, Alford's affiliation with United Way ought not diminish publicity for other charitable organizations.

What kind of policy, then, should journalists adopt regarding membership in community organizations? Some would discourage membership in all organizations: religious, civic, country club, corporate, and so on. Such a policy, however, risks isolating journalists from community affairs. The damage would include loss of leads on important stories as well as frustration over the inability to pursue personal, nonjournalistic value commitments in an active, organized way. Thus, a policy preventing all organizational memberships has little to commend it. On the opposite end of the spectrum, media companies could ignore the question of organizational memberships altogether. They might do so on the grounds that biased reporting stems not from memberships per se, but from underlying value systems, making journalists' memberships in organizations a superficial matter. Using Aristotle's golden mean as an ethical guideline, it is not desirable to preclude all outside involvements, nor is it acceptable for the staff to have no restrictions at all. That leaves the problem of finding strategies for minimizing the conflicts that arise from community memberships. In this regard, the *Morning Tribune*'s policy of not allowing reporters to cover their own activities is sound. Commendably, the *Morning Tribune* took a second step, alerting readers to the staff's external activities.

The boss's affiliations are another matter. His presidency on the Idaho Board of Education and his membership on the Historical Park Advisory Committee would not likely create unmanageable conflicts, but several of his positions in commercial firms are clearly problematic. Potlatch is the largest local industry and is often under public scrutiny for pollution violations. Alford is also a director of the First National Bank and a member of the advisory council for Bonneville Power. These commitments are very questionable. A reporter's interest in pleasing the boss would inevitably conflict with a concern for sound news reporting. Would the reporter be free to investigate discrimination in hiring, irresponsible service, or mishandling of company finances?

The hazards can be minimized. Alford can make it unmistakably clear to the staff that he is a newspaper owner first and a member of Potlatch Foundation second. He can also convey his priorities to Potlatch as a condition for serving. If the *Morning Tribune*'s staff is made up of competent journalists, the message will likely get across. If, however, the staff see themselves primarily as employees and only secondarily as responsible journalists whose obligations are to the public, the point will not get through. Thus, Alford's clarifying his commitments—even in the best of all circumstances—can only reduce the likelihood of damage. His employees could be better "watchdogs" if he would sever his connections with Potlatch, First National, and Bonneville Power. Bitter experience has taught us, for example, that publishers sitting on the boards of utility companies often initiate pro-utility stories when rate increases are requested.

On a more fundamental level, Alford must consider whether he is caught up in a business mentality that subtly weakens his service to the community. William Allen White, an outstanding editor and publisher, once complained, "Too often the publisher . . . is a rich man seeking power and prestige. He has the country club complex . . . and the unconscious arrogance of conscious wealth. Therefore, it is hard to get a modern American newspaper to go the distance necessary to print all the news about many topics."[13] Within the free enterprise system, owners of media institutions often consider themselves entitled to write whatever policy they choose, provided such policies are legal. Ethically sensitive publishers and broadcast executives follow stronger guidelines, however, deliberately adopting specific safeguards against the bewitching power of business allegiances.

3. NBC AND GM'S PICKUP

On 17 November 1992, *Dateline NBC* ran a 15-minute segment "Waiting to Explode." Its focus was the safety of General Motors' full-size pickups in model years 1973–1987. These trucks are designed with gas tanks mounted outside the frame.

The *Dateline* report began with the story of Shannon Moseley, a teenager killed in a pickup given to him by his parents. A law officer described Shannon's screams as he died in the fire. Another segment showed a tearful twenty-two-year-old mother whose two infant daughters died in a similar crash. She could hear their screams as fire engulfed the cab. In this episode, *Dateline* also showed an empty pickup being hit from the side and bursting into flames. NBC called it "an unscientific demonstration" of how the gas would ignite if the tank were punctured on impact or fuel forced out of the cap.

NBC did not tell viewers that the tank had been filled to the brim and an improper gas cap used to seal it. *Dateline NBC* did not inform viewers that toy rocket engines had been taped under the truck to ensure a fire even if the tank did not explode or any gas leak out during the crash test. The incendiary devices were connected to a remote control and activated just before impact. NBC claimed a faulty headlight wire on the old car sent crashing into the pickup had actually sparked the fire, in effect making the flares unnecessary; therefore, they were not mentioned in the program.

And NBC did not tell viewers that its estimates of crash speeds were underplayed for both crashes. All these facts would come to light through the careful investigative work of—not the media—but the corporation whose reputation *Dateline* had impugned.

In a 19 November memo, General Motors blasted the program as "grossly unfair, misleading and irresponsible, . . . vicious and unjust," and charged that it was filled with "inaccurate statements, distortions, and facts wrenched out of context." It asked NBC why viewers were not told that the original crash giving rise to the lawsuit "was caused by a speeding, drunken driver who was convicted and spent time in jail for his crime." It complained that the audience was not informed that GM pickups during this period "actually had the lowest incidence of fatal injury in side collisions."[14]

Dateline producer Robert Read responded on November 20, claiming a fair and balanced report. "As to our crash demonstration," Read wrote, "we did show the public that at about 40 mph there was no leakage, and we feel our use of these demonstrations was accurate and responsible."[15] Now the battle heated up. In early December, GM demanded to inspect the demonstration vehicles firsthand. NBC dodged and avoided GM's request. GM insisted on seeing the test vehicles. NBC replied that the vehicles "have been junked and therefore are no longer available for inspection by anyone."[16]

Perhaps the matter would have died slowly in corporate memos, but for an anonymous call to the editor of *Hot Rod* magazine, informing the trade journal of the real cause of the fire at the crash test site. The caller was probably associated with the Brownsburg (Indiana) Fire Department and was present at the crash simulation; clearly this person did not like what she/he saw.

Immediately *Hot Rod* called General Motors for comment. The new information gave GM the break it needed. Within two hours, company representatives had located the demonstrator in a junkyard near Indianapolis. The videotape taken by firemen who were standing by suggested that only a brief burst of flame had occurred from the rockets and around the cap. The tank had not exploded. GM's examination of the truck's gas tank revealed no puncture at all.

GM outlined the facts about the "unscientific demonstration" in a scalding letter to NBC producer Robert Read, with copies to NBC–CEO Robert Wright and NBC News President Michael Gartner.[17] It was a journalist's worst nightmare: the investigators had done their own investigation, and evidence GM had would show NBC's economical unscientific test (conducted for only $8,000) to be ludicrous and deceptive.

On 8 February 1993, Gartner replied to GM's letter (on the same day GM initiated a suit against NBC), stating NBC's belief that the *Dateline* report "accurately detailed widespread concerns" and was neither "false" nor "misleading." Gartner explained that the sparking device fixed to the crash truck "was intended to simulate sparks which could occur in a collision."[18] NBC was defending itself by admitting to shoddy journalism.

The next day the network apologized. On Tuesday, 9 February, the co-hosts of *Dateline NBC* admitted point-by-point how the crash had been staged. "Within the past couple of hours," Jane Pauley told viewers, "the people at General Motors and our bosses at NBC have agreed to settle GM's lawsuit." NBC has concluded, said co-host Stone Philips, that "unscientific demonstrations should have no place in hard news stories at NBC. That's our new policy."[19]

NBC News President Michael Gartner announced his resignation in March. It was not to take effect until 1 August, so that he could be assured maximum pension benefits.

Gartner had at first defended the broadcast; he ordered an apology only when GM exposed the fraud and threatened NBC through a lawsuit. Thus, Gartner's critics were unimpressed.

> In his belated statement of resignation, Gartner did not seem fully cognizant of the enormity of his role in the near self-destruction of his once trusted and respected news organization. He said only that he hoped his leaving would "take the spotlight off all of us and enable us to concentrate fully on our business. . . . " His handling of the GM fiasco only confirmed the notion that news standards were not high on his list of journalistic imperatives.[20]

Subsequent public opinion polls indicated that CNN had emerged as the most trusted news organization. NBC, which had previously held the top slot, slid to fourth place—behind CBS and ABC. And Hugh Breslin of WHAG-TV in Hagerstown, Maryland, an NBC affiliate, pointed to another disastrous consequence.

> What NBC did with that piece is inexcusable. . . . The affiliates as a body of people are outraged. It was a terrible thing, and they certainly have

heard from me, as well as all the other affiliates who are involved in disseminating the NBC news product.[21]

NBC violated conventional standards and values of a professional news operation. In the initial stages it relied too heavily on parties with an axe to grind. NBC cut corners by hiring a testing company on a bare-bones budget. The story's producer was aware that the crash was rigged, and *Dateline NBC* proceeded even though its own written guidelines do not permit staging news. The best in the news business do not tolerate shoddy information-gathering practices or inaccurate stories—especially not outright fabrication. The guidelines in ABC's "News Standards" book are typical of broadcast news practices generally:

> Everything seen or heard on ABC News must be what it purports to be. We are in the business of reporting what has happened, and we are not in the business of making things happen. Consequently, ABC News has strict rules that prohibit various techniques and devices intended to stage, simulate, or recreate what actually happened. ABC News will not tolerate any practice which misleads the viewer.

There is a fine line between professionalism and ethics. If NBC had strictly followed standard news practices, it would not have acted immorally in this case. In order to prevent another fiasco, on 26 May 1993, NBC's David McCormick added a detailed section on testing procedure and expert credentials to its "News Policies and Guidelines" handbook.

Two trends in corporate thinking set the stage for the mess at NBC. For one thing, it has been assumed in the broadcast business that news operations lose money; but now all units of the media enterprise are expected to be profitable. It is no longer compelling to maintain quality news as a loss leader to enhance a network's credibility. And secondly, CBS's *60 Minutes* proved that there is big money in prime-time news shows. They cost about 50 percent less to produce than entertainment programming. NBC news was just turning a profit—hoping to compete with *20/20, 60 Minutes, 48 Hours,* and the other network magazines. As Everette Dennis of the Freedom Forum Media Studies Center concludes:

> There's enormous pressure on the TV magazines for pictures and hype. Once they become profit centers for the networks, they become susceptible to all of the same pressures that the entertainment divisions always had in keeping the audience and in keeping the ratings up.[22]

In terms of the Potter Box, the problem centers on the first quadrant. Demanding profitability for news operations tends to create a leadership style in which sound professionalism and solid ethics are not paramount. The heart of the issue and its resolution must be concentrated on in step one.

If dramatized news is done in a *cinéma vérité,* eye-of-the-storm way, then it is not surprising that since the GM debacle the ratings for *Dateline NBC* have gone up. As Douglas Gomery of the University of Maryland says: "In the end, I don't think it hurts NBC. The model is Hollywood. . . . 'All publicity is good publicity.' At least more people know about the show. Journalistically it's a disaster. Everybody is up in arms about it. But surprise, surprise, it's making more money."[23] Gartner was the cost-cutter par excellence at NBC News and turned it into an efficient machine. TV news magazines are now netting $1 billion annually, and *Dateline NBC* is one of those cashing in on the profits.

4. THE WICHITA EXPERIMENT

In Kansas, journalists at the *Wichita Eagle*, a Knight-Ridder paper and the biggest newspaper in the state, decided they needed to look more closely at the newspaper's relationship with the community it purported to cover. In the 1990 gubernatorial primary, Democrat Joan Finney, a former state treasurer, won, despite the perception at the newspaper that she did not have a chance. "Obviously, she knew more about what people were thinking than we did," said the paper's editor, Davis "Buzz" Merritt, Jr.[24]

Caught off guard by this development, and then frustrated with the vague rhetoric of the general election, Merritt changed the newspaper's approach to campaign coverage. The new tactics would be aimed at forcing the candidates to reveal their platforms and ventilating issues in such a way that the will of the electorate would not come as a surprise. Reporters were to press for answers aggressively when candidates dodged questions, especially on ten issues that the newspaper had targeted as being of special interest. The ten issues were selected on the basis of 500 interviews (conducted by the newspaper's research department) with local residents. The *Eagle* featured each of the ten issues in an extended background piece, but also reported on them in brief every week, updating the positions of the candidates, and taking note when candidates declined to state a position. The *Eagle* encouraged residents to vote and even arranged for people to register to vote at the newspaper office. The newspaper distributed a simplified election guide to more than 100,000 nonsubscribers and at adult literacy classes. It also cooperated with the local ABC affiliate, KAKE-TV, in encouraging people to register and vote.

These efforts dovetailed with a push for "customer obsession" undertaken chainwide by Knight-Ridder, a push born out of concerns for the future of an industry with sluggish circulation statistics. At a lecture at the University of Kansas, the state's largest university, James K. Batten, Knight-Ridder's chief executive, said that people who feel "a real sense of connection to the place they live" are more likely to read newspapers. He asked, "If communities continue to erode, how can we expect communities to prosper over the long term?"[25] The *Eagle*'s new style of election coverage was aimed directly at strengthening that sense of connection to community and attacking head-on declining voter turn-out rates.

The next year, residents surprised journalists at the *Eagle* in a new way—with their passion over an issue. Operation Rescue, a huge, well-orchestrated anti-abortion protest, came to Wichita. Over the summer almost 1,800 people were arrested in a month and a half as abortion protesters and counter-protesters turned the city upside down. Merritt said, "I don't think we knew enough about our community to know that that many people would invest that much time and energy."[26] This tumultuous "Summer of Mercy" reminded the newspaper of another aspect of "community connectedness"—the need for journalists to have sufficient knowledge of their community to know what issues would stir local emotions.

The *Eagle* extended its efforts at community connectedness with its "People Project": The newspaper published an extensive series of in-depth articles on issues it had already identified as important to its readers. This time, though, the articles were framed in a way intended to encourage responses from readers. Additionally, three times during the course of the series the newspaper rented a hall where those interested in sharing their views could gather to discuss the issues without a leader of any kind directing things. In short, the newspaper (again cooperating with a local TV station and a radio station) was attempting literally to create a public sphere.

In its efforts at community connectedness, the *Wichita Eagle* is taking two professional values usually seen as being mutually exclusive and assuming, instead, that they can overlap. One value is called "spinach journalism": The newspaper's role is to tell people what they *need* to know in order to be well-informed citizens. The other value is that newspapers must tell readers what they *want* to know, or else readers will spend their information budget (of both time and money) elsewhere, and newspapers will perish. Often it is assumed that readers are not very interested in what they need to know—the confusing details of a state budget, for instance. However, what they want to know—celebrity gossip or school lunch menus, for example—is not very important or likely to give them the information they need to act as a responsible electorate. Ordinarily, making readers the source of the newshole results in pandering or "dumbing down."

Under the first commitment (i.e., to give information readers need to be well informed), a newspaper's duty is to society. In a democratic system that gives voters the responsibility to pick their leaders and to decide upon assorted ballot initiatives, it is crucial that voters have access to sufficient facts to make an informed decision. Under the second commitment (i.e., to tell readers what they want to know), the newspaper's duty is to subscribers and investors, those who provide the revenue that allows the newspaper to stay in business.

It is often noted that this dichotomy naively overlooks the inescapable economic fact that newspapers cannot give readers what they need unless they also give them what they want. That is, a newspaper has to remain profitable if it is to have the resources to tackle unpopular issues and causes. What often goes unremarked is the paternalism implicit in this dichotomy, the assumption that readers have to be force-fed the information they need. Editors at the *Eagle* seem to be confronting the second assumption as well as the first in their efforts to improve "community connectedness."

Aristotle's golden mean is helpful in sorting out this dichotomy. At one extreme is the greedy newspaper motivated only by the potential for profit, and thereby giving its readers nothing but titillating, entertaining news that is cheap and easy to gather. At the other extreme is the serious, socially responsible newspaper that is willfully oblivious to its readers' desires on the premise that "we know what's best for you."

The *Wichita Eagle* is trying to find the middle ground between these extremes. It is looking for ways to decide with, rather than for, its readers what the content of the newspaper needs to be. In this process, employees at the newspaper will have to look carefully at how they are assigning their loyalties. "The motivation behind the activist model is not without risk. . . . In their efforts to turn the news agenda over to readers, editors must guard against freezing the agenda."[27] In striving to do right by society, journalists might be glossing over their own obvious responsibilities. Investigative pieces about some political or economic scandal are more important to work on than a story about who made the local high school honor roll.

> Editors, in formulating editorial policy by community referenda, risk losing control over news decisions. Editors often seem alone in believing an issue is important, and their unpopular stands have helped change society for the better. . . . Speaking out against racism was a noble but dangerous tactic, yet the progressive writings of these editors eventually helped bring about change.[28]

Wichita Eagle executive editor Sheri Dill involved reporters in a study of area residents who "ought to be readers" but aren't, people who have strong ties to the community but no connection with the local newspaper. They found that these people were looking for "good news" about their local churches, schools, and charities. One reporter commented that "Some of these people are pretty self-involved; they are not curious about the rest of the world."[29] Certainly, journalism driven by markets can neglect less popular problems. To the extent that reporters dismiss as "self-involved" those interests of readers that do not happen to intersect with reporters' interests, efforts at expanding community connectedness are likely to stall. But to the extent that the staff at the *Wichita Eagle* continue to involve readers in decisions about the content of the newspaper, they are likely to strengthen that connection.

5. NEW TIMES IN LOS ANGELES

In 1952 the *Los Angeles Times* hopped on the highway to the suburbs and became the first metropolitan newspaper in the United States to publish zoned editions for different parts of its circulation area. Many other newspapers followed the *Times* in producing sections catering to suburbanites, providing many of their readers news that hit closer to home—and advertising more in tune with area businesses. But for most of the history of the *Times* publishing zoned sections and editions, the central city was left out. For the two decades after it first published a suburban section, the newspaper offered nothing comparable for the central city. Then, in 1973, it introduced a section, but dropped it a year later because of a lack of advertising. Until 1992, after riots jolted Los Angeles, it did not publish another one.[30]

The *Times* was not alone in focusing on suburban readers. But the newspaper's publisher in the 1970s, Otis Chandler, made it clear that the newspaper had made a conscious choice not to target low-income residents. "We cut out unprofitable circulation, and we arbitrarily cut back some of our low-income circulation," he said in 1977. In a 1978 television interview, Chandler acknowledged that the *Times* fell short in its coverage of the minority communities in the city; he said that targeting low-income readers would not make economic sense, because "that audience does not have the purchasing power and is not responsive to the kind of advertising we carry." This kind of thinking changed in the 1980s at the *Times* and other papers, according to Clint C. Wilson II and Felix Gutierrez; they linked the shifts to increased hiring of minority journalists. However, the central city of Los Angeles remained without a special *Times* section.

There has been support among *Times* editors for providing focused, ongoing inner-city coverage in recent years: Metropolitan Editor Craig Turner said in 1992 (after plans for a special section had been announced) that he and Senior Editor Noel Greenwood had been pressing for "the same level of coverage to the residents and readers of those areas that we do to other parts of L.A. County." "For economic reasons," he said, "it has not been done." In contrast to the situation for the central city, in 1992 the *Times* was publishing five regional editions for areas like Orange County and the San Fernando Valley, along with four weekly or twice-weekly community news sections. The central city was the only part of their circulation area without a special section. The *Times*, the nation's largest metropolitan daily newspaper, had spent tens of millions of dollars on the zoned editions to compete with newspapers like the *Los Angeles Daily News*, its chief competitor in the San Fernando Valley, and the *Orange County Register*.

In 1991, the year before the riots, a zoning task force at the *Times* had paved the way for a change by recommending that a central city section become a high priority. *Times* executives then decided the section would be published. According to management, the driving force behind the recommendation was linked to public service: a recognition that the central city area had changed since the 1970s, becoming more diverse and posing more complicated urban issues that merited more coverage beyond spot news often focusing on crime. No vehicle was available for communities to communicate with one another, and the *Times* could help provide one. The riots in April 1992 hastened the plans for the section, according to Editor Shelby Coffey III.

The *Times* emphasized the public service role of the section over economics in discussing the start-up. "We hope and expect that there is an advertising base there, but our priority really is to fulfill our role as a communications vehicle at this very critical time," *Times* spokeswoman Laura Morgan said. She said this was unlike the decision to drop the previous inner-city section in 1974: "This time, our decision is not driven solely by advertising. . . . We hope we'll be encouraging a dialogue and better understanding of these communities." The editor of the new section, Mary Lou Fulton, said later that the newspaper was committed to publishing the section regardless of how few ads were sold.

The weekly section, called *City Times*, made its debut in September 1992. The section, a tabloid of 32 to 48 pages with a full-time staff of 10 people plus freelancers, was distributed with the full Sunday *Times* in central Los Angeles. In addition to a circulation of 85,000 with the *Times*, 15,000 free-standing copies were distributed free of charge in news racks inside and outside the city.[31]

City Times focused on the kind of intensely local coverage that big-city newspapers often neglect. Each week the section devoted a page to news from each of six areas. In addition to the neighborhood-based coverage, *City Times* ran a weekly cover story related to a topic such as schools or business. Three reporters had assignments to cover subjects that related to community interests and needs, including immigration, housing, education, transportation, and ethnic communities. *City Times* also covered high school sports, listed community events, and summarized City Hall actions that affected the area. Another feature, "Voices," provided local opinion in a variety of forms from commentary pieces and letters to the editor to rap and poetry.

City Times was produced downtown at *Times* headquarters, but the section's staff was based in a strip shopping center in South-Central Los Angeles. As the community began learning of the section, walk-in traffic from the area became common. The section's staff tried to help people understand the ways in which they could gain access to the media by distributing an information sheet that described how to reach reporters.

City Times also tried to foster communication among the diverse cultures of the community by providing a multilingual voice-mail service for comments, story ideas, and letters to the editor. The service was available in English, Japanese, Korean, and Spanish in an effort to reach out to a community in which half of the residents speak Spanish and many were born in other countries. The *City Times* staff was also multilingual.

In the months after *City Times* was introduced, some readers thanked the section's editor for sports coverage and for items about community events and needs. Advertisers also responded favorably. Although the *Times* would not release details of ad volume or financial performance, the section drew far more ads than expected. At the same time, amid continued questioning of L.A. media performance after the riots, the *Times* was criticized for not providing a bigger staff for the South-Central office, and for not distributing *City Times* to all of the paper's readers.

For journalistic decision makers, there is a central issue here: Do newspapers have an ethical obligation to provide coverage to all significant segments of their geographic areas whether they make money from them or not? At the root of this question lies another: Do human beings have intrinsic worth apart from their utility value to individuals or groups? Although other ethical perspectives can contribute to answering this question, the principle of other-regarding care for persons as ends in themselves (expressed in the ethics of agape) provides a powerful motive beyond profit. For agape, meeting human needs is central to a worthwhile human existence; therefore, it points to a journalism that helps to meet these needs.[32]

Agape's emphasis on love for other human beings does not eliminate hard questions that news executives and their employees must face in the rough-and-tumble of economic competition. By calling for loving action without concern for reward, agape creates a tension with the economic motivations that shape the decision making of the commercial news media. What if starting a section for an inner-city area does not yield a strong advertising base and instead costs a newspaper so much money that dozens of newspaper employees lose their jobs? What if some of these employees are those recently hired as part of an effort to diversify the newspaper's staff racially and ethnically? Is serving a potential constituency of readers worth sacrificing the livelihoods of some of the newspaper's own workers and impinging on other goals of the newspaper?

Although the *Times* must make money to stay afloat, its decision to abandon a central city section in 1974 and not to provide another one for nearly two decades is morally unacceptable. If the central city were on the periphery of the newspaper's circulation area, and therefore on the fringes of the constituency it should serve, the decision would be more easily justified; agape does not insist on making bad business decisions in the interest of serving every conceivable community of human beings. But central Los Angeles is at the *Times*'s doorstep and therefore presents a moral obligation to provide consistent coverage.

While the *Times* can be criticized for not acting sooner, it did decide ultimately to create the special section. In fact, the decision, along with the effort to distribute some copies free of charge, was carried out during a year when the *Times* was being buffeted by a recession in Southern California that had cut the paper's advertising revenue. The paper announced in November 1992 that it would stop publishing its distant San Diego County edition, which was losing circulation, and cut 500 jobs through a voluntary employee buy-out program (the second offered in about a year) and attrition. Industry analysts viewed the moves as drastic. During the previous year, advertising linage in the newspaper industry as a whole showed the worst decline since World War II, and linage at the *Times* had dropped 14.7 percent and continued declining in 1992. Faced with these economic realities, the *Times* could have been swayed to postpone the section.

In addition to endorsing the decision to publish *City Times*, the principle of agape applauds its content and approach. Its community news pages have included many stories focusing on people's needs: assistance for homeless families, a computer class at the YMCA, $70,000 in grants for a literacy center, job search help, counseling for men who abuse women, free vaccinations, a shuttle bus service. It has also included stories of healing and good works in the community: a housing project where residents have united, a vegetable garden recovered from the weeds at a high school, mural paintings that let children express their feelings about the riots.

Cover stories in the section have related to social and economic issues in the community: problems with enterprise zones, a lack of ethnic and racial diversity in the Los Angeles Police Department command, the continued pain in the Korean community in the wake of the riots. In addition, the "Voices" pages have offered those in the community an opportunity to express their opinions. A fourteen-year-old African-American girl contributed two poems, one expressing her "courage and pride" and the other voicing her pain after the riots and her desire for equal treatment. Others interviewed for their opinions included a street clarinetist, college students in a community service scholarship program, and two opponents of bilingual education.

City Times also applied the ethics of agape through efforts to build community bonds. *City Times* staff members have promoted their ties with the community by holding meetings with residents, working out of an accessible office, and helping residents understand how to communicate with them. These actions also have the potential to foster bonds among members of the community by enabling them to communicate with one another through the newspaper. The multilingual voice-mail system has been an innovative effort to join diverse groups separated by the difficult barrier of language. In content, too, *City Times* has attempted to foster multicultural bonds by reporting on diverse cultural events.

The litmus test of agape's commitment to persons is whether the *City Times* is steadfast over time. Will there be a commitment of economic and human resources to ongoing coverage, a commitment to stick with efforts to meet needs and build human bonds even if these efforts are not on as large a scale as they could be? Carol Bradley Shirley, assistant editor of the *Times* Westside section and a South Los Angeles resident, pointed powerfully to the importance of this kind of commitment as she expressed her frustration about press neglect of the inner city:

> Let's say you live in Santa Monica and someone wants to put a liquor store on your block. You don't want a liquor store on your block. You and some neighbors get together and make a couple of signs. You go to the city council. The Westside section of the *Times* is right there to report how you feel, and to let people know about the plans for the liquor store. Others read about it and join your little group. Soon your voice grows loud and is amplified by the coverage of the *Times*. Next thing you know, the council decides that a hearing is in order. You may not get your way, but you get a hearing.
>
> If you live in South Los Angeles, as I do, you are on your own. Hundreds of people would have to show up at a council meeting before anyone in the press would take notice of your unhappiness with plans for the liquor store. Another one goes up and there's not much you can

do about it. And then another and another. Sooner or later, you give up. Anyone, it seems, can do anything he wants in the place where you live. . . .

The city government and the press, the supposed public watchdogs, have stood by in silence. Sure, the press steps in when there is a riot or a shooting. Many a Pulitzer has been won by covering the woes of the inner city. But no one is there day to day to cover the issues that are standard in the coverage of any white, middle-class area. While zoning and planning may not be a reporter's dream subjects, they provide the infrastructure of a community. When residents lose control of the infrastructure, they lose control of the community.[33]

By investing in *City Times*, the management of the *Los Angeles Times* provided at least a measure of continuing coverage of the communities and issues in the central city rather than hit-and-miss, reactive reporting. *City Times* challenges editors and reporters to make people-focused, community-oriented journalism the norm for the profession. It also calls on journalists to be sure that they cover their whole communities and do not neglect the disenfranchised among them.

NOTES

1. Fred S. Siebert, Theodore Peterson, and Wilbur Schramm, *Four Theories of the Press* (Urbana: University of Illinois Press, 1956), p. 72.
2. The question is whether one's dual obligation in this instance prevents the fulfilling of both contracts. See Joseph Margolis, "Conflict of Interest and Conflicting Interests," in *Ethical Theory and Business*, eds. Tom L. Beauchamp and Norman E. Bowie (Englewood Cliffs, NJ: Prentice-Hall, 1979), pp. 361–372.
3. Upton Sinclair, *The Brass Check: A Study of American Journalism* (Pasadena, CA: published by author, 1920), p. 436.
4. For a useful overview of concentration in various media, see *Who Owns the Media?* 2d ed., ed. Benjamin M. Compaine (White Plains, NY: Knowledge Industry Publications, 1982).
5. For the quotations and background negotiations summarized in this case, see Bill Saporito, "The Inside Story of Time Warner," *Fortune,* 20 November 1989, pp. 164–210.
6. Sharon Moshavi, "Fire Sale," *Forbes,* 8 November 1993, pp. 96–98; and "Time and Warner May Now Become Time Warner," *Business Week,* 9 March 1992, pp. 31–32.
7. Ben H. Bagdikian, *The Media Monopoly,* 2d ed. (Boston: Beacon Press, 1987), p. x.
8. Charles Thiesen and Barbara Beckwith, "Marketplace of Creative Ideas May Now Go to Highest Bidder," *Los Angeles Times,* 20 November 1989, p. B7.
9. For a description of this problem and the international audience issue that follows, see "Business: The Counterattack," *Newsweek,* 26 June 1989, pp. 48–54.
10. Cassandra Tate, "Conflict of Interest: A Newspaper's Report on Itself," *Columbia Journalism Review* 16 (July/August 1978): 44–48.
11. Ibid.
12. Karen Schneider and Marc Gunther, "Those Newsroom Ethics Codes," *Columbia Journalism Review* 23 (July/August 1985): 55.

13. Commission on Freedom of the Press, *A Free and Responsible Press* (Chicago: University of Chicago Press, 1947), pp. 59–60.

14. For a copy of this memo written by William J. O'Neill, write the authors at the College of Communications, 119 Gregory Hall, University of Illinois, Urbana, Illinois 61801. Copies of all the correspondence between *NBC News* and General Motors between 5 November 1992 and 9 February 1993 are also available from the authors.

15. Letter from Robert Read to William O'Neill, 20 November 1992.

16. Letter from Robert Read to William O'Neill, 4 January 1993.

17. Letter from William O'Neill to Robert Read, 2 February 1993.

18. Letter from Michael Gartner to William O'Neill, 8 February 1993.

19. "No Scandal, No Story," *Newsweek*, 22 February 1993, pp. 42–43.

20. Bob Sunde, "Fake News: A Passing Scandal or Here to Stay?" *Quill* (April 1993): 10.

21. W. Dale Nelson, "Competition Casualty," *Quill* (May 1993): 38.

22. David Zurawik and Christina Stoehr, "Money Changes Everything," *American Journalism Review* (April 1933): 27–28.

23. Ibid., p. 30. For financial details regarding network news magazines, see pp. 27–30.

24. As quoted in Michael Hoyt "The Wichita Experiment," *Columbia Journalism Review* (July/August 1992): 44.

25. James K. Batten, "Newspapers and Communities: The Vital Link," Forty-first Annual William Allen White Speech, University of Kansas, 8 February 1990 as quoted by Jay Rosen, in "Community Connectedness Passwords for Public Journalism," *The Poynter Institute for Media Studies*, St. Petersburg, FL, 1993, p. 4.

26. Hoyt, "The Wichita Experiment," p. 44.

27. John Bare, "Case Study—Wichita and Charlotte: The Leap of a Passive Press to Activism," *Media Studies Journal* 6:4 (Fall 1992): 156.

28. Ibid., p. 157.

29. Hoyt, "The Wichita Experiment," pp. 46–47.

30. Background for this case is drawn from Ben H. Bagdikian, "The Best News Money Can Buy," *Human Behavior* 7:10 (October 1978): 63–66; Felix Gutierrez and Clint C. Wilson II, "The Demographic Dilemma," *Columbia Journalism Review* 17 (January/February 1979): 53–55; Bradley Johnson, "'L.A. Times' Woos Inner City," *Advertising Age*, 10 August 1992, p. 26; Ron LaBrecque, "Racial Resentment Hits Home," *Washington Journalism Review* 14:6 (July/August 1992): 25; M. L. Stein, "Relentless Criticism," *Editor and Publisher* 126: 36 (4 September 1993): 11; Leola Johnson, "Managing Diversity," *Quill* 81:3 (April 1993): 25–26; telephone interviews with Laura Morgan, spokeswoman for *Los Angeles Times* publisher David Laventhol, 12, 29 March and 20 April 1993; Calvin Sims, "The Los Angeles Times in Retreat," *New York Times*, 7 November 1992, p. 35L; and Clint C. Wilson II and Felix Gutierrez, *Minorities and Media: Diversity and the End of Mass Communication* (Beverly Hills, CA: Sage Publications, 1985), p. 56.

31. Details concerning *City Times* are drawn from *Los Angeles Times* publicity materials and interviews with section editor Mary Lou Fulton on 18 March and 20 April 1993.

32. Agape's focus on human needs and its steadfast commitment to persons figure prominently in the ethics of Paul Ramsey, *Basic Christian Ethics* (New York: Charles Scribner's Sons, 1950). Steadfast love is also central to his medical ethics; see *The Patient as Person: Explorations in Medical Ethics* (New Haven, CT: Yale University Press, 1970), pp. xii–xiii.

33. Carol Bradley Shirley, "Where Have You Been?" *Columbia Journalism Review* 31:2 (July/August 1992): 25–26. She wrote after the riots but before the announcement of a central city section.

chapter 2

Truthtelling

The press's obligation to print the truth is a standard part of its rhetoric. Virtually every ethics code begins with the newsperson's duty to tell the truth under all conditions. High-minded editors typically etch the word on cornerstones and on their tombstones. Credible language is pivotal to the communication enterprise.

When Pontius Pilate asked "What is truth?" he posed the question people of every kind have struggled to answer. And as ideas and world views shift, so does the definition of truthfulness. Newspeople must live within the larger ambiguities about truth in Western scholarship and culture today. Their situation is further complicated by budget constraints, deadlines, reader expectations, editorial conventions, and self-serving sources. Journalism is often referred to as "history in a hurry"; providing a precise, representative account can rarely occur under such conditions. At the same time, sophisticated technology generates unceasing news copy and the journalistic gatekeeper must choose from a mountain of options, often without the time to sift through the moral intricacies.

The cases that follow introduce several dimensions of the truthtelling issue. Although not every conceivable aspect is offered, truth is enlarged beyond a simple facts-only definition.[1] One way to broaden our scope, for example, is to consider the antonym of truthfulness and to account for newsgathering as well as newswriting. The opposite of truthtelling is deception, that is, a deliberate intention to mislead. Outright deceit occurs infrequently in the newswriting phase; only rarely, if ever, does a reporter or editor specifically and consciously give the wrong story. But deception in newsgathering is a persistent temptation, because it often facilitates the process of securing information.

The first case in this section, "News Photo Electronically Altered," struggles with the ethical issues raised by the dramatic advances in media technology. Traditionally, a sharp line has been drawn between truth and fiction, between news and entertainment, but this boundary is impossible to maintain in an age of electronic images that can be manipulated mechanically.

The second case, "Abortion Profiteers," illustrates the high stakes sometimes involved in investigative reporting. Whereas several ethical questions are woven through the case, deception is central in the analysis. Gathering news under false pretenses for a noble end is a typical issue occurring in small towns as well as in major cities. When newspapers or stations receive phone calls about violence in an orphanage, maggots in the bandages of patients at a nursing home, mechanics cheating on repairs, deception becomes one possible alternative for breaking the story. The important question, then, is whether deception can ever be ethically justified.

The third case, "Sexism and Hillary Clinton," represents one of journalism's most persistent agonies. Social groups suffering from discrimination are particularly sensitive to stereotyping, and the days of pleading ignorance or making excuses are over. Numerous instances of blatant sexism could have been chosen, but they present no moral dilemma; sexist language dehumanizes and is therefore wrong and unprofessional. This case is entangled by the aggressiveness with which presidential politics are ordinarily covered. From Christine Kraft's dispute with KMBC-TV in Kansas City until now, sexism or alleged gender discrimination is also a point of contention in employment, not just in message content.

The fourth case, "Branch Davidians in Waco," questions our conventional definitions of newsworthiness. Here life and death is at stake, and the moral problem is how to protect lives effectively when confronting the abused, aggrieved, and mentally deranged who thrive on publicity. The Branch Davidian episode helps to establish the ethical parameters that ought to shape journalistic decision making in convoluted, high-tension, and dangerous circumstances.

The fifth case introduces a discussion of Henrik Ibsen's *An Enemy of the People*. Ibsen, the great Norwegian playwright of the nineteenth century, wrote it out of concern for the future of democracy. In Arthur Miller's adaptation to a modern setting,[2] this vivid and troubling drama demonstrates how institutions respond to the painful truth of contaminated springs on which the city's livelihood depends. With skyrocketing public concern over environmental, health, and safety issues, *An Enemy of the People* is a powerful context in which to examine the press's role as a social institution.

6. NEWS PHOTO ELECTRONICALLY ALTERED

Ron Olshwanger was only an amateur photographer, but he took a powerful picture of a St. Louis firefighter trying to breathe life into two-year-old Patricia Pettus. It was published on the front page of the *St. Louis Post-Dispatch* on 31 December.[3]

When Olshwanger heard late in March that this photograph had received a Pulitzer Prize, he went with his wife Sally to the managing editor's office to celebrate. "I don't even drink. I hope they have a Diet Coke down there," he told a *Post-Dispatch* reporter before he arrived. The managing editor sent out for Diet Cokes on ice along with the champagne, and when the assistant director of photography shot a picture for the next day's story, the Coke can was on the desk beside the Olshwangers.

FIGURE 2.1   Photo of Olshwanger and his wife at the office reception (top). In the photo that ran on the front page of the *Post-Dispatch,* the Diet Coke can had been removed electronically (below).

SOURCE: From the *St. Louis Post-Dispatch* (March 31, 1989). Photograph by Ron Olshwanger. Reprinted by permission.

But Robert C. Holt III, director of photo technology, airbrushed the can out of the photo with the aid of the paper's new Scitex system. The managing editor insisted that there had merely been a miscommunication. He had told his staff that the picture would look better without the can and assumed it would be cropped accordingly. Holt remembers somebody suggesting, "Let's Scitex out the Coke can," but in retrospect, he thought that probably meant "Let's crop it out." "For some reason," Holt said, "I airbrushed it out. It was stupid. It was my fault."

The incident was hotly debated internally because Holt himself had a reputation for promoting Scitex but steadfastly opposing image altering. Three years earlier he had warned the American Newspaper Publishers Association not to misuse electronic imaging systems. He was especially chagrined that the Pulitzer Prize–winning photo appeared in the first front-page picture the *Post-Dispatch* produced using Scitex. Even in retrospect, Holt is still not sure why he Scitexed away the can. "It was a more-than-usually hectic day and it was not until [I] went home that [I] realized what [I] had done." To photographers who became upset that the "mistake was made by the very same people who said it would not happen," Holt insists they should "do what I say, not as I do."

The *Post-Dispatch* staff have taken the incident seriously. They have discussed it openly with the public in terms of the technical advances that make abuses nearly impossible to detect. In fact, the staff was in the final stages of developing a company policy on electronic manipulation when the Olshwanger incident occurred.

In George Orwell's *1984* "there were the huge printing shops with their sub-editors, their typography experts, and their elaborately equipped studios for the faking of photographs."[4] Abuses have been common since 1857, when Oscar Gustave Rejlander combined 30 negatives to produce a single image in the "The Two Ways of Life."[5] On the whole, however, Orwell's wolf has been kept from the door. Since early photographic history, the press has denounced manipulated images, and the media continue to draw a hard line in principle between untouched photography for news and documentary, and photo images used in features and advertising. Thus, when *National Geographic* squeezes pyramids together to fit its cover's vertical format, the retouching does not create the frenzy that accompanied a staged photo at the *St. Petersburg* (Florida) *Times* and the *Evening Independent*. It was "a nothing event" in which a veteran photographer etched "Yea, Eckerd" on the bare feet of a teenage baseball fan. The photographer's 17 years with the company was terminated abruptly, according to the executive editor, on the grounds "that there is simply no room for people who don't tell the truth."[6]

The news press operates on the assumption that a picture taken by a photojournalist ought to meet the same standards as a reporter's stories. Just as reporters ought to guard against misrepresentation at all times, photojournalists must not fabricate events. Tom Hardin of the *Louisville Courier Journal* said: "It's tantamount to changing quotes. We're not in the quote-changing business,

I hope." Larry Nyland of *USA Today* agreed: "Manipulating news photos is something we do not do."[7] The moral obligation is to avoid deceiving the public; stories or pictures should carry the inherent meaning and present an accurate account. To do otherwise makes photographers second-class members of the newsroom who need not operate with the same professional standards as writers; they are subtly demeaned as merely providing art or diversion for the printed copy.

Along the lines of this historic distinction between news and entertainment, the *Post-Dispatch* news policy states: "To assure the integrity of our visual reportage, the Scitex system may not be used to distort or change the image in a way that misleads the reader." Scitex can remove dust particles and strike the correct color balance, but moving, eliminating, or adding elements is prohibited. If a picture is altered for a necessary reason, readers must be informed.

Sheila Reaves has argued correctly that this traditional guideline protecting the distinctiveness of news can serve only as a temporary measure while ethicists scramble to develop a more adequate framework in light of the revolutionary technological changes introduced by digital processing. New computer technology based on pixels (a computer term derived from "picture elements") contradicts the 135-year-old view that photography is a slice of reality.

> Because pixels are computer data, they can be moved, cloned, and colored. This new technology turns all photographs into pixel-based images with a new precedent. Anyone with access to the computer has unlimited access to altering the original image. . . . Before the advent of digital photo editing, a skilled printer had to make deliberate choices for manipulation, and it took time.[8]

Historically, a photograph is a record of something that reflects light. As long as Scitex systems cost $2 million and therefore only the major firms can invest in them, news photography may be protected in terms of the credibility with which it is seen to record that reflected image. But when pixel-based equipment becomes as common as personal computers, "Who will set the standards of digitized photography?" "Technology changes, ethics don't" is an old saw, but it is rapidly losing its applicability. And as Robert Gilka—formerly with *National Geographic*—observed about modifying photographs: "It's like limited nuclear warfare. There ain't none."[9]

7. ABORTION PROFITEERS

In May 1978 the *Chicago Sun-Times* received information from a highly reliable source that women were undergoing unnecessary abortion procedures in four Michigan Avenue clinics. The source, a government official who insisted upon remaining anonymous, claimed that each year hundreds of women were being misinformed by clinic personnel that they were pregnant. Apparently over 60,000 abortions were performed at these for-profit clinics yearly.

Working with the Better Government Association (BGA), a citizens' watchdog group, the *Sun-Times* began its investigation by sending female investigators into private agencies that referred women to the clinics. The investigators, pretending to seek pregnancy counseling, brought male urine specimens into the referral agencies for testing. On several occasions the pregnancy tests on the male urine were found to be positive, and the female investigators were referred for abortions to the Michigan Avenue clinics.

In order to pursue the story further, investigators attempted to obtain jobs at both the referral agencies and the clinics. Their employment resumés did not distort their background or qualifications for the jobs, but they did omit any journalistic connection. The first investigator to be hired worked as a receptionist at a swank clinic on Chicago's Magnificent Mile. As part of her job training, she quickly learned that women with negative pregnancy tests were told that the findings were positive or were simply not informed of the results. In the first few weeks of undercover work, she observed that more than 10 percent of the clinic's patients were given "abortions" even though their urine tests indicated that they were not pregnant.

Ultimately, the newspaper was able to obtain salaried jobs in all four clinics and two referral agencies. Several of the investigators worked as counselors or nurses' aides. None became involved in the operating room procedures, but they did have direct contact with patients both before and after the supposed abortions were performed. (At no time were the clinic operators or patients aware of the fact that these "health professionals" were really investigative journalists.) Over a period of four months, they observed abortions being performed on women in advanced stages of pregnancy, anesthetics being improperly administered, clinic personnel practicing medicine without a license, evidence of Medicaid fraud, and other improper practices. Frequent complications and even several deaths were documented.

In order to provide back-up support for their eyewitness observations, the undercover investigators photocopied more than 100 medical records from the clinics. The records were brought to the *Sun-Times,* where the names of the women were deleted. The act of photocopying the records without consent, however, was a violation of Illinois law.

The Abortion Profiteers series was published by the *Sun-Times* in November 1978. Subsequently, the state passed new laws to regulate outpatient abortion clinics. Two of the Michigan Avenue clinics were closed, one permanently, and several of the doctors involved left the state. One physician was ultimately sent to prison. One of the clinics sued the *Sun-Times* and the BGA; the suit was later dismissed.

The sensational charges published in the Abortion Profiteers series were based largely on direct observations of undercover reporters. Throughout the investigation, the *Sun-Times* and the BGA used a variety of deceptive newsgathering techniques to verify the information supplied by the anonymous source. But when, if ever, are journalists justified in lying to get a story? Does the abortion series provide a case of ethically acceptable deception? These are complicated questions that have no easy answers in everyday practice.

One way to assess the use of deception is to examine the purpose that it serves. On Mill's utilitarian grounds, journalists could claim that the misrepresentation served a greater good. After all, the newspaper series informed the general public about a dangerous and illegal scandal. Although the time-consuming news-gathering process may have prolonged some women's exposure to unscrupulous medical practices, ultimately the series enabled greater numbers of women in the Chicago area to make more informed decisions about whether and where to seek an abortion. This was further ensured by the governmental crackdown that occurred in the wake of the series. Given these benefits, the costs of deception may be viewed as justifiable, at least in retrospect.

On the other hand, the newspaper's methods run counter to several philosophical traditions. To Kant, all deception is morally wrong. In this case, the newspaper became involved in a web of deception that pervaded its entire news-gathering process. It is certainly reasonable to question whether the ultimate value of the findings is so great as to justify the many falsehoods that were told in order to obtain them.

Moreover, Kant's categorical imperative—to always treat people as ends and not means—would cast doubt on the strategies used in this particular case. For months, investigators observed nonpregnant women having "abortions." To protect their cover, the investigators rarely intervened to prevent these abuses; worse, they were at times at least indirect agents of the wrongdoing. The decision to continue gathering information for the story was often agonizing, and always made on utilitarian grounds: the newspaper's justifiable need to back up its sensational allegations with solid information. Nonetheless, these justifications may be considered morally shaky in view of the known harm inflicted on women during the months that the investigation was being conducted. Certainly, the sacrifice of scores of women to get a newspaper story would be rejected by the moral tradition of providing help to those in immediate need.

The categorical imperative is also useful for considering the appropriateness of the decision to photocopy the abortion records illegally. Kant's doctrine would not tolerate lawbreaking. Others would argue that lawbreaking is situationally tolerable, such as when it is necessary to speed to a hospital in order to save a life. But a special problem arises in the Abortion Profiteers case. Can journalists, who oppose government searches of newsrooms, justify their own decision to remove records from similarly private, professional institutions? Both law enforcement agents and journalists would claim that their actions were motivated by a utilitarian concern for achieving a greater societal good. On the other hand, Kant's maxim that "what is right for one is right for all" should compel journalists who approve of media but not governmental intrusiveness to examine the consistency of their position.

What standards can the media use for making difficult choices in similar situations? In her book *Lying*, Sissela Bok proposes that honest alternatives be thoroughly considered and debated before any form of deception or impropriety is practiced.[10] In the Abortion Profiteers case, the newspaper began its undercover probe after its source was unwilling to go on record or provide sufficient documentation for his allegations. It may be reasonably argued that there was no way other than through undercover methods to obtain a story of this nature; clinic personnel would obviously deny any wrongdoing and patients were unaware of it.

Thus, the journalists in this situation were left to choose between informing law enforcement authorities of the allegations or engaging in deception to further document them. The selection of the former alternative would run counter to a journalist's professional values and loyalties, and may not even have produced corrective action. However, the selection of the latter threatened to create a fabric of deception that was ethically unjustifiable.

Once undercover techniques were chosen as the least offensive alternative, what could have been done to minimize the moral costs? If the newspaper had retained medical personnel (for example, nurses) to apply for jobs at the clinics, it would have limited the journalistic misrepresentation while increasing the newspaper's participation in the very wrongdoing it was trying to expose. Having journalists pose as patients in the clinics would have reduced the potential for inflicting harm on others while exposing the journalists to the possibility of harm.

Ultimately, the newspaper decided to accept the problems and the risks involved in working in the clinics. Some of the ethical difficulty was relieved by the decision not to change the identities of the undercover investigators. Misrepresentation by commission—the creation of fictional names and backgrounds—was viewed as unnecessary and even dangerous in this case. The use of Aristotle's golden mean—misrepresentation by omission only—was the more ethically tolerable alternative. Although journalists were still going beyond their traditional professional role of recording events openly and neutrally, this use of passive deception enabled them to get the story while they at least minimized the potentially harmful consequences.

The Abortion Profiteers series had a dramatic impact on readers and policymakers. However, the newspaper failed to win a Pulitzer Prize, in part because of its use of deception, a problem similar to that raised by the Pulitzer judges in rejecting the *Sun-Times*'s "Mirage" tavern series that same year.[11] Nonetheless, undercover reporting remains a widely employed and accepted journalistic practice. As Bok directs us, when used under restricted conditions as a last resort to get an important story in a crisis situation, it may be a justifiable tool to inform the public about critical issues that need to be exposed. When used with impunity, however, undercover reporting fuels the public's concerns about the unchecked power and ethical standards of today's news media.

8. SEXISM AND HILLARY CLINTON

In the 1992 presidential election, Americans encountered in Hillary Clinton something they had never seen before: a potential first lady who was a career woman with her own record of public service. The media had a hard time knowing how to report on her. Was she the proper subject of "soft" feature stories about candidates and their families coping with the rigors of the campaign, a wife and mother to be asked about her favorite recipes and haircuts? Or was she potentially the next Bobby Kennedy, a woman who could become the most trusted advisor and confidant of a president, making her an appropriate target of investigative reporting? In the course of the campaign she was both, and more. She was labeled everything from wronged woman to supermom to sorority sister to well-respected lawyer to Lady Macbeth. Much of the reporting about her was interesting and informative and clearly within bounds. Much more of it was of dubious merit. The ultimate affront may have come when *U.S. News & World Report* called her "an overbearing yuppie wife from hell."[12]

Some critics inside and outside the media claimed that Mrs. Clinton was a victim of sexism. Others, mostly reporters, said the media were just doing their job—answering questions the electorate was asking about a potentially powerful public figure.

Mrs. Clinton's first exposure to a national audience came on *60 Minutes* in a joint interview with her husband Bill Clinton, then governor of Arkansas and one of half a dozen candidates in the Democratic presidential primary. Most of the interview was devoted to reports of Bill Clinton's infidelity. Both Clintons insisted that although certainly not perfect, theirs was a strong marriage. In the course of the interview, Hillary Clinton said, "I am not some little woman standing by her man like Tammy Wynette." The press declared her statement a mistake. However, no polls were taken on audience response to the remark, so there was no way to know whether voters reacted negatively or neutrally.

Blunder or not, the interview presented Hillary Clinton in the traditional role of supportive wife willing to say what was needed to further her husband's career. And although some of the campaign coverage framed her as the post-baby boom career wife that she was, many stories approached her derisively from a traditional point of view.

She was accused by the press of another misstep when Jerry Brown, also a Democratic presidential candidate, accused Governor Clinton of improperly giving state business to his wife's law firm. Hillary Clinton responded, "I suppose I could have stayed home and baked cookies and had teas. But what I decided to do was fulfill my profession." The statement was widely reported and cited as evidence that Mrs. Clinton did not respect wives who worked as homemakers. However, few news outlets reported the rest of her remark: "The work I have done as a professional, a public advocate, has been aimed to assure that women can make the choices—whether it's full-time career, full-time motherhood, or some combination." Drawing on such "errors," the media produced a spate of stories questioning whether Hillary Clinton was a liability to her husband's campaign. They seemed to ignore poll results that showed this to be a wrongheaded approach. The polls consistently indicated during the campaign that Mrs. Clinton was an asset, even when her approval rating was at its lowest.

Little changed in the media's relationship with Hillary Clinton when she became First Lady. For instance, in spite of polls showing that the population approved of her in general (and, specifically, was not bothered by her chairing the health care task force), *Nightline* spent not one but two evenings on the question of whether Hillary Clinton had too much power.

Writing in the *Nation*, Katha Pollitt said, "The sexist attack on Hillary Clinton is partly a lazy way to attack her husband." She cited Rush Limbaugh as one in a long line of protagonists who have used sexual slurs to express hostility to someone's politics. Attacking Hillary Clinton, said Pollitt, was one way of condemning "broad social and political transformations without making a case against them."[13] Republican fund-raiser Floyd Brown, in his newsletter *Clinton Watch,* called the president "a captive of the radical left, of which his boss, Hillary, is a member in good standing."[14]

In Pollitt's view, sexism is a broad media problem and cannot be reduced to hot-headed politics. She calls it her "own pet theory":

> The anti-Hillary media types, for the most part men, are protecting their turf. (The female snipers are just jealous.) . . . Journalism is actually one of the last bastions of old-fashioned irrational male privilege. . . . While women have managed to eke out a small preserve in feminist-oriented Op-Ed columns—Anna Quindlen, Ellen Goodman, Judy Mann and many others—the Big Beats belong to the big boys. . . . Could it be that the anti-Hillary pundits and talking heads are motivated by status anxiety and fear for their jobs? . . . Ted Koppel worries about what Bill will do if Hillary does a bad job. He ought to be worrying about what he himself will do if she does a good job, and Cokie Roberts decides she'd like a shot at his.[15]

Karen Tumulty, a Washington correspondent for the *Los Angeles Times*, concurred that women continue to be "denied the plum jobs. . . . Not many women write the big analytical stories, which are really the name of the game these days in political coverage."[16]

However, Pollitt's aside about "female snipers" does not adequately explain why some of the most strident reporting on Hillary Clinton has been done by women. Geraldine Ferraro, who as Walter Mondale's running mate was the first woman on a major party's presidential ticket, observed that women reporters were not immune to sexism: "There were a lot of women assigned to my campaign who had to prove they were reporters first and foremost and women second. And it became a real problem. They were as insecure about a woman running for office as I was in doing it, and it was amazing."[17]

Some of the reporters who have covered Hillary Clinton do not agree that their stories had a sexist slant. Eleanor Clift of *Newsweek* said that Mrs. Clinton was "covered for the most part by women reporters who . . . [are] very sympathetic to her." Michele Ingrassia of *Newsday* insisted that she just meant to "have fun" in an article in which she analyzed Mrs. Clinton's wardrobe, tweaking her advisors who were trying to modify her image through it.[18] The missteps and weaknesses could stem largely from the complexities of contemporary politics, with the press trying to come to grips with the president's "First Advisor," in the heated context of Whitewater. From this perspective, the press generally has been using the same mixture of sympathy and skepticism with which they cover all Washington power brokers. Meanwhile, in an age of radical cultural and social changes, the media must cover a "professional baby boomer" as First Lady—First Lady being a position "framed by the expectations of the nineteenth century."[19]

This case presents an array of interesting and important questions. Have previous First Ladies wielded power comparable to Hillary Clinton's influence? Do working women tend to demean the value of work done by women in the home? Is it appropriate for President Clinton to appoint his wife to lead a task force directing one of the most important policy questions of his administration? Just what do we expect the role of political spouses to be?

But the ethical question in this case concerns the media's treatment of Hillary Clinton. Is she a victim of sexism? Or is aggressive coverage of her the wide-ranging, no-holds-barred reporting that a public figure wielding a great deal of power must expect? Or should one expect and excuse errors that occur when radical shifts are underway in society?

Women have been stereotyped regularly by the press. The problem has long, historical roots. During the women's suffrage movement, for example, news accounts often distorted the issues. Editorials regularly denounced women's "petty whims," spoke of "appalling consequences," and even used labels such as "insurrection." Sample twentieth-century writing of any kind (including journalism) and the failures become obvious: overemphasis on clothes and physical appearance, the glorification of domesticity, the portrayal of women as empty-headed or at least nonintellectual.

Evidence abounds that such problems persist. For instance, the Women, Men and Media project, which monitors media coverage of women, reported in 1993 that for the fifth year in a row women were underrepresented as subjects and sources of news as well as in the newsrooms themselves. In 20 front-page stories, for instance, only 15 percent of the sources were women. Only 34 percent of the front-page stories were written by women.[20] Pay scales are still not equitable across genders. Joan Byrd is an ombudsperson for the *Washington Post* and some women are high-ranking executives now, but women are still underrepresented in influential positions. Jane O'Reilly assails the "pale male" pundits (in skin color and perspective) who dominate editorials and commentary.[21] In fact, the existence of sexism in the media has been proven so repeatedly, and with so little change over time, that one scholar has concluded we should quit doing studies that prove what we already know about media sexism, and start teaching "readers to talk back to their newspapers in ways that make clear their dissatisfaction with how women are represented and portrayed."[22]

Where does sexist language creep into reporting? Where are women missing as sources, and how could they be incorporated? How can we bring more women on staff and into management positions, so that their points of view are more likely to be represented? One beginning would be to consult texts on nonsexist language, for example, the *Associated Press Handbook* entries on "courtesy titles," "persons," "mankind," and "women"; the section on "sexism" in Brian Brooks and James Pinson's *Working with Words*;[23] "Guidelines for Nonsexist Usage" in Francine Frank and Paula Treichler's *Language, Gender, and Professional Writing*;[24] or Casey Miller and Kate Swift's *Handbook of Nonsexist Writing*.[25]

In order to help promote change, readers and viewers ought to monitor closely the media's gender sophistication. Junior Bridge recommends several guidelines for assessing press performance focused on gender expectations:[26]

Traditional Behavior	*Nontraditional Behavior*
• works or acts under the direction of men	• takes risks and acts independently
• is emotionally expressive	• is brusque and aggressive
• is sensitive to others' feelings	• thinks rather than feels
• meets media standards of beauty	• appearance is unconventional or unimportant
• is seen primarily as sex object	• has non-sexual friendships with men
• works with others	• is loner
• cares for children	• takes charge of situations
• provides emotional support for men	• is logical thinker
• engages in home-related activities	• is professional or business leader

Sexism is embedded in our culture and social order. It will take the persistent, thoughtful attention of editors everywhere to identify and expunge it. We could fairly conclude that the best professionals covering Hillary Clinton are not sexist, but instead they are aggressive reporters or sometimes uncertain in their judgment as social mores shift. However, the broader agenda remains. Even if press behavior is improving rapidly in particular cases, there is an urgent need for institutional and structural reform. Otherwise, a long and entrenched history will not be permanently changed.[27]

9. BRANCH DAVIDIANS IN WACO

On Sunday, 28 February 1993, agents of the Bureau of Alcohol, Tobacco, and Firearms (ATF) staged a raid on the compound housing an obscure religious cult near Waco, Texas. Six cult members and four agents were killed, and 16 agents were injured in the abortive action. Fifty-one days later, officers of the Federal Bureau of Investigation (FBI) used tanks and tear gas in an attempt to force the residents out of the compound. During the second raid, the compound was set ablaze and burned to the ground, killing 79 members of the cult, including 18 children. The siege at Waco that resulted in these two dramatically tragic events was conducted under the scrutiny of media from around the world. The little-known religious cult "Branch Davidians" became a household word.

Even before the initial raid on the compound, the media had a highly visible and hotly contested role in the story. Initially, in response to rumors of stockpiling enormous quantities of firearms and later rumors of polygamy and sexual abuse of children, the local newspaper—the *Waco Tribune-Herald* (part of the Cox Enterprises chain)—had begun investigating the secretive cult that had installed itself in Mount Carmel, its 77-acre compound outside of town. The months of reporting had culminated in a seven-part series that was ready for publication in early February; however, federal officials asked editors to withhold the series; by then plans for the ATF raid were underway.

Editors agreed to postpone the series, although only in part because of the official request. *Tribune-Herald* editor Bob Lott said, "We were considering their concerns. The major other concern was security for ourselves—the newspaper and its employees—and the routine things, legal questions and the like."[28] Shortly, before the series ran, newspaper representatives met again with ATF officials; they once more requested that the series be withheld, or that if it did run, they at least be notified ahead of time. Lott said, "After that meeting . . . we decided we had heard nothing that would mess up what ATF was planning. I have always believed you should weigh the consequences of publication, but after listening to the final presentation from them, we decided we had heard nothing that would convince us of the harm to society by publication."[29]

On Friday, 26 February, Lott notified ATF officials that the series would begin on the following morning. He said he did not know at that time when ATF intended to make its move, although he had heard rumors that the raid was set for the first of March. The *Tribune-Herald* opted for beginning the series over the weekend, when fewer workers would be in the newspaper building, out of concern for the security of its employees and its physical plant. Lott said past instances of violence at the compound and the stockpiling of weapons fueled these concerns.[30] Lott told ATF officials that they could pick up a copy of the first installment of the series as soon as it came off the press—shortly after midnight—at the newspaper's loading dock.

The series debuted on Saturday, 27 February, on the front page, under the headline "The Sinful Messiah." In addition, two full pages inside detailed the history of the cult, its beliefs, and the charismatic power that Branch Davidian leader David Koresh seemed to have over the more than 100 followers who lived with him in Mount Carmel. A related editorial entitled "That's Law and Order?" criticized local officials for failing to investigate the cult. Lott said the newspaper "carefully avoided even a hint of our knowledge that the Bureau of Alcohol, Tobacco, and Firearms might be involved," so that the articles would not signal cult members that a raid was in the works.[31]

Later that day someone at the newspaper was alerted that ATF intended to storm the compound on Sunday. The source of the tip and the employee who received the information were not identified. Acting on the information, the *Tribune-Herald* sent five reporters, two photographers, and an editor to the scene. In addition, a reporter and a photographer from the local CBS affiliate KWTX-TV were present during the raid. Neither reporters nor law enforcement officials expected anything resembling the disaster that ensued. Rick Bradfield, news director at KWTX-TV, said, "We honestly didn't think this would amount to more than a knock on the door and a couple of arrests," and a lieutenant in the local sheriff's department said he thought the raid would only take five minutes.[32]

Immediately after the raid, law enforcement officials were accusing the *Tribune-Herald* of giving away ATF's plans, either by starting publication of their series, or, worse, by placing a telephone call to the compound. Both the newspaper and television station have denied those charges. Within a few weeks, one of the ATF agents wounded in the raid sued the newspaper for alerting cult members that a raid was imminent. This version of events was disputed by a Branch Davidian member who said that those in Mount Carmel were alerted to the raid by another cult member who was outside the compound at the time.

After the tragically violent raid, hundreds of journalists descended on the scene. It was immediately apparent that the media's role in the siege was going to be scrutinized. So, within a week of the initial raid, and long before events in the case had played out, the Society of Professional Journalists had appointed a task force to study the actions of the media at Waco. Again, no one could have foreseen that the siege would drag on for weeks, or that it would end in the fiery annihilation of the compound. But it was clear that an intriguing story was unfolding in Texas, and journalists pushed and prodded for interesting ways to report the story, often in ways that were criticized.

Dallas radio station KRLD and CNN both broadcast extensive interviews with Koresh on the first day after the standoff. KRLD did so after consulting with and obtaining the approval of law enforcement officials. CNN acted on its own. Later during the siege, at the request of federal officials, KRLD broadcast a 58-minute statement by Koresh. FBI agents believed Koresh might surrender from the compound if his statement, a mixture of scripture readings and sermonizing, was aired.[33] Also during the standoff, Dallas talk-show host Ron Engleman aired messages sympathetic to the Branch Davidians without consulting federal negotiators.[34] Media outlets were condemned alternately for refusing to consult with law enforcement officials and for failing to maintain a suitable independence from government agents in the case.

During the course of the siege, the tense emotions were not necessarily evident to the naked eye. In an effort to help show the drama, some photographers used telephoto lenses and nightscopes to produce interesting images at the scene. Cult members inside the compound were very likely seeing the pictures about their situation being broadcast. As a result, the media were criticized both on the grounds that their photos might reveal tactics of law enforcement officials, and that they might heighten whatever fear cult members felt at being trapped, and thereby provoke dangerous responses.

Government officials came in for their own share of criticism during the 51-day siege. After the first few days, they removed the media from the immediate vicinity of the compound and clamped down on the amount of information released to the media. Many in the media felt these actions inevitably led to some of their excesses in gathering information.

Besides going to great lengths to get video images for illustrating the story, some media outlets broadcast unsubstantiated rumors as fact. Ray Preston, a reporter for KFOR-TV said, "In the beginning, it was pretty poor because people were not going with the facts. There was a lot of speculation. They were actually [reporting] things that were not substantiated." Apparently, one reporter announced that the siege had ended on the basis of a report that FBI agents had left Waco. "This guy took a rumor and went ahead with it. Rumors are fine, if you check out rumors, but we sat and watched this guy do a live shot from our satellite truck with our mouths open. I was just amazed."[35]

On 26 January 1994, a jury acquitted 11 Branch Davidians of all murder and conspiracy charges. The defendants argued that they acted in fright and self-defense when their group killed four of the 100 federal agents who had raided their compound exactly one year minus two days earlier. Four were acquitted completely, two were found guilty of weapons charges, and five charged with voluntary manslaughter, that is, in legal terms, "acting in the sudden heat of passion caused by adequate provocation." The jury's verdict was a stunning defeat for the Justice Department, which had prosecuted the case for ATF. Despite parading 396 guns from the compound rubble and 120 government witnesses, prosecutors were unable to prove that the Branch Davidians fired first.

The conduct of the media raises an array of questions. The task force marshaled by the Society of Professional Journalists asked: 1) whether the *Tribune-Herald* was responsible because it initiated its seven-part series at an inopportune time; 2) whether reporters from the *Tribune-Herald* and KWTX-TV violated any ethical principle or tipped the ATF agents' hands when the reporters staked out the compound on the morning of the initial raid; 3) whether media coverage of that raid contributed to its tragic consequences; 4) whether the media acted properly in airing messages from and interviews with Koresh; 5) whether the Dallas talk show host was justified in sending messages into the compound; 6) whether the use of pictures obtained with telephoto lenses and nightscopes compromised anyone's safety; 7) whether law enforcement officials contributed to some of the more egregious acts of journalists by keeping them at such a distance; and 8) whether the media protested limits on their access to information loudly enough.

A question the task force did not address but which deserves scrutiny in this and similar cases is how the media can appropriately deal with a character such as David Koresh, someone who is hungry for publicity, shrewd and often articulate, but also demented.

The task force concluded that journalists who covered the siege at Waco "were not perfect. Neither were they responsible for some of the serious allegations of unethical behavior leveled against them."[36] It defended journalists on several specific grounds. It found that the *Tribune-Herald* acted appropriately in choosing when to publish its seven-part series on the cult. It noted that the paper did postpone the series once (at least in part—if not exclusively—at the request of government officials) and that the public's need to know about weapons stockpiling and allegations of child sexual abuse argued against delaying the series further. The task force reported that "no concrete evidence" was found to indicate that reporters tipped off those inside the compound to the initial raid by ATF agents. It noted that both the *Tribune-Herald* and KWTX-TV made efforts to keep from being detected by cult members. The report pointed out that the cult could have learned of the raid from other sources, such as the helicopters flying over the compound on the day of the raid or the "considerable police radio traffic that morning."[37] Finally, the task force concluded that KRLD acted "in a responsible manner" when it cooperated with officials in airing a message from Koresh. It explained that officials at the radio station "were prompted by legitimate expectations that they would help resolve the dilemma and even save lives."[38]

The task force was more critical of other aspects of the Waco coverage. The media were criticized for conducting live interviews with Koresh, and for broadcasting pro-Koresh messages on talk shows, on the grounds that these interviews might have interfered with negotiations going on at the time. They also were criticized for their use of pictures taken with telephoto lenses and nightscopes, and for broadcasting unsubstantiated rumors. The task force chastised the media for not pressing government officials harder for more information and for better access to the site, suggesting that the organization of a press pool might have solved several problems. It also criticized media support groups (including its sponsor, the Society for Professional Journalists) for not being "as proactive as they could have been in intervening on behalf of journalists."[39]

The task force found no evidence that media reporting of events on the day of the first raid did anything to aggravate that situation.

> The coverage of the stand-off at Mount Carmel as it eventually continued for 51 days is more problematical. While journalists had many reasons to be present to cover the story, the extent and intensity of the coverage as the siege wore on may have exacerbated an already difficult situation. Furthermore, it is certainly possible that the media organizations and the public were exploited by the Branch Davidians who sought publicity for their cause. It is also possible that the journalists and the public were exploited by the federal government officials as they tightly controlled the scene and the information pipeline.[40]

In spite of this, however, the task force concluded that "to say that the media coverage contributed to the tragedy is not a supportable criticism."[41]

This conclusion drew some criticism of its own. Deni Elliott argued, for example, that the report lacked internal consistency.

> Few could disagree with the task force conclusion if it means that the media were less morally responsible for the deaths and the lengthy standoff than were David Koresh and some of the Branch Davidians, and some public officials. But it is justifiable to hold journalists accountable for failing to meet the moral requirements of their own profession. In this respect, it is possible, if not likely, that journalistic failing did "contribute to the tragedy."[42]

Elliott also faulted the report for basing some of its conclusions "on a fallacious appeal to ignorance."[43] Pointing to language in the report such as "the charges . . . are not substantiated" and "found no concrete evidence," Elliott wrote, "One wonders which principals—either critics or supporters—the task force interviewed. . . . Who declined interviews? Without this information, the task force's argument comes down to saying, 'We couldn't find that they did. So, we conclude that they didn't.'"[44]

Members of the task force noted that their report was "not intended as the definitive judgment of right and wrong behavior of news organizations and individual journalists."[45] Rather, it was intended as a starting point for analyzing events at Waco and preparing for similar events in the future. The guidelines recommended by the task force offer concrete advice for specific journalistic failings. They leave for the long-term agenda at least two complicated issues about truthtelling.

First, what is the proper role of government authorities in tightly controlling news coverage? Deni Elliott considers this a substantive concern:

> The task force seems to suggest that if law enforcement believes that a news organization's assistance will end a standoff, the news organization is morally permitted to assist. . . . It would be nice if law enforcement officers were always the good guys, but society needs a healthy skepticism about which side is right.[46]

Second, sophisticated technology among competitive news organizations exacerbates explosive situations such as this. Satellite trucks, video through cellular phones, and video computer technology increase pressure to report fast and sensationally.

> Partly managers' eagerness to maximize their investments, partly new expectations of immediacy—often pushes reporters to ignore reporting fundamentals. . . . The considerations surrounding high-tech reporting are . . . confronting news directors across the country. Unless

professionals—and educators, for that matter—address ways of handling this new ethical issue, the questions that haunted the coverage of the Waco siege will crop up in the future.[47]

For all ethical theories, the starting point and overriding goal ought to be protecting human life. The carnage at Waco makes it a tragedy of immense proportions, raising issues often confronted in medical and military ethics.

10. AN ENEMY OF THE PEOPLE

In Henrik Ibsen's *An Enemy of the People,* most of the important players appear in the opening scene. Peter Stockmann, the mayor, stops at his brother's home and meets his dinner guests. Hovstad, editor of the local paper, arrives and tells the mayor that the *People's Daily Messenger* is to print an article by Dr. Stockmann extolling the medicinal value of the town's baths, Kirsten Springs, in Norway. The mayor, who implemented the idea, resents the credit lavished on his brother for founding the baths.

Dr. Stockmann enters his home with another guest, Captain Horster. In high spirits, Dr. Stockmann says that his days of living on starvation wages are over since his brother, the mayor, obtained a position for him with the Health Institute set up by the baths. Peter Stockmann refers to the article to be published, and Dr. Stockmann replies that he may no longer want it printed. The mayor demands an explanation; when his brother declines to offer one, the mayor upbraids him for not subordinating himself to authority and leaves in anger.

Petra Stockmann returns home and hands her father, Dr. Stockmann, a letter. It reveals that the baths are contaminated by bacteria from the discharge of a tannery upstream. His suspicions had been aroused by an excessive number of visitors who suffered from typhoid and gastric disturbances the previous year. Samples of the water that he sent to the university's chemists for testing confirmed his fears. Dr. Stockmann now speaks disparagingly of the Health Institute's board of directors who originally refused to accept his recommendation on how to lay the water pipes to the baths; he condemns them as politicians who reject a doctor's advice. As a result, the entire water system will have to be relaid. He sends his report and the university's results to his brother who is on the Institute's board of directors. When Hovstad hears about it, he realizes the scandalous nature of the news and states that he will print the story because the public has a right to know. He adds that the paper and the people should praise Dr. Stockmann for his discovery.

The following morning Morten Kiil, Mrs. Stockmann's father, drops by the Stockmanns' home. He is skeptical about Dr. Stockmann's report on the existence of "millions of tiny animals invisible to the eye," but gleefully thinks it is a good trick to play on the mayor and the town council. Kiil is still bitter toward the mayor, who was instrumental in removing him from the council.

Hovstad arrives as Kiil is leaving. Hovstad confides to Dr. Stockmann that he desires to use the story to rid the town council of "that smug cabal of old, stubborn, self-satisfied fogies." Aslaksen, the paper's publisher, calls on Dr. Stockmann and assures him of both his support and that of "the solid majority." He wants to stage a demonstration to compliment Dr. Stockmann, but stresses moderation. He brushes aside Dr. Stockmann's protestation that a simple issue is being overamplified. After Hovstad leaves, Dr. Stockmann tells his family that it feels good to have the majority of the townspeople on his side.

Peter Stockmann arrives and informs his brother that it will cost $60,000 to relay the pipes, and it will take two years. In the meantime, the news of the poisonous springs would irreparably devastate the town's financial fortunes. The mayor dismisses his brother's report as hyperbolic; he advises him to be discreet and rectify the problem with his skills as a physician. Dr. Stockmann accuses the mayor of treachery in his unwillingness to acknowledge his error. The mayor admits his concern for his reputation and intends to prevent his brother's report from reaching the board. Dr. Stockmann retorts that the mayor is too late, since the "liberal, free, and independent press will stand up and do its duty!" Peter Stockmann castigates his brother's irresponsibility for habitually expressing his thoughts before he fathoms their implications. Dr. Stockmann maintains that it is a citizen's duty to share new ideas with the public. The mayor argues that the public is better off with traditional ideas. He demands, as his brother's superior on the board, that the report be withdrawn. When Dr. Stockmann refuses, the mayor threatens his brother with dismissal from the Health Institute, points out the dire consequences for his family, and labels him a traitor to society. When the mayor leaves, a distressed Mrs. Stockmann cautions her husband about his brother's political clout. When he states that truth is on his side, his wife warns him that truth without power is useless. Dr. Stockmann nevertheless is confident of victory in the end, and reminds her that the press and the majority are on his side. She urges him to live with injustice and provide for his family. Dr. Stockmann, however, insists on standing by his principles.

In the editorial office of the *Messenger,* Hovstad and his reporter, Billing, conclude that Dr. Stockmann's article will expose the mayor's incompetence. Hovstad hopes that the town council will be replaced by a liberal administration. Aslaksen, the publisher and print shop owner, agrees to print it; but he cautions moderation. He distinguishes between the paper's attack on the national government and on local authorities. Although it is all right to do the former, Aslaksen questions the latter because of the local consequences when a town's administration is destroyed.

Peter Stockmann arrives at the newspaper office's rear entrance. He asks Hovstad about his brother's article and spots it in Aslaksen's hands. The mayor tells them that if the article were printed and it became necessary to change the water system, then the people would have to be taxed. He adds that it will take two years to reconstruct the pipes and the town's businessmen would be without income during that time. Aslaksen, chairman of the Property Owners Association, is horrified by these revelations. The mayor accuses his brother of vindictiveness. Hovstad is also swayed. The mayor offers to provide Hovstad with an article presenting his side of the story.

Just then, Dr. Stockmann arrives and the mayor hides in an adjoining room. He asks for the proofs and Aslaksen replies that they are not ready. Dr. Stockmann notices the mayor's cane and hat on the table, opens the door to the next room, and an embarrassed mayor emerges. Dr. Stockmann realizes what his brother is attempting to do and mockingly tells him that he has the truth, the majority, and the press on his side. Aslaksen and Hovstad, however, say that they are not printing his article after all because it will ruin the paper and the town. Aslaksen asks Dr. Stockmann to consider the consequences for his family. Dr. Stockmann stands by his principles and insists on publicizing the truth at any cost.

In Act 2, Captain Horster offers his house for a public meeting called by Dr. Stockmann. Before Dr. Stockmann can present his case, the rowdy crowd votes on the mayor's suggestion and Aslaksen is elected chairman of the meeting. He calls on the mayor to speak first. Peter Stockmann accuses his brother of wanting to destroy Kirsten Springs and legitimate political authority. The mayor argues that abusing the democratic right to free speech leads to revolution and chaos, and he moves that his brother be prohibited from reading his report. The hostile crowd punctuates the mayor's tirade with uproarious shouts of anger at Dr. Stockmann.

Conceding defeat at the hands of the majority, Dr. Stockmann agrees to drop the subject of the springs and to address a more vital topic. He sarcastically refers to liberals and radicals, like Hovstad, who have fought for the principles of free speech. Hovstad interrupts him and says that he will not impose his will on the majority, especially if they are his readers. Dr. Stockmann passionately lashes out at the belief that the majority is always right, referring to Jesus' crucifixion and Galileo's solar system. When he attempts to read his report, a citizen threatens him with violence. Aslaksen calls for a resolution that Dr. Stockmann be declared an enemy of the people when he threatens to publish his report in out-of-town newspapers. Only Captain Horster and a drunk vote against the motion.

Act 3, the following morning, brings a litany of disasters for the family of Dr. Stockmann. The windows of their home have been shattered. The glazier refuses to fix the windows, and they are also given an eviction notice by the owner. Dr. Stockmann decides to leave for the United States. Petra returns early; she has been fired from her job. Captain Horster comes with the news that he, too, is jobless. The mayor arrives to hand his brother a letter of dismissal from the Health Institute board of directors, and informs him that the people are signing a petition not to seek his medical services. He urges his brother to retract his report on the poisonous waters in order to calm people's fears and be reinstated. When Dr. Stockmann refuses to do so, the mayor charges him with conspiracy. He asserts that Dr. Stockmann has waged a destructive campaign against the springs in order that his father-in-law, Morten Kiil, could buy up Kirsten Springs stock at half its value. Dr. Stockmann is shocked. The mayor threatens to arrest him if he publishes his report outside town.

As the mayor leaves, Kiil enters and places on the table Kirsten Springs stock that he just bought. Kiil states that the polluted waters are coming from a tannery that has belonged to his family for generations. He wants Dr. Stockmann to retest the water and pronounce it clean so that his family reputation is not sullied and the stock will be inherited by Mrs. Stockmann. If his son-in-law refuses, he will give the stock to charity. They are interrupted by Aslaksen and Hovstad's arrival; Kiil leaves. They want to make Dr. Stockmann a hero for buying up stock to force the management to improve public health. They, however, require him to donate money to their paper to offset an anticipated short-term loss of circulation for supporting him. Dr. Stockmann is attracted by the offer to clear his name, but is aghast at the thought that they are merely proposing that he sanctify the springs with medical respectability without rectifying the root cause of the problem. Hovstad excoriates Dr. Stockmann for his refusal, calling him insane with egotism for wishing to put his family through further suffering.

They are interrupted by the arrival of the Stockmanns' children, Morten and Ejlif. Morten's head is bruised. While he was fighting with another boy who called his father a traitor, he was attacked by the whole group. Dr. Stockmann decides to accept the "enemy of the people" label, condemns his opponents as "ambassadors from hell," and resolves to stay. Maybe, he muses, he can teach street kids to be free and independent seekers of truth. Dr. Stockmann tells his family that the reason they are alone is because they are fighting for the truth. As he speaks, a hostile crowd gathers outside his home for further harassment.

For democratic societies, truth is indispensable. Only when citizens know the facts, it is assumed, can they make responsible judgments about public policy. Along this line, Ibsen agrees that truth is a powerful political force. The issue for him is what happens when the truth is painful. When everyone hears good news that will benefit them, the information is welcome and serves as a social lubricant. But Ibsen is worried that when the truth hurts, when it disrupts the status quo, the truth usually creates a crisis rather than promotes the general welfare.

An Enemy of the People is a realistic depiction of the complex human reaction to tragedy. It asks whether any persons or institutions can be depended on when the springs are found to be poisonous and their profitability destroyed. To answer that question, Ibsen examines several democratic mainstays in their response to the scientific evidence. The mayor refuses to take responsibility since he would thereby admit the mistakes of his administration. The newspaper buckles once it learns that the majority of its readers would not appreciate this revelation. The businessmen's council opposes the higher taxes and lost revenue.

Even Dr. Stockmann's last resort—the average citizen—refuses to listen in a town meeting called to discuss the problem. Dr. Stockmann, as an individual with conscience, does generally follow the truth out of principle; yet his own arrogance, his feuds with his brother, and his recalcitrance are Ibsen's way of indicating that even the morally enlightened individual is not pure. Individuals may be the bastion of a democratic society, but even they are not a final and reassuring answer to disturbing truth. The play ends with uncertainty about democracy's future.

Ibsen's play features characters who are not despicable. On all levels, the democratic institutions involved (the press, medicine, politics, and business) are not outrageously evil. They are narrow-minded, spiteful, and defensive, but they are not totally corrupt. Thus, the resolution of Ibsen's concern is extremely difficult; it is not a simple matter of rejecting an immoral practice or two. The current debates—national, regional, and local—over water pollution, acid rain, toxic dumps, garbage landfills, chemicals, and oil spills illustrate the same complexities as Ibsen's drama. They suggest that our penchant for scapegoats and easy fixes is not productive.

NOTES

1. For a classic statement of truthfulness-in-context, see Dietrich Bonhoeffer, *Ethics* (New York: Macmillan, 1955), pp. 363-372.
2. Arthur Miller, *An Enemy of the People: Adaptation of Henrik Ibsen's En Folkefriende* (New York: Penguin Books, 1984). A film version starring Steve McQueen is also available. The play is short enough to make a review essay assignment for students.
3. This case is adapted and quoted from Staci Kramer, "The Case of the Missing Coke Can," *Editor and Publisher,* 29 April 1989, pp. 18-19.
4. George Orwell, *1984* (New York: Harcourt, Brace and World, 1949), p. 43.
5. The history is reviewed by Paul Lester, "Faking Images in Photojournalism," *Media Development* 1 (1988): 41-42.
6. Jim Gordon, "Foot Artwork Ends Career," *News Photographer* (November 1981): 32; for details of this event, see pp. 31-36.
7. Quoted from a survey of editors in Sheila Reaves, "Digital Retouching: Is There a Place for It in Newspaper Photography?" *Journal of Mass Media Ethics* 2:2 (Spring/Summer 1987): 45-46.
8. Sheila Reaves, "Photography, Pixels and New Technology: Is There a Paradigm Shift?" Paper presented to Qualitative Studies Division, AEJMC, Washington, DC, August 1989, p. 5; and Reaves, "Digital Retouching," p. 47.
9. Quoted in Reaves, "Digital Retouching," p. 43.
10. Sissela Bok, *Lying: Moral Choice in Public and Private Life* (New York: Pantheon Books, 1978), pp. 123-126.
11. Zay N. Smith and Pamela Zekman, *The Mirage* (New York: Random House, 1979).
12. For this quotation and several details that follow, see Katherine Corcoran, "Pilloried Clinton," *Washington Journalism Review* (January/February 1993): 28.
13. Katha Pollitt, "The Male Media's Hillary Problem," *Nation,* 17 May 1993, p. 659.
14. Margaret Carlson, "At the Center of Power," *Time,* 10 May 1993, p. 35.

15. Pollitt, "Male Media's Hillary Problem," pp. 659–660.
16. Quoted by Josh Getlin and Heidi Evans in "Sex and Politics: Gender Bias Continues to Plague Campaign Trail," *Quill* (March 1992): 17.
17. Ibid., p. 17.
18. Both Clift and Ingrassia are quoted in Corcoran, "Pilloried Clinton," p. 29.
19. Ibid., p. 27.
20. Karen Schmidt and Colleen Collins, "Showdown at Gender Gap," *American Journalism Review* (July/August 1993): 39.
21. Jane O'Reilly, "The Pale Males of Pundity," *Media Studies Journal* (Winter/Spring 1993): 125–133.
22. Barbara Luebke, "No More Content Analyses," *Newspaper Research Journal* 13:1–2 (Winter/Spring 1992).
23. Brian S. Brooks and James Pinson, *Working with Words: A Concise Handbook for Media Writers and Editors* (New York: St. Martin's Press, 1989), pp. 179–190.
24. Francine W. Frank and Paula A. Treichler, *Language, Gender, and Professional Writing* (New York: Modern Language Association of America, 1989), pp. 137–278.
25. Casey Miller and Kate Swift, *The Handbook of Nonsexist Writing* (New York: Harper and Row, 1981).
26. Junior Bridge, "No News Is Women's News," *Media and Values* (Winter 1989): 22.
27. For a comprehensive review of the issues and challenges, see "The Media and Women Without Apology," a special 250-page issue of the *Media Studies Journal* (Winter/Spring 1993).
28. Joe Holley, "The Waco Watch," *Columbia Journalism Review* (May/June 1993): 53.
29. Ibid.
30. "Waco: What Went Right, What Went Wrong, A Report by the Society of Professional Journalists Waco Task Force on Media Coverage of the Events in Waco" (Greencastle, IN: Society of Professional Journalists, 1993), p. 9.
31. Ibid.
32. Ibid., p. 12.
33. Ibid., p. 17.
34. Ibid., p. 18.
35. Rebecca J. Tallent and J. Steven Smethers, "Feeding the Beast: Waco Coverage Driven by Technology, Competition," *Quill* (November/December 1993): 21.
36. "Waco: What Went Right, What Went Wrong," p. 3.
37. Ibid., p. 11.
38. Ibid., p. 17.
39. Ibid., p. 23.
40. Ibid., p. 14.
41. Ibid.
42. Deni Elliott, "There's Still Hope: We Need Compelling Arguments," *Quill* (November/December 1993): 19 (emphasis is in original).
43. Ibid.
44. Ibid.
45. "Waco: What Went Right, What Went Wrong," p. 7.
46. Elliott, "There's Still Hope," p. 20.
47. Tallent and Smethers, "Feeding the Beast," p. 21.

chapter 3

Reporters and Sources

Well-informed sources are a reporter's bread and butter, and dependence on them creates some genuine complexities. A news medium's pledging to divulge its sources of information would be significant for the public; however, printing names usually results in the sources thereafter speaking guardedly or even drying up. Several tactics are used in confronting this dilemma so that audiences are served and sources remain content. As Hugh Culbertson wrote, "The unnamed news source has been called a safety valve for democracy and a refuge for conscience, but also a crutch for lazy, careless reporters."[1] A *Washington Post* editorial captured some of the struggle in a recent description of "Source's" family tree:

> Walter and Ann Source (nee Rumor) had four daughters (Highly Placed, Authoritative, Unimpeachable, and Well-Informed). The first married a diplomat named Reliable Informant. (The Informant brothers are widely known and quoted here; among the best known are White House, State Department, and Congressional.) Walter Speculation's brother-in-law, Ian Rumor, married Alexandre Conjecture, from which there were two sons, It Was Understood and It Was Learned. It Was Learned just went to work in the Justice Department, where he will be gainfully employed for four long years.[2]

The complications here are not easily resolved. Walter Lippmann noted this journalistic bind more than 50 years ago in *Public Opinion*, where he distinguished news from truth. News he saw as fragments of information that come to a reporter's attention; explicit and established standards guide the pursuit of truth.[3] The judicial process, for example, follows rigorous procedures for gathering evidence. Academics footnote and attribute sources so that knowledgeable people can verify or dispute the conclusions. Medical doctors rely on technical precision and expertise. Reporters, however, cannot compete with these other professions. They have found no authoritative way of examining, testing, and evaluating their information, at least not in a public arena and not under risky, hostile conditions.

The difficulties result primarily because a multitude of practical considerations need to be jockeyed under deadline pressures. On occasion reporters must be adversarial, at least skeptical; at other times, friendliness and cooperation work better. If newspeople become too intimate with important men and women, they lose their professional distance or develop unhealthy biases protecting them. However, to the degree that powerful sources are not cultivated and reporters establish no personal connections, the inside nuance and perspective may be lost. At times, written documents supplemented by public briefings are superior to information painfully dug out by a conscientious reporter. On most other occasions, the official source is blinded by self-interest. But who can predict? Regarding sources, the American Society of Newspaper Editors (ASNE) Statement of Principles correctly warns: "Journalists must be vigilant against all who would exploit the press for selfish purposes."[4] Little wonder that as Watergate documents came to light, for instance, several "scoops" proved to be stories leaked originally by Mr. Nixon's staff.

Most news operations have developed specific procedures to help prevent chaos and abuse. Certain conventions also hold together journalistic practice. It is typically assumed that all information must be verified by two or three sources before it can be printed. Most codes of ethics and company policies insist on attribution and specific identification whenever possible. A few news operations allow reporters to keep sources totally secret, but a majority openly involve editors as judges of the data's validity. The rules also require accurate quotation marks, correction of errors, and an account of the context. However, even with these safeguards, a responsible press must continually agonize over its treatment of sources in order to prevent lapses.

This chapter chooses four entangled aspects of the reporter-source relationship, all of them actual occurrences of some notoriety. The first case, from Watergate, concerns the question of tapping grand jury sources: members and documents. In the second case, the debate revolves around the use of stolen materials. Although few journalistic events have the historic significance of the Pentagon Papers, the decision whether or not to accept valuable stolen materials has to be made frequently. The third case indicates that new understandings of confidentiality are emerging in the courts, forcing media companies to establish guidelines for promise keeping that are undergirded by ethics rather than law. The last case treats the issue of familiarity; it examines the boundary between exploiting friendship and building on it legitimately in gathering news. Cheap answers are not forthcoming, but at every point the ethical issues ought to form a prominent part of the resolution.

11. WATERGATE AND GRAND JURY INFORMATION

After leading the pack on the Watergate story in the early going, *Washington Post* reporters Carl Bernstein and Bob Woodward ran into rough waters.[5] On 25 October 1972, a major coup had turned into a major disaster. They had written that H. L. (Bob) Haldeman, President Nixon's chief of staff, had been personally involved in espionage and sabotage. The charge moved the Watergate break-in to the door of President Nixon. But then, through his attorney, their source for the report denied before a grand jury that he had given such testimony. The White House used the opportunity to respond with a vigorous counterattack on the *Washington Post.*

In an effort to discover how they had gone wrong, Woodward and Bernstein revealed their primary source (an agent of the Federal Bureau of Investigation) to his superior. Back at the office the two reporters and *Post* executives discussed revealing all five sources of their erroneous information, but they decided against it.

After that debacle, Woodward and Bernstein ran into more trouble; now the problem was not erroneous stories but no stories at all. They had hit a lull. The timing was bad. The *Post*'s executive editor, Benjamin Bradlee, became frustrated. The Nixon forces were shooting at him. Charles Colson, speaking to a group of New England editors, said, "If Bradlee ever left the Georgetown cocktail circuit where he and his pals dine on third-hand information and gossip and rumor, he might discover out here the real America." Bradlee told an interviewer that he was "ready to hold both Woodward and Bernstein's heads in a pail of water until they came up with another story." That dry spell was anguish.

Such was the pressurized atmosphere in the *Post* newsroom at the time that Woodward and Bernstein and their editors decided to seek information from members of the Watergate grand jury. They came to the idea by happenstance. One night late in November a *Post* editor told Woodward that his neighbor's aunt was on a grand jury, that judging from remarks she had made, it was the grand jury on Watergate, and that in the words of the editor, "My neighbor thinks she wants to talk."

The two reporters checked the Federal Rules of Criminal Procedure—grand jurors take an oath of secrecy. But it appeared that the burden of secrecy was on the jurors; nothing in the law directly forbade questioning them. The *Post*'s lawyers agreed with that interpretation but urged "extreme caution" in approaching the jurors. Bradlee, nervous, echoed that warning: "No beating anyone over the head, no pressure, none of that cajoling."

All the consultation and advice were for nothing. The woman, Woodward and Bernstein were to learn, was not on the Watergate grand jury after all. But the episode had "whetted their interest." The day after the abortive interview, Woodward went to the courthouse, found the list of Watergate grand jurors, and memorized their names; he had been forbidden to take notes.

After typing up the list of jurors, Woodward and Bernstein had a session with Bradlee, *Post* metropolitan editor Harry M. Rosenfeld, managing editor Howard Simons, and city editor Barry Sussman. They went over the list looking for members "least likely to inform the prosecutors of a visit," eliminating civil servants and military officers. By considering the occupations of the jurors, they sought individuals "bright enough to suspect that the grand jury system had broken down in the Watergate case" and "in command of the nuances of the evidence." "Ideally," Woodward and Bernstein wrote, "the juror would be capable of outrage at the White House or the prosecutors or both; a person who was accustomed to bending rules, the type of person who valued practicality more than procedure." *All the President's Men* describes the mental state of those in the room:

> Everyone had private doubts about such a seedy venture. Bradlee, desperate for a story, and reassured by the lawyers, overcame his own. Simons doubted out loud the rightness of the exercise and worried about the paper. Rosenfeld was concerned most about the mechanics of the reporters not getting caught. Sussman was afraid that one of them, probably Bernstein, would push too hard and find a way to violate the law. Woodward wondered whether there was ever justification for a reporter to entice someone across the line of legality while standing safely on the right side himself.
>
> Bernstein, who vaguely approved of selective civil disobedience, was not concerned about breaking the law in the abstract. It was a question of *which* law, and he believed that grand jury proceedings should be inviolate. The misgivings, however, went unstated, for the most part.[6]

The procedure for interviewing the jurors was agreed upon. The reporters were to identify themselves and say that through a mutual but anonymous friend they understood he or she knew something about the Watergate case. They would then ask if he or she was willing to discuss it. If the answer was no, the reporters were to leave immediately.

Visits to about half a dozen grand jurors yielded nothing but trouble. One of the jurors reported the visit to a prosecutor, who informed Judge John Sirica. *Post* attorney Edward Bennett Williams met with Sirica. After the meeting, he told Woodward and Bernstein he thought they would get off with a reprimand. He was right. The chiding came in open court, in a room packed with reporters. But Sirica did not identify them or the *Post*. The reporters present were out for the story, questioning each other, seeking the identity of the reporters mentioned by the judge. Woodward and Bernstein agreed they would make an outright denial "only as a last resort." A colleague caught up with them as they headed for the elevator. *All the President's Men* describes the scene and thinking of the two reporters:

He [the reporter] caught up with Woodward near the elevator and asked point-blank if the Judge had been referring to him or Bernstein.

"Come off it, what do you think?" Woodward answered angrily.

The man persisted. "Well, was it one of [news media representatives] or wasn't it? Yes or no."

"Listen," Woodward snapped, "Do you want a quote? Are we talking for the record? I mean, are you serious? Because if you are, I'll give you something, all right."

The reporter seemed stunned. "Sorry, Bob, I didn't think you'd take me seriously," he told Woodward.

The danger passed. The nightmare vision that had haunted them all day—Ron Ziegler at the podium demanding that they be the object of a full federal investigation, or some such thing—disappeared. They tried to imagine what choice phrases he might use ("jury tampering"?), and they realized that they didn't have the stomach for it. They felt lousy. They had not broken the law when they visited the grand jurors, that much seemed certain. But they had sailed around it and exposed others to danger. They had chosen expediency over principle, and, caught in the act, their role had been covered up. They had dodged, evaded, misrepresented, suggested, and intimidated, even if they had not lied outright.[7]

This case involves a long sequence of ethical choices. It reveals many of the pressures on the *Post*'s staff. Bradlee's desire, for example, for a story, "any story," to take the heat off the *Post* could be examined as a nonethics of self-interest, principles be damned. In this way, the case is realistic in its reflection of conditions under which journalistic decisions are frequently made. Under most circumstances these pressures are much less strong than they were for the *Post* in this instance. However, knowledge of these circumstances does not help resolve the ethics of the case. Surely the existence of pressures, even intense ones, cannot itself justify a reporter's conduct. At best, the reality of pressure may help one sympathize with a reporter who, feeling it strongly, made bad moral judgments. But that is not ethics in the sense of reaching justified decisions.

Perhaps the best way to begin examining this multisided situation is to identify some of the moral choices made along the way:

1. They decided to reveal the identity of a source to his superior "in an effort to find out how they had gone wrong." But they also decided not to reveal all five sources. The decision to reveal their source likely involved the violation of promises, but the case does not tell us.
2. They decided to seek information from the grand jury. Clearly, they were aware of potential legal problems, as evidenced by their check into the Federal Rules of Criminal Procedure and by their conversation in the planning session.

3. They decided to get the list of grand jurors by memorization rather than by taking notes. This is already a step in the direction of misusing the grand jury system and violating the important ethical principles on which it stands.
4. They decided to do everything possible to avoid being caught in interviews with grand jurors. This was not a case of deliberately violating the law toward the end of changing an unjust law; it was a case of violating the law in order to serve the interests of the newspaper at the moment.
5. They decided to deceive, beginning with their approach to the grand jurors, and said that they got the juror's name "through a mutual friend." This lie was told in order to open the possibility of getting jurors to talk, to use jurors toward the *Post's* own ends.
6. They decided to lie if they were identified by fellow reporters as those reprimanded by Sirica. Admittedly, they would stoop to that only "as a last resort."

Certainly the nation can be grateful to Woodward and Bernstein for the final result of their investigation (Nixon's resignation), but the morality of their investigation was seriously flawed. They did nothing that could not be justified by utilitarian principles. If they had known at the time that issues of overriding national importance were involved, their improprieties could be seen as outweighed by the enormous public benefits. Their lying and their serious tampering with the grand jury resulted in uncovering one of the biggest threats to American democracy in its history. That vital end could be used to justify the immoral means.

The ethical problem is that they employed these immoral means toward immoral ends, namely, the self-interest of protecting themselves and the *Post*. At the time that they chose to lie and violate the grand jury system, they could not have known, and did not claim to know, the final dimensions of the story they would uncover. In this case, then, democracy benefited, but not by their conscious intent to aid society. The benefit was an unforeseen, and unforeseeable, consequence of decisions to violate not only the law but basic moral principles. Their decisions cannot, therefore, be justified ex post facto in light of the fortunate results. Bad choices do sometimes unwittingly evoke good ends. But such results do no more than place us in the awkward position of being glad that immoral people were at work on the case.[8] Journalists cannot morally follow in the *Post's* footsteps as a general rule. Lying must always be justified in terms of some higher value; truthtelling need never be justified.

12. PENTAGON PAPERS AS STOLEN DOCUMENTS

The Pentagon Papers, a confidential report detailing American involvement in Vietnam since World War II, had been commissioned by Robert McNamara when he was secretary of defense. The account of their publication, begun in the *New York Times* on 13 June 1971, reads like a spy story. The *Times* would say only that it received 7,000 pages of the document through investigative reporter Neil Sheehan sometime in March 1971. (It was a former *Times* reporter, speaking on a radio show, who named Daniel Ellsberg as the man who supplied the document to the *Times*.)

The *Times* set about publication with a secrecy worthy of a security agency, according to *Times* writer Jules Witcover. Preliminary work was done in two rooms of the Jefferson Hotel in Washington, DC. Then the operation was moved to a three-room suite in New York's Hilton, eventually taking up nine guarded rooms on two floors. Staff working on the story were told to stay away from the *Times*'s main office. In late May, key production people were told of the project. In a vacant office building, these employees set up a secret composing room to handle the special copy; it included a paper shredder to destroy extra proofs. On 10 June, the first segment of the finished copy was brought from the hotel and punched on tapes. The pages were made up in the secret composing room. At 1:30 P.M. on Saturday, 12 June, the first page of the *Times*'s report was sent to the presses "amid a mood of exultation. . . . One of the great journalistic coups had been achieved with hardly a whisper of suspicion anywhere," Witcover wrote.[9]

The second installment appeared on Monday, 14 June. That evening U.S. Attorney General John N. Mitchell requested that the *Times* stop publication, arguing that the papers contained "information relating to the national defense of the United States" and that publication was "directly prohibited" by the Espionage Law. Two hours later the *Times* read a statement addressed to Mitchell that it also published: "The *Times* must respectfully decline the request of the Attorney General, believing that it is in the interest of the people of this country to be informed of the material contained in this series of articles."[10] Later that day, the *Times* was enjoined from further publication, pending a hearing on the government's plea.

On Thursday, 17 June, the *Washington Post* obtained 4,000 pages of the document, and plans were made for publication. Ben Bagdikian, then assistant managing editor for national news, said the *Post*'s management and lawyers were wary of publishing stories based on the document. The lawyers, posing a question of "propriety," said it would be "wiser to establish the right to publish by allowing the *Times* case to run its course, avoiding indication of a contempt for the court in that case." But, Bagdikian said, "The editors and writers saw it strictly in terms of freedom of the press and journalistic responsibility to the public—if it is authentic and significant, publish it."[11] The editors and writers prevailed. The *Post* began publication on Friday, 18 June. It, too, was enjoined.

While the cases of prior restraint were in the courts, partial copies of the Pentagon Papers cropped up elsewhere: The *Boston Globe,* for example, began publication and was enjoined. The *St. Louis Post-Dispatch* began a series on Friday, 25 June. Contacted by the Justice Department, the *Post-Dispatch* executives said they did not plan to publish an article on Saturday (because of the size of that day's edition) but would resume on Sunday. Before it could do so, it too was required to desist from further publication. Finally on 30 June, the Supreme Court in a 6-to-3 decision ruled in favor of the newspapers.

Three questions must be answered satisfactorily before publication of the Pentagon Papers can be justified morally. The issues are too complicated to allow us to emphasize such professional values as freedom from government interference and then presume that no further debate is necessary.

First, was it ethically permissible to publish classified material? The legal battles centered entirely on that issue and were finally resolved by the Supreme Court in favor of First Amendment guarantees regarding the free press. Typical moral systems would not contradict this type of decision. Nearly all ethical frameworks permit civil disobedience under certain circumstances. Obeying legally constituted authority is promoted as a moral good under normal circumstances (and in this instance the Espionage Law invoked by the attorney general had been duly enacted). However, this act of conscience against the state cannot be dismissed in itself as immoral by any typical set of ethical principles.

Second, should the *New York Times* and the other papers use stolen documents as their source? Daniel Ellsberg had taken the material without authorization. The decision to publish stolen goods raises a fundamental ethical issue.

From a Kantian perspective, theft is always wrong. The categorical imperative suggests that we not permit for ourselves what we do not wish to make a universal law. Obviously, from this viewpoint, societies cannot exist if stealing is allowed. A Kantian would point to the double standard involved, arguing that newspapers do not want government officials stealing their property so why should they condone theft for themselves? Justice Warren Burger reflected this ethical perspective:

> To me it is hardly believable that a newspaper long regarded as a great institution in American life would fail to perform one of the basic and simple duties of every citizen with respect to the discovery or possession of stolen property or secret government documents. That duty, I had thought—perhaps naively—was to report forthwith to responsible public officers. This duty rests on taxi drivers, Justices, and the *New York Times*.[12]

An opposing point of view over stolen property can be built on a utilitarian basis. The various editors who published the Pentagon Papers appealed to the historic circumstances and the enormous consequences of the material. Fifty-five thousand Americans had already died in Vietnam, tens of billions of dollars had been spent militarily, and the nation was acrimoniously divided. Thus, when A. M. Rosenthal, managing editor of the *Times*, gave his paper's rationale, he dismissed simplistic declarations and contended that publication was within the *Times*'s

> constitutional rights and in the best interests of our country. . . . Can you steal a decision that was made three years ago and that has caused

consequences that a country now pays for, good or bad? How can you steal the mental processes of elected officials or appointed officials? . . . I never thought that Americans would buy the argument that you can steal information on public matters.[13]

Unfortunately, in all the lengthy arguments defending the *Times*'s actions, no attention is explicitly paid to ethical theory. Apparently, decisions were based on professional values and legal rights, rather than on a struggle over step three in the Potter Box process.

Third, were the contents of the Pentagon Papers treated fairly and accurately? Not all the documents were printed, since they totaled more than 7,000 pages and covered a 25-year period. Substantial sections were complex and academic. The *Times* staff chose the theme of duplicity, that is, American leaders were saying different things about the Vietnam War in public and private. Edward Jay Epstein did not score the *Times* very highly in meeting their editorial obligations:

> To convert this bureaucratic study into a journalistic exposé of duplicity required taking certain liberties with the original history. Outside material had to be added, and assertions from the actual study had to be omitted. For example, to show that the Tonkin Gulf resolution resulted from duplicity, the *Times* had to omit the conclusion of the Pentagon Papers that the Johnson Administration had tried to avoid the fatal clash in the Tonkin Gulf, and had to add evidence of possible American provocations in Laos which were not actually referred to in the Pentagon Papers themselves.[14]

Clearly, this case represents an important legal triumph for the press. Even though of ancient vintage, it remains as well known in the press as any incident other than Watergate. It takes on historic proportions because the Anglo-American tradition, in principle, has condemned all kinds of prior restraint for nearly 300 years. The ethical questions of "Should the *New York Times* and the other papers use stolen documents as their source?" and "Were the contents of the Pentagon Papers treated fairly and accurately?" warrant consideration nonetheless. The media generally do not traffic in stolen property, and this celebrated situation ought not to dim their conscience.

As was suggested before, a utilitarian defense is possible here but not compelling. Did the editors unequivocally serve the public interest or merely use a noble end to justify desultory means? Ethicists remain uneasy about the duplicity theme also, wondering whether that characterization honestly represents official Department of Defense decision making. Impugning evil motives is not permitted by any moral system that respects human beings. To justify their action, the *New York Times* would have to demonstrate that its presentation faithfully tells the Pentagon Papers story and does not piece together a story of its own.

13. CONFIDENTIALITY IN MINNESOTA

Dan Cohen was director of public relations for the advertising agency handling the political campaign of Wheelock Whitney, an Independent Republican campaigning for governor of Minnesota.[15] One week before the election, Gary Flakne, a county attorney and former Independent Republican legislator, unearthed documents that showed that the Democratic-Farmer-Labor candidate for lieutenant governor, Marlene Johnson, had been arrested and convicted of a six-dollar theft thirteen years earlier.

A group of Independent Republican supporters agreed that Cohen should release these documents because he had the best rapport with the local media. Cohen immediately contacted four journalists: Lori Sturdevant of the *Minneapolis Star Tribune,* Bill Salisbury of the *St. Paul Pioneer Press Dispatch,* Gerry Nelson of the Associated Press, and David Nimmer of WCCO Television. All four subsequently agreed to Cohen's proposal:

> I have some documents which may or may not relate to a candidate in the upcoming election, and if you will give me a promise of confidentiality, that is, that I will be treated as an anonymous source, that my name will not appear in any material in connection with this, and that you will also agree that you are not going to pursue with me a question of who my source is, then I will furnish you with the documents.[16]

The *Star Tribune* editors assigned four or five reporters to follow up the story by contacting members of the two gubernatorial campaigns. The reporter who was directed to verify the authenticity of the court records discovered Gary Flakne's name on the list of persons recently reviewing the records. Flakne admitted to the reporter that he had obtained the documents for Cohen.

The *Star Tribune* editor responsible for the final decision reasoned that the newspaper would be guilty of suppressing information if the story were not run. Sturdevant was asked to see whether Cohen would release the *Tribune* from its promise of anonymity. She telephoned Cohen twice, but he refused to agree to include his name in the story. Sturdevant adamantly objected to reneging on her promise to Cohen and withdrew her name from the article. On 28 October 1982, the *Star Tribune* ran the story on the bottom half of the front page, entitled "Marlene Johnson Arrest Disclosed by Whitney Ally." The article described Johnson's arrest and conviction, named Cohen as the source, and identified him as the agent handling advertising for the opposition campaign. The article did not mention Sturdevant's promise of anonymity. This was the first time the *Star Tribune*'s management had overturned a reporter's pledge to keep the source confidential.

The *Dispatch* also ran an article similar to the *Tribune's* in both 28 October editions. The Associated Press upheld its promise of confidentiality by stating that the court documents "were slipped to reporters." WCCO-TV decided not to broadcast the story at all.

Later in the day, Cohen's employer confronted him and, after a heated discussion, fired him.

On 29 October, the *Star Tribune* published a column criticizing Cohen for his self-righteousness and unfair campaign tactics. The next day it ran an editorial cartoon of a trick-or-treater named Dan Cohen. On 7 November, four days after the election, Cohen initiated a breach of contract and misrepresentation suit against the *Tribune* and the *Dispatch*.

Eight months later, a jury awarded Cohen $200,000 in actual damages and $500,000 in punitive damages, with payment divided equally between the two papers. The jury found that both newspapers had entered into binding contracts with Cohen and that they had breached those contracts. The case is currently being appealed on the grounds that a reporter's relationship with a source is not contractual; the newspapers contend that the issue can be understood only in terms of the press's First Amendment freedom.

In response to Cohen's lawsuit, the *Star Tribune* has issued a set of guidelines for using anonymous sources. It has concluded that eliminating anonymous sources totally would make newsgathering virtually impossible, muzzling the dog rather than leashing it. The newspaper's editors now make a categorical pledge to uphold its promises of confidentiality, just short of a Kantian absolute. Sources will never be revealed, says company policy, with only three exceptions: (1) if the newspaper subsequently discovers that the source lied or unknowingly gave bad information on the grounds that even if some stories must be unattributed they never can be unsubstantiated; (2) if it turns into a life-and-death situation, life will be protected; and (3) if ordered to reveal sources by a court of law, the paper will relent. "We will fight an order all the way to the U.S. Supreme Court if necessary," says executive editor Joel Kramer, "but if the Supreme Court upheld it, the newspaper would comply; we're not above the law." [17]

The *Star Tribune*'s executive editor, Joel Kramer, believes that "anonymity is granted too freely. The problem is that certain promises should not be made." The heart of the issue is not making promises. The paper recognizes that turning back on its word undermines its credibility; therefore, in order to minimize the number of its commitments, the *Star Tribune* has established such written policies as the following:

Reporters must inform editors of the names of anonymous sources. Sources must understand that the right to commit the newspaper to a pledge of confidentiality lies with the management and not solely with individual reporters. Therefore, newspersons must always explicitly review the conditions and not make vague statements, such as "I probably won't use your name."

Anonymous quotations should ordinarily not be used to express negative opinions about individuals or organizations, and never without the approval of the managing editor or executive editor. In other words, personal attacks by unnamed sources are forbidden, such as smear tactics in a political campaign.

If, on rare occasions, anonymous sources appear to be the only alternative, both reporters and editors must be satisfied that the material could not be obtained on the record. In addition, its news value must be significant and the newspaper must have no reason to doubt the information's reliability. When the story is run, it must include the rationale for protecting the source's identity.

Even after promising anonymity, reporters should make every effort to get the information attributable before publication, even if that means asking the anonymous source to reconsider. Should the source refuse, editors retain the option of declining to publish a story if they believe anonymity should not have been granted in the first place.[18]

Historically, anonymous sources have infected nearly all aspects of the news-gathering enterprise. When legal frameworks dominated our thinking about anonymity, the concerns revolved around tighter shield laws and around jail sentences for those disobeying court orders to reveal names. For example, reporter Myron A. Farber of the *New York Times* spent 40 days in jail during a 34-week murder trial in which Farber categorically refused to surrender his notes and names for private inspection by the judge. In fact, Clark R. Mollenhoff concluded his rules on confidentiality with this advice: "If litigation is initiated to force you to disclose your source with threats of jail and fines . . . you should be prepared to serve a substantial jail term, to pay a fine, and to pay legal fees. Your publisher can pay your fine and your legal fees but he cannot serve your jail term for you."[19]

Shifting to an ethical framework, the debates center on the nature of promises. When "keeping one's promise" is recognized as a moral rule, news professionals become far less enamored of anonymity, on the grounds that no one should make promises lightly. On the other hand, when promises are given, the media's integrity suffers deeply unless they are kept in good faith. What is true about the significance of promise keeping in the general morality governing everyday affairs holds for news reporting as well.

14. A TELEVISION REPORTER AS FAMILY FRIEND

Marjorie Margolies, a television reporter in Washington, DC, found herself doubting her own motives while covering a story of a missing twelve-year-old boy. Early in the story, she became an ally of the boy's family. The boy's mother, Rose Viscidi, knew that television publicity might help in the search for her son. She gave television interviews, offering friendship in return. Marjorie Margolies had gained an entrance. She suspected that the nature of her work helped cultivate the friendship. "It is a fact of television newscasting," she wrote, "that we reporters are known to the public already—in effect, we've already been in their homes, as nondrinking guests at cocktail time."[20]

So she and her camera crew were well treated. "The Viscidis welcomed us—they fed us, gave us places to rest out of the hot August sun, and talked." Then came a report that twelve-year-old Billy's body had been found—buried in the Viscidis's garden. Margolies recorded her reaction: "'Oh, darn, the worst has happened—Billy's not coming back.' But there was also a big side of me that said, 'Geez. I've been with the story for so long and this has to happen on a day I was off it.'"

She and her camera crew rushed to the hospital where Rose Viscidi's husband was being treated for a kidney infection. Reporters were barred. But Margolies decided she could still act as a friend. She persuaded an administrator to allow her to pay her condolences to Rose Viscidi (the administrator was subsequently fired). She found Rose sitting alone in a small room. "I bent down and patted her on the shoulders, and planted a kiss on her forehead. 'Do you have any idea how this happened?' I asked her—as a friend."

Developments in the case were to change Margolies's relationship with Rose Viscidi. Police suspected that another son, fifteen-year-old Larry, had killed his younger brother and buried his body in the garden. The Viscidis consulted a law firm and were advised to give no more information to the press. Margolies wrote: "I was torn. I had grown to like Rose very much. But if I did my job as a reporter, the Viscidis would see me as a traitor. It was a no-win situation."

The news media, which had been focusing on the case of the missing boy, now concentrated on his fifteen-year-old brother. "Hordes of newspeople and photographers congregated on the Viscidi lawn and on the neighbors' lawns." Margolies wrote, "At times it took on the air of a picnic, people eating sandwiches and drinking Cokes. I felt uncomfortable."

Margolies and her camera crew, outmanned by members of the print media, attempted to capitalize on their strength—the impact of pictures.

> We would wait hours for the chance to get five seconds of usable tape. Some might think this overkill—that especially in a story of this tragic nature we were intruding too deeply. A number of letters to me complained of this. They said we were all too hungry, but others said we were holding back information. There were times when I would say to myself, "I wish I were not going out there again." But every time, we would come back with something newsworthy. There was incredible public interest in the story. It was news. And we had to report it.[21]

Margolies covered Billy's funeral, being "careful not to disturb the services," but not before delivering a potted plant to the Viscidi home.

Officially, the story hit a lull. Neither the police nor the Viscidis were releasing information. The fact that the suspect was a juvenile further hindered the flow of information. Margolies developed sources and pieced together parts of the story. She explained.

> When you are one-tenth of a television news team, you are expected to produce. There is continual pressure either to produce on that story, or to go on to something else. I couldn't leave the Billy Viscidi story, so I spent every night—after a long day covering other assignments—calling, working sources, into the small hours of the morning.[22]

Margolies found out that the police were sure Larry buried his brother's body, but they were not so sure he did the killing. Billy may have smashed his skull in a fall and Larry, in shock, may have hidden the body to spare his mother grief. Margolies learned that Larry passed a lie detector test. She also learned that Larry was being given a truth serum. Larry's father inadvertently confirmed that report. Margolies told the prosecuting attorney she had the information and was going to use it. She did. The Viscidis concluded she was feeding information to the prosecutor. Margolies asked herself, "Was I crossing the line, inflicting pain on this family with my revelations?"

Finally, police arrested Larry—identified only as "a juvenile." Margolies wrote:

> I resisted pressure to rush to the Viscidi house that evening to take shots. Another station did have someone out there, knocking on the door and attempting to get pictures of the family. It is a matter of taste—and that, I told my superiors, was something I wouldn't do. When the other channel aired its shots, I took some flak for not being on top of the story. When I clued them in on my scoop that Larry was with a psychiatrist taking a truth serum, they wanted me to camp outside the doctor's office and get some pictures. I refused. My bosses began to wonder whether I had gotten so involved with the family that I could not aggressively go after the story.[23]

When Larry was brought to court, the news media had assembled. Margolies called it a "madhouse scene." But she and her crew scored a coup—they got the only pictures of Larry leaving the courthouse through a back door. "I couldn't feel very proud," Margolies wrote. "I felt like a vulture."

Daily the press and television crews waited outside the courthouse for the entrance and exit of the Viscidi family. A bailiff provided Larry with a large bag to wear over his head. On one occasion Rose Viscidi shoved Margolies's soundman and sent him sprawling to the ground. The father, Burton, once passed Margolies's crew and said under his breath, "What do you want me to do—a little jig for you?" Eventually, a county court judge dismissed the manslaughter charge against Larry, holding that the death could as easily have been caused by an accident as by homicide.

And so the case ended. Six months of publicity came to a conclusion, or nearly so. There was one more interview. Rose Viscidi wanted to tell the

family's side of the story. She mended her differences with Margolies, and
she and her husband gave an interview. It was aired as a five-part series.

The most telling phrase appears after the boy's body is discovered. In Margolies's
own words:"Hordes of newspeople and photographers congregated on the Viscidi
lawn and on the neighbor's lawn. At times it took on the air of a picnic with
people eating sandwiches and drinking Cokes. I felt uncomfortable."
     She had reason to feel uncomfortable. The reporters on the scene seemed
oblivious to the grief of the Viscidis. The Viscidis were—to everyone but
Margolies—merely objects to be reported on; they were not people. Because of
Margolies's relationship with the family, she saw them as real people. She could
identify with their needs and be sympathetic to their feelings and frustrations.
Thus, according to the principle that we should always treat others as ends and
not merely as means, her attachment to the family contributed to her morally
responsible conduct—that of restraint and compassion.
     Her discomfort stemmed from what she perceived as a confusion of roles:
reporter (aggressive, analytical, above the fray) and friend (sympathetic, concerned,
involved). It is therefore pertinent to ask whether the attributes usually associated
with responsible reporting are applicable under some conditions and not under
others. When a journalist is functioning as a "watchdog" over a government
agency, something of an adversary relationship exists. Under these circumstances,
a hard-nosed, aggressive, assertive, observer stance may be both necessary and good.
However, when these attributes become so ingrained that they spill over into the
reporter's job of covering the story of a family's tragedy, they are altogether
inappropriate. Under these conditions they only add to the family's grief.
     Margolies was torn between the roles of reporter and friend. She gained
access to Mrs. Viscidi at the hospital, but she did not exploit that occasion to
get special information for broadcast. In fact, she never used her friendship to
get the story. At the end, the interview with the Viscidis benefited the family as
well as the station. The friendship served both quite well.
     Did Margolies intrude too much into family privacy? There is no evidence in
the case that she did, even though she wondered about that in connection with
the information concerning the lie detector and truth serum. But using that
information did not necessarily inflict pain. Moreover, there was reason for the
public to know that the authorities were administering such tests to a juvenile.
     Overall, Margolies made no bad moral choices in this episode. Throughout
the drama, she continued to define the situation as a family tragedy and not as a
"great news story." It was a case where a reporter felt a deep internal, personal
conflict. Since she did not use her friendship with the family to get private
information, she did not behave unethically. Margolies did not permit her career
to determine her actions. In justifying her behavior before a court of reasonable
people, Margolies could rightfully claim that in handling the complexities of the
two legitimate roles, she followed Aristotle's golden mean. The question, then, is
this: Should reporters allow themselves to become personally involved with the
people on whom they report? Yes, when the situation is essentially one of family

tragedy. No, when the situation is essentially adversarial, as in monitoring the performance of public officials.

But these questions only probe into the reporter's responsibility. It could be argued that prurient, leering, blood-thirsty factions of the public are also blameworthy. At least some news directors perceived the viewing audience as clamoring for every detail. That thirst forced Margolies into a predicament. The institutional pressures were obvious, too—reporters must generate some footage and do their share or turn to another assignment. But such inhouse demands cannot obscure the public's apparent fascination with all the details—even though it is not a mad killer or rapist on the loose and thereby does not require up-to-the-minute coverage.

NOTES

1. Hugh M. Culbertson, "Leaks a Dilemma for Editors as Well as Officials," *Journalism Quarterly* 57 (Autumn 1980): 402–408.
2. Editorial in the *Washington Post,* 12 February 1969. Quoted in John L. Hulteng, *The Messenger's Motives,* 2d ed. (Englewood Cliffs, NJ: Prentice-Hall, 1985), p. 79.
3. Walter Lippmann, *Public Opinion* (New York: The Free Press, [1922] 1949), part 7, pp. 201–230.
4. John L. Hulteng, *Playing It Straight* (Chester, CT: Globe Pequot Press, 1981), p. 15.
5. Quotations for this case are taken from Robert Woodward and Carl Bernstein, *All the President's Men* (New York: Simon and Schuster, 1974), pp. 205–224.
6. Ibid., p. 210.
7. Ibid., p. 224.
8. This commentary focuses on the contribution of journalists in uncovering Watergate, though measuring the size of that contribution is debatable. Judge Sirica attempted to document that the judiciary (including special prosecutors) were primarily responsible for developing the case and securing the resolution. See John Sirica, *To Set the Record Straight* (New York: W. W. Norton, 1979).
9. Jules Witcover, "Two Weeks That Shook the Press," *Columbia Journalism Review* 10 (September/October 1971): 9.
10. Ibid., p. 10.
11. Ibid., p. 11.
12. See Ben H. Bagdikian, "What Did We Learn?" *Columbia Journalism Review* 10 (September/October 1971): 47.
13. A. M. Rosenthal, "Why We Published," *Columbia Journalism Review* 10 (September/October 1971): 17–18.
14. Edward Jay Epstein, "Journalism and Truth," *Commentary* 57 (April 1974): 36–40.
15. This case is taken from the *Media Law Reporter,* p. 2209.
16. Ibid., p. 2210.
17. Andrew Radolf, "Anonymous Sources," *Editor and Publisher* 27 (August 1988): 17.
18. Ibid., pp. 17, 19, 33; see also Felix Winternitz, "When Unnamed Sources Are Banned," *Quill* (October 1989): 40. A majority of news sources believe that reconsidering an agreement is understandable when journalists are under pressure; see Bob M. Grassway, "Are Secret Sources in the News Media Really Necessary," *Newspaper Research Journal* 9:3 (Spring 1988): 69–77.

19. Clark Mollenhoff, "Rules for Thoughtful Dealing with Confidential Sources," unpublished manuscript, available from Washington and Lee University, Lexington, VA 24450.

20. Quotations for this case are taken from Marjorie Margolies, "The Billy Viscidi Story," *Washingtonian* 14:8 (May 1979): 125-128.

21. Ibid., p. 127.

22. Ibid.

23. Ibid., p. 128.

chapter 4

Social Justice

Historian Charles Beard once wrote that freedom of the press means "the right to be just or unjust, partisan or nonpartisan, true or false, in news columns and editorial columns."[1] Historically, the media have been conceived as reflecting the world on their own terms and telling the particular truth the owners preferred.

Very few people still have confidence in such belligerent libertarianism. There is now substantial doubt whether the truth will emerge from a marketplace filled with falsehood. The contemporary mood among media practitioners and communication scholars is for a more reflective press, one conscious of its significant social obligations. But servicing the public competently is an elusive goal, and no aspect of this mission is more complicated than the issue of social justice. The Hutchins Commission mandated the press to articulate "a representative picture of the constituent groups of society." The Commission insisted that minorities deserved the most conscientious treatment possible and chided the media of its day for tragic weaknesses in this area.[2]

Often a conflict is perceived between minority interest on the one hand and unfettered freedom of expression on the other. The liberty of the press is established in the First Amendment, and this freedom continues to be essential to a free society. Practitioners thereby tend to favor an independent posture on all levels. Whenever one obligates the press—in this case to various social causes—one restrains its independence in some manner. Obviously, the primary concern is government intervention, but all clamoring for special attention from the press ought to be suspect.

In spite of debate over the precise extent of the media's obligation to social justice, there have been notable achievements. Abolitionist editors of the nineteenth century crusaded for justice even though the personal risks were so high that printing presses were thrown into rivers and printing shops burned down by irate readers. A symbiosis between television and the black movement aided the struggle for civil rights in the 1960s.

This chapter introduces five problems of social justice on a lesser scale, but involving typical issues of justice nonetheless. In all cases, a responsive press is seen to play a critical role. All five situations assume that genuine social concerns are at stake, and not just high-powered special-interest groups seeking their own ends. Each of the five examples pertains to the disenfranchised: the information poor in the first case, the racially stereotyped in the second, the homeless in the third, victims of bureaucratic agencies in the fourth, and Native Americans who had run out of options in the fifth example. In all cases, the reporters felt some measure of obligation. Although press response is sometimes extremely weak, no cause is dismissed out of hand by journalists in these situations.

Social ethicists typically show a strong commitment to justice. We assume this principle here and try to apply it in complicated situations. The heaviest battles in this chapter usually occur over questions in the middle range, issues that media personnel confront along with the larger society. For example, don't the media carry a particular mandate from subscribers and audiences, in the same way politicians may sense a special obligation to represent the people who voted for them—or who at least live in their district? And further, does the press have a legitimate advocacy function, or does it best serve democratic life as an intermediary, a conduit of information and varying opinions? In a similar vein, should the press just mirror events or provide a map that leads its audience to a destination? The kind of responsibility for justice that a particular medium is seen to possess often depends on how we answer these intermediate questions about the press's proper role and function.[3]

15. CLINTON-GORE'S ELECTRONIC HIGHWAY

As a senator from Tennessee, Albert Gore introduced an information highway bill for congressional action. Gore has had a long-term fascination with a technologically sophisticated communication network, an idea that has come into its own as the vice-president joins President Clinton to work toward reinventing government. Through Congress, the administration is developing a plan that harnesses U.S. industry with governmental concern for the public interest. Based on the premise that the United States is a world leader in information hardware and software, Clinton-Gore's electronic highway seeks to capitalize on that superiority by removing technical barriers and coordinating the many disparate initiatives. "Super highway" is an apt label in two ways. It suggests the need to direct speeding traffic toward an appropriate destination. "Put plainly by Rupert Murdoch, the information age is like a steamroller: One must either get on for the ride or become part of the pavement."[4] It also harks back to Eisenhower's interstate expressway project in which the federal government spearheaded a nationwide transportation system for integrating the United States geographically.

This interactive electronic highway combines the storage capacity of data banks with the transmission capacity of advanced cable systems with video imaging with the switching and routing capabilities of cellular telephones.

> Instead of settling for whatever happens to be on at a particular time, you could select any item from an encyclopedic menu of offerings and have it routed directly to your television or computer screen. A movie? Airline listings? Tomorrow's newspaper or yesterday's episode of *Northern Exposure?* How about a new magazine or book? A stroll through the L. L. Bean catalog? A teleconference with your boss? A video phone call with your lover? Just punch up what you want, and it appears just when you want it. Welcome to the information highway.[5]

This merger of computers, telephones, and video is driven by recent technological breakthroughs: (1) the ability to turn all audio and video communications into digital information; (2) fiberoptic channels with nearly limitless capacity; (3) cellular telephony and switching techniques that no longer require rewiring every home.[6] Blue-chip corporations have already launched pilot projects; they are merging and reorganizing their structures to take advantage of what they see as an unprecedented opportunity. An interactive industry of giant companies might well emerge out of today's television, computer, telecommunications, electronics, records, financial service, and book publishing firms. For Vice-President Gore, "'This is by all odds the most important and lucrative marketplace of the 21st century. . . .' Apple Computer chairman John Sculley estimates that the revenue generated by this megaindustry could reach $3.5 trillion worldwide by the year 2001."[7]

Assuming that such an information highway is economically, technologically, and politically possible, what standards should it meet to be ethically sound? According to Everette Dennis:

> There is a genuine concern among many of us about a system largely driven by interests unfamiliar with the basics of information gathering or the ethical processing of news. In a speech last month before participants in the International Institute of Communication's Telecommunications Forum, I urged the development of a telecommunication ethic, one that would draw on the more successful substantive features of news media industries as one step toward truly serving the public.[8]

Such an information ethic would include at least three principles.

First, can a ubiquitous network guarantee privacy for users? Confidential data are already easily available from government agencies and businesses. How can anything important be safeguarded in the macrosystem currently unfolding?

And in another sense, how can users protect themselves from the intrusion of unnecessary and unwanted messages? As William Safire complained:

A society with no place to hide produces people with no secrets worth keeping and no individuals with minds of their own. . . . As communications groupies marry cellular telephony to the computer, they intend to make it possible for each of us to be reachable by anybody on Earth at any time, in any place, with all the data that are currently known to humankind. . . . Being on the end of an electronic leash [does] not appeal to me. Although pundits pride themselves on being in touch, there is no law requiring us to be constantly or instantly in touch. Indeed, the far greater need is to be occasionally, blessedly out of touch.[9]

Second, will noncommercial programs and information services be central or marginalized? Granted, 500 channels are technically feasible. Will they significantly improve the quality of educational material, broaden our political horizons, or make public policy alternatives more understandable? Ellen Goodman concluded:

Before we join this fast lane, we ought to ask where Americans in the '90s want to go and will this technology get us there. I, for one, am glad to help my hospital or office get a quicker dose of data. But I have some reservations about an information superhighway roaring through my front door. For one thing, . . . this highway is not heading for the library; it's heading for the marketplace. The early offerings are going to be in the not-so-wide world of entertainment and shopping. [Automobile] highways took people from Main Street to the Mall. The superhighways hope to turn our homes into domestic versions of the Great Mall of America in Minneapolis. Has anybody asked for this? . . . The superhighways are promoting, indeed betting on, superspending.[10]

Third, will there be universal, affordable network access? Although Clinton and Gore are promoting universal access in the same way health care ought to include every citizen, they are depending on a private sector with little incentive to include the information-poor. Andrew Barrett, appointed in 1989 to the Federal Communications Commission by George Bush, represents a prevalent view that the government ought not guarantee universal access. "I do not accept the premise of general subsidies," he argued recently. "I think that is bad public policy." We could better admit from the beginning that some people will be left behind. Companies are not charitable organizations.

Just as we have poor people today, just as we have homeless people today, just as we have jobless people today, we will have the information-rich and the information-poor. . . . Our job is to provide access, but I don't want to provide it on the basis of companies having to subsidize all of America.[11]

And although Barrett's opinion may be realistic and conservative politics, it is hardly justified ethically.

The important ethical question is whether one can justify allocation of this resource to all parties without discrimination.[12] On what basis can one argue that it is morally desirable to ensure comprehensive information for every person regardless of income or geographic location?

Andrew Barrett, to be sure, does not accede to this concern. He represents a view of social justice based on merit. There are several variants of this approach, but all of them judge on the basis of conduct or achievement and not solely on the inherent value of human beings. Thus, the argument goes, those who have expended the most energy or taken the greatest risk or suffered the most pain deserve the highest reward. Though not all differences in people result from varying amounts of their own effort or accomplishment, in this view, ability to pay is considered a reasonable basis for determining who obtains this service. A prominent canon is whether consumers are at liberty to express preferences, to fulfill their desires, and to receive a fair return on their expenditures. The information structure would be unjust only to the degree that supply and demand or honest dealings are abrogated.

However, another notion of social justice, "to each according to one's essential needs," does validate a concern for universal, affordable access. The contention here is not that all felt needs or frivolous wants ought to be met, but that basic human requirements must be satisfied equally. The basis for judging is not activity or achievement, but on our being human. Whereas there is legitimate argument over which needs qualify, agreement is rather uniform on most fundamental issues such as food, housing, safety, and medical care. People as persons share generic endowments that define them as human. Thus, we are entitled—without regard for individual success—to those things in life that permit our existence to continue in a humane fashion. Whenever a society allocates the necessities of life, the distribution ought to be impartial. Free competition among goods and services has been the historically influential rationale for media practice, but in the case of a total national structure performing a vital function, the need-based criterion appears to be the more fitting ethical standard.

16. BOSTON'S BIZARRE MURDER

On 23 October 1989, the Boston police received an emergency message from a car phone in the reputedly dangerous Mission Hill district: "My wife's been shot. I've been shot. . . . Oh, man, it hurts and my wife has stopped gurgling. She's stopped breathing." The caller broke down crying before police dispatcher Gary McLaughlin could get any clues on his exact location: "You can't blank out on me, I need you, man. Chuck? Chuck? Can you hear me? Chuck . . . Chuck, pick up the phone. I can hear you breathing there, Chuck. Come on, buddy."[13] The police and emergency medical crews had to follow sirens audible over the open phone to find him.

Earlier that evening, Charles and Carol Stuart had left a childbirth class at the Brigham and Women's Hospital.[14] According to Charles, on the way home a raspy-voiced black man jumped in the back seat of their Toyota Cressida at a red light, forced them onto a side street, killed Carol at point-blank range, shot Charles through the abdomen, and made off with her jewelry. Carol's seven-month unborn child was delivered by emergency Cesarean section but lived only 17 days. Politicians attended Carol's funeral out of sympathy for this starry-eyed "Camelot" couple destroyed by an urban savage. Hospitalized himself for over a month, Stuart sent a farewell letter to be read at his wife's burial: "I will never again know the feeling of your hand in mine, but I will always feel you. I miss you and I love you. . . . We must know that God's will was done. In our souls, we must forgive the sinner, because He would." He also pulled himself out of bed to kiss his dying son good-bye.

Boston Mayor Raymond Flynn ordered all available detectives on the case. Following their only lead, they routinely stopped and frisked black men in the Mission Hill area surrounding the crime. Three weeks after the murder, William Bennett, a thirty-nine-year-old paroled convict with a record of violence, was arrested and held on an unrelated charge. Stuart tentatively identified him from police photographs, though he could not single him out in a later police line-up.

Ten weeks later, Stuart's younger brother, Matthew, told Boston police that he had met Stuart right after the childbirth class the night of the shooting and, at his brother's instructions, took Carol's Gucci bag, wallet, and makeup kit tossed to him from the car's open window, and disposed of them in the Pines River outside Boston. Matthew also turned over Carol's diamond ring that supposedly had been stolen. His lawyer claimed that the belated disclosure was prompted by Matthew's concern that an innocent man might be prosecuted.

On 4 January 1990, Stuart reportedly jumped to his death from the Tobin Bridge into Boston's Mystic River, probably having heard that the district attorney had directed the police to arrest him. The night before, he had checked into the Sheraton-Tara Hotel in Braintree, a Boston suburb. Supposedly sometime after 4:30 A.M., he left the hotel, drove ten miles in his new Nissan Maxima, and jumped. A brief note found on the passenger seat said: "I love my family. . . . The last four months have been hell; . . . all the allegations have taken all my strength." In the hotel room, police found a list of defense attorney numbers Stuart had never called and a colostomy bag he was forced to wear after his surgery.[15]

A Boston television station reported that on the night before he committed suicide, Charles confided to a family friend that he had killed his wife for the insurance money. Other reports based on an anonymous source suggested he was involved with another woman. Three days after his wife's murder, Stuart collected a $182,000 insurance payment. As a matter of fact, he had taken out extra life insurance on his wife; in addition to using it for a new car, he purchased a $1,000 pair of diamond earrings. Apparently, Charles had shot himself inadvertently in the stomach when a plan to wound himself in the foot went awry. He reportedly wanted the cash to begin a new restaurant business and believed that his wife and fathering role would deter him.

Boston's mayor was extremely reluctant at first to face up to the issues. But under tremendous pressure, he devoted half of his State of the City message to what he called "a giant fraud on this city. . . . It turned out that we were all victims of a sinister hoax, especially the residents of the good Mission Hill community." And he brought an apology to William Bennett's mother: "I've been on this earth 50 years, and I've read a lot of suspense stories, but I've not heard anything as bizarre and troubling as this." Carol Stuart's parents and brother established a memorial fund in her name to underwrite educational scholarships for Mission Hill children.

In the aftermath, a prominent black pastor accused local news media of overkill that whipped up racial tensions with prejudiced stories "of the worst of what black people are supposed to be." And, indeed, the butchery was often sensationalized, beginning with endless repetition of Stuart's desperate pleas over the car phone. Even the generally circumspect *Boston Globe* oozed over the Stuarts as "rich with potential," saying that their marriage was "so loving it warmed even those at its edge." The media's typical interpretive framework had martyred saints set upon by scum, an epic struggle between good and evil. The Stuarts and their tragedy became symbols in a moral calamity that confirmed stereotypes while the tears flowed. The Boston police, pressured by national headlines, pursued their only lead with a vigor that led to 200 friskings a day in the heavily black areas of Roxbury and Dorchester.

However, the important ethical question centers on the way the issue should be handled once the ruse has been exposed. When the police recovered Charles Stuart's body from the Mystic River, a police spokesman said of his story, "It is not true." Bennett was no longer a suspect and the revelation was greeted with "one part relief and 99 parts outrage." "I'm still outraged," wrote columnist William Raspberry, "that Stuart fingered a black man for the murderous deed. Black America is still angry, and our anger is not moderated by the fact that we aren't quite sure where to direct it."[16] The debate is complicated, of course, by the fact that everyone was duped in the beginning.[17] Now, during the embarrassment of having been taken in by Stuart's damnable lie—itself grounded in a perceived Boston racism—what should commentators and news editors do to enable the public to put this tragedy in a morally appropriate framework?

Many leaders demanded the resignation of government officials, police administrators, and news editors. But Raspberry himself points in a possible direction. He calls for a response in the Aristotelian mode, quoting, in fact, from the *Nicomachean Ethics:* "It is easy to fly into a passion—anybody can do that. But to be angry with the right person to the right extent and at the right time and with the right object and in the right way—that is not easy, and it is not everyone who can do it." In that spirit, he recognized that the Boston police ten weeks later had come to doubt Stuart's account and had begun a stakeout on him as the chief suspect. "Can't we give them credit for not being content to find a credible black scapegoat for the murder? Can't we muster a little gratitude for their refusal to fall for a carefully concocted tale?" Lawyer Howard Alan

Dershowitz noted that physical evidence naturally led the police on the trail of a black male: "They don't want the defense later saying they were looking at other people because they had doubts about your case." And Paul Leary, assistant district attorney of Suffolk County, indicated that black residents themselves—though perhaps under police pressure—had led the police to Bennett as the primary suspect. Presumably, if the assailant had been described as "John Smith," the police would have searched for him.

Even though it is unfair to do psychoanalysis at a distance, the trail of Stuart's spectacular behaviors, beyond his blaming a black gunman, indicates that Boston is dealing with psychopathic behavior and not merely with a white supremacist who tricked a city with a history of racism into believing his story. Perhaps if Aristotle's mean governs our rhetoric in the aftermath, around the nation we will be more judicious when we call for swift justice without waiting for the facts of a crime with racial overtones. A swirl of questions remain, and ethical theorists will play a vital role in resolving them. At least Raspberry's appeal to Aristotle suggests a place to start.

17. THE HOMELESS STORY

When the weather turns cold in the northern climates, and elsewhere on cue around Thanksgiving and Christmas, the homeless show up in the news.[18]

On 17 December 1986, *USA Today* spread 50 mug shots across two pages, one homeless person from each state. A short quotation from each tried to stir emotions and add individuality to an otherwise bland and nameless group.

During a frigid February, Pat Harper of New York's WNBC-TV dressed as a bag lady and spent a week on the streets of Manhattan. With concealed cameras, she filmed a series featuring herself—huddled in a doorway, crying when someone gave her $15, and sitting on park benches next to homeless "friends," drinking alcohol.

In 1968 on New Year's Eve, NBC included poverty as one of four major issues facing America, with 12.8 percent of its people statistically poor. On New Year's Eve twenty years later, however, none of the networks included the poor in its summaries of the year's important stories, even though the poverty rate had increased to 14 percent. Reporter Michael Moss, indicating that perhaps there is compassion fatigue in this country, concluded that reporting on poverty in the United States totals a mere one percent of our news coverage each year—and homelessness is only a fraction of that larger issue. The *Washington Post,* for example, put 28 of its 540-person newsroom staff on the Iran-Contra story but has yet to probe the welfare system in depth.

The *USA Today* spread, "like most other homeless stories in most other papers and broadcasts," ignored the causes and reduced its coverage to the plight of isolated individuals. The WNBC-TV segment exploited "the homeless by not going beyond the pitiful portraits to explore and explain the politics and economics of homelessness."[19] Government policy during the 1980s on public housing,

PROFILES FROM THE SHELTERS AND

FACES OF THE USA's HOMELESS

Homelessness — once a big city problem — now plagues all 50 states. Oil Belt joblessness, prohibitive rents, housing shortages ... the reasons vary. The dimensions are tough to track: Birmingham, Ala., estimates from 2,000 to 12,500; Michigan counts 30,000 to 90,000. In many states, the gnawing problem is suddenly made worse by the "new homeless" — families and people under 40. Thursday in USA TODAY: a report on homeless children. These two pages measure the toll on 50 states — and on 50 human beings: (Story, 1A)

ALABAMA

Homelessness is "so visible now," says Karen Carney of Health Care for the Homeless. "There are more people just wandering around."

By Kim Kulish

Sylvia Towns, 44, left her home and 6-year-old son in Cincinnati 12 years ago. "It was something I had to do. I needed a job, and I was tired of Cincinnati." On the road ever since — Atlanta, Chicago, Cleveland, Detroit, Mobile, Ala., Montgomery and now Birmingham. Has high school degree, typing skills. "But I'm a little rusty."

ALASKA

Rising unemployment and falling oil prices have sent many job-seekers packing, while other residents have lost jobs and homes. Estimated homeless in Anchorage: 600-1,200.

By Dan Smith, AP

Don R. Hughes, 44, from Gaston County, N.C., says he is "just an old hobo who came up Alas⌇ I've ⌇

between mental institutions and group homes for the past four years. Now, she's on the streets of Norwich — waiting for the state to find her a home. "I don't know what I'll do if these people don't have an answer. I know they said it takes time to do this stuff. I want an apartment and job. I can't live off Social Security the rest of my life. Thank God for all the people that have helped me."

DELAWARE

A new study found far more mothers with children (27 percent) and persons under age 35 (65 percent) among the state's estimated 800-1,000 homeless than in neighboring states.

USA TODAY

Matthew Colatriano, 28, has been living at the Wilmington Salvation Army for two months with his wife and daughter. Family was in an accident in Atlanta two months ago. Colatriano left his construction job to be with them. When he returned, his apartment was gone.

D.C.

In 1986, $7.6 million spent for 10 emergency shelters with 1,113 beds, a 17 percent increase in beds available in '85. For 1987, $8.2 million OK'd for emergency shelter, plus another $7 million for preventive programs.

By Greg De Ruiter, USA TODAY

Don Moseley, 64, in Washington, D.C., remembers when he had an apartment in the shadow of the U.S. Capitol. But since the breakup of his marriage 20 years ago, Moseley has lived on the streets, doing yard work, day labor and housecleaning when he can. He sleeps in a parking garage rather than at a shelter because "people are either drinking, gambling or playing their radios loud."

By Mark Jeremy Karell

William Hyde, 24, says he's turned to alcohol and marijuana because it's so tough on the streets. Now homeless in Atlanta, he gets most of his clothes and food at the Samaritan House shelter. He sleeps there when there's space. "I have a dream that I'll eventually find me a permanent job. I pray a lot. I talk to God. He's the only one I can really trust."

HAWAII

Even though unemployment is low, high cost of living and poor tourist industry wages have led to estimated 1,000 homeless. In Honolulu, families now living on beaches.

By Ken Sakamoto, USA TODAY

Dancette Yockman, 33, who lives with her five children in a tent off Waimanalo Beach. Had problems finding home since she was divorced 13 years ago. The children — ages 4 to 14 — sleep on one mattress. She and her boyfriend sleep on another. "I'd be before I would separate my children. I wish my mother were alive. She would never let me stay like this."

IDAHO

Troubles in farming and timber are blamed for worsening homelessness. No statewide estimates. In Boise, homeless sometimes live along the Boise River and in cars.

INDIANA

Estimate: 20,000 hor in Indianapolis ar 4,000 low-cost housi to demolition, rem gentrification in 4 ⌇

By Me

David Haddon, 29, c paint, hang sheet houses, fix plumbin weld, wax floors a — but can't find a Gary shelter, Hadd off 18 months ago, ment a year ago. own place: "I want TV, listen to music things a man can do ⌇ private place."

IOWA

Des Moines has ar 1,200 homeless; ⌇ shelter in abandon In rural towns, f⌇ families aid displace

By Ann Klose.

Ron Canaday, 5⌇ Moines: "I'm sitting ⌇ sion waiting to die. I⌇ living. There's nothi⌇ If a car runs ove⌇ freeze to death, I ⌇ People don't unders⌇ think we're proud t⌇ here, to be winos an⌇ We ain't proud. If I ⌇ my life over, I wou⌇ have gone on the roa⌇ have hung on to that⌇ married. She was ⌇ thing God ever sent ⌇

KANSAS

Wichita estimates less; jobs scarce. A dustry laying off a who failed to find oil⌇ to the south are retu⌇

By Jeff Mitchell, USA TODAY

Gary McCall, 37, of Jacksonville, Fla., a thrice-married high school dropout, says he's homeless in Little Rock by choice. "I'm free, I don't have any strings. (Society) stinks. The rich get richer, the poor get poorer. If a good opportunity walked up, I'd take it."

CALIFORNIA

Estimated 50,000-70,000 homeless, most in L.A. and San Francisco. Over past three years, $17.2 million spent on 211 emergency shelter programs.

By Doug Menuez

Victoria Douglas, 37, has a Ph.D., but is on the streets of East Oakland because she has Huntington's disease. "I'm not crazy. But the police think I am. They take me to the hospital where the doctors strap me down and then they shoot me with Haldol."

COLORADO

Energy bust, airline woes and high rents have led to estimated 6,000 homeless. Half are in Den⌇ ⌇⌇ ⌇ she⌇

FIGURE 4.1

ineptitude in the welfare system, unemployment compensation rules, mainstreaming the mentally retarded, rampant chemical substance abuse, the increasing social disorganization of urban ghettos, and other long-term social issues were never integrated successfully into homeless reporting.

The occasional serious attempt indicates that such public media as newspapers, magazines, radio, and television can be used to communicate homelessness more comprehensively. The *Dallas Morning News* published a sixteen-page story on Thanksgiving Day in 1986 that clarified the kinds of homeless people in their city and connected one segment of them with the state's mental health hospital system. The *Nashville Tennessean* in March 1984 crusaded professionally and competently for weeks until the state legislature finally acted on behalf of a critical matter for the homeless poor and raised welfare payment levels. Nicholas Lemann wrote a powerful account in the *Atlantic Monthly* on the middle-class emigration from black ghettos, which created a social chaos in its wake that jobs, public housing projects, and welfare reform cannot overcome.[20] The *Chicago Tribune* ran a thoughtful "American Millstone" series exploring the socioeconomic upheavals that have been creating a permanent underclass.[21] The *Los Angeles Times* did a front-page story on California's new earthquake law and the prospect that landlords would abandon 34,000 low-income apartments rather than meet the safety standards.[22]

The major news weeklies, networks, Public Broadcasting Service (PBS), and newspapers—in addition to small-town media—have occasionally moved readers and viewers beyond sentiment to city hall and Congress. But Michael Moss's conclusion suggests how the press must improve to become morally acceptable:

> It's hard to prove that the press's generally superficial coverage of the homeless results in superficial political decisions. It's harder still to link news to public opinion. But it stands to reason that if the public associates the homeless merely with a need for emergency shelter, that's what the homeless will get—a band-aid, and no prescription to cure the illness. . . . By and large, the emphasis is on temporary beds in a dorm. And it's a political truism that, as the weather warms up, the homeless issue will melt away.[23]

In addition to engaging the political and economic infrastructure, reporting on homelessness ought to present authentic human beings and not pathological fragments. Leon Dash of the *Washington Post* needed 17 months in a ghetto apartment to earn the confidence of six families and learn local culture well enough to write precisely about the people and their circumstances. Denis Hamill of New York's *Newsday* could write credibly about Manhattan's Third Street Men's Shelter because he regularly immersed himself in reporting on the disenfranchised. From the days of journalism training in largely middle-class institutions, reporters on the whole find it difficult to experience underclass society on its own terms rather than reducing it to a hotbed of human-interest stories.

The agape principle insists on treating human beings with equal dignity, regardless of their merit or achievements. Persons are valued for their own sake— because they exist, and whether they benefit anyone else or not. Reinhold Niebuhr elaborated on the agape principle in terms of justice, demonstrating that it does not simply signify the commitment of one person to another. Agape in its fullest meaning must be understood as righteous institution, both in policy and structure. In the way governments, schools, businesses, and social agencies are organized, the human beings they serve must have unconditional value—not just instrumental value—for these organizations to be considered socially just in both their structure and their policies.[24] Therefore, for the press that seeks to be socially responsible, the litmus test is whether it takes the most alienated seriously. Coverage of the homeless that is politically astute and humanly authentic provides a barometer of the press's overall integrity in serving the public.

18. INVESTIGATING PUBLIC AGENCIES

The police detective was passing his outrage on to the reporter. He pointed to the papers on his desk. "See how thick the file on that kid is!" he exclaimed. "And look where it all ended. A nice girl is dead and this young creep is in the lockup. But too late."

The reporter took notes. The file did, indeed, seem to indict the community's social service and juvenile agencies. The young man behind bars had been charged that morning with the sex-motivated slaying of a twenty-year-old college woman, and he had built quite a dossier in his 18 years. In trouble at age 12, he had been referred to the county mental health agency for counseling. Then came arrests and contact with juvenile agencies, then probation, then the county detention center, and finally a state prison facility. Later came parole, including referral back to the mental health center for therapy. "Every one of those people in the agencies had to smell this coming," the detective fumed, "but they just mealy-mouthed around and wrote up reports with big words in them."

The reporter nodded. "What sort of case do you have against him?" she asked. "I can't give you details," said the detective, "but it's a good case—a damn good case."

Back at the office, the reporter talked with the city editor. She wanted to do a case-study story on the man, a detailed look at what the agencies had done and had not done. At first the city editor objected. "The kid's still presumed innocent, you know. His case has not even gone to a grand jury yet. And we do not report past criminal records—most of his arrests were as a juvenile, too."

"That's just it," the reporter persisted. "We hardly ever examine the performance of juvenile courts and juvenile probation officers—or the mental health center either."

The city editor shook his head. "It smacks of sensationalism."

> "No," the reporter argued, "it's not a crime story, really. I'm talking about a public service story. The community should be aware of how these things are allowed to happen. It's a social issue, not a crime story."
>
> "Why don't we wait till after the trial?" the city editor suggested. "It would still be the same story."
>
> "No, it wouldn't," said the reporter. "By the time the case comes to trial, the murder will have left people's minds. They are stirred up now. They'll read every word. Besides that, the detective is really hot right now—he'll let me get into the records. Later he might think better of it."
>
> The city editor liked the reporter's motives. "Okay," he said. "Go to it. But be thorough."

The editor made the morally responsible choice in this case by letting the reporter see what she could get on the story. He did not decide to publish the story, nor was it a decision on which story to write. There are obviously two stories: One involves the individual's life history, and the other concerns the performance of public agencies that deal with juveniles.

This case points to a very real problem. It is extraordinarily difficult to let the public know about the performance of key public agencies—especially those that deal primarily with juveniles—and at the same time to preserve the anonymity and the confidence of minors. Since that problem is very real and very complex, it puts enormous pressure on the journalist. When, as here, there is an opportunity for examining the performance of these agencies, the temptations are all the greater but the possible gain all the more significant.

In this particular circumstance, journalists should pursue simultaneously and vigorously four important goals or values. The first is that of informing the public about public agencies and about individual crimes. The second is the protection of juvenile anonymity. The third goal is that of monitoring public agencies. The public needs to know how the agencies perform. The fourth goal is a critical one for all citizens, namely to guard the Sixth Amendment rights of the accused. The problem in this case, then, is to find strategies that would allow the pursuit of all four goals at once. Most everyone would agree that the goals are valid. Disagreements would come over strategies and tactics used when pursuing them together.

It seems obvious that the reporter should not publish a case study on this man before the trial. That would be a serious violation of the journalist's moral obligation to protect the Sixth Amendment rights of the accused and to avoid potentially damaging pretrial publicity, such as the prior record of the accused. If the reporter is correct in arguing that by the time the case comes to trial the murder will have left people's minds, then so be it. She is almost surely wrong in that judgment, however. Regardless of the verdict, this man's story will be timely when the verdict is announced and, in the case of a guilty verdict, may be more timely at that point than before the trial. She should therefore, before the trial, get all the information on him she can obtain responsibly.

Should the paper publish this man's life story after the trial is over, including identifying him by name? Probably so, if doing so can be done discreetly. It is a story about a life turned sour, about the forces that impinged on that life, about its tragic consequences. For the local audience, after a guilty verdict, the name would add poignancy to the story without doing significant harm to the convicted. If the verdict is not guilty, there is probably no life story at all. Only the issue of juvenile records would be relevant material, and these do not involve the accusation of murder.

Should she gather and publish the second story, the public service story on the performance of public agencies? Yes. Though it will be a difficult story to do well, the public needs to know about these agencies. The case of this eighteen-year-old provides an important sense of immediacy (and perhaps a lever for gaining access to the agencies) for the public service story. In order to avoid a wholesale indictment of all public agencies dealing with juveniles on the basis of one failure, the life story of this individual should not be published unless the second story can be written and published simultaneously.

In order to write either story, it is important that this reporter gather information prior to the trial, that is, immediately, while the detective may be inclined to provide it. The really difficult issue here is that of possibly violating the moral and legal rights of an accused individual to get access to his past record. The fact that he is a juvenile adds yet another ethical dimension. Laws governing access to juvenile court records, although they may help cover incompetence in juvenile judges, are socially significant since they are designed to help in juvenile rehabilitation. Our society has not found a tactic for monitoring trials by juvenile judges while at the same time preserving the privacy of juveniles. Though that is another matter, lawyers who practice before juvenile judges probably carry the heaviest moral obligation to monitor judicial performance.

That raises the difficult question of whether the reporter has a special obligation to the irate detective. She wants to gain access to records that in some jurisdictions are protected by law and in virtually all jurisdictions are regulated by law-enforcement agencies. She herself recognized that it is the detective's state of mind that might prompt him to give her access to the documents now—an act that upon further consideration and in a calmer moment he might be unwilling to perform.

Thus, important moral considerations arise in the relationship of the reporter to the detective as a key source of information. What kinds of conduct would be acceptable in her strategies for encouraging the detective to give her access to restricted records? Should she, for example, stop short of bribing the detective? Yes, since the public need is not that powerful and overriding. Should she ask the detective for the documents? To do so would encourage him to violate the rules of his agency and perhaps violate the law. If he gives them to her and she uses them, he may later be identified as the source of the leak and thus risk the loss of his job and possible prosecution under the law. How far should she go in encouraging him to incur that risk? If she thinks his state of mind (anger) is such that it would blind him to the risk he would be taking, she does have an obligation to let him cool off or to remind him of his risk. Such a claim would be based on the proposition that we not only have a moral obligation to others to prevent harm, but we also have an obligation not to entice others unwittingly to risk incurring harm to themselves.

Thus, she and the detective should agree before the documents exchange hands just what obligation each has to the other. In order to enable him to assess his degree of risk, she should tell the detective whether she would go to jail if it were necessary in order to protect his identity as her source. The point is that the detective is the key person in her search for information and that she has special obligations to him.

If the reporter does gain access to the records, then she has an obligation to the accused to treat them as confidential documents. She and the paper must not use them in such a way as to jeopardize the chance for a fair trial for the accused.

There is no genuine moral dilemma in this case. Though it does involve different moral goals and principles, they do not fundamentally clash. Strategies can be identified that enable the simultaneous pursuit of several worthwhile goals in order to meet various moral obligations.[25]

19. TEN WEEKS AT WOUNDED KNEE

One of this century's leading civil libertarians, Zechariah Chafee, Jr., once wrote: "Much of our [national] expansion has been accomplished without attacking our neighbors. . . . There were regrettable phases of our history, such as breaches of faith with the Indians, but these are so far in the past that they have left no running sores to bother us now. . . . We have not acted the bully."[26]

If a distinguished Harvard law professor, a man considered a champion of oppressed minorities, could write so casually about the plight of American Indians, little wonder a tight circle of American Indian Movement (AIM) leaders thought they needed a major event to publicize their concerns. And what better event than an old-fashioned "uprising" complete with teepees, horses, rifles, war paint, and television cameras.

On 27 February 1973, some 200 Indians seized the hamlet of Wounded Knee on the Pine Ridge Sioux Indian Reservation in the southwest corner of South Dakota. Tension had been growing steadily for three weeks, ever since a group of Indians clashed with police in Custer, South Dakota, protesting the light charge (second-degree manslaughter) returned against a white man accused of stabbing and killing an Indian there. Thirty-six Indians were arrested in that melee, eight police were injured, and a chamber of commerce building was burned.

But the problem at Wounded Knee was of a different magnitude. Indians had taken hostages (11 townspeople who later declared they were not being held against their will and who refused to be released to federal authorities) and were prepared to hold their ground by violence if need be. They sensed considerable public support as they traded on sympathy for Chief Big Foot's warriors who were slaughtered there in 1890 by the U.S. Seventh Cavalry.

That morbid raid had been the last recorded instance of open hostilities between American Indians and the U.S. government—until February 1973.

As the siege began, news crews rushed to cover the developing story. On 28 February, Indians demanded that the Senate Foreign Relations Committee hold hearings on treaties made with Indians and that the Senate begin a full-scale investigation of the government's treatment of Indians. George McGovern, a liberal Democrat and South Dakota senator at the time, flew home to try negotiations, but to no avail. Meanwhile, FBI agents, federal marshals, and Bureau of Indian Affairs (BIA) police surrounded Wounded Knee, hoping to seal off supplies and force a peaceful surrender.

But the siege turned violent. On 11 March, an FBI agent was shot and an Indian injured as gunfire erupted at a roadblock outside town. On the same day, AIM leader Russell Means announced that Wounded Knee had seceded from the United States and that federal officials would be treated as agents of a warring foreign power. A marshal was seriously wounded on 26 March, and two Indians were killed in gunfire as the siege wore into April. Finally on 6 May, with supplies and morale nearly expended, the Indians negotiated an armistice and ended the war.

An incredible 93 percent of the population claimed to follow the story through television, but Indian attorney Roman Roubideaux did not think they were seeing the real story:

> The TV correspondents who were on the scene filmed many serious interviews and tried to get at the essence of the story, but *that* stuff never got on the air. Only the sensational stuff got on the air. The facts never really emerged that this was an uprising against the Bureau of Indian Affairs and its puppet tribal government.[27]

Television critic Neil Hickey summarized the feelings of many:

> In all the contentiousness surrounding the seizure of Wounded Knee last winter, a thread of agreement unites the disputants: namely, the press, especially television, performed its task over a quality spectrum ranging from "barely adequate" to "misguided" to "atrocious." For varying reasons, no party to the fray felt that his views were getting a decent airing.[28]

The lack of sufficient evidence foiled prosecutors at the subsequent trial of AIM leaders Russell Means and Dennis Banks. Defense attorneys Mark Lane and William Kunstler argued that the Indians were not guilty since they were merely reclaiming land taken from them by treaty violations. But the real defense was an inept offense. In September 1974, U.S. District Judge Fred Nichol accused the FBI of arrogance and misconduct, and the chief U.S. prosecutor of deceiving the court. After an hour's lecture to the government, he dismissed the case.

The occupation at Wounded Knee was deliberately staged for television. AIM leaders knew that the legends of Chief Big Foot and the recent popularity of Dee Brown's *Bury My Heart at Wounded Knee* would virtually guarantee good press. Yet no one can reasonably contend it was not a newsworthy event. The Indians at Pine Ridge had just witnessed what they perceived to be a breakdown in the judicial system at Custer. The American Indian Movement had tried other forums for airing their argument that 371 treaties had been violated by the U.S. government. The Ogalala Sioux were Western Plains horsemen pushed off their land during Western expansion. And while the tribal militants actually precipitated the siege—though numbering only a small percentage of the Pine Ridge population— traditional grievance procedures through the Bureau of Indian Affairs had been tried and to date had failed. Although the event produced several excesses, sympathy for it was aided by heavy doses of folklore and liberal guilt. Yet it was based on a defensible civil disobedience. Joe Ledbetter, a painter in Custer, did not represent the prevailing opinion: "Them Indians learned from the niggers. They got the same tactics." Assuming the distinction between Ledbetter's neurotic behavior and AIM's understandable frustration, media coverage seems warranted.

The moral issue concerns the degree to which the conflicting voices were fairly represented. In fact, the ten weeks of the siege produced so many aggrieved parties that fairness to all protagonists became totally impossible. How accurately did reporters cover the law officials ordered to the scene, for example? After the event, FBI agents and marshals were hissed by hostile crowds near Wounded Knee and ordered to leave lest another outbreak occur. And how could the press treat the Bureau of Indian Affairs fairly? Its policies became the lightning rod of attack, catching all the fury born from 200 years of exploitation. An inept Justice Department, abuses from ranchers and storekeepers, racism from area whites, and inadequate congressional leadership also contributed to the situation but received only a minor part of the blame. How does one evaluate where accusations are appropriate and yet recognize legitimate achievements in a raucous setting? The Bureau contended, for example, that it was not responsible for every conceivable abuse and that it had sponsored nearly all the vocational training and employment on the reservation.

But the hardest questions concern the fair treatment of the Ogalala Sioux grievances. According to the ethical principle that human beings should be respected as ends in themselves, the moral ideal entails an account that clearly reflects the viewpoint of these aggrieved. And even a minimum definition of fairness certainly includes all avoidance of stereotypes. A young Ogalala Sioux bitterly scourged some members of the press in this regard for giving their stories the stilted cast of "wild West gunfights between the marshals and Indians." On 30 December 1890, the *New York Times* warped its news account of the original Pine Ridge battle with biased phrases about "hostiles" and "reds." The story concluded: "It is doubted if by night either a buck or squaw out of all Big Foot's band is left to tell the tale of this day's treachery. The members of the Seventh Cavalry have once more shown themselves to be heroes of deeds of daring."[29]

After 85 years, many newspapers and broadcasters had still not eliminated clichés, prejudices, and insensitive language.[30]

Russell Means complicated the press's rhetorical task with his penchant for quotable but stinging discourse. Years later, in fact, Means was working to erect a monument at the site of the 1876 Battle of the Little Big Horn. In the process, he called for razing the statue of the "mass murderer" General George Custer. "Can you imagine a monument to Hitler in Israel?" he demanded in a news conference. "This country has monuments to the Hitlers of America in Indian country everywhere you go."[31] Means called for a fitting memorial to a battle that "continues to epitomize the indigenous will to resist oppression, suppression, and repression at the hands of European parasites."[32]

Fairness, at a minimum, also requires that the coverage reflect the degree of complexity inherent in the events themselves. Admittedly, when events are refracted through the mirrors of history, separating fact from fiction becomes impossible. Moreover, the Pine Ridge Indians themselves disagreed fundamentally about the problems and the cure. Richard Wilson, president of the tribal council, despised the upstarts of AIM: "They're just bums trying to get their braids and mugs in the press." He feared a declaration of martial law on the reservation and considered the militants Means and Banks to be city-bred leaders acting like a "street gang," who could destroy the tribe in the name of saving it.

"No more red tape. No more promises," said Means in response. "The federal government hasn't changed from Wounded Knee to My Lai and back to Wounded Knee." Raymond Yellow Thunder, after all, had been beaten to death earlier by whites and the charges limited to manslaughter by an all-white jury in Custer. Investigations demanded by Congress, the Justice Department, and Senator McGovern had been to no avail. The average annual wage at Pine Ridge was $1,800, with alcoholism and suicide at epidemic rates. Why not action now? Why were the AIM occupiers, speaking for thousands of Indians, unable to get a hearing for themselves? Maybe the BIA had instituted a corrupt, puppet government after all. Where is the truth in all the highly charged rhetoric?

Some reporters did break through the fog with substantive accounts. NBC's Fred Briggs used charts and photos to describe the trail of broken treaties that reduced the vast Indian territory to a few small tracts. CBS's Richard Threlkeld understood that AIM really sought a revolution in Indian attitudes. ABC's Ron Miller laid vivid hold of life on the Pine Ridge reservation itself by "getting inside the Indians and looking at what was happening through their eyes." But, on balance, journalists on the scene did not fully comprehend the subtleties or historical nuances of tribal government. Reporters covering Wounded Knee complained that their more precise accounts were often reduced and distorted by heavy editing at home. After 71 days the siege ended from weariness—not because the story was fully aired or understood. During that period the press largely became an accomplice of the guns and specter; it got caught up in the drama itself rather than enable a political complaint to be discussed sensibly and thoroughly.

Maybe the principle of fairness can operate only before and after a spectacle of this kind, when the aggrieved knock on doors more gently. If that is true, owners of news businesses in the Wounded Knee region carry an obligation to develop substantial and balanced coverage of the oppression of Native Americans over the long term, even though such coverage may threaten some of their established interests. Often reporters sensitive to injustice receive little support and thus have no choice but to break stories of injustice when they fit into traditional canons of newsworthiness.

This regrettable weakness in Native American coverage did not end with Wounded Knee. A decade later, 100 miles east of the Grand Canyon, the federal government began the largest program of forced relocation since the internment of Japanese-Americans during World War II. Thousands of Navajos were taken from a million acres awarded to the neighboring Hopi tribe. The Navajo-Hopi turmoil is the biggest story in Indian affairs for a century, and "a still-evolving issue of national significance." But, Jerry Kammer complained, major newspapers have hurried past "the way some tourists hurry across the reservations en route to the Grand Canyon. They have regarded the dispute and its people as little more than material for colorful features."[33] Violence is a likely possibility even for years after the resettlement is completed—given the sacred burial grounds involved, disputes over oil and minerals, Navajo defiance, and so forth. Periodically, banners emblazoned with "WK 73" (Wounded Knee 1973) appear to remind everyone that a battle to the death may be at hand with authorities.

> If federal marshals sent to evict Navajos do battle with an unlikely guerrilla force of AIM members, Navajo veterans of Vietnam, and grand-mothers in calico skirts, the press will descend like Tom Wolfe's fruit flies, just as they did at Wounded Knee. They would feast on the violence of a tragedy that was spawned by competing tribes, compounded by the federal government, and neglected by the national press.[34]

Another decade later, in May 1993, journalists from all over the world descended on Littlewater, New Mexico, a small Navajo town on a 25,000-square-mile reservation, the largest in the United States. A disease that doctors had not encountered before had killed six Navajos, as its first victims, but soon infected 39 people in 11 states and left 26 dead (including Hispanics, Hopi Indians, African Americans, and Anglos). "An early front-page headline in *USA Today* called the illness 'Navajo flu,' the *Arizona Republic* labeled it the 'Navajo epidemic,' and *NBC News* referred to the 'Navajo disease.'"[35] The headline stuck, said one man burying his wife, because "people think we live in tepees and our homes are dirty." Navajos chased journalists away from funerals of victims, with the president of the Navajo nation and his press secretary complaining that they "violated many of our customs and taboos. . . . In Navajo tradition, the four days after a burial are especially sacred. That was blasted apart by journalists agressively pursuing a story. They were disrespectful, disruptive, and upsetting to the whole idea of harmony." The mystery illness was later identified as a noncontagious strain of

Hantavirus, a deadly disease carried by the deer mouse.[36] Once again, mainstream media failed to understand the Native American situation thoroughly, some journalists even using offensive terms like "witchcraft" and photographers taking pictures of sacred objects. A tribal council resolution criticized sensational news coverage for inspiring "discriminatory attitudes and activities against Navajo people."

And the beat goes on. Because of this historic pattern of failure, observers predict that the confrontations will move to the state and county level during the 1990s. For example, 72 Wisconsin counties have formed an association to resolve the costly and complex jurisdictional disputes between the Oneida Indians and local governments over fishing rights, timber, minerals and water, property taxes, welfare, and education. Jumbled federal policies, many of them as old as the U.S. Constitution, fan the disputes rather than clarify them. Increasingly, local journalists face the same contentious issues of social justice brought to a head on the national level at Wounded Knee.

NOTES

1. Charles Beard, *"St. Louis Post-Dispatch* Symposium on Freedom of the Press," 1938. Quoted in William L. Rivers, Wilbur Schramm, and Clifford Christians, *Responsibility in Mass Communication,* 3d ed. (New York: Harper and Row, 1980), p. 47.

2. Commission on the Freedom of the Press, *A Free and Responsible Press* (Chicago: University of Chicago Press, 1947), pp. 26-27.

3. For further development of the issues, see Clifford Christians, "Reporting and the Oppressed" in *Responsible Journalism,* ed. Deni T. Elliot (Beverly Hills, CA: Sage, 1986).

4. Andrew Calabrese and Janet Wasko, "All Wired Up and No Place to Go: The Search for Public Space in U.S. Cable Development," *Gazette* 49 (1992): 122.

5. "Take a Trip into the Future on the Electronic Superhighway," *Time,* 12 April 1993, pp. 50-51. For a detailed critical analysis by experts inside and outside the university, see *The People's Right to Know: Media, Democracy, and the Information Highway,* eds. Frederick Williams and John V. Pavlik (Hillsdale, NJ: Lawrence Erlbaum, 1994).

6. "Take a Trip . . . ," p. 51.

7. Ibid., pp. 52-53.

8. Everette E. Dennis, "Looking Critically at the Information Highway," *Communique* 8:3 (November 1993): 2. For a similar conclusion that the ethical protocols remain largely undefined, see Joan Connell, "Virtual Reality Check—Cyberethics, Consumerism and the American Soul," *Media Studies Journal* 8:1 (Winter 1994): 153-159.

9. William Safire, "Wireless Message? Keep It to Yourself . . ." *Chicago Tribune,* 5 November 1993, sec. 1, p. 13.

10. Ellen Goodman, "Driving Ourselves Crazy on America's High-tech Highway," *Chicago Tribune,* 25 October 1993, sec. 1, p. 15.

11. William Grady, "FCC Member: Electronic Highway to Bypass Poor," *Chicago Tribune,* 5 November 1993, sec. 1, p. 13.

12. For elaboration of the ethical framework, see Clifford Christians and Leon Hammond, "Social Justice and a Community Information Utility," *Communication* 9 (June 1986): 127-149.

13. Conversations reported by Associated Press writer George Esper, "Death and Deceit," *Champaign-Urbana* (Illinois) *News-Gazette,* 14 January 1990, p. A9.

14. The details and quotations that follow are summarized from Margaret Carlson, "Presumed Innocent," *Time,* 15 January 1990, pp. 10-14; also p. 30.

15. As the revelations continued to unfold, Thomas Cooper and David Gordon of Emerson College stayed abreast of the details. Write them for a copy of their latest work on it: 100 Beacon Street, Boston, MA 02116.

16. For William Raspberry's analysis, see his "Death and Deception in Boston: Anger in Search of a Target," *Chicago Tribune,* 11 January 1990, sec. 1, p. 11.

17. Apparently Michelle Caruso of the *Boston Herald* was suspicious of Charles Stuart from the beginning. Stuart's responses did not seem frantic enough to her as she reviewed the original 911 call from Stuart's car phone. However, she could not uncover enough evidence to justify a news story identifying him as the assailant. See Christopher Lyon, "The Boston Hoax: She Fought It, He Bought It," *Washington Journalism Review* (March 1990): 56-61; and Bob Sprague "The Classroom and the Street," *Media Ethics Update* 5:2 (Fall 1992): 14, 16.

18. For the examples used below and an overview, see Michael Moss, "The Poverty Story," *Columbia Journalism Review* 25 (July/August 1987): 43-54.

19. Ibid., p. 44.

20. Nicholas Lemann, "The Origins of the Underclass," *Atlantic Monthly* (June 1986): 31-68.

21. "The American Millstone," *Chicago Tribune,* 16 September 1985, 1 October 1985, 20 October 1985, 30 October 1985, 18 November 1985.

22. Penelope McMillan, *Los Angeles Times,* 23 November 1986.

23. Moss, "The Poverty Story," p. 45.

24. See, for example, Reinhold Niebuhr, *Moral Man and Immoral Society* (New York: Charles Scribner's Sons, 1932); his *Beyond Tragedy* (New York: Charles Scribner's Sons, 1937); and his *Love and Justice,* ed. D. B. Robertson (Cleveland: Meridian Books, [1957] 1967).

25. Several legal questions overlap with the moral concerns noted in this case. The reporter would, in some jurisdictions, face possible prosecution for even possessing these documents. In nearly all jurisdictions, there are penalties for enticing. This situation is based on a study of ways to avert damaging confrontations between the bar and the press. See "Protecting Two Vital Freedoms—Fair Trial and Free Press," *Columbia Journalism Review* 18 (March/April 1980): 75-84.

26. Zechariah Chafee, Jr., "Why I Like America" (commencement address at Colby College, Waterville, Maine, 21 May 1944).

27. Neil Hickey, "Only the Sensational Stuff Got on the Air," *TV Guide,* 8 December 1973, p. 34. For details on which this case and commentary are based, see the other three articles in Hickey's series: "Was the Truth Buried at Wounded Knee?" 1 December, pp. 7-12; "Cameras Over Here!" 15 December, pp. 43-49; "Our Media Blitz Is Here to Stay," 22 December, pp. 21-23.

28. Ibid.

29. Arnold Marquis, "Those 'Brave Boys in Blue' at Wounded Knee," *Columbia Journalism Review* 13 (May/June 1974): 26-27; and Joel D. Weisman, "About That 'Ambush' at Wounded Knee," *Columbia Journalism Review* 14 (September/October 1975): 28-31.

30. For a historical overview of photography, see Joanna C. Scherer, "You Can't Believe Your Eyes: Inaccuracies in Photographs of North American Indians," *Studies in the Anthropology of Visual Communication* 2:2 (Fall 1975): 67-79.

31. Daniel Wiseman, "Indians Will Erect Own Monument Over Defeat of 'Murderer' Custer," *Casper* (Wyoming) *Star-Tribune,* 23 June 1988, p. Al.

32. "Statement of Russell Means, Lakota Nation," *Akwesasne Notes* (Summer 1989): 12.

33. For details on this story and the quotations, see Jerry Kammer, "The Navajos, the Hopis, and the U.S. Press," *Columbia Journalism Review* 24 (July/August 1986): 41-44.

34. Ibid.

35. For details and quotations, see Bob M. Gassaway, "Press Virus Strikes Navajos: Journalists Invade Another Culture, Stumble over Traditions," *Quill* 81:9 (November/December 1993): 24-25.

36. Leslie Linthicum, "Of Mice and Mistrust," *Albuquerque Journal,* 19 December 1993, pp. 1E-2E.

chapter 5

Invasion of Privacy

The right of individuals to protect their privacy has long been cherished in Western culture. Samuel Warren and Louis D. Brandeis gave this concept legal formulation in their famous essay "The Right to Privacy" in the December 1890 *Harvard Law Review*. Thirty-eight years later, Brandeis still maintained his concern: "The makers of our Constitution undertook to secure conditions favorable to the pursuit of happiness. . . . They conferred, as against the Government, the right to be let alone—the most comprehensive of rights and the right most valued by civilized man."[1] Since that time, the protection of personal privacy has received increasing legal attention and has grown in legal complexity. Although the word "privacy" does not appear in the Constitution, its defenders base its credence on the first eight amendments and the Fourteenth Amendment, which guarantee due process of law and protection against unreasonable intrusion. The many laws safeguarding privacy now vary considerably among states and jurisdictions. Yet the general parameters are being defined as proscriptions "against deep intrusions on human dignity by those in possession of economic or governmental power."[2] Privacy cases within this broad framework are generally classified in four separate, though not mutually exclusive, categories: (1) intrusion upon seclusion or solitude, (2) public disclosure of embarrassing private affairs, (3) publicity that places individuals in a false light, and (4) appropriation of an individual's name or likeness for commercial advantage.

However, for all of privacy's technical gains in case law and tort law, legal definitions are an inadequate foundation for the news business. Merely following the letter of the law certainly is not sufficient—presuming that can even be determined reasonably. There are several reasons why establishing an ethics of privacy that goes beyond the law is important in the gathering and distribution of news.

First, the law that conscientiously seeks to protect individual privacy excludes public officials. Brandeis himself believed strongly in keeping the national business open. Sunlight for him was the great disinfectant. And while he condemned intrusion in personal matters, he insisted on the exposure of all secrets bearing on public concern. In general, the courts have upheld that political personalities cease to be purely private persons, and First Amendment values take precedence over privacy considerations. In recent years, court decisions have given the media extraordinary latitude in reporting on public persons. The U.S. Supreme Court in a 1964 opinion (*New York Times v. Sullivan*) concluded that even vilifying falsehoods relating to official conduct are protected unless made with actual malice or reckless disregard of the facts. The Court was profoundly concerned in its judgment not to impair what they considered the press's indispensable service to democratic life. In 1971, the Court applied its 1964 opinion to an individual caught up in a public issue—a Mr. Rosenbloom arrested for distributing obscene books. Subsequent opinions have created some uncertainties, though continually reaffirming broad media protection against defamation suits. Thus, even while adhering to the law, the press has a nearly boundless freedom to treat elected officials unethically.

Second, the press has been given great latitude in defining newsworthiness. People who are catapulted into the public eye by events are generally classified with elected officials under privacy law. In broadly construing the Warren and Brandeis public-interest exemption to privacy, the courts have ruled material as newsworthy because a newspaper or station carries the story. In nearly all important cases, the American courts have accepted the media's definition. But is not the meaning of newsworthiness susceptible to trendy shifts in news values and very dependent upon presumed tastes and needs? Clearly, additional determinants are needed to distinguish gossip and voyeurism from information necessary to the democratic decision-making process.

Third, legal efforts beg many questions about the relationship between self and society. Democratic political theory since the sixteenth century has debated that connection and shifted over time from a libertarian emphasis on the individual to a twentieth-century version that is much more collectivistic in tone. Within these broad patterns, several narrower arguments have prevailed. Thomas Jefferson acquiesced to the will of the majority, whereas John Stuart Mill insisted that individuals must be free to pursue their own good in their own way. Two of the greatest minds ever to focus on American democracy, Alexis de Tocqueville and John Dewey, both centered their analysis on this matter of a viable public life. Likewise, Walter Lippmann worried about national prosperity in his *Public Opinion* and *The Public Philosophy*. Together these authors and others have identified an enduring intellectual problem that typically must be reduced and narrowed in order for legal conclusions to be drawn. Professor Thomas Emerson's summary is commonly accepted:

> The concept of a right to privacy attempts to draw a line between the individual and the collective, between self and society. It seeks to assure

the individual a zone in which to be an individual, not a member of the community. In that zone he can think his own thoughts, have his own secrets, live his own life, reveal only what he wants to the outside world. The right of privacy, in short, establishes an area excluded from the collective life, not governed by the rules of collective living.[3]

Shortcuts and easy answers arise from boxing off these two dimensions. Glib appeals to "the public's right to know" are a common way to cheapen the richness of the private/public relationship. Therefore, sensitive journalists who personally struggle with these issues in terms of real people put more demands on themselves than considering what is technically legal. They realize that ethically sound conclusions can emerge only when various privacy situations are faced in all their complexities. The cases that follow illustrate some of those intricacies and suggest ways of dealing with them responsibly. The privacy situations selected below involved a drinking senator, uncovered spy data, small-town gossip, a senior citizen, and a tragic drowning accident. They represent typical dilemmas involving both elected officials and persons who became newsworthy by events beyond their control. The information-gathering and disseminating functions are included also.

Woven through the commentary are three moral principles that undergird an ethics of privacy for newspeople. The first principle promotes decency and basic fairness as nonnegotiable. Even though the law does not explicitly rule out falsehood, innuendo, recklessness, and exaggeration, human decency and basic fairness obviously do. The second moral principle proposes "redeeming social value" as a criterion for selecting which private information is worthy of disclosure. This guideline eliminates all appeals to prurient interests as devoid of newsworthiness. Third, the dignity of persons ought not be maligned in the name of press privilege. Whatever serves ordinary people best must take priority over some cause or slogan.

At a minimum, this chapter suggests, private information in news accounts must pass the test of these three principles to be ethically justified, though the commentaries introduce the subtleties involved. Clearly, privacy matters cannot be treated sanctimoniously by ethicists. They are among the most painful that humane reporters encounter. Often they surface among those journalists with a heart in a recounting of battles lost.

20. THE DRINKING COMMITTEE CHAIRPERSON

Ellen Steenway had covered Washington for 16 years. From the beginning, Washington intrigued her. As a journalism student she had spent her internship on the president's press secretary's staff. She had accepted a position with the State Department's public relations unit after graduation, until the urge for newswriting sent her to a Washington magazine and then a Washington paper before switching six years ago to her latest assignment on the Washington bureau of a New York paper.

During these professional years, she had observed heavy drinking by several public officials, heard well-documented reports on extramarital affairs by members of Congress, watched a cabinet secretary ridicule his wife, and personally knew a photographer who had followed a senator around gay bars. She had never reported any of these private episodes because she believed that these personal affairs were private business as long as they did not interfere with public duties. She also refused to pursue several of these stories for fear she might jeopardize her access to the parties and offices of various politicians.

Then one day Steenway covered the hearings of the Senate Banking Committee when its chairperson was visibly drunk at 10 A.M. He asked rambling questions, interrupted the proceedings, maintained no semblance of parliamentary procedure, and had to be helped from his chair for the noon luncheon. As before, Steenway made no mention of his drinking, even though it clearly interfered with the quality of his committee work and was not merely an after-hour activity. A month later, when the Banking Committee presented a new bill on the Senate floor, Chairperson Williams was again visibly drunk and Steenway explicitly reported his drinking habits rather than use euphemisms such as "the Chairman did not defend the bill successfully." By any standard of fairness, Williams's behavior had now crossed over the line. A major complicated tax bill was involved and its enactment near.

However, Steenway's editor refused to include any reference to Williams's drunkenness. For decades, the paper had a policy that sex and drinking were not mentioned unless there had been arrests with documented evidence available in a public record. In the editor's view, the bill's path through the Senate certainly did not depend on how eloquently Williams defended it. He reasoned that presidential drunkenness might be reported since presidents are responsible for the nuclear trigger, but banking committees could not lead us into World War III. In addition, the editor felt that references to Williams's drinking would sensationalize the story; it was not serious news, and he preferred to focus on the issues. The merit and weakness of the proposed legislation were all that really counted to him. And how did Steenway know for sure? Maybe Williams just had a high fever that day.

Steenway reminded the editor that in 16 years she had not included personal matters nor had she reported Williams's behavior during the hearings. "Then why change your practice now," the editor demanded. "Or are you weakening just because so many cheap papers are printing that drivel." Steenway was upset but did not feel strongly enough to resign. In fact, when the same incident occurred again several days later, she did not even mention it, knowing that her editor would reject the story anyhow and might even consider her insubordinate.

Both decision makers take their responsibilities seriously. Neither can be faulted for outright carelessness or brazen disregard for standards. There is no evidence that the editor is merely protecting an old crony or is concerned about a possible libel suit. Perhaps the editor harbors an artificial reverence for important officials, but his crusty manner makes that doubtful. Steenway does not appear to want to report the senator's drunkenness simply because this will move a page-12 story to page 1.

In fact, Steenway could be held blameworthy for not reporting the incident. Senator Williams, in her judgment, had allowed his personal habits to seriously affect his acumen. Many readers of her newspaper were from New Jersey, the senator's home state, and they had a right to know. No sensational language had been included, though his incoherent speech, tottering, and occasional belligerence were mentioned in a matter-of-fact tone. Given Williams's long record of drinking, Steenway was convinced the cause could not have been a temporary physical ailment.

The editor could also be considered blameworthy if he chose to do nothing. His company policy was explicit, and he upheld the same longstanding reservations about reporting on private matters. He understood the press's vast legal rights regarding public officials, but sincerely felt that the content of the bill and its potential effects were the only relevant story here. Not to overrule his reporter would mean violating his conscience and ignoring his paper's definition of newsworthiness.

In the first phase of this case, both the editor and reporter could justify their actions before reasonable people. The reporter has not wantonly invaded the senator's privacy, but limited her account to his behavior on the Senate floor. The editor, meanwhile, invokes a defensible company policy. Given the fact that the senator is not a personal friend of either the paper's owner or editor whom they were protecting, the reporter's story and the editor's rejection can be considered morally acceptable. In fact, both of them appear quaint, given the current climate. The press reported every detail about Gary Hart's liaison with Donna Rice in his Washington, DC, townhouse and on a boat ride to Bimini; his campaign for the Democratic presidential nomination was finished. Senator John Tower's scandalous personal life was dramatized in the news, and his appointment as Secretary of Defense was defeated. Whereas all boundaries of restraint have seemed to disappear with Senator Packwood, the struggle between Steenway and her editor still represents the morally appropriate way to treat the personal affairs of public officials.

The issue for debate concerns phase two—Steenway's behavior after the editor's decision. The fourth step in the Potter Box process now became inescapable. Where were her ultimate loyalties? Steenway was upset, but she did not resign. When Williams was subsequently drunk on the Senate floor, she made no reference to it. As an employee, she chose not to contradict company policy. Her perceived duty to the paper overrode her concern for her New Jersey readers and her own conscience.

21. SPY DATA AND SUICIDE

On Saturday night, 28 February 1976, the editors of the *Dallas Times-Herald* had a decision to make before the 10 P.M. press time. The Sunday edition would feature an exposé that investigative reporter Hugh Aynesworth had been working on for three months. The article would disclose that Norman J. Rees, a former oil engineer who was retired and living in Connecticut, had been a Soviet spy from World War II until 1975, and that since 1971 Rees had been a double agent working for the Federal Bureau of Investigation.

Rees had twice flown to Dallas and allowed himself to be interviewed by the *Times-Herald*. According to executive editor Ken Johnson, Rees admitted accepting money from the Soviets for technical information and had "voluntarily undergone polygraph examinations" to substantiate his account.[4] But on that Saturday afternoon before publication, Rees had called the *Times-Herald*. He asked if the story would be printed and if he would be identified. Told yes, Rees responded that such a disclosure would leave him "no choice but suicide."

On Sunday morning the story appeared. On Sunday morning Rees's wife found her husband's body. He had shot himself in the head at his home in Connecticut.

That afternoon an Associated Press reporter talked with Rees's son, John, a thirty-one-year-old junior-high-school teacher. He told the reporter he had informed his mother, Ann, of the story, and she was "acting like it's unreal. She didn't know the story was coming out."

After Rees's death, the *Times-Herald* issued a statement:

> From time to time, newspapers receive threats about stories from people attempting to protect their identities. In our judgment, if a story is newsworthy and supported by the facts it is our policy to publish. In this instance it was decided that the story could not be suppressed, even in the face of Mr. Rees's threats.[5]

On 13 March, the *New York Times* printed a letter from a reader questioning the *Times-Herald*'s judgment. Nancy Boardman Eddy of Chevy Chase, Maryland, wrote:

> I cannot comprehend the thinking of newsmen who, when told that Mr. Rees would kill himself if the story identified him, excuse themselves by saying "the story could not be suppressed."
>
> I'd like to ask, Why not? To what higher moral code do newsmen adhere than we mortals do? The First Amendment may give them the freedom to print the news, but why are they somehow obligated to print knowingly a story that may lead to a man's death, and, indeed, what purpose is served? The arrogance displayed is beyond belief.[6]

On 31 March, a second letter was printed, defending the press. John Pyle of Brooklyn wrote: "The threat of just such disclosure has prevented many people from committing just such infamy, knowing that possible disclosure is the price they might be asked to pay. This is possibly a greater deterrent to spying and treason than the law."[7]

Three major choices were made by people at the *Times-Herald:* (1) someone decided the story merited investigation and publication; (2) someone decided to publish it on the Sunday morning originally scheduled; and (3) someone decided to ignore Rees's suicide threat.

What considerations are relevant to each of these decisions? The *Times-Herald* policy was to publish if a story is deemed newsworthy and is supported by the facts. Someone decided that both criteria were met in this case. Presumably, the *Times-Herald,* because of two interviews with Rees, had the details straight and judged them newsworthy. It might have reminded readers that when Rees first began working with the Russians in World War II, Russia was an ally. It might have contained publicly useful reports on the forces and reasons that compelled Rees to continue to supply the Russians with secrets long after World War II was over. It might therefore have given a measure of guidance to some other public official who was contemplating disloyal conduct. Thus, judged by the criterion that it contained information that might conceivably work toward the public good, it is arguable that the story may have been newsworthy. It also is arguable that the story contained nothing that the public *needed* to know but only something the public might *want* to know in the form of an entertaining spy thriller.

On the second question (the decision to publish on schedule), several relevant factors enter the picture. This story is clearly one that would keep. Postponing publication would allow time for negotiation with Rees in order to see what part of the information he had given voluntarily in interviews that he would now prefer to keep off the record. Further conversations with Rees might well have protected those things he wished to conceal while simultaneously serving the public's need to know. In any case, the decision to publish a story that could have been delayed, and to do so under the threat of suicide, appears on its face to be made in indifference to Rees's well-being. The *Times-Herald's* statement about its reason for publication does not address this question, though in an interview 13 years later, reporter Hugh Aynesworth elaborates on the *Times-Herald* decision: "I was willing to give him time to tell his wife, to move, and the editors agreed to give him time as well. . . . At that point, he said that if you use it, I will have to kill myself."[8]

The third matter (ignoring Rees's threat altogether) provides solid evidence of the editors' disregard for Rees's relatives or the authorities who might seek to prevent him from carrying out his threat. The failure of the *Times-Herald* to apprise someone of the threat is remarkable. Any high-school sophomore could have picked up on Rees's apparent instability, and yet the paper ignored his threat even to the point of not alerting anyone that it had been made. Perhaps Rees's suicide could not have been prevented if the story appeared, but the *Times-Herald* should have made an effort. Instead, these editors demonstrated a callous disregard for the life of a human being, a life that almost certainly could have been saved simply by an editor's decision not to publish. The paper violated the basic moral principle that we not only should not cause harm, but should prevent it when doing so does not subject us to a risk of comparable harm. The staff should at least have done everything possible to negotiate with Rees. Sometimes changing the emphasis or clarifying the information removes the objection that triggered the suicide threat. Laurence Jolidon, the metro editor of the *Times-Herald* in 1973 and the last person from the newspaper to see Norman Rees, has concluded correctly that "threats of suicide are extreme examples of what happens when sources feel that the newspaper isn't treating them fairly. . . . You have to keep the dialogue going."[9] He now believes that newsrooms have a responsibility to communicate to sources who are threatening suicide that their interests are being taken seriously.

It is obvious, however, that our duty to prevent harm does not mean that every threat of suicide ought to be honored automatically. As Hugh Aynesworth asked: "If newsworthy information was withheld every time somebody [threatened suicide], what would we have in the papers?"[10] The source's reaction is one component but not the exclusive one in deciding whether to publish. One could imagine another kind of case in which Rees is a wealthy community leader respected for his charity, but he controls a blind trust owning slum property in violation of city codes. A poor family dies in a fire. Rees is unstable and distraught; he threatens suicide if his ownership is ever disclosed. If this situation were considered in terms of Rawls's veil of ignorance, publishing the story would be justified. Or, giving the issues an even harder twist, assume that Rees died of natural causes and there had been no fire: Should his obituary indicate how this rich tenement owner amassed his wealth?

22. A PROSTITUTE ON PAGE 12

Cindy Herbig was a model teenager. A high-school student and the only daughter of a prominent family in Missoula, Montana, she had won a scholarship to Radcliffe. Then on 17 January 1979, she was murdered in downtown Washington, DC.[11]

The *Missoulian,* a daily newspaper with a circulation of 32,000, carried a page-1 story the following day—a tragedy for the community and grief to her family. The sordid details of Cindy's life in Washington were not part of that first local obituary; indeed, managing editor Ron Deckert knew little until his paper was contacted by the *Washington Post,* which was developing the story to its dramatic hilt: promising, talented teenager turned prostitute stabbed on the streets, presumably in the course of plying her trade.

Cindy's transition from gifted musician to streetwalker was first manifest in an uneasy adjustment to the pressures of Ivy League competition and urban Northeastern impersonality. By Thanksgiving 1976 she was out of college and back in Missoula, soon discontented there as well, unable to find interesting work. Six months later she met a recruiter in a Missoula bar, traveled with him to Washington, and entered the seedy world of 15th and K Streets NW. The pimp was known to police, though he was never arrested. In December 1977, Cindy was convicted of solicitation for prostitution.

All this became clear when a *Post* reporter called the *Missoulian* on Monday, 22 January, the day of Cindy's funeral, to get information from the published obituary. In return for the help, the *Post* writer agreed to dictate his story over the phone on Tuesday night.

Cindy's parents, Hal and Lois Herbig, first caught wind of the *Post*'s intentions late Monday when they were also called by a Washington reporter. They were appalled by this encroachment on their privacy and the senselessness of publicizing their daughter's problems. Family friend and Missoula attorney Jack Mudd agreed to help the Herbigs squelch the story. On Tuesday morning Mudd called the *Post* to request a kill. The family had suffered enough, Mudd argued. Further publicity would endanger the parent's health. At least the story should be softened, Mudd contended. The *Post* declined.

Meanwhile, Mudd learned that the *Missoulian* planned to use the story in Wednesday morning's edition. Mudd appealed to Deckert, even making vague references to suicide if the story were printed locally. Deckert told Mudd that a decision to publish would have to wait until the *Post* called to dictate its story later that evening. Deckert hoped the *Post* would not go for the jugular on this one, and he was disappointed when the story came in at about 9:00 P.M. The *Post*'s lead read: "In the 21 years of Cynthia Herbig's life, she received honors and accolades at a Montana high school, mastered the cello, won a scholarship to Radcliffe College, and finally, came to Washington to work as a $50-a-trick prostitute."

Other parts of the story also bothered Deckert. For example, the fifth paragraph read: "Herbig used to talk freely about her work, telling an acquaintance at a party here recently, 'I'm a prostitute.'" After 19 paragraphs describing Cindy's musical gifts and general modesty, the story flipped abruptly into details of her bizarre other life. The *Post* had actually interviewed prostitutes near Cindy's corner and summarized their comments in the twentieth paragraph:

> Several women . . . described her as a bright young woman whose dress was "conservative" and whose manner with customers was "very sweet." "She charged the going rate of $50," they said. A police officer who knew Herbig said he once remarked to her that "she didn't seem like the type to be working out on the street. . . . She responded with a giggle," he said.

Finally Deckert came to the last paragraph—the chilling quotation from Cindy herself, as recalled by an unidentified male acquaintance: "'You see, you didn't believe that I worked the street, and now you know that I'm a pro,' said Herbig."

Deckert finished reading the copy and knew that his paper would have to print the story. It had news value, after all, since much of Cindy's death was still a mystery in Missoula. Deckert also believed that her story would serve as a warning to other Missoula teenagers. The pimp who had recruited her in a bar was still doing business, along with thousands like him. Perhaps Cindy's story would prevent a similar tragedy. Finally, Deckert knew that the story would certainly be distributed nationally and around the region through the *Washington Post/Los Angeles Times* News Service; if he printed nothing, his community would question how often he suppressed other information and on what basis.

In eleven years of journalism, Deckert had never faced a quandary this intense. Local citizens were sure to protest, and in a town of 30,000 it might be hard to find many friends. He decided to run an edited version of the *Post* story on page 12, with other local news. The *Post* headline ("A Life of Promise that Took a Strange, and Fatal, Turn") would be dropped in favor of something more sensitive: "Cindy Herbig 'shouldn't be dead,' friend says." Deckert also killed the *Post*'s fifth paragraph, added four original paragraphs from a telephone interview with a Washington detective, deleted the report of Cindy's giggle, and dropped the *Post*'s last paragraph, including the boast, "I'm a pro." Finally, Deckert put the best light on a minor detail near the end of the story. The *Post* had noted that Cindy kept "a book of regular customers, men she thought she could trust." Deckert's version had Washington police indicating that Cindy's "book of regular customers" was "a way for her to avoid the dangers of working the street when she could."

Deckert called Mudd at 11 P.M. Tuesday to say that the story would run. Mudd voiced a final plea to hold the story until he could prepare the family.

The Herbigs and much of Missoula were shocked at the intrusion. Businesses pulled their advertisements and the *Missoulian*'s law firm dropped the paper as a client. An advertiser boycott was threatened, though it did not materialize. More than 150 letters appeared in the paper in two weeks, most of them bristling with outrage. "The *Missoulian* has shown the public once more what a tasteless rag it can be and is," wrote one reader. "Whether the story is fact or fiction, it should not have been printed in her hometown newspaper for friends and relatives to read. . . . The *Missoulian,* in my opinion, isn't fit for use in 'the little boys' room.'" At least 200 readers canceled their subscriptions.

Yet Deckert's final embarrassment would come from his own staff. Editorial page editor Sam Reynolds, two days after the story, wrote his own letter, headed "A personal note," which began: "It was with shame that I read the story about Cindy Herbig—shame for the newspaper profession, shame for once to be a part of it, shame above all for inflicting additional hurt where hurt already had visited more than enough." Reynolds reviewed for readers the agony of the *Missoulian* decision, then blasted the *Post* story as "blatant sensationalism—the worst of journalism—and my sensation is disgust." Reynolds was also not happy (though he did not say so in print) that Deckert had edited his signed column to soften the mortar shells falling on his own position.

In the aftermath, businesses that had pulled advertising returned to the paper, Hal and Lois Herbig were given the privilege of a last printed letter on the subject, and the *Missoulian*'s publisher admitted that the paper could have handled the story better if it had honored Mudd's request to postpone publication for a day. But Deckert insisted in a later interview that if he had that day to live over again, his decision would probably be the same. Under deadline pressure, journalists do the best they can to get the news out, even news that hurts.

The clash between the outrage of the Herbigs' supporters and Ron Deckert's news judgment arises from the disagreement about whether news value for the community is more important than the privacy of those personally involved. Deckert's utilitarian framework, in effect, argued that the benefit for the many outweighed the bite to the few. But, if one applied the agape principle, what would be considered morally appropriate behavior? Agape is particularly suitable because it has a strong view of personhood. And in order to understand the need for a private inner self in its deepest sense, it requires a sophisticated understanding of the human psyche.

Certainly the agapic mind would eliminate the "fallen angel" story as a totally unwarranted intrusion. Why should victims of circumstance endure punishment through a sensational account? The pimp-in-Missoula angle received only eight words in Deckert's edited version of the *Washington Post* release. Most of the gory details about the stab wounds were included: the number, size, and location on the body. The small-town, rural-virgin-off-to-Ivy-League-and-big-city slant framed the account. All of that was an indecent, sensational, obdurate invasion of privacy. Although Deckert did nothing illegal, his willingness to follow the timing and reporting framework of the *Washington Post* was irresponsible.

However, the opposite extreme—reporting nothing—would also be irresponsible. Agape would suggest that the *Missoulian* had a social responsibility to advance citizen understanding, to investigate pimps and police in Missoula, to get that local story and take whatever additional time might be necessary to do so. There were public dimensions to the case; it was not solely a matter of innocent victims of tragedy. A compassionate story would have inspired readers to confront the community's problem with unwelcome pimps in local bars and would have given the police a public forum in which to fulfill their role effectively. In the process of developing the larger context, Cindy could have conceivably been mentioned by name, if doing so had been materially relevant to the bar-pimp focus and if it could possibly have been judged as a healing story by the Herbigs. But that substantive flavor contrasts sharply with the streetwalking-prostitute tone that was actually published.

The argument from the point of agape can be summarized in this fashion: Protecting privacy is a moral good. Being able to control information about ourselves is essential to our personhood. However, while being a precondition for maintaining a unique self-consciousness, privacy cannot be an absolute since we are cultural beings with responsibilities in the social and political arenas. We are individual beings; therefore, we need privacy. We are social beings; therefore, we need public information about each other. Since we are personal, eliminating privacy would eliminate human existence as we know it; since we are social, elevating privacy to absolute status would likewise render human existence impossible.[12]

23. SPORTS STORIES ON JULY 4

At daily newspapers, the Fourth of July is often a day for happy news, on the theory that people don't like to read bad news on a holiday. Much of the July 4th newspaper is also frequently prepackaged. Most reporters and editors (as well as most institutions and businesses) have the day off. As a result, an unwritten rule is that the perfect Fourth of July story is one that is both happy and able to be written up ahead of time.

By these standards, the *Blade-Citizen*'s lead sports story on 4 July 1989, was nearly perfect. A local woman had called several weeks before, saying that her father, still lucid in his mid-nineties, had been a major league baseball player in the 1910s. In fact, at age 19 he had been the starting catcher for the Philadelphia Athletics in the 1915 World Series. He had lied about his age using his older brother's birth certificates, and went by a nickname during his career.

> "My Father was against my playing baseball," Burns remembers. "He wanted me to be a lawyer. . . . He didn't even know I was playing professional baseball. If he had, he would have broken my neck—until he saw me in the World Series. I guess he figured if I was good enough to play with the best, it was all right."[13]

The sports editors looked in their reference books and indeed found someone with the same last name in the records of that World Series. He was interviewed and told lots of entertaining stories about old-time baseball players and their antics, Babe Ruth and Lou Gehrig among them. By all accounts, it was a wonderful story, perfect holiday reading. It was written up several days beforehand, which allowed the reporter to leave on a two-week vacation before the story actually appeared.

A few days after the story was printed, however, the assistant sports editor (subbing for the sports editor, who was also vacationing) received a phone call from a "sports junkie." The caller said that he had looked up the old player's statistics and biography in the *Baseball Encyclopedia,* which said he had died in 1942. Although this was troubling, the proliferation of sports books in recent years had produced some less-than-reliable references; and the sports department's own reference books didn't contain this information, so the editor was still fairly confident of the story. Soon, however, more calls came in, offering evidence from different sources that the player listed had indeed been dead for 47 years.

The editor then reexamined the story, and some small details suddenly seemed important. First, while using a false name and lying about one's age was a fairly common practice at the time, it now seemed suspicious. In addition, the old man had claimed that virtually all of his keepsakes from the time were lost in an accident when he moved to Oceanside 23 years earlier.

To the editor, this all added up to one conclusion—the old man had been telling false stories over the years to his children and grandchildren. After all these years, the editor reasoned, the man himself probably believed them to be true.

[He]grew up in Berwyn, Pennsylvania, 18 miles outside of Philadelphia. He admits he was a Phillies fan, a nut about baseball, and his hometown team had a reserve catcher sharing his last name. . . . It's possible for a person who holds onto a fantasy long enough to eventually have difficulty separating reality and fiction when their memories fail in later years.[14]

In any case, the most basic professional values demanded that a correction be printed since the story was false. However, publishing a correction might well cause great consternation in the man's family, not to mention what a public disavowal of his stories might do to the man's own self-esteem. The man is in his declining years, thought the editor, why embarrass him in front of the entire community? But at the same time, if the error was not corrected, would that not compromise the integrity of the newspaper, especially to those who had pointed out the error?

After a lot of thought, the editor himself went to visit Franklin Burns and his family. In this follow-up interview, Burns contended the *Baseball Encyclopedia* was wrong.

Burns says he was thought to have been dead once and the error was never corrected in print.

Told there are obituaries on file for the Phillies' Burns, Oceanside's Burns said, "The last time I checked, I was still alive."

He wasn't trying to display his sense of humor. As he sat in his recliner, he was without expression, though he grew more irritable with each question about his past.

"I don't think I want to talk anymore about this; I'm getting tired of it," he said twice.

Burns repeated virtually the same story he had in the original interview. But when told that some of his friends from the 1930s knew nothing of him as a baseball player, he became angry.

"If you're going to dig up my past," he said, "I'll say the hell with it all. If you don't take my word on it, I don't give a damn about it."[15]

The editor spent several days working on a correction story. It was a heartfelt piece, discussing the difficulty of the decision and the newspaper's duty to print truthful information. Under these delicate circumstances, most of the news staff thought it was one of the best pieces of writing ever to appear in the paper. However, the correction generated more hate mail than any other story in recent memory. To some readers who sided with the ninety-five-year-old baseball player, the *Blade-Citizen* reporters had been lazy or incompetent. The necessary reference books were available everywhere; the sports staff could have done its homework rather than a quick and easy interview from the first record book at hand. To them, the paper was at fault, not the old man. Other readers saw it as the typical invasion of privacy they have come to expect from the press, heartless and self-serving as newspapers usually are. A few invoked an ethical principle, even though they may not have used the exact terms: Do not cause harm. In this case, a flesh-and-blood ninety-five-year-old retiree with genuine needs was being harmed in the name of such euphemisms as the press's credibility.

24. DEAD BODY PHOTO

John Harte was the only photographer working on Sunday, 28 July, at the Bakersfield *Californian*. After some routine assignments, he heard on the police scanner about a drowning at a lake 25 miles northeast of Bakersfield. When he arrived on the scene, divers were still searching for the body of five-year-old Edward Romero, who had drowned while swimming with his brothers.

The divers finally brought up the dead boy, and the sheriff kept onlookers at bay while the family and officials gathered around the open body bag. The TV crew did not film that moment, but Harte ducked under the sheriff's arms and shot eight quick frames with his motor-driven camera.[16]

The *Californian* had a policy of not running pictures of dead bodies, so managing editor Robert Bentley was called into the office on Sunday evening for a decision. Concluding that the picture would remind readers to be careful when kids are swimming, Bentley gave his approval. On Monday, Harte transmitted the picture over the Associated Press wire "after a 20-minute argument with an editor who was furious we ran the picture . . . and accused [Harte] of seeking glory and an AP award."[17]

Readers bombarded the 80,000 circulation daily with 400 phone calls, 500 letters, and 80 cancellations. The *Californian* even received a bomb threat, forcing evacuation of the building for 90 minutes.

Distraught by the intensity of the reaction, Bentley sent around a newsroom memo admitting that "a serious error of editorial judgment was made. . . . We make mistakes—and this clearly was a big one." He concluded that their most important lesson was "the stark validation of what readers—and former readers—are saying not just locally but across the country: that the news media are seriously out of touch with their audiences."[18]

For photographer John Harte, Bentley's contrition was "disappointing to me and many of my co-workers." And editorial page editor Ed Clendaniel of the *Walla Walla* (Washington) *Union Bulletin* was not apologetic either about running it in his paper, even though it was out of context. "First, the foremost duty of any paper is to report the news," he argued. "One of the hard facts of life is that the world is filled with tragic moments as well as happy moments. . . . Second, we believe the photograph does more to promote water safety than 10,000 words could ever hope to accomplish."

Later Bentley entered Harte's photo in the Pulitzer Prize competition. "I really don't see any contradiction," he explained. "I think the photograph should never have been published. . . . But the Pulitzer Prize is given for journalistic and technical excellence. It is not given for reader approval."

Michael J. Ogden, executive director of the *Providence Journal-Bulletin,* condemns photographs that capitalize on human grief:

I can understand the printing of an auto accident picture as an object lesson. What I can't understand is the printing of sobbing wives, mothers, children. . . . What is the value of showing a mother who has just lost her child in a fire? Is this supposed to have a restraining effect on arsonists? I am sure that those who don't hesitate to print such pictures will use the pious pretense of quoting Charles A. Dana's famous dictum

FIGURE 5.1

SOURCE: *The Bakersfield Californian,* 29 July 1985, p. 1. Photo by John Harte. Reprinted by permission.

that "whatever the Divine Providence permitted to occur I was not too proud to print." Which is as peachy a shibboleth to permit pandering as I can imagine.[19]

But Ogden is a rare editor. Every day in newspapers and on television, photographs and film footage emphasize grief and tragedy. Though Harte's photo did not win the Pulitzer, in fact, professional awards are regularly given to grisly pictures regardless of whether they pander to morbid tastes.

Defending photos of this type usually centers on newsworthiness. The broken-hearted father whose child was just run over, a shocked eight-year-old boy watching his teenage brother gunned down by police, the would-be suicide on a bridge—all pitiful scenes that communicate something of human tragedy and are therefore to be considered news. Photojournalists sum up a news event in a manner the mind can hold, capturing that portrayal "rich in meaning because it is a trigger image of all the emotions aroused by the subject."[20] Harte in this case acted as an undaunted professional, fulfilling his role as reporter on everyday affairs—including the unpleasantries. From the photographer's perspective, to capture the newsworthy moment is an important self-discipline. Photographers are trained not to panic but to bring forth the truth as events dictate. They are schooled to be visual historians, and not freelance medics or family counselors.

On what grounds, however, can the photographer's behavior be condoned in the Bakersfield drowning? The principals at the scene tried to prevent him from intruding, though, it should be granted, the authorities' judgment is not always correct. The warning bell thesis was generally used by the picture's proponents, asserting that the photo could make other parents more safety conscious. However, this utilitarian appeal to possible consequences has no factual basis.[21] Perhaps in the name of reporting news, the photojournalist in this case was actually caught in those opportunistic professional values that build circulation by playing on the human penchant for morbidity.

No overarching purpose emerges that can ameliorate the direct invasion of privacy and insensitivity for these innocent victims of tragedy. In all jurisdictions, the reporting of events of public concern involves no legal issue of privacy invasion. But it is here that the photographer should consider the moral guideline: that suffering individuals are entitled to dignity and respect, despite the fact that events may have made them part of the news.

Photojournalism is an extremely significant window on our humanity and inhumanity. In pursuing its mission, the ethical conflict typically revolves around the need for honest visual information and for respecting a person's privacy. Bob Greene of the *Chicago Tribune* is only exaggerating slightly in calling the Harte picture "pornography." "Because of journalistic factors they could not control," he wrote, "at the most terrible moment of their lives" the Romeros were exposed to the entire country.[22] The older brother's hysteria for not watching his little brother closely enough is presented without compassion before an audience who had no right to become a participant in this traumatizing event for a suffering family. And even those who find the photo acceptable are upset by the context:

The *Californian* printing the photo right next to a headline about teen killings by a satanic cult.

NOTES

1. *Olmstead v. United States,* 277 U.S. 438, 478 (1928). Brandeis dissenting.
2. *Briscoe v. Reader's Digest Association,* 4 Cal. 3d 529, 93 Cal. Reptr. 866, 869 (1971).
3. Thomas I. Emerson, *The System of Free Expression* (New York: Vintage Books, 1970), p. 545.
4. For a full account of this episode, see the *Dallas Times-Herald,* 29 February 1976, and the *New York Times,* 1, 2, 5, 13, 31 March 1976. For a similar story, see Leslie Brown, "Seattle's Press and the Case of the Judge Who Killed Himself," *Columbia Journalism Review* 27 (January/February 1989): 31-33; in this case, reporter Duff Wilson did not face an explicit suicide threat from Judge Little over an investigation into his sexual activities with juvenile offenders.
5. "Spy Said He'd Kill Himself If Exposed, Then Did So," *New York Times,* 2 March 1976, p. 1.
6. Letter to the Editor, "Of News and Death," *New York Times,* 13 March 1976, p. 24.
7. Letter to the Editor, "Espionage's Price," *New York Times,* 31 March 1976, p. 40.
8. Deni Elliot, "How to Handle Suicide Threats," *Fineline* 1:7 (October 1989): 1.
9. Ibid., p. 4.
10. Ibid., p. 1.
11. Details in Jack Hart and Janis Johnson, "Fire Storm in Missoula," *Quill* 67 (May 1979): 19-24.
12. For further background on the ethics of privacy, see Louis Hodges, "The Journalist and Privacy," *Social Responsibility: Journalism, Law, and Medicine,* vol. 9 (Lexington, VA: Washington and Lee Monograph, 1983), pp. 5-19.
13. Geoffrey Ooley, "Glory Days: Former Major-Leaguer Played in the Good Old Days," *Blade-Citizen,* 4 July 1989, p. 1C.
14. Gary Hyvonen, "A Bizarre Twist to Burns' Tale," *Blade-Citizen,* 23 July 1989, p. 5C.
15. Ibid., p. 5C.
16. "Graphic Excess," *Washington Journalism Review* 8:1 (January 1986): 10-11.
17. For the quotations and details in this case, unless otherwise noted, see "Grief Photo Reaction Stuns Paper," *News Photographer* (March 1986): 16-22.
18. H. Eugene Goodwin and Ron F. Smith, *Groping for Ethics in Journalism,* 3d ed. (Ames: Iowa State University Press, 1994), pp. 211-213.
19. John Hohenberg, *The News Media: A Journalist Looks at His Profession* (New York: Holt, Rinehart and Winston, 1968), p. 212.
20. Harold Evans, *Pictures on a Page* (Belmont, CA: Wadsworth, 1978), p. 5.
21. Obviously beneficent results sometimes follow. As in Stanley Foreman's *Boston Herald-American* photos of a baby and woman falling from a broken fire escape, better safety standards and tighter inspection can be initiated after tragedies.
22. Bob Greene, "News Business and Right to Privacy Can Be at Odds," 1985-86 Report of the SPJ-SDX Ethics Committee, p. 15.

part II

Persuasion and Advertising

Over the years there have been a great many negative things said about advertising and advertising people. For example, after reviewing a number of novels about the advertising business published in the 1940s and 1950s, historian Stephen Fox concluded: "From these dozen novels came a remarkably consistent picture of the advertising world: false in tone, tense in pace, vacant and self-hating, overheated and oversexed."[1]

The picture has not gotten more flattering since that time. For example:

- In 1976, economist Robert Heilbroner called advertising "the single most value-destroying activity of business civilization." Reviewing his remarks more than ten years later, he found no reason to recant.[2]

- After an extensive investigation of "All North American authors known to have written on the culture of advertising," advertising historian Richard Pollay concluded: "They see advertising as reinforcing materialism, cynicism, irrationality, selfishness, anxiety, social competitiveness, powerlessness and/or loss of self-respect."[3]

- Or consider these thoughts from the late Howard Gossage, a member of the Advertising Copywriters Hall of Fame, and one of advertising's most penetrating gadflies: "To explain responsibility to advertising people is like trying to convince an eight-year-old that sexual intercourse is more fun than a chocolate ice-cream cone."[4]

THE LARGER ETHICAL CLIMATE

Of course advertising is scarcely alone on the ethics stage. For example:

- A 1992 cover story of *Time* magazine was entitled, "Lying (Everybody's Doing It, Honest)."
- Professor David Rankin, editorialized in *Newsweek* under the title "A State of Incivility": "We have come to accept as normal broken contracts and broken dates, public display of pornography and profanity and, I fear, even theft."[5]
- Virtually every day the media inform us of the ethical improprieties of congresspersons, sports figures, Hollywood deal makers and, of course, media reporters and entertainers.
- And of course, there are the everyday volatile concerns of right-to-life, right-to-choose, right-to-death, the homeless, gene splicing, etc., etc.

So advertising can be categorized as being in good (or bad) company with its other counterparts in the media, as well as on the larger scale of societal ethics. This is not a new perspective. In 1927, advertising pioneer Bruce Barton observed: "If advertising persuades some men to live beyond their means, so does matrimony. If advertising speaks to a thousand in order to influence one, so does the church. If advertising is often garrulous and redundant and tiresome, so is the United States Senate."[6]

THE BUSINESS PERCEIVES ITSELF

Rather than taking Barton's we're-no-worse-than-the-other-guy position, the trade organizations that represent the advertising business frequently emphasize what they perceive to be advertising's *social responsibility*. Apart from the expected litany of serving the sovereign consumers and lubricating the economy, they point to the following:

1. *"Enforced"* social responsibility through

    - a Federal Trade Commission that is more of a presence under the Clinton administration than its relative inactivity during the Reagan/Bush years;
    - a proactive Food and Drug Administration that has become quite assertive about advertisers' health claims, such as "light," "low fat," "reduced calories," "natural"; and

- a Congress quite interested in exploring possible methods of restricting or qualifying advertising in such sensitive areas as cigarettes and alcoholic beverages.

2. *"Voluntary"* social responsibility through

- codes of advertisers, media, agencies, and trade organizations;
- a much-respected National Advertising Review Board, a major force in advertising self regulation;
- the Advertising Council, and its more than $1 billion efforts dealing with such causes as crime prevention, arresting high blood pressure, the Negro college fund, AIDS education, and racial intolerance;
- the "Partnership for a Drug-Free America," with its $1.5 billion in donated space and time over a three-year period;
- the American Association of Advertising Agencies' $25 million effort to combat functional illiteracy;
- virtually daily goodwill efforts on the part of advertisers, agencies, and media for a host of state, regional, and local concerns.

THE ETHICAL BATTLEFIELD

Thus, we have a business that is commonly under attack, yet generally perceives itself to be involved in responsible activity, both voluntary and enforced. Why these starkly different perceptions of reality? This is, in part, because there are at least seven areas of ethical confrontation that are *inherent in advertising practice.*

1. *The advertising business is rationalized predominately by classical liberal philosophic assumptions.*

The basic assumptions of self-interest, the individual as a competent decision maker, and the virtue of competition leading ultimately to the good of all concerned through a "natural harmony of self-interests," are central to a classical liberal orientation, and the ensuing ideology of the market system.

Now, if one *accepts* these positions (as practitioners generally do) there will also be an acceptance of:

- consumer sovereignty; and
- advertising as a mirror, a socially passive force.

But if one *questions* these positions (as critics generally do) there will generally be an acceptance of:

- the advertiser as sovereign, with the consumer open to manipulation; and
- advertising as a shaper, and/or selective reinforcer, a socially influential force.

Thus, at a very fundamental philosophical level, practitioners and critics are "seeing" advertising from divergent reference frames. Thus, a clash of what constitutes "ethical" behavior is inevitable.

2. *The advertising message is one-sided communication, with the inherent potential of deception by omission.*

In his important work, *The Making of Modern Advertising*, historian Daniel Pope addressed the issue of the bias of the advertising message: "For advertising to play a large part in market strategy, consumers had to be willing to accept this kind of self-interested persuasion as a tolerable substitute or complement to more objective product information."[7]

Thus, advertising is seen as a trade-off, sacrificing value-free information for a form strong on convenience but laced with persuasion. The ethical minefields in volatile areas seem apparent: for example, disclosure of relevant health and nutrition information, the intentional blurring of the similarities of many consumer products, and the essential question about what constitutes adequate information from ads.

3. *The purpose of all advertising is to cause us to think or act in accordance with the advertiser's intent, whether it be noble or venal.*

Legendary advertising practitioner Theodore MacManus (creator of the much honored "Penalty of Leadership" ad) was an eyewitness to what several historians consider the beginnings of the "culture of consumption" in the 1920s. His 1928 thoughts on advertising's role are insightful:

> The cigarette has become almost a health food—certainly a weight reducer [as in "Reach for a Lucky Instead of a Sweet"]. The humble cake of soap has risen far above its modest mission of cleansing, and confers the precious bloom of beauty upon whomsoever shall faithfully wash. We are all glowing, and sparkling, and snapping, and tingling with health, by way of the toothbrush, and the razor, and the shaving cream, and the face lotion, and the deodorant, and a dozen other brightly packaged

gifts of the gods. Advertising has gone amuck in that it has mistaken the surface silliness for the sane solid substance of an averagely decent human nature.[8]

Here, MacManus is pointing to advertising's alleged ability to shape the consumption agenda. But contemporary critics also contend that advertisements contain relentless cues in such noncommercial areas as

interpersonal and family relations, the sense of happiness and contentment, sex roles and stereotyping, the uses of affluence, the fading of older cultural traditions, influences of younger generations, the role of business in society, personal autonomy and persuasion, and many others.[9]

Thus, it seems inevitable that since advertising has an explicitly persuasive agenda—like preaching, politics, and numerous other activities of our civilization—as well as an implicit agenda, frequently linking the acquisition of products and services to the "good life," it will be accused of unethical practice by those who disagree with its subject and/or its intent.

4. *Frequently, advertising seeks out the individual rather than the individual seeking it.*

Except for catalogs, classifieds, directories, the food ads in the midweek newspaper and the like, we are frequently the ones being sought. Not surprisingly, this raises a host of questions with ethical dimensions in areas such as timing, privacy, and frequency.

Now, it can be contended that some of this potential conflict will subside as market and media fragmentation continue apace (i.e., advertising for golf clubs will be compatible for a reader of *Golf* magazine, and messages about low-cost insurance policies may be welcomed by the readers of *Modern Maturity*). Even television, clearly the lightning rod in this and other areas of advertising/ethical encounters, is finding it easier to match viewer interests with appropriate advertising as cable watching becomes even more routine, with appropriate selectivity in program (and advertising) content.

Yet, it is clear to all that advertisers will be seeking us perhaps more relentlessly than ever before through the mass media, as well as through increasingly untraditional forms. The ethical signals are apparent.

5. *Advertising continues to be a controversial third party with the mass media.*

From the mid-to-late nineteenth century with newspapers and from the early twentieth century with magazines, shortly after the earliest days of radio and from the outset of the American television system, advertising has been an important third party with the traditional publisher/reader and broadcaster/audience relationship. The ensuing tradeoffs are the ongoing stuff of pride (advertising helps the media to be available less expensively without possible dependence on government subsidy), as well as controversy. Among the more common ethical charges are the following:

- that advertising can change the *subject* of the media coverage. The most obvious case is television, where the availability of advertising dollars for some kinds of programming in particular time slots has proven a seductive lure. It is common, for example, for college football and basketball teams to reschedule their starting times for games—almost oblivious to the wishes of the spectators—in an effort to maximize the audience for advertisers.

- that advertising can alter the *content* of the media coverage. This is one of the most common criticisms, and deals with the media allegedly "selling out" to advertisers. For example, a 1992 study in the *New England Journal of Medicine* concluded that "magazines become increasingly reluctant to cover smoking risks as their revenue from cigarette ads rises."[10]

- that advertising can affect the *type* of available media. Media follow markets, so it seems self-evident that we are more likely to imagine advertising-supported magazines with titles such as *Self-Indulgent Jogger* and *Young and Possessive* than *Ghetto Life, Migrant Worker*, or *Old and Poor*.

6. *The advertising agency commission system still continues to reward agencies for what they buy (media space and/or time) rather than what they produce (ads).*

Historically, the advertising agency receives a commission (usually 15% or less) on the cost of the advertising space and/or time it buys with the advertiser's money. This venerable system is now somewhat in decline as compared with fee and other arrangements, but it still represents a significant force in the process. Former practitioner Howard Gossage observed:

You show me a business where one's income is dependent on the amount of money spent rather than the amount of money that comes in and I will show you a business that is doomed, even with the very best of intentions, to mutual distrust and enormous psychological barriers.[11]

It is, for example, hard to imagine an advertising agency recommending that an advertiser *cut* his or her advertising budget and devote the savings to some other aspect of marketing activity—say, building up the sales force. In addition, some claim that the value of the advertisement itself is diminished because the best ad and the worst have equal (media-cost) value. Of course, the counter-argument would assert, the "good" ad is likely to be repeated more often, thus benefiting the agency's income.

Ethical concerns in and about such a compensation arrangement are apparent and—judging by the ongoing squabbling from advertisers about what constitutes "fair value" for advertising service—still quite real.

7. *Finally, the underlying uncertainty regarding the outcome of the advertising process leaves it wide open for differing interpretations of the same event.*

This is a central factor in understanding advertising philosophy and practice, as advertising's outcomes frequently remain uncertain due to the quixotic nature of consumer behavior and the many other variables in addition to advertising that could affect that behavior. As veteran advertising observer Edward Buxton noted:

The advertising business is rife . . . with baffling intangibles. Nobody knows for sure how it works in many cases. The ad-making process itself is highly subjective, opinionated—and largely unprovable as to what is a good ad and what is not. Such pervasive uncertainties are breeding grounds for disquietude.[12]

And these pervasive uncertainties are breeding grounds for ethical ferment as well. For, given the ambiguity of the process, critics and supporters will "see" different advertising realities as individuals "see" different shapes in the classic inkblot test.

If, for example, a critic and a supporter assess such topics as advertising to children and advertising of cigarettes, the following may result: In one "reality" these activities can be seen as a highly principled meshing of the self-interests of sellers and buyers in a strictly voluntary relationship, while in another perception they can be seen as the unprincipled actions of manipulation and exploitation involving a crafty communicator and a hapless, if not helpless, audience.

PRELIMINARY OBSERVATIONS

These seven areas of ethical confrontation are likely to be an ongoing presence for advertising practitioners and critics for the foreseeable future. Some of these areas of concern are simply not high on advertising's ethical agenda. For example, studies by Rotzoll and Christians as well as Hunt and Chonko[13] have revealed that practitioners' primary areas of concern are: (1) agency/client/vendor relations, and (2) the advertising message. At the very least, these don't touch such sensitive areas as advertising as a third party with the media, and advertising as the seeker rather than the sought.

Therefore, critics will tend to regard advertising practice as unprincipled to the extent that (1) they regard advertising practice in any of these areas as *not* being based on ethical principles, and/or (2) that the ethical principles that the practitioners *do* choose to invoke to support their decisions are different than those the critics would deem appropriate.

NOTES

1. Stephen Fox, *The Mirror Makers* (New York: Vintage Books, 1985), p. 206.
2. Robert L. Heilbroner, "Advertising as Agitprop," *Harpers* (January 1986): 71.
3. Richard W. Pollay, "The Distorted Mirror," *Journal of Marketing* (April 1986): 18.
4. Howard Luck Gossage, *Is There Any Hope for Advertising?* (Champaign, IL: University of Illinois Press, 1987).
5. David Rankin, "A State of Incivility," *Newsweek*, 8 February 1988, p. 10.
6. Fox, *The Mirror Makers,* p. 108.
7. Daniel Pope, *The Making of Modern Advertising* (New York: Basic Books, 1983).
8. Fox, *The Mirror Makers,* p. 117.
9. William Leiss, Stephen Kline, and Sut Ghally, *Social Communication in Advertising* (New York: Methuen, 1986), p. 3.
10. Ronald K. L. Collins, *Dictating Content* (Washington, DC: Center for the Study of Commercialism, 1992), p. 41.
11. Gossage, *Is There Any Hope for Advertising?*
12. Ed Buxton, "Fear & Loathing on Agency Row," *Adweek*, 5 September 1983, p. 34.
13. Kim B. Rotzoll and Clifford G. Christians, "Advertising Agency Practitioners' Perceptions of Ethical Decisions," *Journalism Quarterly* (August 1980): 425–431; and Shelby D. Hunt and Lawrence B. Chonko, "Ethical Problems of Advertising Agency Executives," *Journal of Advertising* 16, 4 (1987): 16–24.

chapter 6

Special Audiences

Analysts of American society have commonly noted our pride in plurality, and the ensuing premise that, somehow, the whole becomes greater than the sum of its parts. Within the last several decades, however, the idealized "melting pot" concept has been replaced with the idea of the societal "salad bowl," wherein all parts contribute to the whole, yet still maintain component identity.

It is hardly surprising, then, that at a recent meeting of the Association of National Advertisers, a special panel on ethics spent a great deal of time dealing with the thorny issues of advertising's relationship to "special audiences," and the overarching issues of whether or not advertisers have a special responsibility to treat some audiences (e.g., children, the "market illiterate," minorities, the elderly) with greater sensitivity than their other constituencies.[1]

Advertising practitioners tend to believe that the pursuit of their craft is generally socially beneficial, and that for most people, most of the time, advertising performs a useful service. Those carrying the banner of special audiences, on the other hand, contend that the advertising system is simply unfair to those who may be potentially more vulnerable and, hence, must be treated with greater sensitivity.

It is appropriate, then, that the advertising section of this book begin with the ethical questions raised by the concept of special audiences. In the mid-1990s, this issue remains among the top concerns of advertising's critics.

25. THEIR MORE VULNERABLE SIDES

Cynthia Marx, a thirty-five-year-old specialist in market research for one of the country's largest advertising agencies, faced a potential challenge. One of her agency's clients, a nationwide fried chicken chain, was anxious to develop some edge in its ongoing competition with Colonel Sanders and others in the field. Impressed by the star quality and marketing prowess of Ronald McDonald, someone suggested that a search begin for a fantasy character who might create the same competitive pull. Not surprisingly, the agency had suggested a chicken. That's when Cynthia entered the picture. She had been asked to set up and supervise research to assess the appeal of certain chicken characters to an appropriate audience—the important market segment of children.

This would be a new experience for her, as her previous research work had not involved children. In order to work efficiently with the agency group responsible for the account, and to be properly informed for directing her research, she examined some of the prominent literature in the general area of marketing to children through advertising. She found, of course, considerable controversy, with vehement criticisms that advertising to children (particularly preschoolers) was simply a moral abomination, and/or that the products advertised to children were frequently unhealthy, expensive, or unrealistically represented.

But there was certainly no question about marketers' attraction to this particular audience, as she found in the recent *Advertising Age* special report on "Marketing to Kids."[2] Page after page offered hints to researchers on how to learn more about kids as consumers (e.g., "They aren't pint-size adults") as well as ads on how to reach them with greatest efficiency (e.g., "Get a Lion's Share of the Kids' Market with Delta Airline's *Fantastic Flyer* magazine").

There was, above all, one indisputable conclusion: Children can be influenced by advertising (particularly television advertising), and that influence can be strongly affected by the presenter of the message. So Tony the Tiger and company have become highly recognizable—and, many would argue, highly *credible*—figures in the oft-visited television world of the child.

Well, she reflected, the company and the agency seemed on the right marketing track, and nothing in the message itself, or in the use of the chicken figure, would violate any business, media, or government stipulations.

Cynthia could imagine the appropriate research design: the right sample size and composition; different actors in different costumes, different theme songs, and chicken voices from high tenor to basso profunda; the chicken in a typical restaurant, in kids' homes, in a special chicken coop. She considered approaches from clownish to dramatic, including the chicken as an adventure hero.

Cynthia had no doubt that she could ultimately discover the most effective character. And, market experience would suggest, it would help sell their client's product. But what would she be using her considerable research skills to do? She kept being nagged by the advice of a prominent child research specialist quoted in that special *Advertising Age* report—"By interviewing kids alone, their more vulnerable sides are more easily brought out."[3] Is that what I should be doing, she wondered, using research to try to discover what makes kids *vulnerable*?

Somehow, she thought, that just doesn't seem right.

Cynthia is a researcher. She has been trained to gather information in a systematic way in order to help answer some particular question. In this case, the assignment is to investigate children, to find the way to get them to develop a preference for the client's product. Yet, she is troubled by the prospect. Why?

Perhaps she could develop her thinking by starting with *ends*—in this case, the proposed advertising campaign using the chicken figure. To begin to define the issue, she apparently recognizes the legality of the client's intent. Nothing in the formal stipulations of or about the advertising business—including the Children's Advertising Review Unit, the television networks, or the Federal Trade Commission—prevents the advertiser from using this particular approach on this particular audience, as long as the message is not deceptive. Cynthia could also reason that the results of an advertising and promotion effort using the chicken figure could be generally positive (or at least not harmful) since, first, parents will usually make the purchase decision, and second, chicken is relatively wholesome, particularly when compared with the crinkly snacks and sugar-laden products that have so irritated groups such as Action for Children's Television. She could, of course, also justify her efforts with the simple observation that fantasy characters have worked for others, with the implicit understanding that children and/or parents apparently found their self-interests served by the purchase of the product or service.

But is it right to use the best tools of market research to "get at" children, some of whom are still too young for school? Do these ends justify these means?

Perhaps Cynthia could sharpen her thinking by focusing on *loyalties,* for, as the Potter Box emphasizes, choosing loyalties frequently stands at the heart of many vexing issues. She could consider whether she is troubled by advertising to children in general, by the use of fantasy figures, or only by her potential involvement as a researcher. If Cynthia concludes that advertising to children is wrong under any circumstances, then she could be assuming that moral duty is owed to the vague population of potentially "vulnerable" children. She could then refuse to lend her expertise to the project, and, depending on the depth of her feeling, also protest whenever the agency considers working for a client who will advertise to children.

If her discomfort is merely the device of the fantasy figure, then she could attempt to persuade agency strategists to take another approach. Her moral duty here would then seem to rest with the advertiser and the agency, *except* when a particular advertising strategy offends her sensitivities under special circumstances. Thus, here she could presumably operate comfortably with other advertising approaches to children, and freely participate in the preliminary research.

If she simply wishes to beg off the project for the moment, and thereby avoid her ethical discomfort, Cynthia would be asserting that moral duty is owed to herself, based solely on the quandaries of this particular situation, and her desire to escape it. She would, of course, be left with no guidelines for future ethical encounters, other than to "take them as they come."

All of these choices do, of course, leave unanswered questions concerning the reactions of her employer to her requests—scarcely an issue to be treated lightly. (For example, one of America's largest advertising agencies routinely asks candidates for employment in their research department if there are *any* of the agency's clients they couldn't work for. If the answer is yes, no job is offered.)

Cynthia faces a moral choice. Thinking through the ethical dimensions of complex situations requires reflection. If that is lacking, the routine of standard professional expectation frequently prevails as the alternative of least difficulty—in the short run at least.

26. TRADING ACCESS TO KIDS FOR MONEY?

Well, Charles Farling reflected, there's no shortage of opinions when it comes to "Channel One" is there? Charles, a member of the school board in a midwestern community of 40,000, was thinking about the service offered by the Whittle Educational Network, and its entrepreneur-supreme, Chris Whittle. The network, currently in more than 10,000 schools and reaching more than 6 million junior and senior high students,[4] involves the offer to schools of a color television set for every 23 students, two videocassette recorder/players, a satellite dish, and installation, all of which is free with the agreement that they will show Channel One each school day—a 12-minute video program consisting of 10 minutes of current events and features, and 2 minutes of advertising.[5] Tonight Charles's school board will be taking a vote on whether to sign a contract with Channel One.

The existing evidence suggests that the program has generally been well received by the teachers and students currently using the system, but there's still no shortage of controversy, primarily over the presence of advertising, an opportunity for product promotion currently utilized by such brands as Pepsi, Clearasil, Gillette, Gatorade, and M & Ms. (Burger King runs public-service messages rather than product commercials.)

The rationale has always been that the schools would acquire valuable equipment that they might not otherwise be able to afford, and that the students' awareness of current events would be enhanced. That's an appealing combination, Charles thought, in spite of the National Education Association's recent denouncement of those who "seek to commercialize the classroom" and exploit the "captive audience" of students.

Yet, a recent University of Michigan study (funded by the Whittle organization) indicated that Channel One had little impact on students' knowledge of current events. Based on a study of 3,200 students at 11 sites in the 1990-1991 school year, the writers of the report concluded that Channel One's effect on the measured current events knowledge of the average viewer was "quite small" when compared with the knowledge of students in comparable schools not carrying the program.[6]

That was all the critics needed to raise the volume of their protests. Longtime opponent Peggy Charren, president of the advocacy group Action for Children's Television, commented, "The only people this is working for are the advertisers and Chris Whittle," while Bill Honig, Superintendent of

Public Instruction for the state of California, reasoned that the Michigan study offers more evidence that Channel One is a "flat-out commercial deal. It's trading access to kids for money."[7]

Well, Charles thought, so it didn't make a great difference in what the kids knew; the school certainly couldn't afford that video equipment without it. And it wasn't the only commercial presence in the school: There was the Coke sign on the scoreboard, and for years teachers had welcomed any number of other "educational" materials from reputable outfits like McDonald's, Nutrasweet, Chef Boyardee, and Polaroid.[8] He even remembered seeing an ad directed to advertisers from a company called "Modern" that said, "She's in her tenth grade classroom nine months a year. Modern can make sure your sponsored video plays there. If she's in your target market, call us." And *Scholastic* magazine boasted how through "corporate sponsorships like 'Extra Credit' magazine by Discover Card, 4 million junior and senior high school kids are learning about money."[9] Charles even remembered the rulers from the local hardware store when he was in elementary school. So we're not blazing new ground here, he thought. And the schools sure could use the equipment. . . .

One way of probing the ethical depths of this murky issue is to consider the matter of consequences. For example, would it have made a difference to Peggy Charren or Bill Honig if the Michigan study had concluded that Channel One *was* elevating the students' knowledge of current events? Almost certainly not, since both have been longtime critics of the program based, apparently, on the assumption that the practice is simply wrong regardless of its potentially positive outcomes. Charles, on the other hand, seems very concerned with consequences, albeit selectively. For him, the dominant factor seems to be the opportunity to acquire the equipment, and that is a powerful lure for financially strapped school districts. He seems willing to dismiss, or at least minimize, the consequence that there may be little or no educational gain from Channel One. There is also a somewhat unformulated rationale—"Well, this process has been around a long while," "Everybody's doing it"—suggesting first, that no harm seems to have been done by earlier commercial incursions in the classrooms, and second, that others are doing it, so it can't be all that bad.

Basically, the only consequence Charles deems of importance is the acquisition of the equipment, while the critics apparently see this—and would probably see even a *positive* result in educational gain—as irrelevant.

Both sides seem to be oblivious to evidence that exists. The critics seem willing to dismiss reports that the existing users of Channel One—both teachers and students—are satisfied. Charles seems unimpressed by the apparent failure of the program to substantially increase the students' knowledge of current events. For Charles, the ends (the acquisition of the equipment) justify the means, whereas for the critics they clearly do not.

One fact seems unassailable: Channel One is not just business as usual in the classrooms. It brings what many consider to be the most powerful audio and visual symbol package available to advertisers (the television commercial) into the classroom intact, and, as in the case in regular television programming, as part of a larger package of entertainment designed to attract and keep the attention of an audience. This is, then, an unprecedented venture of commercial interests in the schools. To begin to come to grips with its ethical dimensions, both detractor and supporter must start with that.

27. SAYING "NO" TOO OFTEN

Stan Clark had expected a routine evening. As the program director of a network station in a middle-sized midwestern city, he always had his ear to the ground for any rumbles of discontent that might become serious during the period when station licenses were reviewed by the Federal Communications Commission (FCC). The invitation to speak to a local parent-teacher association (PTA) on the subject "Children and Television" hardly seemed threatening. He anticipated the usual complaints about kids logging more time watching television than studying. He would agree, and would joke that this seemed to be a problem in his house as well.

Teachers, and some activists who always seemed to show up at these events, would probably argue that the quality of most programming available for children is poor. That complaint Stan could not dismiss so lightly. There was certainly not an overabundance of children's programming that approached the capability of the talented people associated with American television. The so-called kidvid of Saturday and Sunday mornings was populated by fantasy or television heroes or their clones, moving through often-violent confrontations by means of production-line animation, all too often encouraging sales of the matching "action figures" or dolls. (In this mixed media bag, Stan found the height of hypocrisy in Arnold Schwarzenegger's stand to ban toy guns from the Mattel line of action figures based on his then-current hit *Last Action Hero*. The figures wouldn't have guns, but would be able to raise havoc with flying axes, hooks, and dynamite!)[10] Virtually nothing notable was available for kids during after-school hours either—Stan's own station offered cheap but popular syndicated programs, such as *Hogan's Heroes, Gilligan's Island,* and *The Brady Bunch.*

He imagined that he might get some questions at the meeting about the 1990 Children's Television Act, which empowered the FCC to demand that owners of local stations serve the "educational and informational needs" of young viewers or risk losing their licenses.[11] Well, he would certainly have to admit that the immediate reaction of the station owners had not been exemplary. Many simply reinterpreted their current programming as having plenty of educational girth; for example, an episode of *Bucky O'Hare* was described this way: "Good-doer Bucky fights off the evil toads aboard his ship. Issues of social consciousness and responsibility are central themes of the program." We're not *that* transparent, Stan reflected, but the television networks have not exactly outdone themselves in providing new programming in keeping with the spirit of the FCC directive. For example, the television version of *The Addams Family* featured bondage, decapitation, flea-eating, and torture.[12]

If there was too much flack, Stan thought, he could always talk about the simple economics of television: expensive time and programming supported by advertisers at no direct cost to the viewers. No one seriously wanted to cut back on the total hours of television available. And there was always cable, with fine alternatives such as Disney, Nickelodeon, and The Learning Channel. Things could be improved, he thought, but, all in all, this is a workable system.

Stan's speech went according to plan until he opened the floor to questions. What happened then was something for which his administrative position and socioeconomic background had not prepared him—a cry for help from those desperately trying to make ends meet. Perhaps it was the time of the year—early December—but a large part of the audience came alive with this question from a parent: "Can't you do anything about the stuff our kids see advertised? The ads drive me nuts!"

Almost immediately, another sounded off: "That's right. My kids watch TV as much as anybody else's, and they see all these wonderful toys and expensive snacks and they bug us." "Yeah," came another protest, "and when they get to school, they hear their friends talking about the same things. But there's one big difference. Their friends will probably get those toys, and my kids won't." From yet another parent:

> You know how much some of that stuff costs? Those He-Man and Jurassic Park things? Sorry, friend, but there's no way I can buy that stuff. And, oh yeah. Charles Barkley comes on and says "I'm not a role model." Well, thanks a lot! That hasn't stopped Nike from pushing those damned expensive shoes has it? But that's what the kids want because they saw it all on TV. Do you know how that makes me *feel?*

Then came another frustrated voice:

> Damn right! I work, and when my little ones get home I want them to stay in the house. So they watch TV. And they get a *big* dose of what the kids in those ads are playing with and eating. Hell, my kids are human. Why shouldn't they want it all? And I'll tell you, brother, I get damned tired playing the heavy.

Stan was getting uncomfortable. Finally he responded:

> You folks are really asking for a way to prevent some advertisers from reaching into your homes. Obviously that's not possible, unless advertisers totally withdraw from children's programming. And if that's what you want, you'll also get a drastic cutback in the time

devoted to children's programming, and lower production quality of what little might still be offered.

The audience obviously did not like that alternative. But, with television viewing in low-income households consistently higher than in the affluent, and with only a shrinking percentage of American households fitting the "Beaver Cleaver" model of a working father, a housewife mother, and children younger than 18, the frustration was deep seated. Stan tried to end on an upbeat note: "I hear what you're saying. The system isn't perfect, but given the way it's paid for, it seems to work out reasonably well most of the time."

"That may be," a woman said as Stan sat down. "But it wears you down saying 'no' so often. And some of us have to say it a lot more than others."

When this case was shown to a senior advertising executive, he commented, "Is there an answer to this question?" Most observers see something harmful here, but what can be done about it? What is the ethical focus?

First, we need to understand that the issue here is presumably not the programming, but the prevalence of advertisements—particularly those for products or services that are beyond the financial reach of those protesting. There is no argument that some excellent children's programming comes without ads (e.g., *Mr. Rogers, Barney, Sesame Street*), but they don't appeal to all kids, and are certainly not as readily available as commercial fare. So as long as television is in business to "gather an audience together for advertisers," the programs and the ads will come as a set.

Is Stan Clark's station at fault? It is a network affiliate and carries a high percentage of network programming and the accompanying advertising. Why? Because they're obligated to, and the programs are popular, making it easier to sell television time around them. As for the late afternoon programs run on his station (e.g., *Gomer Pyle, The Munsters*), children watch them, and because they do, advertisers like them.

Is it the advertisers? As we have observed, most companies operate on the assumptions of the market system that if firms take actions in their own economic self-interests, they will by the very nature of the system end up satisfying the needs of others. So an advertiser pays for television time on programs to reach the largest number of potential customers, and he or she advertises products or services that are likely to have appeal to that same audience. No advertiser wants to waste money trying to sell to someone who can't buy. But television is an indiscriminate medium, and reaches the poorer families as readily as the more affluent.

Are the parents to blame? Certainly they could forbid children to watch certain kinds of programming, and most parents do. But the problem here is not the programming, but the advertising. Short of saying, "Watch the show but not the commercials," many parents are left with the alternative of encouraging their children to watch only the public television channel (if the community has one) or ruling out television altogether. Given the importance of television in American life (an average of 70 hours a week for children), particularly as a babysitter in homes with working parents, the latter hardly seems a palatable solution.

Where, then, is the ethical testing ground? These parents are protesting one result of the television system: the continuing stimulation of their children with messages for products beyond the parents' financial capacities. (Apparently even relatively affluent parents object. For example, Barbara Kantrowitz, a senior writer for *Newsweek,* wrote: "Of course, it's my job to say 'no' and I do, over and over again. But that job seems to be getting tougher every day as the siren songs on the TV become more and more alluring.")[13] Yet at the same time the parents register at least implicit support for the programming underwritten by the advertising. They don't want to let the salesperson into the house to tantalize their children, yet this salesperson also entertains, occasionally enlightens, and quite often provides a needed babysitting service.

Stan Clark acknowledges that the complaints are legitimate, but he is well accustomed to the existing system. His initial response ("It seems to work out reasonably well most of the time") is pure utilitarianism—the greatest good for the greatest number—which certainly underlies capitalist economics and the system of commercial television in this country. Can an issue like this be addressed within this system?

One possibility, following the perspective of John Rawls, is to abandon the mandate of "the greatest number" and attempt to better account for the frustrations of at least the sizable few in a context of fairness. There is little that Stan's station can do with the network programming it is provided, but it can act with the airtime it does control—particularly the after-school hours. For example, they could select the most popular of available programs that would be regarded by the FCC as "educational and informational" and make them available commercial-free, while compensating for the lost commercial time with slightly higher rates elsewhere. They could also consider offering "consumer education" segments aimed at kids, which might help them to understand a bit more about the selling game but without driving off advertisers. (This seems a rather unlikely balancing act, but there might be considerable community goodwill generated by the attempt.) The *Buy Me That!* series underwritten by *Consumer Reports* might be a possibility and/or something produced by the station's own news department.

As Stan Clark drove home that night, he reflected on the genuine frustration he had heard. The primary obligation in the commercial television system is to advertisers, and, implicitly, to the viewers through the programs that those ads support. It is, he reminded himself, a game that most enjoy. But, obviously, the "tyranny of the majority" doesn't work for everyone. To ignore what he had heard that night would be to leave unquestioned the "greatest good for the greatest number."

Somehow, he felt, there must be room for some compromise—particularly for those who have to say "no" more often than most.

28. THE BIG SELL FOR A "PURELY REGRESSIVE TAX"

"Hey, you never know."

"Somebody's always winning."

"Play Little Lotto. The odds be with you."[14]

You bet, thought Brenda Kravitts, the odds are really with you in the state lotteries—odds for winning the big prize that make getting hit by lightning seem like a sure bet.

Brenda sighed as she leafed through the latest reports on what was surely becoming one of America's growth industries. She knew that by the end of the 1990s it was likely that every state except Utah and Nevada would have lotteries. The lottery advertising alone accounted for $286 million in 1992, a total budget that surpassed Nissan USA, Colgate-Palmolive, American Express, and Nike.[15] No question that her organization, the National Coalition to Control State Lotteries, was fighting an uphill battle.

Addiction to games of chance—and the frequent escalation of debt, the families and friends lost—is one of the major byproducts of these boons to state economies. "Lotteries," asserts a Penn State sociology professor, "are the most habituating forms of all gambling."[16] Brenda also knew that they were a severely regressive "tax" as well. For, according to another corroborating study, state lotteries "place a greater burden on low-income families because low-income groups spend a higher proportion of their income on lottery tickets than do high-income groups."[17]

And is the advertising particularly aware of those target markets? Well, as Dr. Eileen Epstein of the John F. Kennedy Medical Center observed, "Advertising feeds into the fantasy."[18] The fantasy of what? Big financial rewards, of course. The freedom to have and exercise options. The thrill of beating the odds and reaping the enormous benefits. In its most crass form, there was the infamous 1986 outdoor board on Chicago's depressed West Side. That message from the Illinois State Lottery?—"Your way out." Even trade publication *Advertising Age* recognized the problem: "Lottery ads regularly target the economically depressed, mislead consumers about their chances of winning, and generally glorify lottery playing as harmless fun."[19]

Well, there are *some* guidelines now, Brenda admitted. For example, Texas has the guideline that "advertising should avoid language and visuals that are directed to the economically disadvantaged."[20] But that hardly covers all the appeals for low-cost instant gratification, some even suggesting that the lottery is a reasonable alternative to sound investing, education, or hard work: for example, the New York City subway poster that read in Spanish, "The New York Lottery helped me realize the American dream."[21]

A somewhat disturbing side issue is that, in general, lottery advertising is not regulated by traditional federal or government agencies, since it's the governments that authorize the advertising. Even the ad business's most significant self-regulatory arm—the National Advertising Division of the Council of Better Business Bureaus—ignores the genre.

John O'Toole, then president of the American Association of Advertising Agencies, seemed unconcerned. He was recently quoted: "The lottery passes the two tests—it is a legal product and the advertising is truthful. . . . Advertising is not in the business of protecting people from themselves."[22] Brenda wondered—what about at least letting them know the whole picture?

She thumbed through a recent study by two Duke University economists who found that only 20 percent of all lottery ads—and just 12 percent of radio and TV spots pushing the lotteries—accurately report the odds.[23]

That's what Brenda's group was currently agitating for—federal or state requirements that accurate odds be made a prominent part of *all* forms of lottery advertising. That would, she hoped, clarify that a claim that one's "chance of winning is 1 in 30," means *any* amount, not the jackpot, where the odds are closer to 1 in 13 *million*.[24] These are, after all, people who are acting unwisely, and she thought they should at least be given an obtrusive warning flag.

Was that too much to ask for people who might "sell food stamps to buy lottery tickets"?

"This is not an advertising problem," an American Association of Advertising Agencies executive has said. "The moral dilemma has been passed by the states' acceptance of the lottery."[25] What is ethical, then, is apparently to be equated with what is legal. Is it that simple? Brenda and her co-workers don't think so. They contend that lottery advertising encourages addiction, particularly among those who can least afford it.

It would seem that there are two starkly contrasting views of "human nature" at work here. The representatives of the American Association of Advertising Agencies are apparently assuming a model of the sovereign individual, master of his or her own choices, and quite capable of dealing with skillful attempts at persuasion. Brenda and her organization, on the other hand, consider the vulnerability of the individual, a person relatively easily swayed by the verbal and visual symbols of advertisements, particularly those who are in the lower-income groups.

Advertising, John O'Toole tells us, should not have to "protect people against themselves"[26]—a statement that, at least, requires some qualification. For advertising commonly does do that now—voluntarily. For example, hard liquor is not advertised in the broadcast media; the major television networks generally refuse to carry condom advertising; at least some in the cigarette industry attempt to avoid outdoor advertising close to schools and churches. Would it be "protecting" people against themselves to support the prominent inclusion of the odds in all lottery advertising? Is it proper to maintain that individuals should be encouraged to take an action—potentially expensive and possibly addictive—without being fully informed as to the nature of that choice?

Advertising is self-interested information, but should the same *laissez-faire* standards apply when the potential outcome of the successful advertising can be psychologically and sociologically dysfunctional, particularly for some population segments? In other words, is there no room whatsoever for social responsibility in this particular segment of advertising?

And what of protectionism? Is there implicit elitism here, with the assumption that some are far more vulnerable than others and that the only way to stem the swelling tide of lottery promotion and advertising is to at least force the states to include the odds, thus presumably stimulating more pause for thought than currently exists?

Several facts seem clear: Lotteries are on the rise, and advertising is seen as an essential element to stimulate and reinforce behavior. This is a form of gambling encouraged by states as an income-producing tool, and rationalized as entertainment and diversion for its citizens. It clearly has, and will have, dysfunctional effects for some of these same citizens, and these citizens are likely to be those least able to afford it.

The attraction of utilitarianism as an ethical principle is obvious. Some people enjoy gambling, and the fact that the lotteries have grown so prodigiously is unassailable proof of that popularity. Following these positive signals, more and more states will offer lotteries, with participation encouraged by heavy advertising budgets and ads produced by some of the most talented advertising agencies in the country. All that, from a utilitarian perspective, would seem to proceed naturally.

Brenda's organization is apparently opting for a different ethical principle, one potentially running counter to the best interests of the states. Few would argue that full disclosure of the odds is not important information to be imparted. Whether or not it would curb participation is by no means certain, but disclosure has been required in cigarette advertising for decades, and many would like to see it become commonplace in alcoholic beverage advertising as well. The subjects in both cases are, after all, potentially addictive products.

Is there an ethical problem here, or should we simply let business take its course? Judging by the soaring advertising budgets, advertising is apparently deemed necessary to (1) stimulate participation, and (2) maintain it, particularly with creative new variations of the basic lottery pattern. Almost by its nature, this advertising will promise more than will be delivered: for every big winner there are 13,000,000 losers. If investment bankers gamble, we may shrug our shoulders. But what of the "greater relative burden on low-income families"?

Or, as John O'Toole implies, is it ethical to attempt to protect [some] people from themselves?

29. "IF THEY KNEW THE FULL STORY, I BELIEVE THEY WOULD STOP THIS OUTRAGE"

Those were the words of Dr. Carlos Ferreyra Nunez, president of the Argentine Association of Public Health.[27] The "outrage" he refers to is how American "[tobacco] companies and government are promoting smoking among the world's children." He is apparently not alone in his outcry. *Reader's Digest* staff writer William Echenbarger has written with considerable passion about what he calls "America's New Merchants of Death." He offers these and other examples:

- In Germany, three women in short skirts set up a display table beside a Cadillac in the center of Dresden. In exchange for an empty pack of local cigarettes, the customer is given a pack of

Lucky Strikes with a leaflet that reads "You just got a nice piece of America." Adolescents are apparently common participants.

- In Buenos Aires, a jeep decorated with the Camel logo parks in front of a high school. The driver, a blond woman in safari gear, hands out cigarettes to the students on their lunch break.
- American cigarettes are strewn atop each game in a video arcade in Taipei. "Before the United States entered the Taiwanese cigarette market such give-aways directed to adolescents were uncommon."
- In Malaysia there is a comic book, *Gila-Gila*, popular with elementary school students. It carries a Lucky Strikes ad.[28]

Worldwide sales for American tobacco companies have tripled since 1982, whereas domestic sales have declined for eight straight years. Smoking in the third world is apparently rising at about 2 percent a year. In the Philippines, it is estimated that 22.7 percent of people under 18 smoke, and in some Latin American cities teenage smoking is at 50 percent.[29] Given these sales figures, it is hardly surprising that American tobacco companies should be aggressive marketers in these and other countries.

And what of the governments? In at least some cases, the American government has attempted to pressure foreign governments into opening their markets to American tobacco companies, presumably as part of the larger goal of addressing the balance-of-trade deficit. (In this country, of course, there are still agricultural subsidies that support the growing of tobacco.) Other countries may or may not have laws dealing specifically with the marketing of tobacco products, but even if they do, the marketers are commonly adept at ways to circumvent the more obvious restrictions on media advertising. Then there is the fact that for many countries cigarette sales bring in vital tax revenues: for example, 22.5 percent of all tax revenues in Argentina; 16.7 percent in Malawi.[30]

Yet according to Echenbarger,

> Smoking is one of the world's leading causes of premature death, linked to cancers of the mouth, lung, esophagus, kidney, pancreas, bladder, and cervix, as well as heart disease. More than 50,000 medical studies have demonstrated these hazards.[31]

Or, as the Dean of Harvard's School of Public Health observed, "Cigarettes are the only readily available consumer product *which is harmful when used as intended.*"[32]

Should there be "outrage" here?

Dr. Nunez, put it bluntly: "American tobacco companies know their product causes death. Yet they promote smoking among children. What must these people think?"[33]

This case lends itself to the Potter Box model, but it will be necessary to define the situation precisely. We are dealing with individuals in other countries—particularly those considered "under age" for smoking. Yet, these individuals present "markets" for various forms of advertising and promotion.

In this country, we have become accustomed to learning that cigarette smoking carries risks. We learn it in school, from the media, and from the ads and packages of the cigarette companies themselves (they are required to provide a warning label even as they provide us with the product, or an inducement to buy it). We are, in many ways, quite protected in these matters. For example, can you imagine an American tobacco company running an ad in a comic book? Or distributing cigarettes outside a high school? Not likely. You may recall protests in recent years about the advertising of cigarettes near schools and churches in many of our inner cities. The advertisers and the media (primarily outdoor boards) eventually agreed to restrict such marketing activities.

We have become quite used to the association of cigarettes with risk, and cigarette companies are not allowed to let us forget it, even while they encourage us to ignore it. But the "rules of the road" are often different abroad. Tobacco sales bring in needed government revenues, and regulations about marketing may be somewhat lax by our standards.

So, Dr. Nunez's tobacco company marketer is probably not involved in anything illegal. After all, if *you* were a tobacco marketer, would you include warning labels on your packages and in your advertising if you didn't have to? The issue, of course, is not about "could," but about "should." Should tobacco marketers think and act differently than they do in marketing to other countries, particularly to groups considered "under age"—even when they are not legally restricted from doing so?

Consider the following facts:

- American tobacco companies are involved in marketing activities abroad, particularly in third world countries, specifically targeting those who might be defined as "children."
- These activities are not apparently considered illegal.
- These activities would not be allowed—legally or ethically—in this country.

Dr. Nunez hoped that, "If [the American people] knew the full story, I believe they would stop this outrage."[34]

Are *you* outraged? If so, why? If not, why not? Are these potential customers in other countries to be considered a "special audience," to be treated with ethical standards that transcend the legal?

"What must these people think?" This is a question of ethical analysis and self-examination.

30. TIME FOR CONDOMS?

The television spot opens with two couples leaving a restaurant at sunset. They go to shoot pool in a nearby bar and, while playing, one of the men assists his date as she takes a shot. As he stands beside her, guiding the pool cue, the camera zooms in on his wristwatch: the Protech II, which comes equipped with a condom hidden in a compartment under the watch. It is promoted as "Life insurance you can afford." The commercial then informs the viewer that some portion of the purchase price of $39.95 will be used to help fund AIDS-related research, education, and treatment.[35]

The company tried to air the commercial in Florida, but most stations refused to run it, at least during prime time. NBC-affiliate WESH-TV agreed to run the spot between 11 P.M. and 6 A.M., explaining that "It is not that we choose not to advertise condoms in prime time. But there is a certain sensitivity in the market that we have to take into consideration when deciding when to run sensitive ads, whether they be for condoms or other personal products." When the commercial did run, it resulted in the sale of about 500 watches through a toll-free order number.[36]

For most of television's history in this country, condom advertising has been not only unwelcome, but banned from the premises. Even though various kinds of sexual encounters were occurring with high frequency in the programs carried by the stations, condom advertising was considered an open invitation to sexual promiscuity. That might still be the case were it not for AIDS.

As the true proportions of the AIDS epidemic became clear, so did the means of prevention. High among them was the use of condoms for sexual acts. Thus, it was argued that condoms could be advertised as a means of preventing sexually transmitted diseases, AIDS high among them. Some manufacturers tried anew, and some stations (and one network) loosened their acceptance standards to at least consider advertising the product, while still reserving judgment about the style of an individual message—for example, the Fox network does not ban condom advertising, but has thus far run only one and rejected several because of creative executions.[37] CBS, NBC, and ABC still refuse to accept any condom advertising, preferring instead to let local affiliates determine their own policies.

Jocelyn Elders, President Clinton's Surgeon General, has joined her immediate predecessors in encouraging the big three television networks to accept condom advertising. "I find it rather strange," she has said, "that we can advertise [products like] beer to the young but then get nervous when there is talk of something that can save lives."[38]

And it is the "young" who are the primary audience here, not only because they are more sexually active than other age groups, but because they are, perhaps, at greatest risk, not only from sexually transmitted diseases, but unwanted pregnancies as well. And through which media are young people most accessible? The broadcast media, of course.

"TV is the most powerful medium there is," Dr. Elders asserts, and "not to use it says that we don't care enough about the problem [sexually transmitted diseases] to use our best weapons against it to make a difference."[39]

And what of those who may be offended or embarrassed? A current *Redbook* magazine poll indicated that although 81 percent of the women polled say ads are "too sexy," and have been embarrassed in front of their family or lover when a sexy or particularly intimate commercial appears on

TV, 57 percent said they would support the airing of condom commercials. "I think women are more tolerant of condom advertising than men are," said Ellen Levine, editor-in-chief of the magazine. "Men don't want to wear them, and they don't want to hear about them. But [condoms] protect women. . . . The networks are going to wake up one of these days."[40]

Business executive Susan Young recently put the subject in a provocative context:

> I don't get it. Why is there such a problem about airing a commercial for a condom/wristwatch and not a similar problem for airing commercials about vaginal itch, vaginal yeast infections, vaginal douches, sanitary pads, diarrhea, constipation, incontinence and hemorrhoids?
>
> I've yet to see a commercial for these products that was handled in a "sensitive" manner.[41]

Condom advertising on television, even in an age of rampant and insistent sexual expression, is still largely regarded as beyond the realm of "acceptable" commercial content. Yet, Dr. Elders contends, "because of the spread of AIDS and teen pregnancy, we can't watch while our young people get washed out to sea."[42]

Is it time for condom advertising on television?

This could easily be considered an argument that pivots on utilitarianism. Consider that the major networks and most stations seem to be arguing that the greatest good for the greatest number is served by keeping advertisements for condoms off television, presumably to protect the sensitivities of their viewers. By contrast, Dr. Elders and others seem to be contending that many will be well served if condom ads lead to "safer sex" and, in the process, reduced transmission of diseases—particularly AIDS—and fewer unwanted pregnancies.

Who stands on firmer ethical ground? If the existing policy of banning condom ads was defended on the basis of audience sensitivities, the networks and stations would then have to explain why some apparently offensive product classes (particularly feminine hygiene products) are allowed to peddle their wares while condoms are not. Because they might "promote" sexual activity among the young? What defense could there be for the sexually provocative content of numerous programs?

We have seen that the majority of the women respondents in *Redbook*'s poll were open to the idea of condom ads on television. But how would a poll of, say, a heterogeneous group of CBS viewers respond to the question of the acceptance of condom advertising? Arguably, they would probably be marginally in favor of the ban, but in favor of extending it to other sensitive product classes as well.

So does utilitarianism support the existing practice? If the focus is purely on the audience of a network or station offering the traditional mix of entertainment, sports, and news, that perspective might hold. Many people *are* likely to be embarrassed by condom advertising on such a largely indiscriminate medium as television, just as they are embarrassed by some other television advertising. Yet condom advertising on more specialized networks and stations (e.g., MTV) would probably be received quite differently.

Those opposed to the ban could argue that the "greatest number" transcends a particular audience for the greater cause of a healthier and more humane nation. And, it is argued, television (particularly the big three networks) is the only delivery system capable of reaching large enough populations (particularly the young) with the message of "safe sex," albeit while serving the self-interests of particular condom producers.

History tells us that changes in what is allowed to appear in the television time devoted to advertising is largely determined by what are perceived to be changing audience tastes and economic imperatives, not necessarily in that order. One could argue, then, that television advertising of condoms is inevitable, as was the elimination of the ban on advertising feminine hygiene products. It is unlikely that we will become *less* interested in and become tolerant of sexual activity.

Yet, for those who argue that AIDS and teenage pregnancies have reached epidemic proportions and require, as Dr. Elders asserted, "crisis intervention,"[43] this gradual evolution is too slow, and far too costly in human terms.

To provide a position for debate, one could contend that a utilitarian defense of the existing condition seems particularly vulnerable to arguments that existing acceptance practices clearly do not always serve the best interests of the "many" in the audience. A call to change, then, could arguably be best promoted on the level of, "Look, you're already doing it [failing to consider the sensitivities of your viewers; 'promoting' sex] so why not at least be consistent—and for a good cause." This would, then, move the ethical frame from utilitarianism to some sort of Aristotelian middle ground.

This is clearly an ethical, rather than an economic or functional, issue. And the stakes, according to some, are very high indeed.

NOTES

1. "Panel Delves into Ad Ethics," *Advertising Age*, 19 October 1992, p. 53.
2. "Special Report: Marketing to Kids," *Advertising Age*, 10 February 1992, pp. S1–S24.
3. Betsy Spethmann, "Focus Groups Key to Reaching Kids," *Advertising Age*, Special Report, p. 5–24.
4. Scott Donaton, "More Turbulence for 'Channel One'," *Advertising Age*, 18 May 1992, p. 48.
5. Peter Rooney, "Channel One Finding Audience in Area Schools," Champaign-Urbana *News-Gazette*, 12 July 1992, A-3.
6. Donaton, "More Turbulence for 'Channel One'."
7. Ibid.
8. See "Selling to Children," *Consumer Reports* (August 1990): 518.
9. Both ads from *Advertising Age*, Special Report.

10. Kate Fitzgerald, "Arnold Becomes an Anti-Gun 'Hero'," *Advertising Age*, 31 May 1993, p. 8.
11. Harry F. Waters, "On Kid TV, Ploys R Us," *Newsweek*, 30 November 1992, p. 88.
12. Ibid., p. 89.
13. Barbara Kantrowitz, "Saturday Morning Classroom: 15- and 30-Second Lessons," *Adweeks Marketing Week* 30 (November 1987): 58.
14. 1993 Lotto slogans for the states of New York, Kansas, and Illinois.
15. From Iris Cohen Selinger, "The Big Lottery Gamble," Advertising Age Extra, *Advertising Age*, 10 May 1993, pp. 22–28.
16. Ibid., p. 22.
17. Ibid., p. 23.
18. Ibid., p. 22.
19. "Clean Up Lottery Ads," *Advertising Age*, 17 May 1993, p. 20.
20. Selinger, "Big Lottery Gamble," p. 23.
21. Ibid.
22. Ibid., p. 26.
23. Ibid., p. 23.
24. Ibid.
25. Ibid., p. 28.
26. Ibid., p. 26.
27. William Echenbarger, "Tracking America's New Merchants of Death: The Smoking Gun," Champaign-Urbana *News-Gazette*, 9 May 1993, p. B-1, excerpted from a longer treatment in the April 1993 issue of *Reader's Digest*.
28. Ibid.
29. Ibid.
30. Ibid.
31. Ibid.
32. "Harvard Public Health Dean Asks Ban on Cigarette Ads," Champaign-Urbana *News-Gazette*, 22 April 1985, p. 15.
33. Echenbarger, "Tracking America's New Merchants."
34. Ibid.
35. Riccardo A. Davis, "Condom Wristwatch Shows It's Time for Safe Sex," *Advertising Age*, 29 April 1993, p. 17.
36. Ibid.
37. Scott Donaton, "Women Hit 'Sexy' Ads, But Say Condoms on TV Would Be OK," *Advertising Age*, 12 April 1993, p. 29.
38. Steven W. Colford, "New Surgeon General Backs Condom Ads," *Advertising Age*, 11 January 1993, pp. 3, 39.
39. Ibid., p. 39.
40. Donaton, "Women Hit 'Sexy' Ads."
41. Susan V. Young, Letter to the Editor, *Advertising Age*, 7 June 1993, p. 19.
42. Colford, "New Surgeon General Backs Condom Ads," p. 39.
43. Ibid.

chapter 7

What to Advertise

$\mathbf{A}$s a way to approach the cases in this chapter on content, consider the following three premises:

1. Because some consumer advocates, special interest groups, and legislators are skeptical about the ability of individuals (other than themselves) to make wise decisions, the subjects of advertisements are matters of concern. That is, if we all believed that people can make up their own minds about the products and services they want, we would not be concerned about them being "targets" of advertising's persuasive appeals.
2. Given the nature of advertising as a potentially powerful form of mass persuasion, individuals, groups, and organizations will desire to use it on behalf of their products, services, and ideas.
3. The real dilemmas in this area arise because of the alleged effect of advertising content on the thinking and/or behavior of individuals. But because of the complex environment in which advertising operates, there is often no proof of either the presence or the absence of these effects.

Our approach to case studies in this chapter also requires that we recognize certain regulatory structures. In addition to consumer choice, the following serve to a greater or lesser degree as gatekeepers:

1. Government. Federal, state, and local governments regulate the advertising of some types of products and services. For example, certain regulations deal with the advertising of particular types of

drugs and firearms, in addition to the well-known ban on cigarette advertising in the broadcast media.

2. Media. Regulation by the media occurs on two levels. The first is represented by media codes such as those of the American Business Press, the Direct Mail/Marketing Association, and the Outdoor Advertising Association of America. The second level consists of particular media vehicles such as CBS, the *New Yorker,* and the *Los Angeles Times,* which have specific acceptance criteria. It can be contended that this is the key pressure area concerning what is advertised. If a media vehicle assents or demurs, advertising opportunities are affected accordingly.

3. Individual Enterprises. Particular advertisers and agencies take stands regarding the appropriate forums for their advertising or appropriate contexts.

   For example, Kraft, Procter & Gamble, and several other large advertisers have adopted guidelines concerning the types of television programming in which their advertising will appear. These companies will generally advertise on shows perceived as "family fare" rather than excessively violent or sexually oriented programs. Also, some advertising agencies refuse to accept certain types of accounts, most commonly politicians and cigarettes, although the majority are not so discriminating.

This backdrop should allow complex ethical confrontation. In some cases, the issue concerns the advertising of a subject per se; in others, it concerns whether a particular medium or vehicle provides an appropriate forum. In the absence of clear cause-and-effect data, heat is often generated by passionate conviction, colliding with equally intense economic interests and, as we shall see, different assumptions about nothing less fundamental than human nature.

31. A MAGAZINE AND ITS CIGARETTES

Sue Chord had recently accepted the position of assistant advertising manager with one of the country's leading magazines for the "modern" woman. She was justifiably proud. Sue thought her new employer was several cuts above the *Cosmopolitan* vision of the woman as a sexually obsessed, narcissistic, clothes-and-recreation zealot. *Women,* in contrast, prided itself on sensitivity to the triumphs and tragedies of American women through thoughtful editorial content, ranging from case histories to provocative interviews, serious features, and a smattering of well-balanced self-help articles. It was, in short, a magazine worthy of the name, and Sue was happy to be on board.

Women, she knew, was also extremely popular with a wide range of advertisers interested in reaching the magazine's generally well-educated audience—the people called "opinion leaders" by media buyers. But she had not realized how much advertising was carried in a particular product category—cigarettes. The pages were festooned with colorful ads extolling the virtues of brands aimed directly at women. None were what she would call sexist—the magazine simply wouldn't accept ads like that. But the abundance of cigarette advertisements certainly made cigarettes seem like an appropriate element in the lifestyle of the modern woman.

Now beginning to identify with the publication's editorial mission, Sue found the presence of these ads troubling. She was a nonsmoker, but recognized the rights of others to choose for themselves. What bothered her was the seeming incongruity between the careful and respectful treatment of women in the editorial pages and the seeming disregard for their well-being in the advertising material. She recognized that there are differences in tastes, as well as in the kinds of products and services individuals prefer. However, in her judgment there was no longer any reasonable doubt about the hazards of smoking in general, and for women in particular. For example, she knew that:

- Advertisers are increasingly singling out women as a distinct market.
- Women have now achieved virtual equality in a formerly male-dominated area—lung cancer.
- In addition to its linkage with gastric ulcers, chronic bronchitis, emphysema, and heart disease, it is now known that smoking may cause hazards for unborn children.

Because cigarettes are a harmful—potentially lethal—product, Sue felt they should perhaps not be advertised at all, but certainly not in *Women.* To do so was simply inconsistent. If the magazine staff chooses editorial material with the goal of helping modern women live more fulfilling lives, should they advertise products that work contrary to the best interests of these same women?

It was not a matter of trusting the readers (as if the ads might lure them into smoking) but rather of bringing the caring attitude from the editorial pages over to the advertising pages. Sue's approach was that this magazine should not promote habits that have been proven harmful. Such a policy seemed reasonable enough to her. Was she the only one who thought so?

Sue approached the advertising manager with her observations. She was pointedly reminded that cigarette advertising constituted a significant part of *Women*'s advertising revenue, which in turn helped finance the vigorous editorial side she found so attractive; that cigarettes are still legally sold in this country and can be legally advertised in the print media; and that *Women* readers are wise enough to make their own decisions.

During the next six months, Sue's dilemma became more and more discomforting. Cigarette advertising directed solely at women was increasingly plentiful, and *Women* was a marvelously efficient, even prestigious, vehicle. Meanwhile, many magazines—though not always *Women*—reported new studies on the health-threatening effects of cigarettes. She remembered a study published in 1992 in the *New England Journal of Medicine* that indicated that magazines become increasingly reluctant to cover smoking risks as their revenue from cigarette ads rises—and that women's magazines were particularly prone to this self-censorship.[1] (She even learned that five of *Adbusters* "Dirty Dozen" of "magazines hooked on tobacco ad revenues" were magazines directed to women.)[2]

Eventually, Sue reached the point where she couldn't live with what she considered to be the magazine's schizophrenic editorial/advertising attitude toward its readers. She resigned.

There is no disagreement between Sue and the advertising manager about the facts of the case. First, the presence of large amounts of cigarette advertising is acknowledged, as is its profitability. Second, the manager does not debate the potential dangers of smoking. Therefore, this is a genuine ethical conflict—not merely a disagreement about the interpretation of facts.

One perspective might be to see the issue as a disagreement about consequences. Sue, despite her disclaimer, does seem concerned about the types of choices the readers will presumably make as a result of exposure to cigarette advertising. The magazine staff, by contrast, seems indifferent to the direct effects of the cigarette advertising, but rather sees it as the means to the ends of financial support for the editorial dimension and, ultimately, profits.

From this perspective, Sue could see the greatest good for the greatest number served by eliminating cigarette advertising from the magazine. (Implicit in this assumption seems to be a lack of faith in the decision-making po wer of the readers.) For the magazine staff, the greatest good for the greatest number could be seen as being achieved through accepting the advertising of legal products and using the revenue to produce a high-quality editorial product. (Implicit in this assumption seems to be a belief that individual decision making should not be guided, at least in relation to advertising content.)

Yet Sue may find it difficult to justify her position on utilitarian (consequentialist) grounds, given (1) the indifference of the magazine staff to her concern, and (2) the apparent lack of protest from the readers. The magazine, on the other hand, is apparently operating in a split-level ethical house. On the editorial level, there is concern for what is best for its readers, with certain normative values implicit. Yet on the advertising level, guidance is left entirely to the individual readers.

Sue forced an ethical dilemma for herself by noting that the concept of what was "right" in her area of concern—advertising—was incongruous with the concept of "right" on the editorial side. Given the depth of her concern, and her clear belief in "right" as defined by the editorial philosophy of concern for its readers, she could be seen as acting on ethical principle: the principle that this practice was simply wrong, regardless of clear consequences.

Meanwhile, *Women* continued to function with coexisting credos of (1) responsibility in journalistic content, and (2) a *laissez-faire* ethic in advertising content. This split-level ethic is not uncommon in the media. Neither, then, are the ethical questions that ensue.

32. SENATOR THURMOND TRIES AGAIN

On 14 April 1993, Nancy Moore Thurmond, 22-year-old daughter of the senior senator from North Carolina, died from head injuries after being hit by a car. The driver was charged with felony drunken driving.[3]

There is deep irony as well as tragedy here, for Senator Thurmond has been active in introducing legislation to regulate the alcohol industry. He was responsible for authoring a 1988 bill (now a law) that requires health warning labels on all alcoholic beverage containers. A similar bill to include health warning labels in all alcohol advertising was introduced several years ago, but has languished. Now called the Sensible Advertising and Family Education Act (SAFE) of 1993, it has achieved new momentum in Congress due to the personal tragedy involving the bill's author.

Recently, Senator Thurmond and Senator Conrad Burns made their cases for and against the measure. Here are what may be considered their main arguments:

Senator Thurmond
- Alcohol is this country's most widely used and abused drug— particularly among young people.
- The alcoholic beverage industry spends nearly $2 billion each year on advertising and promotions that associate drinking with active, handsome, and beautiful people, good times, and good fellowship. And this same advertising is the primary source of alcohol information for most Americans.
- More than 100,000 Americans die annually from preventable, alcohol-related causes. Its association with fatal automobile accidents is well known, and alcohol-related problems cost our health care systems millions of dollars each year. Directly or indirectly, it is one of the leading causes of death among young adults and is the leading factor in Fetal Alcohol Syndrome, affecting almost 40,000 babies each year with birth defects and accompanying mental retardation.
- Initiatives to curb advertising and promotion of alcoholic beverages have had support from national health policy leaders, the National Commission on Drug-Free Schools, the American Medical Association, Mothers Against Drunk Driving, and others.
- The proposed legislation would require that seven rotating health messages be included in all alcoholic beverage advertisements and promotional displays in both print and broadcast media. It is thus not meant to prevent either the advertising or consumption of alcoholic beverages.
- The bill faces strong opposition from the alcoholic beverage and advertising industries and the broadcast media. They argue that it's an encroachment on free speech, but their opposition is clearly

generated less by concern over the Constitution and more over the balance sheet. Commercial speech simply does not enjoy the same vigorous protection as other types of speech.

- Basically, this is an attempt to make sure certain consumers are aware of the pitfalls associated with attractively packaged and advertised products—pitfalls that could prove disabling or deadly.[4]

Senator Burns

- In recent years this nation has developed a coordinated response for dealing with the acknowledged problem of alcohol abuse—for example, major educational efforts, tougher laws, uniform and high drinking age. In addition to specific tasks—for example, to curb drunken driving—these efforts also hope to develop a new social attitude that looks down on overconsumption.
- These efforts seem to have borne fruit—over the last 10 years the number of deaths in alcohol-related automobile accidents has dropped 40 percent; awareness levels around alcohol's dangers to pregnant women have climbed dramatically; the term "designated driver" has become part of our common vocabulary.
- Senator Thurmond's proposed legislation, though well meaning, raises serious constitutional questions. The Supreme Court has repeatedly ruled that forcing a speaker to use private property to disseminate someone else's content-specific message is unconstitutional.
- The requirements of this bill—the rotated health warnings—will lead to a de facto ban on this type of advertising, particularly in the broadcast media. And if the ads won't run, neither will the warnings, thus defeating the purpose of the bill.
- There is no evidence that suggests advertising leads to alcohol abuse or that warnings of this sort would work.
- Alcohol advertising is not intended to increase overall consumption of alcohol, but rather to build brand awareness and brand sales.
- The loss of revenue to broadcasters would be substantial and significant—for example, fewer nonpay sports broadcasts, diminished public service campaigns that have been subsidized in part by advertising revenue.
- Although the bill's authors are well intentioned, their legislation is simply the wrong solution to the problems.[5]

There are some important facts here. For example, we can assume that Senator Thurmond's statements about the harmful effects of alcohol and alcohol-related activities are accurate, as are Senator Burns's claims pointing to an improvement in at least some areas of alcohol abuse. And there is the fact of the bill itself— particularly the requirement that virtually all advertising and promotion of alcoholic beverages include one of seven rotating health warnings.

There is also a good deal of speculation. On the part of Senator Thurmond, there is the assumption that individuals exposed to the advertising in question will (1) get the message, and (2) act on it. For his part, Senator Burns apparently assumes that the proposed legislation will result in a decrease in advertising of alcoholic beverages, and that the resulting decline in revenue—particularly with the broadcast media—will result in the curtailing of programming (e.g., sports) as well as the time made available for public service announcements. It is especially important that he feels the courts would find such a law unconstitutional.

One approach to sharpening the ethical focus would be to define the situation from the two perspectives in this way:

- Is it ethical to promote a product whose use has negative health and social consequences for sizable segments of the population in a manner that extols—even idealizes—its physiological, psychological, and sociological associations without a word of caution about its potentially dangerous consequences?
- Is it ethical to require a company to include in the advertising paid for by that company words that are meant to discourage the use of their product and, hence, diminish their legal self-interests?

Clearly, Senator Thurmond feels that social responsibility must be mandated, force fed to consumers and potential consumers in the same forms of communication. He offers no proof here that those who currently abuse alcohol are not already aware of its possible dangers. In other words, the unstated directive here may be "Help them," for his arguments do not include even an oblique reference that might be interpreted as "Help us."

Senator Burns, on the other hand, suggests that social responsibility on the part of the alcoholic beverage industry and the media should not be melded to the responsibility to produce an honest profit from the sale and/or the promotion of a legal product. He does not object to the dissemination of cautionary information about alcohol consumption; indeed, he applauds it and its presumed results. He simply doesn't want it mixed with the clearly self-interested form. (It is interesting that Senator Burns seems to see some positive effects from the "moderation" campaigns of the alcoholic beverage industry, but dismisses the idea that warnings within ads will have similar effects.)

Senator Thurmond could be seen as occupying Aristotelian middle ground—we don't want to ban the ads or the consumption, merely to see that everyone is reminded of the risks along with the pleasure. Senator Burns, by contrast, offers both an ethic of self-interest (leave the ads as they are) and one of social responsibility, through campaigns of moderation.

Unlike cigarettes, which are harmful when used as intended, the consumption of alcoholic beverages can have adverse effects on some and not others although the national consequences are clearly wide and deep. Would warnings curtail abuse? It could certainly be argued that they could be easily ignored in print, and they have certainly not inhibited vigorous cigarette advertising and promotion. But to see a tableau where the television slogan "It doesn't get any better than this!" is followed by a grim warning about interaction with other drugs, or high blood pressure? This is a different dimension indeed.

Is the current situation of self-interest and social responsibility ethically defensible? *If* consumers and potential consumers already know the risks of alcohol abuse (as in Senator Thurmond's seven warnings) then it could be contended that the current mix of group/media/industry moderation efforts and the ongoing inducements to consumption can be seen to coexist, if not in harmony then in uneasy truce.

If not, then it could be contended that the clear and present dangers of alcohol abuse, and their wide direct and indirect personal and social costs, justify a mandated caution along with the inducement to consume. In either case, it could be argued that informed individual judgment is championed—in the latter case, of course, the judgments of consumers are given preference over the self-interest of producers, a not inconsequential precedent given the other "clear and present danger" arguments that could be made against a host of other products and services.

Ethical analysis encourages the establishment of principles to guide future decision making as well as rationalize current choices. This seems particularly important in the volatile areas of cigarette and alcohol advertising practices—and consequences.

33. THE 30-SECOND CANDIDATE?

"Look, Jason, I don't see what the problem is. This guy is smart, liberal, has a great media presence, and stands a damn good chance of going into the convention with enough delegates to get him in on the first ballot. You'd join the agency ad hoc group and stay in it until our guy gets as far as he's going to go. And who knows how far that could be?"

"Phyliss, you know what the work load on this thing would be. I mean we'd have to be constantly on call to revise our strategies and media buys depending on what the other candidates do. And, God knows, we'd have to react fast if someone throws out a charge that could hurt him. And just think of getting our ideas approved! Some of the Bush media advisers are still moaning and groaning about their suggestions being ignored by his 'handlers,' and George Lois is apparently still convinced that Dukakis could have won in '88 with the right advertising strategy!"[6]

"OK. I admit that it won't be easy, but since when is advertising easy? One of the reasons we want you on board is because of your skills in dealing with difficult clients—selling them on good creative stuff that's going to be in their best interests, even if they can't see it. Besides, Jason, how many opportunities do you have to promote the ideas of someone who could be the next president? Pretty heady stuff."

"But damn it, Phyliss, we'd still have to sell him like a can of soup in those abominable television spots. They're great for detergents, my soft drink account, and lots of other products and services, but we're talking here about ideas and positions that just can't be communicated with any understanding at all in 30 seconds or less. And certainly the stakes are a tad higher for a wrong decision. Surely you can't disagree?"

"No, I don't disagree, but you know that people don't get all their information for voting from TV spots. Look at Perot's infomercials, Clinton on *Arsenio Hall,* even poor, uncomfortable George Bush on MTV! And remember all the talk show appearances. Was Dan Rather as important in that election as Larry King? And then there are the papers, TV news, special reports. Sure the TV-spot campaign is important—but primarily for awareness and a few simple positions and slogans. The rest comes out in other places."

"Sure, there's a lot more going on, but you know and I know that the spot campaign is very important, and you know it's been proven effective in producing awareness, not to mention a very, very simplistic impression of the candidates. And, face it, Phyliss, there are an awful lot of voters out there who don't go to the trouble of being informed. They want it all to come to them—and in easily digestible doses. And nothing does that better than a TV spot."

"So, it's OK for the other candidates to get across their simplistic awareness and simpleminded issues and slogans, but you don't want the guy you admire to play the game?"

"Phyliss, it's OK for them and OK for our guy because that's just the way things are now. But I still think it's a travesty to have presumably the cream of our political crop using 30-second and 15-second bits of television to present themselves and bash each other. What kind of a system is that? I'd enjoy the action and the challenge, Phyliss, but I'm afraid I don't want to help perpetuate a system that sells politicians like commodities. I'd better stick to colas. The stakes are a lot less important."

The selling of political candidates via some type of advertising has been around for the better part of this country's political life. But it was really with the successful use of television spots by Dwight Eisenhower in the 1952 campaign that the modern dimensions of the political sell began to take form. (It is said that during the filming of these short and simplistic messages Eisenhower was overheard to murmur, "To think an old soldier should come to this.") Now the use of television and radio spots (usually 15 or 30 seconds long) is commonplace in today's political campaigns at the federal, state, and local levels, and not surprisingly, discussions on advertising's role in politics almost inevitably focus on television advertising.

As you might expect, this has not been a subject in which ethical dimensions have been ignored by the advertising business. For example, among other material presented in a much-acclaimed 1983 session in the Senate Caucus Room was the American Association of Advertising Agencies (AAAA) "Code of Ethics" concerning political advertising:

1. The advertising agency should not represent any candidate who has not signed or who does not observe the Code of Fair Campaign

Practices of the Fair Campaign Practices Committee, endorsed by the AAAA.

2. The agency should not knowingly misrepresent the views or stated record of any candidates nor quote them out of proper context.
3. The agency should not prepare any material which unfairly or prejudicially exploits the race, creed, or national origin of any candidate.
4. The agency should take care to avoid unsubstantiated charges and accusations, especially those deliberately made too late in the campaign for opposing candidates to answer.
5. The agency should stand as an independent judge of fair campaign practices, rather than automatically yielding to the wishes of the candidate or his authorized representative.
6. The agency should not indulge in any practices which might be deceptive or misleading in word, photograph, film, or sound.[7]

Jason's decision not to join the agency team is based on a generalization about the relationship of broadcast advertising to politics. He could have reflected on the issue a bit more by investigating the specific situation. For example, several others in the task force may also have worried about the increasing trends toward political ads of 60 seconds or less, but then reasoned that each situation must be evaluated on its own terms. The question for them may not have been whether the selling of politicians using television spots is a broad problem, but whether a campaign could be designed with integrity for a particular politician.

But for Jason this issue centered on his perceived complicity in weakening the democratic process, and he therefore declined to participate. Was this an act of principle or a simple cop-out? In light of the fact that his complaints were apparently serious and sincere, the simple act of not joining the team seems incongruous and even meaningless. A vital aspect of social life is being threatened, he declares, and yet he reacts in a way that costs him little. At a minimum, should he not protest his own agency's involvement? Several advertising firms in the United States refuse all political accounts. For some, this policy is one of self-protection, arising from the poor credit risk that most campaign accounts represent. But a few object on grounds similar to Jason's.

Perhaps the question he ought to face is whether he has a responsibility to pursue every means possible until his agency adopts more enlightened guidelines. Some television stations have chosen to refuse to allow anything less than five minutes for paid political broadcasts. Jason could urge his agency to enact a similar standard for any political campaigns it would undertake. He might even become active in broader issues of reform, such as promoting the adoption of the British system.

Great Britain has had a longstanding policy that prevents anyone from buying commercial time for election campaigns. The major parties are allocated an equal amount, and television stations are required to broadcast the programs free. All other exposure occurs in news coverage, over which politicians have no control.

Regardless of the options proposed, should such possibilities of reform be on the forefront of Jason's agenda?

Precisely what is Jason's ethical objection to political advertising? In working through the problem, he thinks largely in sociopolitical terms about the need for enlightened citizens. He warns against slick and simplistic ads in a complex world. Apparently these concerns represent strong political values, but the ethical issue could be focused better. Has he concluded that political commercials of 30 and 60 seconds are inherently deceptive? Even if no outright lies are permitted, he could contend that short spots inevitably and fundamentally distort both the style and content of the candidate, thus violating at least two of the AAAA's political "Code of Ethics."

A form of deception seems to be the moral issue here, and if Jason defined the question in those terms he might be motivated not simply to decline participation in the task force, but to demand changes in his company, and in public policy as well.

It is not difficult to find situations where self-righteousness overwhelms sincere ethical conviction.

34. FEMININE HYGIENE IN THE LIVING ROOM

Former advertising practitioner Jerry Mander wrote more than a decade ago:

> Most people are aware that advertising is an invasion of privacy; this is not a new revelation. But the fact that we can be aware of it and not be furious about it, and do nothing about stopping it, is not so much a sign that it's an unimportant issue as it is a sign of the level of our submission.[8]

"Well," Dr. Josh Farleigh asked his class in media ethics, "was Mander right?"

The first response hit a common theme: "We have a choice. We don't have to pay attention to ads, or any other media content that we don't like."

"That may be," Farleigh responded, enjoying his role as devil's advocate, "but doesn't most advertising seek us out rather than the other way around? And we really don't have all that much choice about whether we want to encounter some ads, particularly on television or over the radio, not to mention billboards."

"Well, the ads are there because they help pay for the media, and besides that, we all get used to shutting out ads we don't want to see, particularly with the broadcast commercials—and we can always surf to another channel."

"But," Farleigh probed, "why should you have to work at avoiding them? If you had a friend that constantly tried to 'get at' you, whether you were interested or not, you wouldn't tolerate him or her very long would you? Then why should you tolerate unwelcome advertisers, particularly in the privacy of your home?"

"OK, but if you're going to choose to have a television set, and watch commercial television, you know you're going to see ads. It's a compromise we all understand, so I don't see it as an ethical issue. It's simply a matter of choice."

"Well, then, let's get specific. Here's an article from *Advertising Age*. Look at the headline: 'Feminine Hygiene Ads Are Rated Most Hated.'[9] It's based on a nationwide survey of 1,000 adults who were asked to name TV commercials they find really objectionable. The article says the research 'turned up a clear winner: the whole feminine hygiene product category. For men and women alike, these commercials made them squirm with discomfort.' Listen to that— 'squirm with discomfort.'[10] Why should we have to do that, in our own homes, because of a commercial form we can't anticipate and find it very difficult to avoid when it does intrude?"

Jerry Mander, facing the general issue of advertising's invasion of privacy, wrote: "Why do we tolerate this? What right do advertisers have to treat us that way? When did I sell the right for them to run pictures in my mind? Why is it possible for people who are selling things to feel perfectly free to speak to me, over public airwaves, without my permission, all day long?"[11]

Is there an ethical problem here? Jerry Mander, who Farleigh quoted, is obviously operating from what is, for him, a very strongly held value—it is simply wrong, apparently under any circumstances, for advertisers to "invade our privacy." That statement, of course, probes the essence of one of the inherent characteristics of modern American advertising—that is, it seeks us out rather than the other way around. And it's abundantly clear that the media frequently think of themselves as the means to the end of gathering potential customers together for advertisers.

Now, it could be contended that Mander would find it less comfortable to operate at the consequentialist level. For example, it could be argued that advertisers feel that the present arrangement offers them a chance to put their messages before potentially interested individuals.

The media would argue that individuals do have choices, and that the presence of advertising—sometimes welcome, particularly with more specialized media—is simply a trade-off that most readers, viewers, and listeners seem ready to accept.

Even the viewers, listeners, or readers themselves would probably contend that the presence of advertising is occasionally illuminating, sometimes entertaining, and generally a reasonable subsidy for some of the nonadvertising content.

So Mander remains (properly, it seems) in Kantian territory, asserting that to the extent that advertising seeks us out so relentlessly through the media it is inherently flawed.

But, as we've learned, one of the steps in ethical analysis is to define the situation properly. And perhaps this issue might take on a slightly different cast if we narrow the scope. First, there is no clear evidence that many find ads in most of the print media objectionable, so the argument is primarily about television, the most intrusive of the forms. Second, it seems likely that certain kinds of television advertising, regardless of execution, are more likely to promote disquietude than others. Obviously, feminine hygiene products rate high in that group.

So the issue is narrowed down to the advertising of certain product categories on television being seen as objectionable by some segments of the population.

In the absence of overt viewer objections, advertisers could still rely on utilitarian arguments, although they could find it difficult to make that case for the advertising of feminine hygiene products. Still, they could fall back on the comfort of the "natural" signals from the market—that is, if they really object to us, they won't buy our products, and we'll do something different.

The media are, of course, the gatekeepers, but they seem increasingly inclined to open the doors wider—for example, by at least experimenting with accepting ads for condoms, and now routinely allowing bra commercials with live models.[12] Why? Well, as we have seen, condoms have been justified as products of disease prevention, and television as one of the few media that guarantee sure access to appropriate population segments. The presence of bra-wearing models is justified on the basis of the growing liberality of the audience. And there is always money. These advertisers buy time. (It would have been difficult for network television to make a "public need" case for information on feminine hygiene products in order to justify lifting their self-imposed ban on that product category a number of years ago.) And given the response to the *Advertising Age* poll, as well as simple grass-roots sampling, it must be evident that viewers dislike this form of advertising more than virtually any other. Therefore, simple economic self-interest looms large.

Perhaps there are Rawlsian dimensions of fairness here that could be explored, such as restricting the feminine hygiene product advertising to late prime-time or daytime shows, when the adult female audience is likely to dominate, an audience potentially more appreciative of the ad's content. The medium's income would be maintained, and at least some of the irritation level might be diminished.

Is there an ethical problem here? Having a significant portion of a television audience "squirm with discomfort" because of an intrusive advertising form dealing with a sensitive subject area would certainly suggest so.

NOTES

1. Kenneth Warner, "Cigarette Advertising and Magazine Coverage of the Hazards of Smoking—A Statistical Analysis," *New England Journal of Medicine,* 30 January 1992, p. 305.
2. "Stop the Dirty Dozen," *Adbuster* (Summer/Fall 1992): 77.
3. Steven W. Colford, "Tragedy Revives Alcohol Ad Threat," *Advertising Age,* 10 May 1993, p. 8.

4. Senator Strom Thurmond, "A Reality Check for Alcohol Ads," *Roll Call,* Roll Call Associates, 7 June 1993.

5. Senator Conrad Burns, "Alcohol Abusers, and Abuse Won't Stop by Labeling Ads," *Roll Call,* Roll Call Associates, 7 June 1993.

6. For a particularly illuminating perspective on the Bush-Dukakis campaign, see "The Campaign You Never Saw," *New York,* 12 December 1988.

7. "Responsibility in Political Advertising in 1984," presentation by the American Association of Advertising Agencies in the Senate Caucus Room, 9 December 1983.

8. Jerry Mander, "Four Arguments for the Elimination of Advertising," in *Advertising and the Public,* ed. Kim Rotzoll (Urbana: University of Illinois Department of Advertising, 1980), pp. 14-21.

9. Scott Hume, "Most Hated Ads: Feminine Hygiene," *Advertising Age,* 18 July 1988, p. 3.

10. Ibid.

11. Mander, "Four Arguments," p. 21.

12. "Ads That Shatter an Old Taboo," *Time,* 2 February 1987, p. 63.

chapter **8**

How to Say It

Advertising is, by definition, communication with a purpose. It seeks to alter the thinking and/or behavior of those receiving the message in a manner beneficial to the advertiser. In the previous chapter, we examined some of the ethical controversies centered on the subject of that message. Here we consider some of the decisions about execution, the host of verbal and nonverbal symbols that can be arranged in virtually infinite combinations to attempt to achieve advertisers' ends.

Whether this potential is considered a problem or not depends to a great extent on what assumptions are made about human nature (about whether or not an individual is deliberate and calculating, for example), as well as the ultimate fairness of the market system within which advertising flourishes. Compounding the issue is the powerful reality that for most advertising, most of the time, its actual effects are often quite difficult to determine, even when there is agreement as to what "effect" means (for example, does it mean awareness? attitude change? an increase in sales?).

What is to be advertised is, then, one of advertising's thornier ethical battlegrounds. How it will be presented is, as we shall see, no less taxing.

35. A MINUSCULE (AND TASTELESS) DIFFERENCE?

Cynthia Brace was the newly appointed Advertising Manager for Brandco, a large, regional soft drink company, one of many in a highly competitive market. She had just been promoted from the assistant advertising manager position and was anxious to establish her credibility in this responsible job.

Brandco had been successful through intelligent "niche marketing," refusing to go head-to-head with the big bottlers with traditional or clear colas and

173

the like, but instead concentrating on their well-regarded fruit-flavored beverages. Their line leader was a strawberry soda, and that, Cynthia found, was the current bone of contention she inherited along with her new position.

Brandco's advertising agency had recently finished a comprehensive study of the company, its competitors, and the soft drink market in general. Its basic conclusion was complimentary—Brandco offered products consumers associated with consistently good taste. This confirmed what the company thought was one of their assets—quality control throughout the processing and bottling process. The problem was that virtually every competitor was claiming "great taste," and the idea of "quality" might have little impact on consumers. Quality was, at best, an elusive concept, perhaps better associated with cars or television sets than an essentially taste-dominated product such as a soft drink. So the agency had been searching for another way of asserting a competitive edge. In essence, it sought a proxy for "high quality."

Finally, they thought they had found it with a "natural" theme, expressed in the slogan, "A little bit of natural flavor in every drop." After an initial screening, the legal department, extremely sensitive to themes involving the use of the term "natural" because of concerns of the Food and Drug Administration, asked, "Can you prove it?" The agency turned to Brandco's new Advertising Manager for the anticipated verification that the company's strawberry soda did indeed contain natural flavoring.

But it did not, Cynthia told them, for the simple reason that natural strawberry juice simply tastes awful. All of Brandco's other flavors did contain varying degrees of natural flavoring, but not strawberry, its bestseller.

The agency was adamant. The "natural" theme would not only imply Brandco's high quality, but it also tied in nicely with the country's move toward healthier lifestyles. "Natural" had highly positive connotations, and the agency felt certain that a competitive edge could be gained through using that theme.

After some frenzied conferences, Cynthia was asked if Brandco could add *some* natural strawberry flavoring to verify the claim. She pointed out that any amount that could be tasted would result in a negative change for the popular soda. So then they asked, what about adding a minuscule amount, just enough to support the slogan, "A little bit of natural flavor in every drop," but not enough to affect the taste?

Her boss would have to decide that, Cynthia knew. After all, it would represent the first change in the formula in the 70-year history of the brand. (Shades of "Classic" Coke, she thought cynically.) But what should she recommend to the president?

Ultimately, she decided to propose the change, on the basis of the attraction of the promised competitive edge, as well as her assessment that no real harm would be done to anyone. The media could accept the advertisement. The agency could stand behind the slogan. The customer could continue to enjoy the taste of a soft drink that had become a bestseller on the basis of its flavor.

And, finally, the company could continue to offer high-quality soft drinks in an extremely competitive market.

Brandco apparently has a good-quality product. The initial problem here is to discover some way to get across the idea of quality without stating that theme explicitly, since it apparently has little motivating power for consumers. Eventually, "natural" was seen as the best alternative. It was necessary to add only enough natural strawberry juice to verify the claim, but not enough to change the taste.

Cynthia's decision to support the addition seems to be based on her belief that the end (Brandco's success in the highly competitive soft drink market) justifies the means (a willingness to potentially mislead, but without any appreciable effect on the consumers' use of the product).

Let's examine her assumptions a bit more closely. Presumably, Cynthia's company will benefit from increased sales. But what of the consumers—present and future? It would be difficult to argue that their experience with the product will somehow be enhanced. Indeed, it could be argued that new consumers may be drawn to the product on a false premise, even though their taste experience would still be satisfactory.

Cynthia could have relied upon the categorical imperative of truthtelling. She could have concluded that it is simply wrong to misinform, whether by what is included in the message—or by what is omitted.

Utilitarianism could be valuable in this and many other business decisions, but only if the absence of any obvious "greater good" to present and future customers could be rationalized in some manner.

Basically, it would seem that Cynthia acted without any overriding reflection on what is "right," short of what is best for the company. This position is expedient for an employee in terms of her or his business career, and one can certainly understand the conditions when "What's good for General Motors is good for the country," to use a former business executive's classic utterance. For, simply put, one of the enduring premises of capitalism is that the good of the company (in terms of profits, etc.) can only be achieved when it satisfies its customers.

It can be argued that Cynthia's loyalty to the company, and the underlying premise of belief in the mechanisms of the market system, are sufficient justification for her recommendation. If present and future customers will not be favored, neither will their experiences be diminished. In other words, this is not a decision with earthshaking consequences. Of course, she could have responded differently by thinking along Kantian, or even utilitarian, lines but she did not.

What of her future decisions in her new job? Lacking any apparent set of working premises that do not end with the company's well-being, Cynthia could be destined to confront each issue with increasingly predictable results. As her career in management grows, past decisions may well solidify into an operative set of company-serving rules that shortcut thoughtful ethical considerations, perhaps in matters of greater consequence than this particular "strawberry dilemma."

Making an ethical decision requires reflection on alternatives. In this case, Cynthia placed heavy emphasis on company loyalty. If that focus remains her only reference point in future encounters, very little of the ethical complexity associated with the Potter Box will cross her mind.

36. JOE CAMEL

Early in January 1992, *Advertising Age* ran an editorial with the headline "Old Joe Must Go."[1] The editors were referring to the camel "spokescartoon" that had been in use since 1987 on behalf of all advertising and promotion for Camel cigarettes, and had recently come under staunch attack from the Surgeon General as well as other anti-smoking groups. The controversy had become particularly heated after the *Journal of the American Medical Association* published several studies that alleged that the use of the Old Joe figure encouraged children to smoke.[2]

Subsequently, *Advertising Age* solicited two opposing views on the issue and published them in their 27 January 1992 issue. They are reprinted here.

FOR OLD JOE: Free Speech Is the Issue
By James W. Johnston, Chairman and CEO of R. J. Reynolds Tobacco Co.

By calling on R. J. Reynolds to withdraw its Camel advertising campaign ("Old Joe Must Go"), *Advertising Age* has, perhaps unwittingly, adopted a position that could deprive the tobacco industry, or any industry, of its right to commercial free speech.

It is difficult to launch a broad assault on commercial free speech, but this editorial chips away at this right through a selective attack on a specific advertising campaign. The fact that children see and recognize tobacco advertising is not a justification for eliminating those ads or for depriving a company of its right to advertise a legal product.

For the record: Contrary to the conclusion that some people have drawn from a series of articles in the December 11, 1991, *Journal of the American Medical Association*, there is no evidence whatsoever that Camel's campaign causes anyone to start smoking. Moreover, the fact that some children recognize the Camel character and understand that it is linked to tobacco products is hardly "scientific proof" that the Camel is targeted to children.

It is true that since the "Smooth Character" campaign was introduced in 1987, Camel has reversed its downward slide and has held stable at 4.4 percent of the cigarette market. But, according to U.S. government reports, the incidence of underage smoking has not increased during those four years. So claims that Camel's success is the result of causing children to smoke are blatantly false.

I believe your editorial staff and your readers should be aware that the *Journal of the American Medical Association* studies contain a number of serious flaws. For instance:

- The assumption that anyone between the ages of 12 and 19 who smokes is an "underaged smoker." By assuming this, one of the studies reported in *Journal of the American Medical Association* conveniently ignored the fact that, of the five states studied, one has a legal age of 17 (Georgia); one (New Mexico) has no age restriction; and in the other three states the legal age to smoke is 18. Consequently, many of the smokers classified as "underaged" in that study were, in fact, of legal age to smoke. If you adjust the data in this study to reflect this fact, the study will then show that between 91.6 percent and 95.3 percent of Camel smokers appear to be adults. That clearly refutes the claim that Camel advertising is aimed at youth or that there is a significant unintended spillover.

- The equally false assumption that early logo recognition leads to premature smoking. A recent Gallup survey asked smokers why they began smoking. Only 1 percent cited advertising. The largest reasons the survey specifically cited were peer pressure (48%) and family influence (15%).

So why is Camel advertising under attack? Because of another widespread assumption that is equally false—that animal caricatures appeal only, or primarily, to children.

In their need to break through clutter and impact competitive adult customers, advertisers have used animation since the earliest days of advertising. Video Storyboard (a video production company) reported in 1989 that animation and animals were quickly replacing celebrities as the most popular form of advertising among adult consumers. The Energizer Bunny, the California Raisins, the Kibbles'N Bits dog, even Ernie Keebler, have enormous appeal with adults. At one time or another, each of these campaigns has been considered great adult-directed advertising.

Not surprisingly, Video Storyboard Tests (in an article carried in *Advertising Age*) reported that the "Old Joe" Camel campaign has been one of the 10 most popular print ad campaigns among adults for the past three years. For better or worse, the use of animation and animals in advertising is here to stay.

If advertising were the true culprit, then perhaps all ads should be banned. Possibly the automobile industry should be blamed for advertising fast, sleek cars and have the responsibility for someone who drives without a license or exceeds posted speed limits.

We do not want children to purchase cigarettes or to smoke, and we believe that enforcement of existing laws is an effective way to accomplish those goals. In fact, there is evidence, even in the same *Journal of the American Medical Association* issue, that through enforcement, underage cigarette sales and consumption can be cut by more than 50 percent.

So there are solutions to the problem of underage smoking, and we are working on them. Last year, R. J. Reynolds began a youth non-smoking campaign that will be expanded and accelerated by 50 percent in 1992. Other voluntary steps are underway to concentrate on better enforcement of existing state minimum purchase laws. Through these actions, we believe underage smoking can and will be reduced.

But suggestions like *Advertising Age's* proposal to "lose the Camel" don't do anything to reduce the incidence of underage smoking. All they do is further chip away at the First Amendment, one campaign at a time.

In every war, there are casualties that result from so-called "friendly fire." Let's hope that commercial free speech does not suffer that fate.

AGAINST OLD JOE: It's the Final Straw
By Dr. Elizabeth M. Whelan, President of the American Council on Science & Health

Historians may record that it was the confluence in time and space of two events—the unprecedented success of the "Old Joe" Camel ad and the anticipated U.S. Supreme Court ruling against tobacco companies—which triggered the beginning of the end for cigarette advertising in America.

- At a December 1991 press conference in New York, Dr. George D. Lundberg, editor of the *Journal of the American Medical Association*, announced that there was now solid scientific evidence that children recognized "Old Joe" as readily as they did Mickey Mouse. Indeed, the evidence of cigarette awareness among young kids is so startling that the geniuses behind this campaign should step forward and take a bow.

  Unfortunately for the advertising industry, the ad's "success" ignited outrage in the medical community. "Old Joe," Dr. Lundberg said, "will turn out to be the metaphorical straw that broke the advertising camel's back," one which would start the dominoes falling on *all* cigarette advertising.

- In October 1991, the U.S. Supreme Court heard opening arguments in the case of *Cipollone v. Liggett*. The survivors of Rose Cipollone, a smoker who developed lung cancer, claim the manufacturer is responsible for her health. The industry disagrees, arguing that Congress "pre-empted" it from liability when it mandated warning labels. The court will decide not on the merits of Mrs. Cipollone's case, but on whether or not cigarette companies are immune from lawsuits.

  After the October arguments, the eight-member High Court was apparently deadlocked (they usually take a preliminary vote after the opening arguments) and decided to re-hear the case in January with Justice Clarence Thomas as the tie-breaking vote. Judicial bookies give odds that Thomas (given his states' rights orientation) will rule against federal pre-emption, thus removing the industry's shield of legal immunity. The result: a growing number of lawsuits. [The Supreme Court found in Cipollone's favor, but the case was subsequently dropped.]

Whether or not smokers prevail in later court actions for damages is problematic. However, in any scenario, cigarette advertising itself will be on trial: The cornerstone of the plaintiff's argument for product liability will be that the industry was and is actively involved in a strategy of deception to negate the effects of warnings by using ads associating smoking with sex, "machoism," youth and the good life.

Courtesy of press coverage of these trials, Americans will get unprecedented insight into how the manufacturers of the leading cause of death manipulate the media and consumers through misleading advertising to entice the public into using an inherently dangerous product. The long simmering public contempt for cigarette advertisements, recently further fueled by "Old Joe" and the proof that ads reach children, will boil over. The call for an advertising ban will assume new momentum.

Under another scenario (with the same end results), should the plaintiffs be awarded damages in jury trials, tobacco manufacturers may seek to minimize future losses by admitting that cigarettes present health risks, offering to feature skull-and-crossbone labels and promising to market only on an "informed consent" basis, whereby smokers assume all responsibility for the consequences of smoking. Continued advertising, at least as we now know it, would be incompatible with this new "here's the truth, you're on your own" strategy.

Thus, cigarette ads will disappear—either due to consumer-driven congressional action or in the industry's desperate quest for survival.

But, inevitably, there will be those who still defend the "right" to advertise. To them I ask:

How can you rationalize advertising a product which, *when used as intended*, maims and kills, claiming the lives of 1,300 Americans each day?

Because cigarettes are the *only* inherently hazardous legal U.S. product, current-day analogies don't exist. But consider the patent medicine Radithor, a radium water widely marketed and advertised in the 1920s: In ads Radithor's manufacturer promised consumers that daily consumption would give them extra energy and make them feel good all over. Radithor users paid for their "glow" of health with prolonged and grisly deaths from leukemia, bone cancers, and other radium-induced malignancies.

The only difference between radium water and cigarettes is one of historical accident, in that cigarettes gained an economic and biochemical stranglehold on this country before scientists established them as hazards. To modern-day champions of cigarette advertising I pose this question: If Radithor were approved for sale today, would you defend the "right" to spend over $3.5 billion advertising it to both children as well as adults?

What do *you* think of the ethical merits of these two positions?

37. MAKING THE SAME DIFFERENT: PARITY PRODUCTS

Harry Feldner was a Creative Supervisor with more than 23 years' experience in the agency business. He paused over the question on the form before him. Some researchers were trying to find out something about the ethics of the advertising business. Talk about old wine in new bottles! The question read, "Do you feel that you encounter ethical decisions in the practice of your job?" Harry immediately wrote, "Not really. All our work is carefully scrutinized by lawyers internally, as well as the client and the networks." He stopped, thought a bit, and then added, "I have not yet decided whether 'puffery' is unethical. Yet I do feel that if an advertiser has to tell the whole truth he may as well not advertise—there would be no competitive advantage since most products are parity, with only minor shades of difference."

Harry reflected on parity products, advertising's bane and triumph. Face it, a very large number of the mass-advertised mass-consumption brands are substitutable for one another without any noticeable difference in performance. Hadn't the Batten, Barton, Durstine & Osborn (BBDO) Worldwide study revealed that two-thirds of the consumers in 28 countries considered brands in 13 major product categories to be *virtually identical?* Hell, Harry thought, parity products are all over the home-medication shelves in the drug store, not to mention deodorants, margarines, VCRs, "natural" and synthetic vitamins, household cleaning aids, bottled waters, as well as a great number of laundry products. And what of beer and cigarettes? Test after test has demonstrated that even the most brand loyal could not consistently pick out their brand from other, unidentified samples. *Consumer Reports* wrote: "As far as we can tell, relatively inexpensive shampoos contain perfectly adequate cleaning and conditioning ingredients. If you want to spend money on an expensive shampoo, do it knowing that you're indulging your psyche, not your hair."[3] And, on another subject, "When it comes to ordinary cleaning, all soap is created equal. . . . One real difference is price. The most expensive of the bars we tested sells for nearly 45 times the price of the cheapest."[4]

In some cases, the products are identical because of government requirements (for example, some drugs), or because producers commonly sell some of their output to retailers for marketing under their brand name(s)—for example, it was recently reported that 6 tire producers sell their products under more than 17 brand names. The intriguing thing about parity products, he thought, is their curse and their challenge. The curse is best summed up by that memorable quotation from the old master of the hard sell Rosser Reeves: "Our problem is—a client comes into my office and throws two newly minted half-dollars onto my desk and says, 'Mine is the one on the left. You prove it's better.'"[5] The challenge, of course, comes precisely from the lack of physical or functional difference. It enables the copywriter and art director to move with considerable ease into the realm of the consumer's emotions—to manipulate symbols, to create moods and distinctive product identities:

> A green giant? A doughboy? A marching rabbit? A rugged cowboy? Lovers brought together over an instant coffee? Boy meets girl through beer? Attach them successfully to generally indistinctive brands and behold, there's more projected than the functional performance of the item.

> Or have recognizable personalities speak for the product and let their charisma wash over. (Just think of the "celebrity wars" waged by Pepsi and Coke, and certainly this must be the era of the spokesathlete!)

> Or sing. Yes indeed, sing about the beer, about toilet paper, about the joys of carpet, the rhapsody of the open road in that new "sport sedan."

The challenge was, then, Harry knew, to suggest a difference where none in fact existed in any real sense. A former colleague, the late Howard Gossage, used to make much of the distinction between image and identity. "An *image*," he often said, "is how you want others to see you. An *identity*, on the other hand, is what you really are."[6] Obviously, Gossage felt one is on much firmer ethical ground dealing with identities. But, Harry thought, the essence of a great deal of advertising involves images. And, until the government tells us we can't sell differences where none exists, he thought as he turned back to his work, I'll lend my talents to the cause.

In a review of several books by advertising professionals, the *New York Times*'s Roger Draper put the ethical issue succinctly. Much consumer goods advertising, he asserted, attempts "to suppress an important fact: the similarity among competing brands. If 'some of the truth' in this sense is an acceptable alternative to all of it, the value of truth itself becomes puzzling."[7]

Our not-so-mythical Harry was responding to the first question on a form we sent to advertising practitioners. His initial response tended to equate "right" with what is considered "legal." In other words, if the lawyers at the agency, the client, and the media consider it acceptable, then it is. But Harry knew there was more. His response about puffery seems to address the more fundamental question in this case: Regardless of specific consequences, is it wrong to imply differences where, functionally, there are none?

This question strikes at the heart of parity products, as Harry knew. His wanderings in difficult ethical territory were short-lived, however. He was soon reflecting on the curse and challenge of parity products—but his reflections were focused on the *advertising practitioner*, not on the public. Parity products, Harry seems to be saying, are a curse in the sense that it is hard to provide a successful difference where none exists, but they are also a challenge in that the advertiser has to create a difference that establishes brand loyalty. Harry seems to shrug aside concern over the effects of this type of advertising by implying that we're all creatures of symbolic meaning and are therefore not ill-served by communications that suggest more than they may ultimately deliver. Of course, we may in fact feel more "comfortable" with one virtually identical brand over another—such as Bayer versus generic aspirin—because of the symbolic content that makes a difference for us. (After explaining how consumers could save $2,500 a year at the supermarket buying store brands rather than national brands, *Consumer Reports* noted that a poll revealed most of *its readers* "opt for buying name-brand products despite the cost.")[8] So it could be argued that this is an ethical issue without a constituency—if customers in fact want to perceive their brand choices as different, so be it.

But are customers aware of the parity in many of their choices? Would it make a difference if people knew that certain brands were virtually identical in performance? Would they then say, "I don't care if my brand is the same as another, less expensive option, I want to buy it anyway"? Perhaps. But if knowledge of the parity nature of some brands *would* make a difference in purchasing decisions, then the comfortable utilitarian justification of the greatest good for the greatest number is weakened.

What other ethical justifications for continuing to "make the same different" would be available to Harry? Certainly there are options: to be convinced that moral duty is owed specifically to the advertiser ("I need to establish a difference for the client's product because it's my job"), or, more generally, to advertising as a communication form ("That's the essence of a great deal of advertising" or "That's the way the game is played"). And, perhaps, there could be an expanded vision of utilitarianism in this context to show that—beyond purchase consequences—the greatest good for the greatest number is served through allowing individuals freedom of choice, including the freedom to choose to pay more for a functionally identical product if it suits their particular needs.

Harry's experiences as a seasoned practitioner could have led him to confront two premises: (1) What is good is what is legal; and (2) What is legal is not necessarily what is good for the public. Basically, Harry refused to address the second challenge and, in the process, left his ethical thinking stalled at its current business-as-usual level rather than attempting to resolve—at least for himself— one of advertising's most challenging ethical issues.

38. TRICKS OF THE TRADE IN MARKETING TO CHILDREN

"Buy Me That!," "Buy Me That Too!," and "Buy Me That 3" were three 30-minute programs produced by Consumer Reports Television and aired on Home Box Office (HBO). They were promoted as "Survival Guides to T.V. Advertising" for kids. Hosted by Jim Fyfe, the programs included:

- A comparison of the commercial for the toy Typhoon II with the real-life experiences of children using it. (The toy sank rather than skimmed across the water, was much harder to operate, and had a short battery life.)
- A comparison of the commercial for GI Joe Battle Copter with the real experience. (The toy flew a short distance into the air and crashed, unlike the models in the commercial that were kept aloft with fishing line and powered by small electric motors to simulate ongoing flight.)
- A comparison of the promises for the Burger King Kids Club with reality. (One interviewed child described it as a "rip-off.")
- A look at the commercial asking "Who's the Number One Fan of New Kids on the Block?" (If a child were to buy all the items celebrating the singing group featured in the commercial it would cost $341.84.)
- A look at celebrity-endorsed athletic shoe advertising—for example, "Gotta be the shoes." (Tests with kids indicated that they couldn't help kids to run faster or jump higher.)
- A look at cereal toys, featuring the offer of "3D" baseball cards found in special boxes of Kelloggs Corn Flakes. (It was estimated that it would take 73 boxes to acquire all 15 cards in the set.)
- A test of 72 devoted Coke and Pepsi drinkers to see if they could identify their favorite brand (with RC Cola added to the test) in unmarked glasses. (50% of Pepsi drinkers guessed wrong, 75% of Coke drinkers.)

> The Consumer Reports Television programs also asserted that:
> - A can of regular Coke contains the equivalent of 10 teaspoons of sugar.
> - "Gushers" and "Fruit Roll Ups" are implicitly and explicitly promoted as "wholesome fruit snacks," yet contain no fruit.
> - Heavily promoted orange beverages such as Capri Sun, Tang, and Minute Maid Orange Punch contain less than 15 percent juice.
> - The odds of winning the Cookie Crisp cereal sweepstakes are 1,999,999 to 1.
> - The popular and heavily advertised cereal Golden Crisp contains the equivalent of 67 teaspoons of sugar in a 10-ounce box.
> - Heavily promoted sport drinks (e.g., "Gotta be like Mike") are "high-priced sugar water with fancy names."[9]

The trade magazine *Advertising Age* asked prominent practitioners to review one of the programs ("Buy Me That Too!").

Bob Garfield, Editor-at-Large of the publication, said that it provided "an illuminating inside look at the tricks of the trade in advertising to children," but was concerned that "kids are apt to leave the show with an *unhealthy* suspicion about the Business World." The ultimate responsibility "for dealing with slick 'n sleazy kids marketing," he observed, lies with the parent.

John O'Toole, former president of the American Association of Advertising Agencies, asserted he would "give the concept a thumbs up, the execution a thumbs down," observing that "there is nothing wrong with commenting on advertising to children." "It's reality," he continued, to "caution that advertising is really there to sell you something, that it's not going to tell you everything that's wrong with the product." But, he contends, "kids already know that," and if the producers' "goal was to take on the mantle of protecting kids, it's naive." Like Garfield, he wondered, "Where are the parents who are saying 'no'?"[10]

Even a casual examination of the *Consumer Report* magazine for children, *Zillions*, or its predecessor, *Penny Power*, reveals a staunch "Be on your guard!" stance in relation to advertising. So, then, does its television version, the "Buy Me That" series. They are implying an ethical system in striking contrast to that pervading the advertising business in general, and those who advertise to young children in particular. Garfield may be exaggerating when he cautions that the program(s) "portray the idea of selling as essentially sinister and portray commerce as very nearly an evil force," but there are no examples of helpful advertising presented. Keep in mind that the examples selected for the programs were from prominent companies and major advertisers, and none of the advertisements had been rejected by the television networks or stations as being potentially deceptive. Yet, clearly, the message from the programs is that these ads *do* mislead, in part through exaggeration and in part through information not included—for example, sugar content, cost, battery life. There is also no clear message as to where to get more complete information, but rather the warning that "You don't have to listen to [advertisers]."

The "Buy Me That" programs seem to suggest that if the child is the target (an appropriate word in this context) of the advertising, then he or she must also be ready to deal with it, presumably by ignoring it. So these advertisers, and presumably virtually all others, are perceived as acting unethically by over-promising and underinforming the audience they address.

By contrast, the quoted practitioners (and virtually all those who speak in defense of advertising to children) point to the role of the parent as gatekeeper, if not of what is watched, then certainly of what may or may not be bought. Therefore, it can be argued that advertising to children is an ethical practice because there are others to prevent unwise actions from being taken.

This stance raises some interesting questions. If the parents are to provide a dampening effect on presumably unwise requests from the children, how will the parents be able to make an informed judgment when they are not likely to have seen the advertising? Would they know, in the wisdom of their years, that the Typhoon II wouldn't perform as advertised? (Or even what a Typhoon II is?)

Or that Fruit Roll Ups contain no fruit? Or that it would take 73 boxes of corn flakes to acquire all the desired baseball cards? And if, as John O'Toole suggested, "kids already know that" (that advertising doesn't present all of the information), then why are parents needed in this role at all?

Notice, however, that both perspectives accept the presence of advertising and promotion to children, often very young children. This has not always been the case, and, indeed, the prominent special-interest group Action for Children's Television was founded more than 20 years ago in large part to pressure for the *elimination* of advertising directed toward very young children. So, if "Buy Me That" urges children to devalue the advertising directed to them, and spokespersons for advertising contend that parents should add an appropriate caution, perhaps another way of framing the ethical core might be by addressing these questions:

- Is it ethical to advertise to young children at all?
- If so, how can it be accomplished in a manner that provides a realistic picture of the value gained in the possible commercial exchange?

These questions are at the heart of one of the most controversial areas of modern advertising.

39. LARGER THAN LIFE

One of the accounts of a medium-sized West Coast advertising agency is a major regional potato chip company. The agency is preparing to launch a new campaign for the chips, and has sent commercial scripts to the production department. Mike Skillings, television production coordinator, reviewed the scripts and made preparations for taping. The script called for a party scene in which an attractive woman opens a bag of chips and pours them into a bowl. Mike made the necessary arrangements for the needed properties and talent, setting the videotaping for one week later.

Two days before, Mike received a phone call from Marsha Young, the account executive, who wanted to know if everything was ready. Mike assured her that the schedule looked good and that she should have the commercial on time. Marsha was pleased and explained that the new campaign was expected to play a major part in the success of the chips in an increasingly competitive snack food market.

At the taping the actors and actresses were briefed, and they rehearsed the scene. When the actress opened and emptied the bag of chips, some were, predictably, broken and discolored. At the end of the scene, Marsha called Mike aside and suggested that they open several bags of chips, collecting the light, unbroken chips to make one perfect bag. She argued that consumers know what to expect from chips, so no harm would be done by this simple exaggeration. After all, she said, think what the "food stylists" on the fast food accounts do to make an ordinary hamburger look irresistible:

cooking the meat only 20 seconds on a side to assure plumpness, painting the patty just so with food dye, using carefully iced lettuce, the "perfect" bun, and only the very best fries, chosen from dozens and dozens of trays. Puffery, Marsha concluded, is certainly an acceptable element of advertising expression.

She's right there, Mike thought. A certain amount of puffery is regarded as part of the advertising process, even by the Federal Trade Commission. Just leaf through a magazine and look at some of the headlines and slogans:

"In a League of its Own"

"It Just Feels Right"

"Sophisticated"

"The Symbol of Imported Luxury"

"A New Standard of Value in Sports Sedans"

So there was certainly plenty of verbal puffery. And Mike knew it was there in a visual sense as well. Not much attention had been paid to puffery through nonverbal symbols, but it was all around—exaggeration, a symbolic boast, a bit of presumably acceptable wishful thinking on the part of the advertiser—"promising what the people out there really want," as one advertising practitioner had put it. And with extraordinary talent and finesse as well. (Social historian Roland Marchand once observed that future historians would look to the American culture of the twentieth century and ask what kind of art commanded the greatest resources, the best talent: The answer, he asserted, would be advertising.) Consider just a few of the common dimensions of nonverbal advertising expression:

- The models chosen. Memorable. Frequently handsome, beautiful, muscular, slender, articulate, cute—as needed.
- The settings. Awful or splendid as the selling argument calls for. Quite often simply fanciful. Exotic or gritty. Elegant or pedestrian. Well chosen to stimulate the right mood.
- The colors. Show the girl with drab hair in somber colors, the one with revitalized no-fuss hair in brights. Paint a scene with emotion-evoking hues.
- The mood. Upbeat/exciting or dull/flat—at least until an application of the sponsor's product. Artfully orchestrated by music and setting.
- The graphics. Absolutely brilliant photography or cinematography. Crisp editing. Deft retouching. Careful matching of type of music with the mood desired (the colas were masters here).

These are common and acceptable practices, Mike knew. Sure they exaggerate. Advertising is almost always larger than life, isn't it? Perhaps because people want it to be. He remembered what Pierre Martineau, the researcher, had said: The consumer doesn't feel that he is being victimized or cheated by the retailer and the producer. On the contrary, he loves his stores and the mechanical triumphs of his age—the colorful automobiles, the pink washing machines, the garage doors with electric eyes. He is far, far more interested in the people who make Polaroid cameras and power tools, color TV sets and low-cost air conditioners than he is in what the intellectuals and politicians have to offer. This is what he works for; this is what he wants from life—not the frustrated pouting of some university hermit.

OK, Mike reflected, puffery may not be real life, but it doesn't seem to victimize either. So let the commercial's potato chips be a little better than they would normally be. The consumer's previous experience with chips—and advertising—should provide enough safeguards against deception.

Now, let's look for those "perfect" chips. . . .

Scholar Ivan Preston has noted that puffery in advertising receives forgiving legal treatment because it is assumed to have no effect, although it is used by advertisers because they believe it does. A "puffing" of claims about a product or service is generally to be expected in advertising, the courts have decided, and is presumed not likely to have any detrimental effect on even a relatively naive consumer. In short, the reasoning goes, when an advertiser says his product is the greatest, no one *really* believes it.

This perspective on puffery is based largely on assumptions rather than facts, but this situation may be changing. Several research studies have cast doubt on puffery's presumed noneffect and have demonstrated that the common form of puffery called "implied superiority claims" (e.g., "Nobody does it better") can have potentially misleading effects.

It is doubtful that this potato chip advertisement would result in any legal challenge, unless a competitor raised objections. This is, after all, a visual (rather than verbal) puff, and potato chips are not a product closely linked with health or safety concerns, such as, for example, a cereal extolling its contributions to lower cholesterol. No, most likely Mike would be able to offer the public a commercial with perfect chips without any legal ripples.

The ethics of the situation are somewhat more problematic. Deciding that "everybody does it," Mike is in essence embracing misrepresentation as part of the nature of that self-interested form of communication called advertising. In the process, he is apparently making certain unreflective assumptions about the audience, their capabilities, and their priorities: (1) People *are* deliberate and calculating. They have had previous experience with potato chips and will carry that experience over to this commercial. They realize that advertising is paid propaganda, and they will weigh their own experience against the advertising in favor of experience. (2) People are *not* deliberate and calculating. They live in worlds of symbols where colors, moods, design, and psychological and sociological suggestions are very real parts of their lives. Hence, they frequently confront exaggeration in many facets of their lives and may, in fact, like it. (Scholar Theodore Levitt suggested that advertising serves the function of "alleviating imagery" for many consumers and thus should not be relegated to transmitting mere product information.)

Buttressed with these all-encompassing assumptions, it is not surprising that Mike could conclude that puffery is not likely to victimize the individual. In the first case, an individual is constantly on guard against advertising's exaggerations, and this defensive posture is usually adequate. In the second case, the individual apparently *welcomes* the blandishments of the advertisements, a willing seduction. Here the encounter is between not adversaries, but friends.

In the *first* case, Mike is shifting the moral burden of what is right to potential consumers. Let them be on guard. Let them filter advertisements through their own experiences and make appropriate judgments. Here, Mike sees humankind as deliberate and calculating, as envisioned under classical liberal philosophy: Let the buyer beware, *caveat emptor.* But should Mike endorse the *second* set of assumptions, the responsibility shifts back to the advertiser, for he is dealing with a vulnerable public, one open to the spinning of symbolic meanings and the manipulation of priorities. Here, Mike justifies his decision with greater difficulty.

In any case, he has refused to examine his assumptions in light of the conditions of the situation. He could, for example, ask that a rough cut of the commercial be tested with both a perfect and a normal bag. If individuals are left with the impression that these chips are more likely to be lighter and unbroken than those of competitors, then it is clear that normal chips must be used if the public is to be served. If there is no difference reported in the test, however, then no practical harm (or good) would seem likely to occur. There would, however, still remain the more fundamental question of whether, *regardless of the consequences,* it is right to misrepresent the experience an ordinary consumer is likely to have with this or any product.

From the perspective of Preston's observation that puffery is not extensively regulated because it is assumed that it *doesn't* work, and it is used by advertisers because it *does* work, it could be contended that Mike made his decision about puffery in an extremely casual manner. With further consideration, Mike might have concluded that (1) if it *does* make a difference, then it is at least wrong on ethical grounds and probably on legal grounds as well; and (2) if it does *not* make a difference, why indulge in the exaggeration anyway, particularly when its effect in the long run may be a further devaluation of advertising as a credible medium of market information.

Simply put, the chips do *not* look perfect under normal circumstances. Mike concluded that it was permissible to suggest they do. In the process, he apparently assumed both a "guarded" and an "open" model of potential consumers, yet he also assumed that the responsibility should rest with the consumer in both cases. However supported, expediency triumphed over reflection.

NOTES

1. "Old Joe Must Go," *Advertising Age,* 13 January 1992.
2. J. R. DiFranza, J. W. Richards, P. M. Paulman, N. Wolf-Gillespie, C. Fletcher, R. D. Jaffe, and D. Murray, "RJR Nabisco's Cartoon Camel Promotes Camel Cigarettes to Children,"

Journal of the American Medical Association 266, 11 December 1991, pp. 3149-3153; P. M. Fischer, M. P. Schwartz, J. W. Richards, A. O. Goldstein, and T. H. Rojas, "Brand Logo Recognition by Children Aged 3 to 6 Years," *Journal of the American Medical Association* 266, 11 December 1991, pp. 3145-3148; J. P. Pierce, E. Gilpin, D. M. Burns, E. Whalen, B. Rosbrook, D. Shopland, and M. Johnson, "Does Tobacco Advertising Target Young People to Start Smoking?" *Journal of the American Medical Association* 266, 11 December 1991, pp. 3154-3158.

3. "Shampoos," *Consumer Reports*, (September 1984): 194.

4. "Hand and Bath Soaps," *Consumer Reports*, (January 1985): 52-55.

5. Rosser Reeves, quoted in Martin Mayer, *Madison Avenue, U.S.A.* (New York: Harper Brothers, 1958), p. 3.

6. Howard Luck Gossage, *Is There Any Hope for Advertising?* (Urbana: University of Illinois Press, 1986), p. 61.

7. Roger Draper, "The Faithless Shepherd," *New York Times*, 26 June 1986, p. 18.

8. "How to Save $2500 a Year at the Supermarket," *Consumer Reports* (March 1988): 163.

9. "Buy Me That!" Consumer Reports Television, shown on Home Box Office, December 1992.

10. Bob Garfield and John O'Toole, quoted in "Kids Ad Special Raises Some Eyebrows of Critics," *Advertising Age,* 10 February 1992.

chapter 9

Media Considerations

For most of this century, U.S. newspapers and magazines have relied heavily on advertising revenue as a source of income. Virtually from their inception, radio and television networks and stations sought their funds for operation and profit from advertising subsidy. In this arrangement, the media exist in part as conduits of advertising messages to particular audiences—serving to gather them together for advertisers.

The larger consequences of this accommodation will be discussed in the next chapter. Here we concern ourselves with the ethical confrontations faced by some who work for the media in their unique and sensitive positions between advertisers and audiences. The very nature of these positions is central to many of the problems raised in this chapter. Among the more important:

- Which advertisers will be granted access to the pages or to airtime in order to expose their message to a particular audience?
- What are the ethical considerations when the interests of the media channel and those of the advertiser conflict?
- How should media personnel use confidential information gleaned from their normal exposure to advertisers who are often competing for the same business?
- Are all media appropriate vehicles for advertisements?

The answers, and the ethical consequences, are very important indeed.

40. GATEKEEPERS I: NONE OF "THOSE ADS" IN THIS PAPER

Some days, Andy Scott thought, being an advertising manager for a newspaper is a lot more painful than it seems. Today was one of those days. Andy was responsible for the advertising content of the *Telegraph,* a monopoly newspaper in a northeastern city with a population of 100,000. The matter causing him anxiety at the moment was a relatively innocuous ad for a local group of gays. It was a straightforward announcement of the availability of a "Gay Switchboard" in the community. He was now ready to reject the ad, but not without some second-guessing.

The issue had some history. Several years earlier, a similar ad had been brought to the paper. A representative from the advertising department had deemed it controversial and had taken it to the owner of the paper. The owner declared he wanted none of "those ads" in his paper. Subsequently, the board of directors supported the position, although there was not then, nor was there now, a written policy.

The gay organization took its case to court—and lost. This outcome was hardly surprising, since the courts have generally interpreted freedom of the press to mean freedom to publish or broadcast, not freedom of access, even to the "rented" advertising space or time.

Now the group was trying again. Its arguments were basically:

- The *Telegraph* provides the only print medium to reach virtually all of the community with any degree of efficiency.
- The information in the ad is not inflammatory. It simply offers a telephone number to facilitate counseling and other support activities.
- The paper has run ads from the organization before—both in display space and in the classified section—although they were not as prominent as this particular message.
- The paper runs news stories about gay groups.

Andy had even agreed to meet with a local Presbyterian minister, who was speaking on behalf of the group's request to send what it considered to be a reasonable message (the availability of the telephone number) to the community at large. Andy had explained that policy was policy and that any previous appearance of an ad by a gay group was due to lapses in the gatekeeping system—for example, new employees accepting ads, or the owner being out of town. This was simply one of those categories of products or services (along with ads for massage parlors, X-rated movies, real estate scams, etc.) that were simply rejected because the owner did not want the readers exposed to them.

There is, Andy knew, the argument that the "rented" space of a newspaper should be open to all to ensure that the "marketplace of ideas," held dear by libertarians, could function properly. After all, they argue, the newspaper controls the editorial content, so shouldn't the advertising spaces be available to anyone with something legitimate to say? Indeed, if the paper trusts people to make up their minds when faced with divergent positions on the editorial page, should it then assume that these same individuals cannot cope with some diversity in the advertising content?

But it may not, Andy thought, be all that simple. Where, for example, were those ideals when the liberal campus newspaper recently pulled an informative ad from the White Aryan Resistance after "adverse reactions," or when the campus paper publicly apologized to outraged feminists after running a Miller beer supplement with a tongue-in-cheek guide to sun, surf, and sexual conquests over spring break? What happened to the cherished "marketplace of ideas" then?

Well, the law is certainly on our side, Andy thought. There's no doubt about that. This is, after all, a privately owned newspaper, and the owner can decide what does—and does not—get in, based on his particular standards as well as those he perceives to be in "the community interest."

Well, the policy and the law are clear. Might as well get on with the rejection. . . .

There is no question of the *Telegraph*'s legal right to control both the editorial and advertising content of the newspaper, and the existing "policy" could certainly be seen to lie solely on an assertion of ethical egoism: It is right to reject ads from gays because the owner says it is right. (The board of directors was brought into the picture only after the fact.)

Andy recognized that there were other categories of products and services that the paper would not accept—solicitations of one sort or another, massage parlors, and so forth—but this "no exceptions" absolutism was not carried over to other potentially sensitive product or service categories, such as cigarettes or liquor. (Apparently all of the other advertisements submitted are accepted or rejected solely on the basis of individual content.)

A utilitarianism rationale would certainly seem to require a thoughtful consideration of the newspaper's audience (as in "the greatest good for the greatest number"). Was there any assurance that the newspaper readership would, in fact, find the advertisement objectionable here? If this issue was put to a test, the ad could be run and the "market" would speak, in terms of indifference, protests, canceled subscriptions, and so forth. But in this case, considerations of the audience seem to be implicit rather than explicit—the publisher may have assumed that the readers of his paper would find this advertising objectionable.

There was certainly no attempt to establish a middle ground through compromise or accommodation. Following this perspective might have involved evaluating each advertisement for gay or lesbian organizations on the basis of its own merits, perhaps rejecting those that were perceived as provocative but accepting those with strong informational content.

Yet, regardless of how relatively straightforward this particular situation may seem, it must be emphasized that Andy's decision to reject the ad on behalf of the publisher's unwritten "policy" has serious practical and ethical consequences. Practically, it denies a potential advertiser access to tens of thousands of readers that can not be reached through any other print vehicle.

Ethically, an intriguing perspective is the issue of where loyalty is owed. The owner of the *Telegraph* could contend that the policy is based on loyalty to the paper's audience, but there is no evidence that the audience members share his particular biases. Indeed, they are denied the opportunity to express an opinion. If the loyalty could be seen as wholly subjective (i.e., it's right because the publisher says it's right), we are confronted with the power of private property (the newspaper) as a vehicle to serve public needs, but driven by the perspective of a single individual.

The owner is clearly on solid legal ground in his role as part of the largely privately owned media system of the United States. In that role, he and his staff are gatekeepers to determine content for often powerful vehicles of mass information and entertainment, including that found in the "rented" space and time. They determine what their audiences will see, or not see.

Where does—and should—loyalty lie for these advertising gatekeepers?

41. GATEKEEPERS II: TAKING THE HEAT ABOUT ABORTION

Well, Alice Jeffers thought, this is what is to be expected when you make a decision about an issue that sharply divides people. She had just completed a telephone conversation (more a monologue than a conversation) with a listener of her central Ohio radio station, serving a town of about 50,000.

"How dare you," the caller had begun, "run those horrible right-to-life commercials!" By this time, Alice knew the commercials well:

- One noted that there were more than 1.5 million babies killed by abortion annually, and more than 18 million since 1973—"More than all the American solders killed in all our wars." "The most dangerous place in America today," the announcement concluded, "is inside a mother's womb."
- Another played an eight-week-old fetal heartbeat, followed by a period of silence.
- One stated that a beating heart, brain waves, organs, and so on are all functioning shortly after conception.
- Still another asserted that when a 7-pound, 2-ounce baby was born it wasn't the first day of her life—"just the first time we get to *see* her."

Alice had expected feedback—predominately negative, as those in agreement with something rarely take the time to let us know their opinions. And so far she had taken about half a dozen calls, including this one. Well, they should have heard *another* ad that the local right-to-life group had wanted to run but that Alice had rejected:

"Gee Mom, did you notice that I have fingers now, and . . . can you feel me kicking? And Mom, I can hear what's going on. Could you tell me, when you were talking to the doctor, what 'abortion' means?"

Alice explained her position to each caller: She knew the subject of the ads was controversial, but she found the ads honest, and she and the station management were trying to treat their listeners as adults. In order to be fair, she had contacted pro-choice groups to see if they would be interested in running responses, but they were not, even though she knew that the National Organization for Women probably had prepared pro-choice ads for local groups, just as these spots being used by the local pro-life group had been prepared by National Right to Life.

She knew that print versions of these same ads had run in the local newspaper, but she knew that the radio spots were particularly likely to strike a response because of the "guest-in-your-home" nature of radio, as well as the impact of the human voice, sound effects, music, and so forth. Still, she felt confident in her rationale and her station's policy. It was, after all, an election year, this was a controversial and topical subject, and she had tried to be fair.

What were some of Alice's options in this situation?

1. to refuse to accept the right-to-life spots because of their controversial topic, or their execution;
2. to accept all the spots, letting the audience members—not the station management—make their own judgments about the subject matter and treatment;
3. to accept some of the spots, but eliminate those considered most likely to offend;
4. to accept some of the spots, and also seek out opposing points of view.

In accepting the fourth option, Alice was apparently seeking a middle ground by, first, refusing to air at least one of the spots, thus presumably protecting her audience, and second, alerting the pro-choice groups that these ads would be running and inquiring whether they wished to use advertising of their own. (Of course, it could be contended that she was not being idealistic at all, that she was simply interested in increasing the station's revenues, although both pro-life and pro-choice groups tend to operate on extremely limited budgets.)

By "protecting" her audience, even with the rejection of one radio spot, Alice was not, of course, being entirely true to the ideal of the "marketplace of ideas," but was certainly motivated by that standard, albeit tempered by a sense of "social responsibility." She permitted a partisan position on a controversial (but important) subject to be aired, and made an effort to air the other contending point of view as well. Her critical assumptions of "human nature" clearly include the ability of individuals to make their own judgments, and the idea that the "greater good" is served by exposing individuals to all ranges of opinion (at least "paid" opinion) on issues—particularly controversial ones—even though some listeners will be offended in the process.

It is, we feel, helpful to note Alice's actions in relation to those of the *Telegraph* in the preceding case, particularly given the intrusive nature of the commercial time on radio versus the relatively passive presence of print forms.

Should an audience be protected from some types of advertising? This is, in many ways, the most central of the issues facing the gatekeepers of the media's "rented" time and space.

42. ADVICE FROM A BIASED SOURCE?

The advertising manager for retail accounts had just issued the marching orders. Given the tight economic times, increasing pressure from the free-subscription all-advertising shopper, and the aggressiveness of television salespeople, the newspaper was beginning to see a decline in its retail advertising. The message was clear: We need to be more assertive in promoting the use of our newspaper's advertising space by the community's retailers. Sell them on the idea of

- the newspaper as a preferred advertising medium;
- this newspaper as the best of that breed;
- frequent advertising versus infrequent;
- big space versus small space.

That, Dick Lutz thought, is the nature of the business, at least in his 10 years in selling advertising space to retailers. Newspapers are convinced that they need substantial advertising subsidies in order to function. As retailers' budgets become uncertain and competition becomes tighter, that income source is threatened, and then comes the call to the barricades. Sell harder! Be more creative! Become indispensable to your accounts!

There, Dick reflected, may be the heart of the dilemma that virtually all media salespeople face—at least those who think beyond the task at hand. Advertising, by its very nature, is an uncertain process. Most advertisers, most of the time, are not able to determine with any accuracy just what they are getting for their advertising dollars. And although retailers are closer to the actual sales transaction than a manufacturer like Procter & Gamble, the problem is no less real.

For example, maybe the ad was fine, but the timing was lousy. The timing may have been fine, but the ad was not. Both may have been great, but competitors were more effective. In addition, few retailers are able to use the expertise of advertising agencies, so they often handle advertising in their free moments or delegate it to some idle employee. Sometimes this practice works to their advantage; frequently it does not.

As the professional selling advertising, Dick can offer at least the appearance of expertise to retailers struggling with the question of advertising—and at no cost. The actual preparation of a newspaper ad—the writing of copy and the physical layout—can be provided by the paper's staff, without charge. Within this set of expectations—a desirable service offered in an ambiguous area—it was hardly surprising that Dick and his colleagues would be consulted for answers to more fundamental questions such as: "When should I advertise?" "How big should my ad be?" From the paper's economic perspective, the answer to these questions was simple: Advertise as much as you possibly can. (Dick also knew that it would be desirable to encourage advertising in the paper's advertising-light editions, Monday and Saturday, rather than the popular Wednesday and Friday issues.)

Of course, his own financial future was linked to the paper's prosperity, both directly (in terms of the commissions he earns) and indirectly (in relation to the paper's overall financial health). Ideally, as retailers prosper through increased advertising, so will the paper. But those reasons rarely allowed Dick the opportunity to move beyond his self-interest to suggest, for example:

- "You don't need to advertise as much as you're doing now."
- "You can get by with smaller space than you're using."
- "I honestly think you'd be better off in radio."
- Or (horror of horrors), "Jack, I really think you'd be better off not advertising at all and putting the money into hiring better salespeople."

In the land of the blind, Dick mused, the one-eyed man is king. He may not have all the answers about advertising's effectiveness, but his experience can certainly be helpful to uncertain retailers. But should his advice be followed when his motives are so clearly directed by self-interest? What kind of person can rise above self-interest when it conflicts with the well-being of another? Perhaps a salesperson who is thereafter unemployed?

The ethical dilemma Dick Lutz faces is common for media personnel dealing with unsophisticated advertisers. Under the best of circumstances and intentions, advertising is an uncertain process. Because of the host of other variables that can confound a simple cause-and-effect assumption, even giant advertisers with state-of-the-art research are often unsure exactly what they should be saying, to whom, and with what size and frequency. And, for every advertising colossus, there are thousands of small producers and retailers whose advertising savvy is extremely limited. They represent a potentially vulnerable population.

It is often difficult to get some retailers to advertise at all ("I tried it once and nothing happened") or to switch from one medium to another ("I've had good luck with radio; why should I use television?"). Once an account has been established, a salesperson can become a regular partner in the advertising efforts of the store, and the door is open for him or her to become something more than simply an order taker.

Dick can satisfy himself with the knowledge that the services he and his paper provide—particularly the actual preparation of the ads—are valuable to many retailers, and may well increase their advertising efficiency. Indeed, the advice and services that he offers often approach the ideal of enlightened self-interest for all parties ("We help you because you're advertising with us, and if you succeed you'll advertise more with us). But Dick knows full well that the formula (Big Ads + High Frequency = Success) does not work for all retailers all the time. Then what are his options?

His first choice is to seek the self-interest of the newspaper in all situations. Often that results in sound advice for the advertiser as well. If not, the decision to advertise still belongs to the retailer, who is certainly aware that an ad salesperson is a biased advisor. Therefore, moral duty is owed first to the paper, and second to the retailer, assuming the harmony of self-interests.

Dick's second alternative is to serve the best interests of the retailer in all situations. As the retailer perceives that in some situations Dick may be operating against the newspaper's short-term interests, respect may grow. The result could be more business in the long run, either from that retailer or from others who come to respect Dick's advice. Then when Dick does recommend a major campaign that would obviously benefit the newspaper, his suggestion may be taken more seriously. The *potential* market payoff can be long term rather than short term.

Dick's dilemma is intensified by the reality of the marketplace. His media competitors—salespeople for the weekly newspapers, radio and television stations, and others—are likely attempting to persuade the same retailers from their own narrowly defined self-interests. Thus, if Dick pursues the retailer-sensitive option, the newspaper may suffer losses on some of his accounts, at least in the short run. Since the advertising manager's call to the barricades was stimulated by current losses, how receptive will he be to Dick's argument that unbiased advice will benefit the paper in the long run? "If they want unbiased advice, let them hire a consultant," may well be the manager's reply.

Depending on the depth of his moral convictions, that may be another option Dick could pursue. By quitting his newspaper job and becoming a hired consultant to retailers, he could use his knowledge of the local advertising scene to benefit all of his clients, and in a far more objective manner.

But that is a difficult and uncertain way to earn a living.

43. INSIDE INFORMATION—I

As a food advertising specialist for a northeastern city's dominant newspaper, Kristine Larrimore called on the supermarkets and specialized food stores of the area. Depending on their needs, she would simply take their prepared advertising and arrange for scheduling, or get information for an ad to be turned over to the paper's copy department for layout and production. Given the monopoly position of her paper, little hard selling was necessary. Rather, she simply pointed out opportunities in upcoming food supplements and the like, and when necessary downplayed the growing number of free shopper papers that some advertisers were beginning to find attractive.

In the course of her job, Kristine acquired a great deal of inside information concerning promotional plans and general advertising philosophies of her regular advertisers. One morning a few weeks before Thanksgiving, a manager in one of the city's largest supermarket chain stores made clear just how much that information was worth.

First, Joe Gibbons reminded her of the cutthroat nature of food retailing, particularly during uncertain economic times. Second, he pointed out that the ultimate beneficiary of all this competition was the consumer. Then came the clincher. Joe offered Kristine $500 for one small piece of information: the Thanksgiving turkey prices of his chief competitor, Saveco. "Frankly," Joe pointed out, "we don't want to go any lower than necessary. But if we knew Saveco's price, we could at least match it, if not undercut it. The customer wins, and you'll be $500 richer for helping."

In that awkward moment, Kristine refused. (She wondered later if she would have done the same thing if her paper had not been in a near monopoly position, and Joe had had someplace else to go.) First, she told Joe that the paper explicitly forbids the leaking of confidential information to interested parties. (She knew, of course, that there were breaches of that policy.) Then she told him that if she shared such information with him there was no guarantee she would not share his prices with someone else when it was in her interest to do so. To work efficiently for both of us, she said, we have to trust one another.

Joe was embarrassed and angry. Without the information he wanted so badly, he set his turkey prices and found them two cents a pound higher than those of Saveco. His chain suffered relatively heavy sales losses on turkey and related sales during this peak period.

Kristine's subsequent dealings with Joe could be best characterized as strained, but over time they regained much of their previous rapport.

This case provides an opportunity to use relatively structured ethical criteria for examining four fundamental questions for ethical analysis:

1. What makes a right act right? Joe apparently felt it was right to offer a bribe to Kristine because it was in his company's best interest to do so. (His allusions to a public benefit are a point to be examined later.) Kristine initially equated "right" with her paper's policy: Her employer explicitly forbids sharing information from another client. Her second argument, however, transcends that limited standard. The criterion that violating the trust of advertisers is simply wrong, regardless of the consequences or the guidelines imposed by others, depends on universal principles such as justice and fairness. Does it say anything about her own standards to note the order of her argument?

2. To whom is moral duty owed? Joe felt that he had a moral duty to his company. By serving his food store, he argued, he would ultimately be serving others, namely his customers. Kristine first suggested that her duty was to her

employer. Second, she asserted that she had an obligation to her clients, those advertisers she contacts on behalf of the paper.

3. What kinds of acts are right? The contrast here is particularly instructive. Joe was concerned with the consequences of the situation. His self-interest is evident, but he also argued that the public would benefit; in other words, it offered the greatest good for the greatest number. The strength of this conviction weakens, however, with his admission that he has no desire to price his turkeys any lower than necessary. His profit margin was an important factor. There was the unspoken concern that, without Kristine's information, he might price his turkeys too low (for him, not the public). Kristine, by contrast, argued on a relatively more formal level. Regardless of the consequences, she felt the bribe was wrong, specifically because her paper forbids it, and generally because it would represent a breach of faith. Obviously, the second rationale is more fundamental than the first.

4. How do rules apply to specific situations? Joe was stressing the importance of this particular set of circumstances. Kristine, in the first instance, was equally concerned with this particular situation since it was covered in her employer's rules. Her fairness argument, however, touched on basic standards of human conduct that transcend specific circumstances.

Both parties felt guilty: Joe, because he recognized that his action transgressed accepted norms and he was held to account on their behalf; Kristine, because her client had been compromised and, perhaps, because she was uncertain how much of her decision was due to leverage created by her newspaper's monopoly position.

Kristine's initial reliance on the situation-specific criteria to make her decision suggests that her ethical standards could be compromised in the future. How will she decide when the company's rules do not cover a particular situation? Are her more universal standards of fairness and justice strong enough to stand the pressure of a moment without the support of her employer's rule book?

Ethical thinking requires reflection and analysis. Lacking that, an individual may assume a mantle of righteousness when one is, in fact, a prisoner of events, without a reliable moral compass.

44. INSIDE INFORMATION—II

The classified advertising section of any reputable daily newspaper comes as close to the ideal of pure market information as any advertising is likely to provide. Sellers and buyers find it a constantly renewing forum of exchange, generally free from the verbal and graphic hyperbole of the more pervasive display advertising. As such, its information is frequently prized.

Martha Louwens, a twenty-eight-year-old mother of two, had recently reentered the work force as a classified advertising salesperson for the town's only paper. Actually "salesperson" was misleading. Basically she was an order taker. Individuals would call when they had decided to place a classified ad. Martha and her colleagues would then tell them the rates and take down the exact wording for the ad or, rarely, help the customer compose the ad over the phone.

In this role Martha acquired a great deal of timely information. She learned of the availability of items prized by herself and her friends: used Nintendos for the kids, room air-conditioning units, used children's clothing, home furnishings in good condition, and so on. Then there were the job openings. Frequently employers listed a telephone number and placed priority on a first-come first-served basis for qualified applicants.

Since Martha had this information a day, or at least several hours, before the paper's next edition, she got into the habit of sharing the news with friends who she felt might be interested. (On some occasions she would follow up herself.) As a general rule she asked her friends to wait until just about the time the paper hit the streets. That way no suspicion could be cast on her or her department. Such caution had caused her friends to lose a few good opportunities to sharp-eyed early readers, but usually not. When someone can plan an action in advance, she or he can usually operate with considerable advantage.

Martha's caution indicated the presence of an ethical, if not administrative, question. Though there were no specific prohibitions, she knew that the information in the classifieds was intended for all the newspaper readership, not simply a select few and their friends. Indeed, some people out there could possibly use the items or jobs a great deal more than Martha or her friends. The classifieds as an open forum were less open when she handed out information in advance. She knew that.

Still, Martha was not troubled enough to stop. First, it happened with only a small fraction of the material she handled. Also, it was the purpose of a classified to sell the item, fill the job, or whatever, wasn't it? She was certainly facilitating that. Finally, she had to admit, there was the special feeling of being an insider who could offer her friends favored treatment. She might not be able to give them inside information on Wall Street, or tips on a "hot" restaurant, but at least this was something.

Martha is scarcely a shaker and mover in the advertising business. Yet, even in an ordinary job dealing with matters of little economic significance, she confronts ethical decisions.

Apparently, she feels vaguely guilty. Why? It is not clear whether her co-workers offer similar favors to their friends, but the basic cause for her uneasiness may be that she knows she is violating the spirit if not the letter of the newspaper's policies. Would she have acted in the same way if the ethical dimensions had been made explicit? Since it was her first venture into the workplace since her children were born, her desire to feel important may have proven too strong even then. In any case, the absence of a specific rule has allowed her the latitude to act on her own.

Who is served by her actions? Without doubt the seller, who is usually not concerned with who buys, merely that someone does, and as rapidly as possible. Her friends benefit, of course—an inside track on bargains or a desirable job is extremely valuable. And, at the heart of the matter, Martha benefits by feeling she is important to others in a job whose objective dimensions are not likely to impress.

Martha has apparently constructed her rationale so that her decision making has become routine. She will provide information to friends unless it is of no use to them. Thus, her rule of serving the relatively small universe of self, friends, and seller supersedes the spirit of fairness.

Suppose Martha encountered Rawls's veil of ignorance, and was unsure whether she would emerge as the ad taker with inside information or as a member of the public at large, interested in good buys and good jobs; would she choose the course she now follows, or assure access to the marketplace for *all* the newspaper's readers?

Given that the purpose of the classified ad is to sell, never mind to whom, and the relatively elusive notion of fairness in this case, it may be that responsibility lies with the newspaper's administration to develop an ethical code that explicitly protects the interests of all the readers of the paper.

Yet, Martha's personal ethical code raises questions, not only about her own moral integrity, but about the effects of her actions on others. Jules Feiffer called his book about the day-to-day tribulations of living in New York City *Little Murders*. Similarly, it is the little compromises of people such as Martha that establish and maintain a working environment where short-run advantage triumphs over long-term integrity—and personal gain over potential fairness.

45. THE CAPTIVE AUDIENCE

Susan Lomax put down the phone. As an executive in a large American motion picture chain, she and her company were under virtually constant pressure to accept cinema advertising (screen commercials or advertiser-related music videos featuring popular music performers to be shown before features).

It wasn't as if they hadn't given it a try, she thought. Over the years, they had experimented with advertising for national and regional advertisers in the United States, in addition to local merchant advertising during the Christmas season, and even audio spots, advertising messages played over the theater sound systems behind a blank screen.

A decision to accept cinema advertising assures virtually "found money" for the theater owners, who receive about a third of the income paid by national advertisers such as Hasbro, who for the 1992 Christmas season backed their popular Transformer action figure with an "unprecedented multi-million dollar campaign debuting strictly on movie screens"—in this case, 800 Cineplex-Odeon and Screenvision theaters.

Some survey data indicate that theatergoers respond favorably to big budget ads made specifically for cinema presentation, with Screenvision claiming that although two-thirds of those polled objected to the idea of cinema advertising going into the theater, two-thirds said they liked the spots after they had seen them.

As might be expected, the very nature of the cinema advertising experience promotes extremely high advertising recall for advertisers. As a recent ad for Cineplex-Odeon's "Cinespot" trumpeted to national advertisers:

> A Clutter-Free Environment. Fully Integrated Marketing Programs. *Featuring* Creative Freedom.
>
> A Captive Audience. No Zipping or Zapping.

All true, reflected Susan, but since the early 1990s her company had decided on a policy against any commercial advertising on the screen except those promoting other films. This decision, she knew, was based at least in part on the corporate judgment that advertising was simply not something that patrons expected—or appreciated—as part of their motion picture experience.
Susan liked that.

This case gives us the opportunity to examine the situation from the viewpoints of the interested parties: the advertisers, the theater owners, and the audience.

THE ADVERTISERS

The "captive" nature of the audience in the viewing situation can certainly result in much greater attention being paid to an advertisement than in the often distraction-laden environment of television viewing. There is also ample evidence that cinema advertisements are generally remembered longer and in more detail than the typical television commercial. Costs are a bit of a concern. The production costs for an advertisement that will do justice to the cinema setting are high. This may, however, be offset to some extent by cutting out shorter versions of the ad for television, thus stretching the production dollar. In a relative sense, buying exposure on screens for cinema advertising is more expensive than buying television time, but the virtually assured impact of the message may more than compensate. And what of possible theatergoer backlash? Well, there is certainly concern about adverse reaction, but it can be rationalized by the creation of "special," more entertaining commercials.

THE THEATER OWNERS

The foremost advantage is obvious: a source of income without direct expense. Yet, only a minority of theaters in this country carry cinema advertising. This might seem curious, since theater owners are pressured by rising costs and uncertain revenues from ticket sales and concessions, as well as often demanding arrangements from major suppliers—for example, agreements to run a feature at least so many weeks, and so forth. Thus, an additional source of income—particularly one of virtually "pure profit"—could be compelling. Yet many theater owners have chosen not to participate—at least at the moment.

THE AUDIENCE

Cinema advertising would seem to have two distinguishing characteristics for the movie-going audience:

1. Cinema movies are probably the only major mass medium that people have traditionally been accustomed to experiencing *without* advertising, other than that for other films.
2. It is, arguably, the only prominent form of advertising that does not in some way require the assent of the potential receiver. And it provides no reasonable possibility of choice concerning exposure to the message. With magazines, newspapers, radio, and television, individuals are aware that they will be exposed to advertising. They can, if they wish, choose to avoid it in one manner or another. With cinema advertising the individual is neither forewarned, nor able to choose not to participate without extraordinary action—for example, leaving the theater or closing one's eyes and plugging one's ears. There have been reports that "hoots and howls are common when commercials flash onto screens in New York City," and columnist Donald Kaul urged nothing less than an audience revolt—"When people treat you cheap, it's important to let them know you notice."

Susan's company's decision to decline the obvious financial benefit of cinema advertising was presumably based on concern for the audience. Given that many polls about public reaction to cinema ads are based on the *absence of hostile reaction*—for example, 65 percent "don't mind them" or two-thirds are opposed going in but tolerant of what they've been forced to see going out—it is difficult to argue that the theater-going public is well served by this advertising form in a previously commercial-free environment.

To decide to accept cinema advertising ethically, then, would seem to require a relatively narrow conception of who is benefited—the advertiser, the theater owner, and the company supplying the ads, rather than the "captive audience": moviegoers.

Apparently, for at least one motion picture chain, the equation was solved in favor of the audience.

chapter **10**

Macro Issues

In this final chapter of our inquiry into the ethical dimensions of advertising, we present not case histories, but issues that are inherent in the practices of advertising. That is, all advertising must face questions of setting priorities; all advertising must face questions of whether or not its presence is welcome, or an intrusion; all advertising in using the mass media must face questions of the effects of that usage; and all advertising is intended to affect resource allocation.

These aspects are simply part of the advertising process, which gives us a great deal to grapple with here. As we shall see, whether advertising is considered good or evil is determined in large part by the assumptions made by individuals about such fundamental concepts as human nature, the proper role of the individual and the state, and so on. Predictably, these are not issues with starkly clear resolutions, but it is hoped that highlighting several of these overarching dynamics will stimulate discussion of these complex and important ethical dimensions inherent in the omnipresent institution of advertising.

46. THE PRIORITIES OF ADVERTISING

Sometime during the mid-to-late 1990s, the Pontifical Council for Social Communication of the Roman Catholic Church will conclude a study concerning the moral dimensions of advertising. "Because of the importance of advertising in all areas of communications," Archbishop John P. Foley stated, "a number of [Council] members thought it was important to examine the ethics of advertising." The trade paper *Advertising Age* reports that "the industry appears to be more apprehensive about the investigation of advertising by the Catholic Church than by almost any other group, including the federal government."[1]

There will certainly be no shortage of subjects for inquiry, but among the more important is also one of the most elusive—the question of whether or not advertising has a significant affect on fundamental priorities of the citizens of this society. Consider:

- Social observer Christopher Lasch contends that advertising "manufactures a product of its own: the consumer, perpetually unsatisfied, restless, anxious, and bored. Advertising serves not so much to advertise products as to promote consumption as a way of life."[2]
- Social reformers Michael Jacobson and Ronald Collins warn that "Value alternatives beyond those of the marketplace are disappearing. The very idea of *citizen* has become synonymous with *consumer*."

Jacobson and Collins elaborate that "rampant commercialism," works *against* such desirable priorities as:

- "psychological well-being"—where advertising "purposefully promotes envy, creates anxiety, and fosters insecurity";
- "communal values"—where "civic-mindedness is an alien concept to a people mesmerized by consumer goods"; and
- "egalitarian values"—where "differences between the commercial 'haves' and 'have-nots' become synonymous with one's rank in society."[3]

How do we begin to address these far-reaching concerns? First, perhaps, by asserting that, individually and collectively, advertisers are certainly attempting to alter priorities—to get their product, their brand, their idea, their suggested lifestyle, to the top of our mental priority lists. To get us to think: "I *must* see that movie. I *must* try that brand. *That* is a great way to live." (As a particularly arresting current example, it is estimated that the videotape version of *Jurassic Park* will be promoted to 98 percent of the adult population of the United States approximately 25.2 times for each individual in a 6-month period.)[4] Clearly, none have the power to compel, no matter how vast their promotional efforts. They do, however, have the power to *prevail*—prevail in our magazines and newspapers; prevail in our radio and television programs; prevail on the shelves, and in the store windows; ultimately, perhaps, prevail in our priorities.

Virtually all advertisers wish to do this. It is, again, part of the system. And so, then, are the ensuing ethical consequences.

As we have noted many times, advertising tends to thrive in economies that feature strong market dynamics: private property and private gain, the assumption that overt persuasion is permissible, and so forth. It is hardly surprising that practitioners of advertising frequently use the ideology of the market to defend and promote their craft. Thus, advertising is championed because it promotes competition among self-seeking advertisers who are always held in check by the inherent rationality of consumers and the relentless forces of competition. The mechanism of this constant interchange of self-interest is thought to be the "invisible hand," leading self-interests in directions that will ultimately serve the best interests of all.

To the charge that advertising by its nature attempts to direct human consciousness to serve the advertiser's self-interest (commonly commercial), the practitioners could easily respond that what works well for the successful advertiser also works well for customers—it is, they would say, the consumers who set the agenda, not us.

Consider by way of example the shifts in product planning/marketing/advertising strategy brought on by a single factor—the move toward lighter diets. Fast food outlets now routinely feature (and advertise) offerings such as salad bars and baked potatoes, while entire new chains are starting to specialize in "natural" foods. Low-calorie products are carried in any food store, no longer relegated to "dietary foods" sections. Products—and advertising—*followed* this growing national endorsement of healthier eating.

It is illuminating to note the "Trends to Watch in 1994" as predicted by the editors of *Advertising Age*. Among them are

Ready-to-drink iced tea;

Ethnic condiments;

On-line interactive services;

Preventative health care;

E-mail;

Family films;

Home shopping; and

Home voice mail.[5]

Changing public life conditions and styles, driven to a great extent by social/economic dynamics within the society, are certainly responsible for many of these consumer trends. To assume that they were created out of whole cloth by the direction of advertising requires a considerable leap of faith.

Then why the ethical concern? Perhaps because two of the key assumptions underlying the assumed harmony of interests of the market system (the rationality of the individual and the beneficial effects of competition) can be contested. We can also examine the inherent fairness of the system.

First, there is the matter of presumed rational decision making by the consumer. It has been well documented that most people, most of the time, are not careful shoppers by normative standards, and do not have extensive knowledge about alternatives, including the advantages of not buying at all. The continued success of brand-name products in the face of countless lower-priced and functionally comparable competitors serves as a case in point. Heavily advertised movies are frequently rewarded by strong initial patronage, regardless of the quality of the film. And so on. Thus, if consumers are not always driven by an internal voice of a deliberate and calculating nature, the argument for humankind's inherent good sense weakens, and the contention of manipulation is strengthened.

And what of the safeguard of competition? The ideologues of the classical market system assumed a large number of competitors offering virtually identical products, all competing on the basis of price, with no one big enough to influence the outcome. Today's market system is not one of diffused economic power; instead, we are confronted with growing evidence of *concentration* of economic power by giant firms at the production, service, and retail levels. Consider, in a casual example, the prepared cereal industry (where three companies dominate), the cigarette industry, the soft drink market dominated by the giant Pepsi and Coke power blocs, the enormous retail presence of Wal-Mart and the "anchor stores" of the shopping malls of our commercial landscape, and so on. It is instructive to note that the ten biggest mergers in U.S. history have taken place since 1981. Enjoying market power, the giant firms have enormous competitive advantages, including a rich supporting cast of symbolic dimensions contributed through packaging, advertising, and merchandising, driven by budgets commonly counted in the hundreds of millions of dollars.

If one takes seriously the erosion of these two assumptions of the market's supporting ideology (the rationality of the individual and the beneficial effects of competition), then advertising emerges with the potential for exploitation— for example, the biggest advertiser, not necessarily the producer of the most efficient or satisfying product or service, is able to attract patronage due in large part to the pervasiveness of the symbol packages we call advertisements.

Defenders of the market's implicit mechanisms assert that advertising cannot compel. The self-interest of the advertiser requires that the product or service be interpreted in terms of the self-interest of potential consumers. So constituted, advertisements serve complex individuals as handy guides for buying—sometimes based on "objective" criteria, frequently value-laden, mirroring the ambiguity of the human condition.

As historian Stephen Fox concludes in his history of American advertising, "The people who have created modern advertising are not hidden persuaders pushing our buttons in the service of some malevolent purpose. They are just producing an especially visible manifestation, good and bad, of the American way of life."[6] If the buyer is not interested, this reasoning goes, the effort fails and the producer is left to ponder new advertising or, perhaps, a new product.

Frame the issue in terms of moral responsibility. By asserting belief in the rationality of consumers (consumer sovereignty) and the basic fairness of the market, the advertisers are in essence pressing responsibility onto the consumers themselves. *They* are the final judges. *They* can best make the decisions between competing stimuli. *They* know what they can afford, what satisfies them.

Those who raise questions about advertising's overwhelming priorities, on the other hand, are arguing that moral responsibility is not served by simple reliance on the values of the market. The system, they contend, is not working for the good of all concerned. People are more driven than they need to be, and are spending their money less wisely than they could be. It is unethical to assume that responsibility rests with individuals alone.

The priorities of advertising underscore the question of who should set that agenda. And this will undoubtedly remain a central issue to all those concerned with the ethical dimensions of advertising.

47. THE PRESENCE OF ADVERTISING

Now, no matter what priorities the advertisements may want to press upon us, their messages are simply a growing part of our lives. In short, advertisers are constantly trying to get at us, and the advantages are strongly on the side of the advertiser. Simply, with the exception of market information forums like the *Yellow Pages,* classifieds, catalogs, weekly supermarket ads, the cable shopping channels, and various interactive systems, advertising seeks us out rather than we seek out advertising.

As former adman Jerry Mander saw it, the essence of the advertising process is that the advertiser talks and we listen.[7] In most cases, we have very little opportunity to alter the monologue or even avoid it. Now, if someone talked at us and we were not interested, we could tell him or her to change the subject, ask for an opportunity to respond, or walk away. Advertisers, however, monopolize the subject in whatever manner, frequency, and volume they choose. It is also certainly uncontestable that they seek us out in virtually every facet of our lives, make it extremely difficult for us to avoid them, and commonly provide us with no opportunity to respond except at the point of purchase. The result is a system destined to intrude.

The term "behavioral interdiction" in advertising circles refers to putting an advertisement in front of someone who is going about his or her daily affairs in the hope of delivering a (usually) commercial message. Examples abound—and expand. As advertising practitioner Rod Miller observed, we now have:

Ads in toilet stalls, both on the ground and in flight.

Ads on parking meters and garbage cans on city streets.

Ads on grocery store shopping carts (including tiny video screens and safety belts), ads on shopping bags, even television monitors playing commercials at checkstands and in the aisles.

Commercials on movie screens, on rented videocassettes (even little billboards on the box they come in), on giant screens at sporting events, and on television monitors at airport baggage claim areas.

Advertisements sent to fax machines.

Telephone sales calls to people at home (usually during dinner, it seems) from other people or—heaven forbid—computers.

Commercials on the telephone while you're on hold.

A wealth of specialty items from T-shirts to sunshades for windshields to fortune cookies.

The much-publicized Channel One, in which school systems force-feed students commercials in exchange for a few television sets and VCRs.

And that's not to mention increasing clutter in traditional media: 15-second TV spots, more commercials on cable TV, more and more free-standing inserts falling out of newspapers, magazines stuffed with bound-in and blown-in response cards, mailboxes overflowing with unsolicited advertising, and so on.[8]

There has even been serious publicity given to an "Environmental Billboard," the size of more than 100 football fields, destined to orbit the earth: "At an altitude of up to 250 miles above the equator [it will] look about the same size as a full moon to the naked eye, or large enough to carry the brand name and/or logo of a deep-pocketed advertiser."[9] In spite of shrill criticism from astronomer Carl Sagan, as well as critical comments on the editorial pages of *Advertising Age*, "clients are intrigued with the idea."

As for the increasingly indistinct line between advertising and nonadvertising content in newspapers, magazines, television, radio, and other media of entertainment and enlightenment, essayist Michael Kinsley satirized the growing commercial presence:

[A] Shakespeare production, still in the planning stage, involves the rise and fall of a Scottish king and offers a variety of rich product-placement opportunities. Three elderly sisters will be cooking onstage throughout the play, sometimes even reciting recipes. A single product reference—"eye of newt, toe of frog, one-quarter cup ReaLemon reconstituted lemon juice"—will be $20,000. An entire couplet will be priced at $40,000. For $60,000 the sisters will say, "Heck, let's just dump this mess and call Domino's."[10]

The result of all this commercial presence, Jerry Mander would say, is that we develop a defensive posture; we shut ourselves off, or wallow in cynicism. But at what cost? And why should we have to? In Mander's words: "Why do we tolerate this? What right do advertisers have to treat us this way? When did I sell the rights for them to run pictures in my mind? Why is it possible for people who are selling things to feel perfectly free to speak to me . . . without my permission, all day long?"[11]

From the perspective of our system of business, these are insignificant complaints, as the right to persuade is assumed. From the perspective of ethical reasoning, the question of advertising's ubiquity is harder to dismiss.

The basic defense of this form of advertising practice could be found in the assumed harmony of the self-interested advertiser with the equally self-interested potential consumer. Thus, "It's in my [advertiser] best interest to put a message in front of you [consumer] that you might be interested in, and thus serve my self-interests while serving your own by buying my product." In practice, however, there are at least two important qualifications.

1. The media that carry advertising messages in this country are often indiscriminate with regard to advertising purposes. Thus, those consumers barraged with many forms of advertising are likely to be uninterested in the product or service advertised in spite of the best intentions of the advertiser to be precise. The appeals of certain product and service categories are often broad enough that harmonious matching of subject and interested audience is the exception rather than the rule.

2. Advertisers control both the content and the frequency of the messages.[12] Rather than having the messages appear at our convenience with a message content that reflects our needs, the advertiser decides what is in his or her best interest to say (and not to say) and how often and where to say it. Sometimes (as the harmony-of-self-interest ideology would suggest) this system works well for all parties. Sometimes it does not, leading to frustration from inappropriate timing and irritating repetition, exasperation from mindless content, and/or annoyance at the intrusion of commercialism into more and more facets of everyday life.

Now, under normative conditions, attempts to persuade should embrace certain basic understandings: for example, that an individual has a perfect right to attempt to persuade another as long as (1) the targeted party initially accepts the attempt to persuade; and (2) after making the best possible attempt at persuasion, the initiating party accepts the judgment of the other and ceases his or her efforts.

Can advertising meet either or both of these criteria? Perhaps it can deal with the matter of invitation to persuade in the sense that any astute individual in this culture who picks up a magazine or newspaper, or tunes in a radio or television station is aware that a sizable portion of the content will be persuasive appeals. Of course, it is easier to avoid this element in print than in the broadcast media, but, in any case, forewarned is forearmed. This is certainly *not* the case with some other forms, including cinema advertising, airplane banners, T-shirts, and advertising in videotapes—not to mention orbiting billboards.

In terms of advertisers being more restrained, it is difficult to see how the current state of the art offers much hope. No advertiser, no matter how zealous, wishes to waste money attempting to persuade someone who will not be budged, but the often indiscriminate reach of the media and the complexity of consumer behavior encourage a certain "more is better than less" mentality that, when fueled by large advertising and promotion budgets, can easily lead to excess.

Now, if advertisers could neatly reach only those interested in their offerings, they would surely do so—and this may be increasingly possible with interactive systems such as Prodigy, the cable shopping channels, various forms of direct marketing using increasingly precise data bases, and so forth. Yet even in the far reaches of the "electronic highway," there will be many who are simply not connected, or are disinterested or resistant. Thus, countless advertisers will, for the foreseeable future, continue to rely on "conventional" media for delivering their advertising messages. And, even with highly specialized publications, such as *Jogger's World,* some readers will not be interested in the content of a given message. A great deal of advertising will continue to reach individuals who are disinterested in the general or specific content, and this will increase the likelihood of irritation.

Of course, as all advertisers know, consumers can be fickle. An old advertising axiom is, "Your customers are a parade, not a mass meeting." Thus, advertisers may feel reasonably justified in attempting to reach the apparently unpersuadable with the expectation that, perhaps, one day soon their attempts will prove successful.

Yet, for all its obvious successes, advertising can be seen as a potentially wasteful form of communication for both advertiser and receiver. The advertiser frequently pays to reach disinterested individuals and is unsure how often to advertise to achieve the desired ends. The consumer does not always find advertising when he or she is interested, and when it is accessible, it may not be in a form that serves his or her particular needs. Perhaps, in order to address this often contentious area concerning the balance between advertiser and consumer interests, the advertiser needs to pose a simple question and consider it inherent in any attempt to persuade, particularly through indiscriminate channels: Am I welcome here?

The future will certainly allow advertisers more precision in matching their self-interests with those of potentially interested individuals. But there will still be mismatches, in spite of (or because of) often ingenious strategies of interdiction. And, finally, there is the simple reality that, as one sage observer commented, "For some advertisers there is simply no 'Off' button."

Advertising's presence on the media landscape of the twenty-first century, then, seems likely to be every bit as pervasive—and confrontational—as its late twentieth-century counterpart.

48. THE PRESSURES OF ADVERTISING

If one were asked to describe the mass media of the United States, one of the first phrases offered would be "privately owned," and close behind would be "advertiser supported."

The two have not always been so closely linked. For the better part of the eighteenth and nineteenth centuries in this country, publishers were essentially producing low-cost convenience goods. Their efforts were supported largely by reader subsidy, with the readers paying the entire cost of the newspaper or magazine. By the early twentieth century, however, the pattern had been altered. Rather than continue to raise the price of their commodity to reflect increases in production costs, many publishers chose to keep the cost low and use the contented readership to attract more advertisers. Thus, financial support from advertising increased as that of the readers diminished. The outcome was predictable: Publishers became "brokers in blocs of consumers" of interest to advertisers.

Today the vast majority of the media vehicles in this country look for their financial well-being to advertisers first and readers/viewers/listeners second (Although Professor Vincent Norris of Penn State offers compelling evidence that, at least in the case of magazines, the advertising "subsidy" may be more myth than substance).[13] Presumably, one constituency could not be satisfied without the others, for if the readers/viewers/listeners are not attracted, advertisers will not be interested, and the media vehicle's financial fortunes will decline. Yet, it is undeniably clear that the needs of these three central parties—publishers/broadcasters, advertisers, and listeners/viewers/readers— do not always harmonize.[14]

Publishers/Broadcasters
How far does the publisher/broadcaster go to accommodate the advertiser? For example, is it ethical to do any of the following:

- attempt to accommodate more advertisers either by adding more advertising pages or by (as in broadcasting) reducing the length of a standard commercial so that more may be aired?
- create new units (for example, home-buying sections, network news breaks) largely for the purpose of selling more advertising?
- arrange the magazine, newspaper, or radio or television programming largely for the benefit of the advertiser: (e.g., spread editorial material throughout the magazine so overall advertising readership may be higher), break into televised movies at points of advertiser rather than viewer convenience, stop televised football games at predetermined times, and so forth?
- attempt publishing and/or broadcasting ventures only in terms of market-dominated criteria (e.g., Are there enough advertisers willing to pay to have me gather these people into an audience)? Consider the sentiment expressed in Figure 10.1. It could be argued that there is a need for a mass-media vehicle dealing with the concerns of the urban poor, but can you imagine an advertiser-supported vehicle called *Down and Out,* or *Homeless?*
- stop publication of a newspaper or magazine because of weakened advertising support without even questioning the readers as to whether or not they would be willing to shoulder more of the cost to keep the publication in business?
- purposely blur the division between advertising and nonadvertising material by accepting "editorial" style advertising or "advertorials" in print, or "infomercials" in cable–TV programming?
- give in to advertiser pressures to kill stories, or be more accommodating when advertisers withdraw their support in protest? (A recent major study of newspaper editors reported that 90% had been "pressured by advertisers because of the type and content of

Calvin and Hobbes   by Bill Watterson

FIGURE 10.1

the stories carried by the paper.")[15] Or, as a prize-winning reporter commented:

> When you write about government, the attitude of [editors] tends to be "no holds barred." When you write about business, the attitude tends to be one of caution. And for businesses who happen to be advertisers, the caution turns frequently to timidity.[16]

Advertisers
What are the ethical dimensions if advertisers do the following:

- withhold support from magazines or newspapers whose editorial treatment of company-sensitive issues is not supportive?[17] (Mercedes-Benz of North America recently received a rash of negative publicity for attempting to implement exactly such pressure.)
- regard the audience as individuals who are gathered to read/view/listen to nonadvertising material and are therefore due no particular respect? (In such cases, advertisers may feel free to repeat, shout, badger, seduce, or frighten as the advertisers' priorities dictate.)[18]
- select media vehicles predominantly on the basis of impersonal readership/viewership/listenership criteria rather than making an attempt to determine the degree of commitment that exists between the vehicle and its audience, while knowing that withdrawal of advertising support for a particular magazine, newspaper, or program may be partially responsible for depriving loyal readers/viewers/listeners of the pleasure they receive from that media experience?

Listeners/Viewers/Readers

Audiences are consigned to a passive role if advertisers seek them out rather than the other way around. The audience must realize that its patronage of particular media vehicles sends messages back through the system. If they respond positively (or at least passively) to particular television/radio/ newspaper/magazine content, they are likely to get more of the same. If they watch "whatever is on," they are clearly responsible for perpetuating the television forms so favored. If they find it less demanding to read *People* than *Harpers,* the consequences are predictable. If they silently tolerate advertising abuses in terms of volume, content, taste, or sheer leverage, they encourage these abuses to continue.

If one assumes that the sole purpose of media vehicles in this country is to make money, then the ethical issues are simplified considerably. The publisher or broadcaster simply produces an editorial or entertainment package that attracts the largest possible audience of interest to advertisers. Advertisers and their agencies, in turn, select those vehicles with the lowest cost-per-thousand or those that cover the most efficient demographic segments. Both can rationalize their single-mindedness by assuming that they are supporting media vehicles that offer the public what they want. And the attraction of listeners, viewers, and readers completes the circle.

If, however, one raises questions of whether reliance on advertising revenue leads to a vigorous and satisfying mass media for society, other questions emerge. For example, how might advertising support be related to the quantity of media vehicles in this country as well as the quality of their content?

QUANTITY

The media landscape in the United States is certainly abundantly populated. Daily and weekly suburban papers have flourished even as the number of urban dailies has declined. Magazines appeal to countless vocations and avocations, and a great many are supported by advertisers grateful to reach a homogeneous audience of (for example) professional wrestling addicts, antique buffs, or science fiction enthusiasts. Specialized programming abounds on both AM and FM radio; television, still the most indiscriminate of the mass media, continues to fragment through ad hoc networks, cable, pay cable, interactive forms, and other accommodations to the laws of competition for advertiser money and viewer tastes.

Of course, as media vehicles serve advertisers they commonly seek out not simply interest blocs, but "markets." Since markets are usually associated with the kind of disposable income needed to buy the baubles of our consumer society, it follows that the media will follow markets. Thus, those who can buy things (e.g., often the young, affluent, and well educated) will generally be overindulged with media attention, while those with less disposable income will be generally less favored.

QUALITY

Regardless of the quantity, is the *content* of these media vehicles strongly affected by advertising? If so, for better or worse? Here the critic and supporter fail to reach even tentative agreement.

The Critic of Advertising:

The media in the United States are, regrettably, in the business of gathering audiences for advertisers. As a result, they try to attract as many from a desirable market as they possibly can. This is typically accomplished with lowest-common-denominator content that emphasizes the titillating and sensational rather than the substantive and thoughtful. In short, the media "attract the eye without engaging the mind," while offering a degrading diet of truncated news, violence, sex, and simplistic comedy and drama.

The Supporter of Advertising:

The media in the United States are diverse and vigorous, their content ranging from the profound to the profane. The variation in content is a reflection of the interests and tastes of the American people. The media, after all, are surviving in a market system. If they do not serve the needs of an audience, they will falter and disappear. The reader, listener, or viewer has the ultimate veto authority. Finally, support from a variety of advertisers is far more likely to produce a press free to criticize the government than would be the case if government supported the media, as it does in part or in whole in many other countries.

Advertisers are, without debate, an increasing presence and force in the media of this country. As such, they represent an enormously influential "third party" to interact with the publishers/broadcasters and the readers/listeners/viewers. Whether the ensuing trade-offs are, on balance, positive or negative will surely continue to be a topic of sometimes volatile debate.

It cannot be otherwise. As a country we consume enormous quantities of media content. We would, then, be well advised to appraise the substance, and style, of that diet.

49. RESOURCE ALLOCATION

In their 1994 calendar,[19] the editors of the magazine of critical commentary *Adbusters* offered two arresting reminders of the inexorable fact of resource allocation.

In the first (Figure 10.2), a variation of the famous World War I recruiting poster, we are asked to curb our consumption because: "A North American consumes five times more than a Mexican, 10 times more than a Pakistani, 15 times more than a Nigerian and 30 times more than a person living in Bangladesh."

FIGURE 10.2

First published in *Adbusters Quarterly,* 1-800-663-1243.

FIGURE 10.3

First published in *Adbusters Quarterly*, 1-800-663-1243.

In the second (Figure 10.3), we are asked to consider "American Excess": "Five percent of the people in the world consume one-third of the planet's resources and produce almost half of the non-organic waste. . . . Those pigs are us!"

Any planet, any continent, any society, any city, home, or individual, faces the problems of resource allocation. There is only so much time, so many raw materials, so much money. Decisions must be made and resources allocated appropriately. Advertising has been both criticized and championed as playing a significant role in this allocation process, either through reinforcing existing values or, far more ominously, through altering the old and shaping the new. This is a matter laden with ethical questions.

A favorite classroom gambit is to suggest to students that the instructor will be visiting them in their hometowns and wishes to be taken for a ride around the city. The only stipulation is that "somewhere along the line we travel past the homes of the most successful people in town." Asked where their tour would go, students almost inevitably offer descriptions of well-manicured lawns, large and impressive houses, ample driveways, and so on. And then the sting: "I didn't tell you to include the homes of the *richest* people in town, only the most *successful.*" What, they are asked, of the school janitor in his inconspicuous home? He has worked hard all his life to support a family and make their lives better than his. He gives his time and money (such as it is) to others and, after 35 years of thick and thin, is still devoted to the same wife. Why is he not "successful"?

One answer would be that those are not the values that our market system has come to honor. And advertising, critics assert, is very influential in setting those values, since its overall effect is to equate achievement with things, and fulfillment with the consumption of goods and services. If the market has no goal except to meet consumers' demands, advertising can be said to help direct that demand toward a warped system of values that sees more spent on the advertising of pet foods than on many social programs.

By contrast, assume for a moment that advertising is merely a reflection of consumer sovereignty. Here, if we have too many cars and not enough beautiful drives, it is the consumers' will that it be so, and advertising is only following the market directives.

At the time of this writing, many secondary and elementary schools are in deep financial trouble. Library acquisitions are being cut, educational programs curtailed. Suppose that for a period of one year the amount now spent for advertising and promoting cigarettes (well over $2 billion) was spent (with similar expertise) on advertising school bond issues. Would we have better schools?

Or, as Canadian advertising practitioner John Dalla Costa recently mused: "What would happen if McDonald's used its incredible marketing smarts, advertising budget, promotional dollars, and instore materials to create more environmental sensitivity in kids?"[20]

Many thoughtful projections for the remaining years of this decade and the opening of the next century raise the specter of widening gaps between the haves and have-nots, both domestically and internationally. This is a highly complex issue, but it is not unreasonable to think about advertising's possible role.

Does advertising accentuate the situation? Can advertising improve it? Or is it merely a passive element totally dependent upon other, more fundamental forces such as political systems? Should those who work in advertising be concerned with these matters?

More than two decades ago, Carl Ally, one of advertising's more outspoken (and respected) figures, proposed that advertising should take upon itself nothing less than the task of helping to solve the world's economic ills. He noted that the condition of a small percentage of the world's population consuming an enormous share of the world's products cannot long endure, particularly with the rising aspirations of many developing countries. Advertising, Ally suggested, can help by leading the more affluent countries to accept a new ethos featuring curtailed consumption, assuming that the resources thus conserved could be more equitably distributed.[21]

Most of us can remember being admonished by our parents to finish the food on our plates because of the starving children somewhere else on earth. It was never made clear how eating our remaining food, which was to be thrown in the garbage if we did not oblige, would fill the stomachs of children half a world away. Yet the idea was right: Waste less and there would be (potentially) more to share.

Some would certainly regard Ally's idealistic message as right-minded, but essentially hopeless to implement. For, as we have seen throughout this section of the book, if one endorses the motivating force of self-interest inherent in the market system, and also assumes that the safeguards of a rational humankind and atomistic competition are in place, then it can be assumed good will be the ultimate result *without* heroic efforts of social responsibility. Thus, the producer of a cheese-flavored dog food can believe he or she is behaving ethically by seeking the firm's best interests, which will in turn affect the well-being of the company's employees, contribute to the viability of the domestic economy, and keep the country in an economic position that will enable it to respond to the less fortunate of the world through foreign aid, charitable giving, and the like. Resource allocation, then, is determined from the bottom (consumer sovereignty) rather than the top (government planning), and the market simply follows existing demand.

On the other hand, if advertising, fueled by self-interest, helps to *shape* that demand and direct the market, then two conclusions may follow: (1) To the extent that advertising encourages private consumption, particularly of products and services high in social costs such as pollution potential, it can be held to account for a shameful misallocation of resources to the few at the cost of depriving the many; (2) If advertising is, in fact, powerful enough to direct this allocation of resources, it could also be used to *redirect* it to more socially beneficial ends. There are examples, both large and small, of such efforts, including:

- the efforts of the Advertising Council on behalf of such noteworthy causes as aid to black colleges, AIDS education, the prevention and treatment of high blood pressure, anti-drug themes, etc.;
- the advertising of the foster children programs and the various relief organizations;
- the numerous charitable promotions for hospitals and research on crippling diseases; and
- daily examples of advertising in support of local, state, regional, and national causes.

To the argument that these and other efforts are woefully underfinanced, there are two answers. The first is yes, they are underfinanced, but even a little of the right advertising can make a difference. For example, a *single* ad in each of the following cases played a major role in:

- the reintroduction and subsequent passage of a rat extermination bill for the city of New York;
- killing of a bill that would have led to the damming of the Grand Canyon in order to provide hydroelectric power for the peak-hour needs of Phoenix; and
- asserting the independence of the tiny Caribbean island of Anguilla in the face of a pending landing by the Royal Marines to establish British sovereignty.

And, generally, advertising for good causes stands out from the commercial milieu and has potentially greater impact.

The second answer is yes, it *is* just a drop in the bucket, and the only real solution is to introduce a more authoritarian political and economic system than we now have. In essence, government should then take control of the market to direct it in ways deemed desirable by those in power.

For advertising practitioners, there are three possible courses of action: (1) to endorse the values of the market system and assume that what is good for all will ultimately prevail because of the motivating force of private interest and the basically fair allocations produced by the market system's presumed implicit mechanisms; (2) to find (or encourage) work in companies, agencies, or special-interest groups that promote socially helpful causes; and (3) to agitate for change in the political and economic system to replace the market as a resource-allocation device with a more authoritarian system, expecting that the subsequent direction of resources will be more just.

NOTES

1. Michelle McCarter and Judann Dagnoli, "Is Advertising Moral? Vatican Looking Into It," *Advertising Age,* 6 September 1993, p. 1.
2. Christopher Lasch, *The Culture of Narcissism* (New York: W. W. Norton, 1978), p. 72.

3. Michael F. Jacobson and Ronald K. L. Collins, "Commercialism Against Culture," *The Advertiser* (Association of National Advertisers) (Summer 1993): 58-60.

4. Peter M. Nichols, "Jurassic Video," syndicated from the *New York Times* in Champaign-Urbana *News-Gazette,* 24 June 1994.

5. "Trends to Watch in 1994," *Advertising Age,* 1 November 1993, p. S22.

6. Stephen Fox, *The Mirror Makers* (New York: William Morrow and Company, 1984), p. 381.

7. For a provocative statement of many of the issues in this chapter, see Jerry Mander, "Four Arguments for the Elimination of Advertising," in *Advertising and the Public,* ed. Kim Rotzoll (Urbana: University of Illinois Department of Advertising, 1980), pp. 17-28.

8. Rod Miller, "No Escaping Ads," *Advertising Age,* 11 December 1989, p. 34.

9. See "Advertising Enters Cosmic Phase," *Advertising Age,* 12 April 1993, p. 3; "Blasted Space Ad!" *Advertising Age,* 7 June 1993, p. 16; "Space—the Final Frontier," *Advertising Age,* 5 July 1993, p. 16.

10. Michael Kinsley, "These Foolish Things Remind Me of Diet Coke," *Time,* 11 June 1990, p. 88.

11. Mander, "Four Arguments," p. 21.

12. See Paul Keller and Charles T. Brown, "An Interpersonal Ethic of Communication," in *Messages,* ed. Jean Civikly (New York: Random House, 1974), pp. 41-50.

13. See Vincent P. Norris, "Consumer Magazine Prices and the Mythical Advertising Subsidy," *Journalism Quarterly* 59 (Summer 1982): 205-211.

14. See, for example, Rebecca Ross Albers, "When Is News Not News," *Presstime* (April 1993): 52-54; Rader Hayes and Herbert Rotfeld, "Infomercials and Cable Network Programming," *Advancing the Consumer Interest,* 1:2 (1989): 17-22; and Michael Hoyt, "When the Walls Come Tumbling Down," *Columbia Journalism Review* (March/April 1990): 35-41.

15. Lawrence C. Solely and Robert L. Craig, "Advertising Pressures on Newspapers: A Survey," *Journal of Advertising* (December 1992): 1-9.

16. Bill Lazarus, quoted in Ronald K. L. Collins, *Dictating Content* (Washington, DC: Center for the Study of Commercialism, 1992), p. 61.

17. See Eugene Secunda, "Ad-Editorial Wall Crumbling," *Advertising Age,* 4 October 1993, p. 34.

18. For a discussion of the advertiser's concept of "audience," see Kim Rotzoll, "Gossage Revisited," *Journal of Advertising* (Fall 1980): 6-14.

19. "Adbusters Spoof Calendar, 1994—The Year of Culture Jamming," The Media Foundation, Vancouver, British Columbia.

20. Ian McGregor-Brown, "The Greening of Corporate America," *Adbusters* (Winter 1989-1990): 53.

21. "Advertising Must Help Solve World Economic Woes: Ally," *Advertising Age,* 29 July 1974, p. 1.

part III

Persuasion and Public Relations

The ancient sages would not be surprised by our modern interest in public relations. A citizen of Athens was by nature an advocate, salesperson, purveyor of ideas. Perhaps their only surprise would be the professionalization of this common human enterprise. Even at that, the Sophists might be expected to regard this development as merely an extension of an old, if not honorable, calling.

Public relations is now ubiquitous and omnipresent. The need for advocacy and information extends from PTA councils to councils of war. Dwight Eisenhower recalled in his memoirs of the D-Day invasion that soon after his arrival in London in the summer of 1942, he recognized that the Allied plan to break into Germany through France would impose immense hardship on British families and farms as American sailors and soldiers gathered in preparation. His solution was to establish early "an effective Public Relations Section of the headquarters."[1] The general went on to describe battle plans, so readers were left to wonder what role public relations played in the success of the Allied cause and in the continuation of pluralist democracy in the West. We suspect that this part of the untold story is complicated and considerable.

Histories of modern public relations usually follow the contours of communications technology and progressive capitalism. The need to fill columns of newspapers generated press agents paid to supply words that would serve purposes similar to the words in adjacent advertisements. But the genius of press agents was to shield their advocacy in the paper's news functions. Ivy Lee and Edward Bernays, and perhaps

P. T. Barnum, expanded agentry to encompass the creation of cultural archetypes to explain the ways and means of their mostly corporate clients. Big business needed this crucial help, especially as Congress moved to curtail capitalism's excesses and the muckrakers rushed to expose them. Nowadays, along with farming and health care, public relations seems like the profession we could least imagine living without.

Are public relations professionals advocates or information specialists? The debate rages. Journalists have jealously regarded their own role as informational, whereas public relations engages in the task of persuasion. Advertising professionals clearly define themselves as pacesetters in the advocacy function—people who know attitude change and consumer behavior and apply that knowledge in campaigns to promote the special interests of clients. Does this leave P.R. professionals somewhere in the middle?

The answer is that the work of this important profession is clearly informational and decidedly persuasive. And why not insist on both at the same time? Truth is never neutral, so why should the telling of truth be any less the professional mandate of someone paid to communicate a particular perspective? In one important sense, this is a more honest mode of media work, since one's biases as a communicator in a P.R. setting are usually transparent. Shedding pretenses is normally the first lesson in public relations training.

The two chapters in this section cannot claim to be encyclopedic. We have selected cases representative of the dilemmas encountered in corporate public relations and its counterpart in public agency charity and nonprofit work. We suspect that the contours of media ethics scholarship will be shaped more and more by the needs, pressures, contradictions, and promises of this expanding influential profession.

NOTE

1. Dwight D. Eisenhower, *Crusade in Europe* (New York: Doubleday, 1948), p. 58.

chapter **11**

Corporate Public Relations

Perhaps the fastest growing field in communications today is public relations. Ambitious writers and producers are attracted by its multitiered challenge, its chance to be where corporate decisions are made, and its frequently generous salaries. An enormous amount of news appearing in each day's newspaper comes from public relations writers.

Yet the field of public relations is full of ambivalence. A recent cartoon in *Punch* shows a couple seated in an exquisite restaurant being instructed by a waiter who explains: "Chicken nouvelle cuisine is the same as roast chicken, but we get a graphic designer to lay out the veg." Is public relations the specialty of putting old information into new form? Newspaper journalists often consider P.R. writers as "hired guns" yet depend on their releases for leads and even stories. Public relations professionals claim they are in the information business pure and simple—not neutral information surely, but information that clarifies and educates the public on the role and mission of the client firm. Both reporters and P.R. specialists are persuaders and providers of news, advocates with a professional's sense of obligation to truth and fairness. By their numbers and their expertise, P.R. professionals are some of the most powerful information sources in the world.

It is no longer responsible to dismiss such an important field as "all flacks and liars," as did one recent speaker.[1] Public relations professionals have made noteworthy efforts to provide fellow workers with a code of ethics (introduced already in 1950) and with agencies to monitor that code. The dilemmas inherent in the dual role of advocate and information source make a professional's training in applied ethics all the more important to the long-range health of the firm, the client, and the culture.

The cases in this chapter echo dilemmas found in news and advertising. "Lambert, Voss and Broadbent" looks at the serendipitous nature of information gathering and considers how much one can use such surprises to one's own advantage. "Regal Holding" worries over the encroachment of P.R. duties onto the inviolate news function. "MCB Corporation" raises concerns about the internal processing of information. Are there thin walls between the P.R. office and the sales office next door? Under what conditions is marketing information put to the advantage of the firm that gathered it? "Acme Parts" puts the public relations professional in the most humane role—as mediator and conciliator. Since when do P.R. people need a college degree in counseling? Finally, "Disney World's Birthday Celebrations" raises old ghosts from Dante's level reserved for freebie-takers.

50. LAMBERT, VOSS AND BROADBENT, INC.

Alan Broadbent was a principal and account executive for the public relations agency Lambert, Voss and Broadbent in Seattle. Broadbent had recently been sent an invitation by Airtran, a large aircraft manufacturer in the area, to make a presentation for the company's account. If Alan's agency could get this account, he estimated, it would double the agency's billings.

Airtran had sent him a document outlining its strategic communications objectives for the upcoming fiscal year as well as a host of documentation about the company itself. He was invited to spend a day at the company in order to meet the key corporate communication personnel and tour the corporate offices and plant site. Broadbent had heard through the grapevine that his firm and one from Washington, DC, were the main competitors for the account. He was worried because he felt that the Washington agency, which served several international accounts, had a competitive advantage.

The day arrived for Broadbent and several of his colleagues to visit corporate headquarters. He hoped that this visit would provide important political and strategic insights for making the all-important presentation.

After a tour of the plant and several meetings with corporate management, Broadbent was asked to take a seat in the senior corporate communications manager's office while the manager attended to a small emergency. Several minutes passed in the office, and Broadbent was getting nervous. He began to pace about. His eyes scanned the office, the credenza by the window, the certificates and photographs on the wall, then the manager's desk. What! He thought he saw there the formal written proposal of his Washington competitor. His eyes quickly moved away from the document toward the office door. All was quiet. Most of the employees had left for home.

"Should I just take a quick look at it?" he thought to himself. "It's not as though I would be going through any files or desk drawers. And I really need to get this account." Nervously, Alan scanned the document and made mental notes. He found several intriguing strategies. He quickly placed the document back on the desk, just as he found it. Only a minute of speed reading, but what a difference a minute can make. Soon after, the corporate communications manager returned and the two men summarized the day's events.

Broadbent did not tell anyone what had happened. When Lambert, Voss and Broadbent, Inc., completed its proposal, it clearly contained some of the insights that Broadbent had seen in the Washington agency document.

The formal proposal to Airtran was well received, and the agency was awarded the account. Alan Broadbent was the hero of the day. At the end of the first year of the relationship between Lambert, Voss and Broadbent and Airtran, the agency's contract was renewed with great enthusiasm.

Alan Broadbent was not a newcomer to public relations war games. He was a full partner in the firm, and he was the company's choice to represent it at the most important new client visit of the year. Broadbent was a home-run hitter on a Triple-A franchise, but he was up against a barnstorming bunch of major leaguers from the East Coast. A little nervousness was understandable.

Broadbent needed something to give him a competitive edge. He had made some of his biggest deals with old Seattle friends. On some clients he could work his native gift of schmooze. The graphs, charts, and diagrams—data generated by his firm—could bedazzle hard-core numbers-or-nix types, usually recent graduates from marketing schools. But that afternoon at Airtran the competitive edge required "intelligence"—not the common-sense type, more the kind associated with collars-up trenchcoat snoops.

And there he was, temporarily sidetracked while his corporate host attended to a late afternoon emergency. Alan had not pilfered the files or photocopied anything. He had just looked, as he would have done with the magazines outside the office door had his host been less collegial. The intelligence he gathered that afternoon could have come to him in other ways, too. In fact, some of the ideas in that file had filtered out in tidbits of conversation he had during the day. He was not raiding the Watergate; this was just competitive information gathering that Alan subsequently used to win the account and build it into one of his firm's prize winners.

Alan had every right to feel proud of his work at the one-year anniversary of the account. Serious questions about purloining information—stealth or stealing—were part of the past. Of course, someday he wanted to tell his story to his new Airtran friends, just to get their reaction. He wondered if they would slap his shoulder in admiration of his spy skills, or laugh it off as part of the craziness of the P.R. business, or perhaps, though not likely, show some irritation at what could be interpreted as invasion of corporate documents.

Alan also wondered at times whether that emergency and the strange willingness of a corporate manager to let him occupy an office alone for all that time, and the coincidental availability of that important file were all a setup, a kind of test of his and his firm's integrity under fire. What a twist, he thought. Had Airtran concocted a fake file and purposely left it in the open just to see how much of it would get reproduced in Alan's proposal? No, Alan mumbled, that's too sophisticated for these busy corporate types; things like that happen in Paul Newman films, but not in Seattle. Nonetheless, Alan admitted that he would have felt like the world's biggest chump had his claim to an original creative proposal been challenged by the very people he was trying so hard to impress. Thank heavens Airtran is not a devious type of company, Alan surmised, or he would not have gotten away with his ploy. He wouldn't care to work for such people anyway.

51. REGAL HOLDING COMPANY

Over the years, Saul Harper had been a very successful businessperson in a southwestern city. From his family he had acquired a bank that had grown to be the largest in the community. He also had acquired the town's most popular television station (KBNK), popular at least in terms of local news programming. Its 12 noon, 6 P.M., and 10 P.M. news ratings were three times higher than those of the competition. Both the bank and TV station were operated under the Regal Holding Company.

Vinita Compton was the public relations professional for Regal and was responsible for all public relations activities for both the bank and the television station. Compton and the television news staff had met over the years to discuss what she thought the relationship should be between the news department and the bank. She always stressed that the news department should act in a completely independent manner even when it came to news concerning the bank.

In January 1990, a competing television station was about to air an investigative report on local bank policies, accusing the three leading banks in town, including Harper's, of engaging in discriminatory lending practices toward minority groups. It was alleged that these banks engaged in redlining: not offering mortgages or business loans to specific geographic areas of the community, the areas that contained mostly minority individuals and businesses.

As soon as the story broke on the competing station's 6 P.M. news, Compton called the KBNK's news department and asked them not to air a report on the story until the bank's officers could prepare a reply. That might mean missing the 10 P.M. news, but a reply would be ready early the next day.

When the news director protested, Compton said: "All we are asking for is a small delay so that the bank can put together some important numbers to repudiate the charges. A bank's reputation is all it has. To have that reputation damaged by irresponsible reporting is unacceptable. We'll respond to this sensationalistic muckraking as quickly as we can."

"But 10 P.M. gives you four hours. That's time enough," the news director insisted.

Compton replied, "Mr. Harper is not at a phone just now. We're trying to find him. Hold the story until I get back to you."

Vinita Compton knows she is stepping where every textbook tells her to fear to tread. She is trying to muscle into the news operation of the company's station, in the interests of her boss and his reputation in the community. Despite the advice of textbooks (and she read plenty of them in journalism school), Regal is not a university and Mr. Harper is not a professor. Her grade in this stretch of life is her paycheck, and the world on this side of the classroom is generally called "real" for good reason. Now she has interests and a negative media campaign to mitigate. And she needs all the help she can get.

Vinita is careful not to demand cooperation. She knows the newsroom/public relations tension too well to try a frontal power play. But she hopes her not-too-subtle suggestions will carry the weight of Mr. Harper's own words. If KBNK *News* thinks she is speaking for the owner, they will at least think twice before rushing on camera.

Vinita is also careful not to avoid the story. She is engaged in damage control, not censorship. There is no way Saul Harper can simply take a pass on this story; he will have to respond. Her job is to design the best possible response: sincere, to the point, aggressive, nothing said that would have to be retracted later, nothing mentioned to give ammunition to the muckrakers for a counterpoint. The story is coming, she assures KBNK, so let it come right from the top.

Vinita is also careful to cover herself, and this may be her greatest professional triumph here. If KBNK goes on the air with the story at 10, at least the story airs over her protest. Mr. Harper cannot blame her for not caring about his image and business reputation. If he sullies himself by firing employees in a rage over the negative coverage, he will have little reason to fire her—unless, of course, he is provoked that this chief P.R. specialist did not know beforehand what the media were working on.

Vinita knows she has "bought time" at KBNK. At least, her urgent requests will cause some confusion in the newsroom, and perhaps by 10 o'clock she will be able to find Mr. Harper and put together a bona fide reply. That would make her a kind of mini-hero, except of course to the muckrakers, and perhaps to the minorities whose concerns this news story is supposed to promote. There will be time enough for that. She will recommend that Saul Harper head up a citywide commission to address minority banking problems. "Hey," she realizes, "that's just what the KBNK 10 o'clock news needs! An announcement! A call to action! Now . . . where does that old man spend his evenings?"

52. MCB CORPORATION

Jason Smith was head of the public relations department of a large multinational corporation located in Boston. The company's products ranged from those sold to individuals through retail outlets to those sold to other businesses. One of his main tasks was to gauge how these different groups felt about MCB: its corporate image, the reliability of its product design, its market support system, its advertising, and its sales program.

It had been several years since MCB had done any survey work to measure attitudes of purchasing agents toward MCB. Since MCB was considering a major sales campaign in the business-to-business area, it made sense to conduct the survey not only for public relations purposes but also to help the sales force in the new campaign. After a suggestion to management, Smith received approval to proceed.

The meeting did not go as smoothly as Smith expected. Although all felt the project was necessary, they insisted (1) that the questionnaire be disguised (that is, respondents would think they were in a phone conversation only), and (2) that corporation people be allowed to see the answers along with the names and phone numbers of the respondents. Management did not want the intention or the sponsor of the project to be revealed to the purchasing agent respondents. They argued that to identify MCB would bias the results and alert competitors that MCB might be "up to something."

Smith argued that disguising the questionnaire and sponsor of the project was unethical. He stated: "By calling someone at his or her office and attempting to gather information from them under false pretenses, we are invading their privacy. We are eavesdropping on their thoughts." He also argued that a sales representative should not be allowed to see any questionnaires that identified a respondent. He said: "The only purpose of the project was to gather research data. Its intent is not to develop leads or provide information about the private thoughts of a particular customer. Sales representatives would be more than welcome to see the completed research report, which of course would not identify any specific customers."

How confidential is the information in your briefcase, or notebook, or head? The question is pervasive. News reporters usually know more than they tell. Ad salespeople know things about competitors that could turn some firms into eagles, others into gnats. In almost every case, how a professional media person uses information depends on how it was obtained, whom its dissemination would hurt, and what the repercussions would be should the "leak" be revealed.

For example, information obtained under conditions of strict confidentiality is often not disclosed directly. Newspeople do not run to police departments with every tip. Sports writers do not rush to print with every inside detail of trades and contracts. True, the ultimate goal is to print and broadcast news, but successful news reporting in the long range requires careful handling of information—ethical judgments on what's ready for public viewing, and how it should be framed. Raw information can be explosive, and while truth heals and helps, information can also hurt and destroy.

Jason Smith stands in a solid tradition when he insists that trade information gathered by his office is not necessarily company property for indiscriminate use by salespeople and management. He rightly argues that company credibility depends on careful control of his survey results. It is one thing to ask buyers about their attitudes toward MCB, but the sales force is shortsighted if they think buyers would naively surrender specific details of their purchasing plans to an "anonymous" survey only to welcome a sales call from MCB that pinpoints their plans with almost psychic precision. The mind of the sales force is muddled by visions of short-range profit.

Although some of Jason's results will hardly be hot news (the general image of MCB), some findings could make trade sector headlines. Therefore, Jason would do well to search for an appropriate middle ground in his response to the MCB sales force. He is not a lone ranger at MCB, and his company benefits from his work only if sales increase. If Jason wants to gather information for its own sake, he should become a librarian. Aristotle would remind him that information on market trends, appropriately collected with subsequent usage reasonably clear to all respondents, could be put to strategic use by MCB without his sacrificing the ethical high ground.

For example, Jason could restructure his approach so that respondents know they are talking directly to a corporation that will claim "first use" privileges to the specific product information its survey uncovers. He could wrap the promise of a cordial sales visit into his first approach to a respondent, clarifying up front any conceptions that his salespeople will receive only summaries and not specific questionnaires. He could promise to release his survey results at a trade convention, as a service to that corporate sector, but a month after MCB sales leaders have had their own briefing. He could offer to distribute survey results simultaneously to all respondents and to other corporate clients willing to purchase his findings. He could call a press conference.

Jason's worries over gathering information "under false pretenses" need not be an insurmountable barrier. He should make his pretenses public and truthful and avoid the moralistic posturing that claims his project is "only to gather research data." If that is really his purpose, he should take that university teaching job he has always dreamed of and leave the tumult of corporate competition to the sly and the wary.

53. ACME PARTS, INC.

The history of Acme Parts, Inc., reads like the history of a number of privately held U.S. companies in the 1980s. Established in 1932 by the Johnson family to produce drive shafts, clutches, and other transmission components for the off-and-on highway markets, it prospered and showed steady growth during its first 50 years of existence. It grew from one to three plants, all located in the Midwest.

In the early 1980s, the Johnson family decided to sell the company to a large American firm, ANOVA, which was also in the off-and-on highway business. The transition was a difficult one for employees, who were used to the Johnsons' rather *laissez-faire* management style.

Within a year of its purchase by ANOVA, the employees decided, in a very close vote, to join the United Auto Workers. As one employee said: "You need some protection around here. The new bosses are only concerned with production quotas and expenses. It just ain't the same without the Johnsons." After three years of ownership by ANOVA, a bitter strike ensued over wages, fringe benefits, and working conditions. The six-month strike ended with a compromise settlement that left negative feelings between management and the employees.

Shortly after the strike settlement, it was suddenly announced that ANOVA was selling Acme Parts, Inc., to a West German firm. Within six months, most of ANOVA's management teams had been replaced by both American and West German managers. New production techniques and management styles were rapidly introduced without employee or union consultation. Grievances, anger, and confusion became the watchwords during this transition period.

After a few years, conditions seemed to be returning to "normal" at the plants when it was announced on 2 July 1990 that some elements of the existing management team—the American managers plus several outside investors—were going to attempt a leveraged buyout of Acme Parts, Inc. The deal was completed in October 1990. New managers were again brought in to the company along with a new public relations person. The public relations function was established at the insistence of a major outside investor, who had been involved in a public relations firm; it was the first time such a function existed at Acme.

Among management's first acts was to change the company name to Brighton Parts, Inc. Another was to hire a team of production consultants from Boston to evaluate existing production techniques and pay schedules at the three plants. Management considered all options to be open, from closing and consolidating plants to a major reorganization of production procedures. Employees were not to be informed of the consulting group's existence, however, since it was felt that it could cause great uncertainty and anxiety.

The first assignment for the new public relations person was to deal with the employees. Sandra Eble initiated an employee survey with the input and consent of the union. The public relations person's objectives, as given by management, were (1) to inform employees about the changing conditions, (2) to build employee morale and develop a sense of belonging, and (3) to prepare the employees for some difficult times ahead.

The results were devastating. Over 80 percent of those surveyed had a negative perception of their job and the company. Comments included: "Here we go again." "The only way I know who I work for is by the name on my check." "I seem to have a new boss every few months. Everyone wants to do things differently. No one ever asks me, and I have been here 25 years." "I am afraid and worried about my future here." "They will probably want some wage concessions, given all the money they borrowed." "It is just insane around here—no one ever tells you anything; everything is a secret."

On the one hand, Acme was long overdue for a public relations office. It had already had 58 years of corporate life with only the owners and managers, apparently, to represent the company to the community and articulate corporate concerns to employees. On the other hand, the emergence of public relations professionals as part of a new management team could create the impression that the company was taking a turn toward appearances over substance, toward snow jobs instead of clutch jobs. Much of the P.R. staff's image, both inside and outside the reorganized company, would depend on their integrity and openness as they explain and clarify changes already underway. That's what made Sandra's survey so important.

From her first week on the job, Sandra could already see that she would have to choose between limited-objective utilitarianism or a Kantian first duty that included the Judeo–Christian others-as-self concerns. Under the utilitarian option, she could adopt a role as part of the new management team with a mandate to achieve the long-range goals of Brighton Parts' owners, even if those goals were not harmonized with the style to which workers were accustomed. The needs and desires of some senior workers would have to be sacrificed to the greater good of the new company. Although some people might feel exploited or ignored, new workers would come in to advance the new agenda. On the other hand, Sandra could choose a prior duty of establishing the communication channels that would alleviate worker anxiety and enhance the mutuality of each part of the Brighton team. Transmissions are not made by managers, she reasoned, but the skilled machinery operators need direction for the company to stay viable and competitive. In other words, an interdependent company needs a modicum of trust and mutual goodwill to the benefit of all, and she could be the universal joint, so to speak, that keeps the drive shafts turning.

Sandra decided on the latter course, partly because of concern about her own future. If management wanted to conduct its campaign and reach its decisions in isolation, there could well come a day when she too would be part of the isolated crowd. In fact, maybe she already was like a pawn and didn't know it. In an environment where a few determine the course for all, everyone is vulnerable. Just as Sandra hoped her own advice would get a fair and professional hearing, so she reasoned that other workers could and should have input, too.

Her survey was a first step, but much work remained, both above her and below her on the corporate ladder. She could proceed with stated objectives 1 and 2 (to inform employees about the changing conditions and to build employee morale and develop a sense of belonging) only if management granted an ear and a voice to workers who would be first to feel the difficult times forewarned in objective 3 (to prepare employees for difficult times ahead). She would also insist that management not mislead or seek advantage over workers. Sandra knew that surveys could signal a new attitude of openness, or a subterfuge for sudden announcements and pink-slip notices. Her top priority would be a corporate communication environment in which workers could gradually shed their sense of isolation, and managers their sense of bottom-line profits—wrenched from the company at all human costs. It would not be an easy task, since each group was suspicious of the other's real interests, but she felt that if she kept before her the ideal of caring for others as if she herself shared their status (and their problems), Brighton Parts could become, if not a family again, at least a company where people could say, "I was treated like a human being, not a drill press."

54. DISNEY WORLD'S BIRTHDAY CELEBRATIONS

To celebrate its fifteenth birthday, Disney World invited 10,500 guests to a three-day party. Half of them were media representatives and the other half a personal guest of each. A financial group of the Walt Disney Company, airlines, Orlando-area hotels, convention bureaus, and state and local governmental agencies contributed approximately $8 million to underwrite the event.

Disney did not disclose how many of those attending paid nothing. A face-saving offer of $150 per person was billed to those requesting it. A few news organizations that prohibit all gratuities paid their own way. On the bus ride back to the hotels after the last party on Saturday night, one fan of central Florida's hospitality announced to all: "My wallet's been in hibernation all weekend. That ole Walt Disney is some party animal."[2]

Disney estimated that during their visit, crews from radio and television stations broadcast more than 1,000 hours of coverage to all parts of the United States. Also, as gifts from Disney's public relations army, media personnel left with material for months of possible stories. The three days featured spectacular parades, air and water shows, food extravaganzas, and Disney employees catering to every request. Some of the nation's top entertainers, such as country singer Dolly Parton, provided broadcast-quality material while endorsing Disney World's glamour. Disney's management made no effort to shape the reporting but, given their expertise at generating publicity, it correctly presumed that the results would be overwhelmingly positive. As the *Chicago Tribune* reported: "One Orlando TV reporter interviewed a woman from a Colorado TV station and asked if she uncovered anything negative during the weekend. The Coloradan said she did find the weather very humid and might mention that in her next report."

Most of those in the crowd were talk show hosts, travel writers, station owners, radio disk jockeys, publishers, and magazine staff. A small percentage represented the working press, and news conferences for them dealt with Disney's future plans for its 28,000 acres and its international ventures. No one mentioned the dispensations given to Disney by the Florida legislature for developing its land, though a former Orlando newsman wryly observed, "They could have been building nuclear weapons for years at Disney World and nobody would have bothered them."

In spite of some minor criticism in the press and from journalism educators, Disney celebrated its twentieth anniversary in high style once again. This time NBC's *Today* came under fire for sending 30 staffers and producing a flattering show, including endorsements from Disney executives and satisfied visitors. When the *Washington Post* columnist John Carnody blew the whistle on the excursion (estimated at $50,000), NBC issued a formal reply:

> The Disney anniversary was not hard news or journalistically significant and we disclosed through on-air credits that facilities and air fare were provided to us. Nonetheless a strict adherence to NBC

News guidelines would not allow accepting these services and to avoid even the appearance of conflict or compromise, NBC *News* will reimburse the costs in question.[3]

The problem in a situation such as this one is obviously to record faithfully both the good and bad associated with the trip. However, to expect reporters on free trips to report carefully on both sides is to assume that reporters are willing to "bite the hand that feeds them." That is more than one should normally expect of mere mortals. Thus, agreeing to free trips is tantamount to accepting the proposition that it is morally permissible to write puffery.

The question, then, turns on company policy regarding free trips for travel writers. To examine the matter of policy, one must inquire about the reasons for having a travel section or broadcast segment at all. Since people are interested in traveling, the paper's self-interest encourages coverage of this subject. If the public's fascination with travel stories were purely one of entertainment, no journalistic question would be involved at all. There would be no need for balance or accuracy, and the more fanciful and entertaining the story the better. But some people are interested in reading or hearing about travel in order to determine where to go and how to do so most efficiently. Such readers and viewers turn to travel sections for important information on which they will depend rather heavily. The role of travel material to inform places special moral responsibility on reporters assigned to it.

What then should the media's policy be regarding the acceptance of free trips? The ethical problem is immediately apparent, because accepting free trips may involve a conflict of interest whereas refusing them does not. Certainly the logic of this ironclad guideline from Society of Professional Journalists (SPJ/SDX) is obvious: "Gifts, favors, free travel, special treatment or privileges can compromise the integrity of journalists and their employers. Nothing of value should be accepted."

In the final analysis, nothing in life is free. The agency or organization that picks up the tab expects some return on its investment. Sponsoring organizations such as Disney pay the bill in order to get relatively inexpensive and very effective publicity. That expectation converts the role of the reporter from journalist to public relations agent. John McClintock, Disney's supervisor of publicity, is a former reporter with the Palo Alto *Times Tribune*; he is fully aware that reports in travel columns can be more influential than a paid commercial advertisement. In light of those circumstances, it seems clear that media policy should flatly prohibit participation. If a company cannot pay for the reporter's trip, the reporter should stay home.[4]

For some papers such a policy would, in effect, eliminate stories on travel. The consequence would be to deprive readers and viewers of information in which they have a justifiable interest. The question then becomes whether it is possible to adopt a strategy to meet the legitimate public need for travel information while accepting the gift of trips from outside organizations. Can ways be found to minimize the likelihood of deceit?

Two things can be done. First, the editor or station manager can insist that reporters who take trips report as accurately as possible without considering the effect on possible future trips. Editors are more likely to be successful, of course, if the reporter is not just a travel specialist but a carefully trained journalist.

Second, an editor can notify the public that the trip was in fact underwritten by some outside organization. The specific name of the party need not be reported, but the article should identify the kind of enterprise it was (a travel agency, hotel, airline). The information enables the reader or viewer to assess the story more intelligently.

The decision to accept outside sponsorship of such trips nevertheless runs the risk of biased reporting that deceives the public. As travel writer Jeremy Alderson puts it, asking hard questions of travel industry executives when they are paying the bill "is considered as tasteless as . . . a television news anchor asking our vice-president about allegations of criminal conspiracy."[5] On the other hand, if the paper or station or magazine cannot pay for a trip, the decision not to accept free trips in effect deprives certain social groups, that is, the readers and viewers in those communities. Thus, the absolute policy of forbidding free trips is not always in the public interest.

It might be useful to examine a situation in which a free trip involves more serious journalism. Suppose Hotwire Electric is contemplating construction of a nuclear generating facility in your area. Your television station has been reporting carefully about the benefits and risks of that facility. The utility, right or wrong, believes that reporters have not given an accurate picture of the alternatives. The utility operates a nuclear facility in a distant state and has asked the station to send a reporter to that area to get firsthand information on the operation of the facility and on public attitudes toward it. The station cannot pay the bill so the utility offers to pay it. Should the station send a reporter at the utility's expense?

"Yes" seems to be a reasonable answer. The station should send its best-informed reporter, and it should make clear that Hotwire Electric paid for the trip. In this case, the public has an overriding need for the most accurate information available. If that news story cannot possibly be obtained without the acceptance of the gift, the station should take Hotwire's financial assistance and find strategies for avoiding a co-opted report.

NOTES

1. Quoted in Donald K. Wright, "Individual Ethics Determine Public Relations Practice," *Public Relations Journal* (April 1985): 38.
2. Quotations and details are from Charles Storch, "Disney Does Its Magic for the Media," *Chicago Tribune,* 8 October 1986, sec. 3, pp. 1, 7.
3. Adapted from "Reporter Tourists," *Quill* (November/December 1991): 31.
4. Additional examples and commentary on the importance of avoiding even the appearance of impropriety are in John L. Hulteng, *Playing It Straight* (Chester, CT: Globe Pequot Press, 1981), pp. 25-33. See also Charles W. Bailey, "Conflicts of Interest:

A Matter of Journalistic Ethics," Report to the National News Council, Minnesota Journalism Center, Minneapolis, 1984.

5. Jeremy Weir Alderson, "Confessions of a Travel Writer," *Columbia Journalism Review* 26 (July/August 1988): 27–28. For elaboration, see Ed Avis, "Have Subsidy, Will Travel," *Quill* (March 1991), pp. 20–25; and Eric Hubler, "Freebies on the Tribe," *Quill* (March 1991): 26–27.

chapter 12

Public Relations Beyond Corporate Walls

At a Department of Energy experiment station in northern Illinois, high-energy physicists are discovering the behavior and makeup of nature's building blocks. This is science of the first order, and the teams assembled are international in scope. Most of the action occurs underground, in the particle accelerator, and in above-ground Quonset huts packed with computing gear and neutrino-sensing devices. To most of us, it is a netherworld of research, vital but distant, probing the *Urstuff* issues that are arcane and esoteric. We need help to take even a first step toward understanding.

Fortunately for nonphysicists, Fermilab is an open facility. Guard gates greet visitors off the Batavia Road entrance, but the guard is rarely on duty, and when she is, it is mostly to provide directions. Once on the grounds, visitors can roam nearly at will, and the miles of paths on this former farmland are used often by joggers and cyclists seeking reprieve from suburban highways.

Serious visitors at this multi-billion-dollar operation, however, are hard pressed to find guidance. If the guard is not in, it is difficult to find the one public relations professional who writes the press notices, conducts the tours, organizes briefings, develops brochures, produces videos, edits the inhouse publication, etc. She is a busy P.R. specialist, whirling around this sedate preserve like an electron around the nucleus. When fire is reported at Fermilab, it is usually because someone has mistaken this one-person P.R. staff for a small atomic explosion. She is an accelerated particle the cyclotron cannot contain.

In stark contrast, charities, hospitals, social service agencies, churches, and private schools have tight budgets, lean staffs, and little left over for public relations. In these settings, the P.R. professional discovers that versatility and resourcefulness are prerequisites that the textbooks could not teach.

Public relations in the noncorporate world ranges from the dingy hallway where political hopefuls first assemble their leaflets to the Washington restaurants where lobbyists shape public policy, from the police spokesman explaining a drug bust to the monsignor urging support for an inner-city school.

Habitat for Humanity enjoys a national reputation because former president Jimmy Carter helps with its carpentry—but would we know of it apart from the work of a public relations professional? The Jewish Guild for the Blind has been rated the most cost-effective social service charity of the nation's 100 largest, but who would know of it if not for public relations?

Cases in this chapter explore the difficult P.R. challenge of the many non-corporate agencies that sprout like wildflowers, reach for the sun, and either find a constituency or wither for lack of support. Case 55, "The Empty Chest," asks whether the gripping appeals that tug at heartstrings have a role in meeting a community's needs. Case 56, the "St. Luke Hospital" case, approaches fund-raising from a different angle—how much of the truth needs to be told. "Fudging on the Future," Case 57, is a common problem in the competition to find students still willing to pay to learn history and literature. Case 58, "Spin Doctors," takes up the tough calls of a political campaign under pressure. Chemical and nutritional issues are increasingly complex; in "Pesticide Panic," Case 59, the media's competence in covering them is the central question. In Case 60, "A New Kind of War," the massive public information operated by the Pentagon is examined in terms of the Gulf War.

This is only a beginning, not a comprehensive set of cases to settle all the issues of our varied volunteer culture. The wildflowers of noncorporate P.R. will never be a formal garden, but neither should we assume a trillium only to pick a stinging nettle. Public relations is at the center of decisions by donors to give money, by volunteers to give time, by neighbors to give support to worthy causes; the cases in this chapter help us distinguish the important commitments.

55. THE EMPTY CHEST

The Empty Chest is a charitable organization run by Barb and Stan Adams. They collect clothing, canned goods, and money from individuals and businesses in the community to assist low-income individuals and the elderly. They organize tutorial programs for underachieving youngsters and provide a job placement file for single parents of preschoolers. The organization has three employees handling clerical and service chores; Stan and Barb run the organization with the advice of a board composed of prominent citizens, clergy, a school principal, and two elected county officials.

With recent changes in the income tax laws and skittish securities market, gifts had fallen by over 35 percent in the previous two years, making it very difficult for Empty Chest to maintain its normal level of service, much less take on the care of those additional needy who had felt the secondary effects of the market slowdown. At a board meeting in June, a member suggested that Empty Chest attempt to seek a "public relations type" to assist in fund-raising efforts. The board quickly agreed to the suggestion, saying that Empty Chest could no longer rely solely upon its reputation, no matter how good that reputation was. Barb and Stan Adams were skeptical but agreed that the matter should be pursued.

At the July board meeting, Sue Lyons, an executive vice-president of a local public relations agency, indicated she would be willing to assist. The board was delighted and gave her the charge of developing a fund-raising campaign that would increase donations by 25 percent for each of the next four years.

Sue spent considerable time developing the campaign, drawing upon her experience with the United Way and the American Red Cross. She felt that the Adamses were possibly in "over their heads"—that is, their charity work had grown past their capacity to maintain it. But she also knew that on average, more pennies of every dollar given to Empty Chest found their way to the poor than was the case in many similar organizations. The Adamses, it seemed, were genuinely caring and honest people.

At the next board meeting Sue made her presentation. Although it was warmly received, some board members and especially the Adamses felt that Sue's campaign proposal painted a rather bleak picture of Empty Chest, bleaker than it really was. The Adamses said it focused too much on what the Empty Chest had not been able to do rather than on its many positive accomplishments. The campaign was based on an extremely pessimistic forecast of donations for the coming year. Certainly, if present trends continued some services would have to be curtailed, but not so severely as the campaign implied.

Sue defended her plan: "You sometimes have to stretch things just a little to get the public involved in a particular charity. Sometimes you have to get a little emotional. You have to focus on unmet needs. You have to touch people's hearts."

The Adamses knew that there was a thin line between "stretching things" and telling a lie. They insisted: "This community has trusted us for almost ten years to do the right thing with their contributions. That's why they have been so generous to us."

Sue replied: "To broaden the constituency, and to get them to dig deeper into their pockets, we can't treat Empty Chest like an old family pet. We have to show need, concern, and potential—but especially need. We need to make some people cry, some others cringe."

The board agreed with Sue and gave permission to move ahead with the campaign. The Adamses reluctantly gave in and told Sue they would offer whatever support she needed.

There was a time, perhaps, when goodwill and a good reputation were all it took to be successful in the charitable field. Churches seemed to be particularly trustworthy then, and private citizens who wanted to help their neighborhoods could often do so without a lot of people raising eyebrows, suspicious of whose pocket was being filled. The situation has changed. Ministers are in jail for major-league pilfering. Charities are as likely to be asked for a copy of their annual audit as for their list of needs. Board members of most charities carry omission and errors liability insurance to protect themselves from charges of malfeasance. Many contributors to worthy charities feel fortunate if half of their dollar gets to needy recipients. Goodwill programs are facing a much more complicated and cautious market than they did a decade ago.

The Adamses have felt the pinch. There is never enough to go around, but now their receipts are declining while calls for their services are increasing. Who, if not Empty Chest, is to fill the crevices of our culture where disadvantaged people, for reasons often summarized in the peculiar phrase "hard luck," do not have adequate housing, food, shelter, or medical care? Government programs are one avenue of solution, surely; but organizations such as Empty Chest show another face: local agencies doing good, often thankless, work within a square-mile radius, a city's ethnic neighborhood, or a rural county. Sue Lyons has every reason to do her best work for Empty Chest.

And perhaps she has. Each charity ought to have a personality, she can rightly argue. People expect faceless agencies and foreboding bureaucracies from government social services, but a private charity should have a distinguishable personality. If Sue designs a fund-raising campaign around the cluster of people and projects (current and potential) that make up the Empty Chest family, she has done so because that kind of campaign tells the Empty Chest story as truthfully as stories can be told. Exaggerations are acceptable within that story, as long as a potential donor could call the Empty Chest office some sunny July afternoon and conceivably meet the type of needy person Sue Lyons will highlight. Just as social science researchers use "maximized comparisons" to develop types of social interactions that press away from the statistical middle ground, so public relations specialists may responsibly use "extreme need cases" that are legitimately within an organization's orbit of concern. Even pessimistic forecasts are acceptable, if a potential donor who cares to ask can be shown how those projections were developed, without losing credibility.

Sue needs to listen to Stan and Barb more empathetically, however. They are not beggars and never have been. They do not want to hang their heads like someone off skid row. Sue needs to provide a campaign that the Adamses, their staff, and their volunteers can be proud of. Sue's gift to the Adamses, above and beyond the four-year goals of the campaign, is to give them the tools to look a new donor squarely in the eyes, set out the needs, ask for a contribution, accept it gratefully, and know that an honest transaction has been accomplished that serves everyone's interests.

Stan and Barb may need Sue's pushiness to bring them into the 1990s. Sue may need the Adamses' conscience, honed against the poverty they have seen firsthand and tempered by the dignity of the poor they have served. False humility and pseudo-righteousness won't get the job done; Sue's specialty is a campaign that extrapolates from the present into the future, and that seeks to make that future better. If a tear is shed along the way by someone who comes to under-stand poverty as an unnecessary condition of people of great dignity and honest ambition, there is no moral fault in that.

56. ST. LUKE HOSPITAL

St. Luke Hospital, located in the southern part of Chicago, had existed for over 80 years. It had seen its patient base change over the years from a community of Eastern European immigrants to one of poor Hispanics and Afro-Americans. Its mission was to serve all who came to its door for help. A major part of its service to the community was through its emergency and trauma units.

Chief financial officer Frank Bailen had always felt that reimbursements from Medicare and Medicaid for emergency room and trauma treatment were inadequate; he made a suggestion, or what really seemed like a demand, that St. Luke no longer provide these services. At a board meeting, he presented objective financial evidence that the emergency room and trauma services were literally driving the hospital out of business. Since two other hospitals in the area had recently been forced to close their doors, Bailen's statement had an added impact. Bailen stated that it would be better to provide a more limited array of services than to provide none at all.

> Our mission is to service this community, and we are the only hospital left in this area. We should not close our doors because we were trying to do too much. Why can't we educate people to use our outpatient clinic rather than going to the emergency room for every little thing? Anyhow we can't even begin to serve all these people in the emergency room given that we will get the spillover from the two hospitals that have closed.

A spirited debate ensued at the board meeting about this conflict between serving the community and remaining in good financial health. A compromise was finally reached: to keep the emergency room and trauma unit open but allowing the hospital to go on pass-by when needed. Pass-by is an alert condition, lasting a few hours or even a few days, in which the hospital will not accept emergency patients arriving by car or ambulance. Pass-by would be instituted when there was severe overcrowding or the possibility of exceeding a daily quota of emergency room patients. The daily quota concept was a compromise between Bailen and the board to reduce the emergency room's negative cash flow.

Mary Jones, the public relations officer, was to help institute the program. She was to set up a system that would let the community know when a pass-by condition existed at the hospital. She was also to explain these new policies to the press. Although the board felt that the overcrowding dimension of the pass-by system was legitimate, they were worried about the quota dimension. They told Mary not to devote a lot of time on it with either the press or the community. One board member told her: "Smooth over the quota side of the problem. Not everyone will understand. It is either this or no emergency room service at all. We're trying to do our best to serve this community."

Public relations specialists are constantly called upon to present information to various groups, and occasionally to *not* present information to various groups. Should P.R. professionals conspire to hide valuable information?

Generally, no. A society that treasures justice also requires that information be widely shared and readily available. Tyrannies enjoy monopolies on information. But sometimes information is hard to come by, and rightly so. Checking account numbers and salary figures are not so accessible, and with good reason. Mary Jones must decide whether the quota system devised by the hospital board is information vital to public justice, or merely inhouse financial maneuvering that every business and service enterprise uses to keep the doors open and the bills paid.

The test devised by Sissela Bok for judging cases of deception might be helpful to Mary. Professor Bok insists that truthtelling is mandatory unless a jury of disinterested peers can agree that the lie is justified. (The proposed lie must also reckon with the conscience of the teller and that of the teller's trusted associates.)[1]

Mary could accept the hospital board's judgment and keep the quota system out of the newspaper if she could reasonably anticipate that most readers would misunderstand and misconstrue the system. Such a judgment is fraught with potential for abuse, but if community interest is foremost (and hospitals, like hardware stores, must show black on the bottom line), the possibilities for abuse can be minimized.

One way to minimize the abuse of withholding information is to find an appropriate jury of peers and lay out the hospital's case before them, quota system and all. Mary should insist that St. Luke Hospital present its innovative and questionable system at a convention of hospital administrators. Such conventions do not typically receive thorough press coverage, and there her peers could critique the plan, judging its merits on the basis of their own expertise.

What if such an informal jury were to assail the quota system as inhumane and contrary to the hospital's pledge of providing medical services unilaterally? Mary could then effectively promote the development of alternative strategies for keeping the hospital afloat, such as cutbacks in peripheral but not trauma services. A sensible board would have to listen.

What if such a jury were to applaud the plan in health care delivery? Mary could prevail upon the chair of such a group to join her in a press conference explaining the plan to reporters and interested community constituencies. Outside help might not settle the case for the quota system, but Mary could at least rest on the claim that she and St. Luke Hospital had not jumped off their own private gangplank, impervious to the judgment of professional colleagues. (The jury system is not a final answer to all questions of secrecy, of course. Juries can be virulently self-interested and callously self-protective.)

There will be occasions when a duty to tell all the truth must prevail over outside expert advice. Such duty will likely arise from claims of nonnegotiable human rights, or from compelling, theologically based moral responsibilities. Kant's imperative may come to bear on a secrecy question. Also, the love-justice continuum of Jewish and Christian (and other religious) morality may compel publicity of certain sensitive information, in order to prevent injustice and human suffering caused by greed and power.

Mary's problem is not that acute, however. She has not been told to lie, only to guard the facts. A morally sensitive guardian in this case would release and rehearse the facts before responsible groups who can render an appraisal in the interests of the whole community. If such a jury were not available, or if Mary's board prohibited her from locating one, she would have every reason to worry that a cover-up was the actual agenda here. Mary should propose her convention presentation to the St. Luke board without delay. The board should be as eager to utilize Mary's professional skills at such a presentation as they are for her services at the upcoming press conference.

57. FUDGING ON THE FUTURE

Just as magazines and ad agencies have discovered that specialization is the key to the future, so have some of the best public relations firms begun to narrow their range of clientele, or to hire "experts" to serve specialized clients.

Thus, Jeri Sanders had forged her path into the industry. Her doctorate was in geography, and she had taught in the field at a branch of the state university. But her real love was promotion. So when she decided to leave academia for public relations, naturally she presented herself as just the sort of account representative who could serve the interests of smaller colleges struggling to locate and recruit students.

The personnel officer at Buxter-Heide knew an asset when he saw one. Jeri was hired and soon thereafter began to work on the "Better Person" campaign, a brainchild of the new president of Maple College, Kenneth Hermann.

Jeri's role was to advise Hermann and the board of trustees at Maple on how best to expedite their plan to draw students toward a traditional liberal arts college at a time when most students were keenly interested in learning job skills. Maple College had a proud 75-year tradition of liberal arts education, and its leadership was committed to the idea that the most capable worker in any field is broadly trained in science and the humanities, though now that included learning computer software too. The "Better Person" idea had come to Hermann as a way of distinguishing Maple's approach to higher education from that of vocational schools and community colleges.

The week after Jeri's first meeting with Hermann, she began to do the kind of research that she sensed Maple's board had neglected. Would the "Better Person" idea work? Would employers buy it? As she inquired among her friends in the business world, she began to have misgivings. "History is fine and dandy," one contact told her, "but we're not fighting the French Revolution, we're selling apple sauce!" Another contact who did employee interviewing emphasized that his company had the highest regard for "theories and stuff, but if the youngster doesn't know numbers, we can't look at him."

By the time of her next meeting with Hermann, Jeri was well prepared to argue her case: Whatever appeal the "Better Person" campaign might project, its bottom line must be the preparation of trained workers with saleable skills—that is, if Maple College really wanted to tap today's student pool.

Despite Jeri's thorough homework, she could not convince Hermann to modify the direction of his campaign. He was determined, in the face of her impressive research, to insist that Maple could produce a "Better Person," and he wanted Jeri to develop the idea to the hilt.

Well, it was her first assignment with Buxter-Heide, and who could do a better pitch for higher education than someone like herself with firsthand experience in the field? Jeri accepted the president's directive and set to work on the campaign.

Jeri knew that she was no longer a professor in a classroom, able to say and do pretty much what she wanted without outside interference. She had entered the business world, and in that larger classroom the client is king, or queen. Jeri had done her duty by presenting research to President Hermann, research that suggested his plan needed serious revision if Maple were to realize its recruitment goals. But Jeri was not obliged to surrender the account if Hermann's plan was slightly misconceived. Or was she?

Jeri continued with Maple's campaign under the assumption that in a free marketplace, her highest goal was to generate business and to do it honestly. "Let the buyer beware," was modified in her case to "let the buyer decide," and she had done her part to influence the client's decision. With that duty to honesty accomplished, she could now spend Maple's P.R. budget on a campaign she believed was almost certain to fail.

But Jeri had lost something in the transaction. As a professor she had taught her courses well, knowing that her students needed the basics of geography before they could fully understand issues such as overpopulation, urbanization, and ecology. As a public relations professional, however, she had allowed the student to write the syllabus. Her pursuit of the business had clouded her sense of professional responsibility.

As a consumer, Jeri deplored shoddy products put out by manufacturers intent on quick sales. As an active member of her community, she had protested when the community cable franchise wanted to double its rates for subscribers, knowing that lower-income families would be that much further removed from important information sources. But with Maple College, Jeri had agreed to pursue a costly plan that her own research had indicated was out of touch with the future. The obligations that she unhesitatingly applied to other products and services were forgotten in her own profession. She had become a "hired gun," churning out material she did not believe in, generating excitement over the objections of her own studied beliefs. Jeri had forfeited the benefits of her own liberal arts training, a living example that the "Better Person" campaign might be more fluff than substance.

58. SPIN DOCTORS

The 1988 Democratic race for the presidency began with a menagerie of hopefuls, all eager to displace a Republican machine that had been one of the most popular, but arguably among the least effective, administrations to occupy the White House in this century. Among the contenders was the senator from Delaware, Joseph Biden.

Not a dream candidate in every sense, Joe Biden had assets that gave him early momentum. He was articulate, known for biting one-liners and populist rhetoric, a quality public speaker. His team of political consultants (the black belts of political public relations) were talented veterans. And Biden had an intuitive sense for the blue-collar, farmer, laborer, voter—he was a "Heartbeat of the American people" candidate: direct, honest, and classy.

But Joe Biden ran into trouble with the press—the big Eastern press first, all others quickly thereafter—and it proved to be terminal for his campaign. The problem was plagiarism.

"I kinda thought I could just do it off the top of my head," Biden explained on the *Today Show* in response to reporters' charges that he had used a speech by British labor leader Neil Kinnock in his own presentation at the crucial Iowa Forum. Biden had been looking for a dramatic close, but his choice was on the wrong side of "borrow," a hairbreadth away from "copy."

Kinnock

Why am I the first Kinnock in a thousand generations to be able to get to university? Why is Gladys the first woman in her family, in a thousand generations, to be able to get to university? Was it because all our predecessors were thick?

Did they lack talent?

Those people who could sing and play and recite and write poetry.

Those people who could dream dreams—see visions.

But why didn't they get it? Was it because they were weak?

Those people who could work eight hours and play football weak?

Those women who could survive eleven child bearings— were they weak?

Biden

I started thinking when I was coming over here. Why is it that Joe Biden is the first in his family to ever go to a university?

Why is it that my wife, who is sitting over there in the audience, is the first in her family to ever go to college? Is it because our fathers and mothers were not bright? Is it because I'm the first Biden in a thousand generations to get a college and graduate degree that I was smarter than the rest? Those same people who read and wrote poetry and taught me how to sing verse.

Is it because they didn't work hard?

My ancestors who worked in the coal mines in Northeast Pennsylvania and who would

Does anybody really think that they didn't have the talent or the strength or the endurance or the commitment? Of course not. It was because there was no platform on which they could stand.[2]

come up after twelve hours and play football for four hours.

No, it is not because they weren't as smart. It is not because they didn't work as hard.

It's because they didn't have a platform on which to stand. That's what my party's always been about. We provide people a platform upon which to stand. That's what government is for.[3]

Long before the Iowa debate, Biden had been using the Kinnock close, each time with attribution. But at the crucial moment in Iowa, he dropped the attribution. And on subsequent occasions, too, the senator seemed so accustomed to these words that he in fact made them his own.

Borrowing words and appropriating ideas is fair political strategy, but in this case, strangely miscalculated. The Kinnock material was from a 10-minute video distributed to all the Democratic candidates—so it took no monumental feat of investigative reporting for the *New York Times* to headline its coverage: "Biden's Debate Finale: An Echo from Abroad." A follow-up story documented other Biden "lifts" from Robert Kennedy and Hubert Humphrey. The Kennedy material was the result of speechwriter Pat Caddell's hasty work, Biden claimed. Not a real problem—just campaign clumsiness.

Then the law school matter surfaced. While a student, Biden had used five pages of a law article in a paper of his own without attribution. He received an F for the course, took it again, and passed with a B. Together with the campaign speeches, this new revelation began to make his plagiarism look like a character trait, which hurt the proud politician deeply.

As the allegations mounted, and further instances of inaccurate self-puffery were reported, Joe Biden sought the advice of his ace staffers. All but one knew his candidacy was over. Pat Caddell, alone, urged that Biden take the offensive with an anti-press campaign. Beat them off with charges of bias, he urged. Salvage a run for the presidency by going on the attack—and by watching his words with great care the rest of the way.[4]

Public relations can make or break a political campaign. Candidates for most every office beyond county coroner depend for image, speeches, and press contacts on professionals who follow in the illustrious footsteps of Ivy Lee and Edward Bernays, founders of the idea that realities beg to be constructed and reconstructed by people trained to build modern Babels out of symbol and icon. Bernays went so far as to claim that P.R. professionals constitute a braintrust behind and above government—the apparatus of democracy being a gameboard for players who hold the magic keys to mass persuasion.[5]

Nowadays, after every debate, forum, or speech, P.R. professionals gear up to "explain" the candidate's words to an eager press corps. With an intuition for hermeneutics that some might call fanciful, the "spin doctor" interprets the meaning of the speech, correcting its minor flaws, underscoring its prescient themes. It is heady territory for a new class of communication experts, yet their task is justified by the vengeance of reporters looking for a candidate's flaw, scrutinizing for a flinch that becomes a damaging angle in tomorrow's headlines. The public may forget the ephemeral TV appearance, the doctors advise, but they will not forget the press's retelling of it. In reports about the debate, a candidacy is either made strong or undermined.

In this complicated interplay of story and image, first impression and afterglow, the key to moral action is the golden mean called integrity. It stands as the virtue between manipulation and rigid stenography.

Does a spin doctor have the right to remake a candidate, to revise the meaning of the office seeker's message, to add meanings not present in the candidate's personal appearances, to create a mirage candidate based on possibility and potential but disconnected nonetheless from Mr. Mayor himself?

No. Reporting based on such a massage of the candidate invariably deceives; it is tantamount to seeing a different face while looking in a mirror. Citizens of the city have a right to know the candidate herself, not a mannequin image of her. Virtue demands that a public relations specialist interpret her subject in terms consistent with her subject, so that the real person, not a shadow image, achieves clarity and distinction in the public mind.

Is a spin doctor then obliged to merely rehearse and repeat a candidate's own words for the sake of accuracy? No, no more than a reporter is obliged to insert in quotation marks all the uhs, ohs, and profanities that might find utterance in the course of an on-the-record conversation. Stenographic exactitude is not a news story's glory. Public relations specialists may rightly enhance, expand, and occasionally clean up their candidate's rhetoric—provided the real candidate comes through. Integrity requires that the report the public depends on to make informed voting possible is a truthful account of the person named on the ballot. Spin doctors act with moral resolve when their efforts at interpretation serve to sharpen the distinctions that make their candidate unique.

Did Biden's P.R. staff have reason to believe that the senator—whose success was their own ticket to Washington power—had carelessly appropriated the words and life experiences of other people as his own? Should they have counseled a counterattack with the press as viper? Biden's advisors, all but one, had apparently come to realize that national exposure had accentuated a flaw the public would not condone. They counseled retreat with integrity, a morally virtuous and personally painful path. All the citizens who constitute the polis we call American democracy owe that P.R. team a small debt for an honest day's work.

59. PESTICIDE PANIC

In February 1989, the television show *60 Minutes* aired a story that apples treated with the chemical Alar were dangerous to small children. It was initiated by a report from the Natural Resources Defense Council, a nonprofit environmental group, stating that Alar could raise the levels of daminozide dangerously high in children.

Since 1968 Alar had been important to the apple industry for making apples redder and slowing ripening. "Without Alar," explains one of the growers, "we must get in and pick four to six days sooner, before the apples drop." Without Alar some of the varieties go to market green and lacking visual appeal.[6] But when scientists reported in 1985 that Alar and one of its breakdown products could cause cancer in animals, many growers stopped using it. Now the NRDC was extending the possible danger to small children.

Actress Meryl Streep immediately picked up the cause as part of her ongoing crusade against pesticides. She was quickly booked on *Donahue* and other major talk shows and invited to testify at an emergency hearing on Capitol Hill.[7]

An apple scare followed. School cafeterias in Los Angeles, Chicago, and New York City ordered apples removed from the menus and storerooms. An official of the International Apple Institute received a call from a panicky consumer asking whether their apple juice could be poured down the drain or had to be taken to a toxic waste dump. Signs were posted above bins stating that the apples therein were Alar-free. Washington State, which grows 50 percent of the nation's apples, faced crippling economic losses.

Said one school official, "It was overreaction and silliness carried to the point of stupidity." Kenneth W. Kizer, director of the California Department of Health Services, said the panic created a "toxic bogeyman." And, in fact, at the height of the apple furor the U.S. embassy in Santiago, Chile, received a phone call that a grape shipment on the cargo ship *Almeria Star* headed for Philadelphia had been laced with cyanide. Having been chided for inaction with Alar, the Food and Drug Administration impounded 2 million crates of fruit at U.S. airports and docks, and advised consumers to avoid all Chilean fruit. That included most of the peaches, melons, green apples, pears, plums, blackberries, and blueberries on the market in early spring of that year. Japan and Canada followed suit. Fruit worth $15 million piled up on Chilean docks with no buyers anywhere. Twenty-thousand Chilean food workers were laid off and another 200,000 placed on temporary assignments. FDA Commissioner Frank Young, accused by Chileans of overreacting, insisted he would rather be safe than sorry. Given the apple frenzy the week before, the public fruit phobia was a foregone conclusion. Dramatic government intervention in that climate was the only alternative.

David McDonald, head of the National Food Processors Association, condemned the Natural Resources Defense Council for seeking visibility rather than seriously facing the scientific evidence. Scientists had not produced convincing conclusions as to whether Alar was poisonous for humans, but rather than presenting its findings to experts for debate and evaluation, the NRDC, through its public relations counsel, negotiated an "exclusive coverage" arrangement with *60 Minutes*. The news people, in McDonald's view, did not make clear that only 5 percent of all apples grown are still sprayed with Alar. It also staged the story as a confrontation between a money-hungry commercial industry and inept government agencies. In addition, critics consider the news media part of the problem, because they are not adept at covering complicated issues in science and economics. Saying a chemical is toxic without clarifying the meaning of that phrase, for example, leads the public into thinking that by eating an apple one gets cancer.[8]

In order to keep modern society from becoming terrified and immobile, one body of opinion insists that strong government surveillance and more detailed consumer information in the supermarket should carry the responsibility. On this view, the press should not consider itself the guarantor of public health but should play an adjunct role to those social units that can treat issues in a more discriminating way—in this case, the local retailer—without creating a social crisis. At the other extreme, some media advocates insist that media warnings about potential dangers are essential in a fast-paced and complex age, even though they often lead to societal dysfunction. From this perspective, if the media give too much deference to economic and legal interests, the public will be lulled into a self-destructive complacency. The "watchdog function" is never so important as when powerful industries stand to save millions of dollars by equivocating on the safety of their products.

John E. Cox, president of the Foundation for American Communications in Los Angeles, has proposed a set of guidelines based on Aristotle's golden mean that he believes place risk-reporting in an appropriate context.[9]

1. Journalists should delay the presentation of a story until all the facts are in. As McDonald complained, "We have in our laboratories the largest database available on pesticide residue; we offered the information to *60 Minutes* and they wouldn't listen to us."
2. Journalists must put risk in perspective, not by simply reporting two points of view but through presenting careful analysis. Figures from the National Safety Council, for example, show that less than one dozen people per year die in the United States directly from food poisoning—though approximately 1,500 perish annually from disease connected to food contamination. With 46,000 dying each year in motor vehicle accidents, 12,000 in falls, 5,000 in fire, 5,000 in drowning, and so forth, the public needs a broader picture of risk and safety, not one centered predominantly on warring regulatory agencies or confrontational politics.
3. Reporters must have the training and education to deal with complex data and ask tough questions, particularly in such areas as toxicology, chemistry, and medicine.
4. Journalists must develop neutral sources of information other than industry and public interest groups. Their concern should be seeing the viability and competence of such neutral agencies over the long term, rather than periodically traumatizing the citizenry. At least to some observers, if the news media had shown adequate sophistication, the issues regarding Alar could have been focused on the Environmental

Protection Agency (EPA), giving them an opportunity to act. As a matter of fact, EPA has now banned Alar as a potentially dangerous pesticide, though available scientific evidence is not conclusive.

Accepting any data blindly is irresponsible, but the public is entitled to know of tests systemically gathered in a non-industry laboratory.

60. A NEW KIND OF WAR

On 17 January 1991, some newspaper headlines were set in type that was three, four, or even five inch high. Others were printed in red ink. "IT'S WAR!" they proclaimed. "U.S. Bombs Baghdad."

What became known as the Gulf War had begun, and Americans were transfixed by the news. Some described themselves as "war news addicts," tuning in at all hours to CNN's around-the-clock coverage, and buying up newspapers by the millions.[10]

The nature of the news from this conflict differed from other war news in several ways. On the one hand, this war came directly into living rooms around the globe as it happened, making it the first truly "televised war."[11] On the other hand, U.S. media coverage was more tightly managed by the Pentagon on the battlefield than during other wars and its public information office was highly successful at home.

Pete Williams, assistant secretary of defense for public affairs, handled the press briefings in Washington. He trotted out U.S. and coalition officials, showed "Buck Rogers" videos, and coordinated backgrounders. Meanwhile, Colonel William L. Mulvey operated the U.S. military's Joint Information Bureau in Dhahran on the Persian Gulf 200 miles northeast of Riyadh. With a master's degree in literature from Duke University, he was appointed in 1988 as chief of media relations for the Army. Mulvey assigned reporters, photographers, and camera crews day-by-day to the Gulf War operations, choosing from available journalists approved for the pool system. "In Dhahran, Mulvey was the boss. He was the city editor of the Persian Gulf War who decided what got done and what didn't."[12]

The roots of this situation can be traced back to the Vietnam War, the loss of which some policy makers still blame on the media. Sydney Schanberg, who won a Pulitzer Prize for his coverage of the fall of Cambodia, explained: "Many politicians and senior military men cling tenaciously to the myth that the press, through pessimistic reporting, tipped public opinion and cost us the war in Vietnam."[13] Determined to control its image after Vietnam, the Pentagon clamped down on the media so tightly that during the U.S. invasion of Grenada in 1983 no reporters were allowed on the island for the first three days, completely blacking out all coverage of the most crucial moments of that brief engagement.

The media restrictions imposed during the attack on Grenada were so clearly inappropriate that Defense Secretary Caspar Weinberger convened a commission headed by retired Army Major General Winant Sidle to address the matter. The panel was asked to recommend how to give the press access to the early phases of military maneuvers without jeopardizing their chances of success. The Sidle Commission came up with the concept of the press pool.

The first official pool was put to work in 1987 covering the U.S. Navy's escorting of Kuwaiti tankers in the Persian Gulf. The arrangement was regarded by both the media and the military as a workable solution to the legitimate tension between military planners' desire for secrecy and the media's mandate to bring news of military action to the public.[14] That may have been the last pool that was considered a success.

When in December 1989 the United States invaded Panama, the existence of the pool was used as an excuse to keep other journalists already in the country confined at Howard Air Force Base away from the action. The pool itself arrived at the scene late. Reporters in the pool also were kept away from the fighting, and they were required to stay together, rather than fanning out to capture diverse aspects of the battle.

This tactic of using the pool to restrain journalists was refined in the Gulf War. The pool was institutionalized as a tool for controlling the flow of news, and journalists were subjected to an array of restraints that an attorney for the Society of Professional Journalists called "unprecedented—even in time of war."[15] Pool reporters were not allowed to go anywhere without being accompanied by military officials, who frequently read and made changes in reporters' copy. Transmission of reports was often delayed for several days, sometimes rendering the news contained in them moot. John S. Driscoll, editor of the *Boston Globe*, called the restrictions a "black hole" that kept news from reaching *Globe* readers.[16]

The purported reason for the restrictions was to protect national security, but often William Mulvey's constraints seemed to have more to do with image than security. In one widely cited example, a reporter's description of pilots returning from their first bombing mission as "giddy" was changed to "proud." Foibles such as these might have been laughable had they not been so ubiquitous. The Pentagon tried to control every aspect of reporting about the war, not just events at the front. In one case, a *New York Times* reporter's credentials were revoked by the military for conducting an "unauthorized" interview without a military escort present—the reporter was interviewing Saudi merchants 50 miles from the Kuwait border.[17] The Pentagon even banned any coverage of the arrival at Dover Air Force Base of the bodies of U.S. soldiers killed in the war,[18] prompting Sydney Schanberg to comment in an article published while the war was in progress that, "it's all too clear that the current restrictions have nothing to do with military security and everything to do with political security."[19]

Schanberg contrasted the tight restrictions imposed during the Gulf War to the order issued by General Dwight Eisenhower right before D-Day, which said reporters should be given "the greatest possible latitude in the gathering of legitimate news. . . . They should be allowed to talk freely with officers and enlisted personnel and to see the machinery of war in operation."[20]

Even the most steadfast defenders of press freedom agree that the exigencies of war may necessitate imposing unusual restraints upon the media. Information that would jeopardize the lives of soldiers or undermine military strategy arguably should not be revealed to the enemy. This does not mean, however, that a democratic society abandons its principles at the very time that it claims to be fighting to preserve freedom. The public still has a right to know why a war is being fought, who is being asked to fight, and, if not what war strategy is planned, at least how the fighting is progressing. So to the extent that military information officers try to control information to cover up civilian casualties, allied deaths at the hands of friendly fire, equipment failures, or just sagging morale (in other words, news likely to embarrass), they are abusing their power.

Schanberg called the excuse of censoring the media for security a "red herring":

> With very rare exceptions, the press has never breached any of the security rules—not in World War II, not in Korea, and not in Vietnam. Barry Zorthian, who was the official spokesman for the United States Mission in Saigon from 1964 to 1968, said recently that though roughly 2,000 correspondents were accredited to cover Vietnam in those years and hundreds of thousands of stories were filed, only five or six violations of the security guidelines occurred. He recalled most of these as accidental or based on misunderstanding. To his knowledge, he said, none of them actually jeopardized any military operations or personnel.[21]

Schanberg quoted Henry Kissinger, who, Schanberg noted, "certainly has shown no tolerance for press criticism." For Kissinger, while some leaked information out of Washington jeopardized security, he could think of no such incidents that occurred on the battlefield.[22]

One reason given for the strict rules Mulvey used to govern the media was that the military would have been overwhelmed by the hordes of reporters covering the war if the media had not been reined in some way. Charles J. Lewis, Washington bureau chief for Hearst newspapers, dismisses this as a "fallacy" used as a rationale by the Pentagon to cover up less honorable motives for censoring the news.[23] Pentagon spokesman Pete Williams, claiming this was "the best war coverage we've ever had," gave conflicting accounts of the number of reporters in Saudi Arabia covering the war, all of them inflated, to bolster his defense of pools. Williams claimed that up to 1,600 news personnel were deployed through the pool system, when the peak was probably 400 to 700.[24]

But censorious information officers are not the only ones who must account for failures to fully inform the American public on the nature and progress of the war with Iraq. The media themselves dropped the ball in at least two crucial and oddly contradictory ways. On the one hand, they did not protest the Pentagon-imposed restrictions with appropriate vigor. On the other hand, they remained far too preoccupied with the stories the Pentagon was keeping them from, while neglecting to report sufficiently on the crucial aspects of the war occurring far away from the front. In other words, while they tended to allow the Pentagon to direct their focus to events at the front, they failed to challenge seriously the general control the Pentagon maintained over the coverage.

Even before the fighting began, some in the media protested the pool arrangement. On 10 January 1991, several small weekly and monthly media outlets filed a lawsuit against the Pentagon in a New York federal court claiming that the military's rules governing the press were unconstitutional. Although members of the mainstream media were alerted to the suit and asked to support the effort, they declined to join the suit or even to file friend-of-the-court statements supporting it. As John R. MacArthur, the publisher of *Harper's Magazine*, explained, the major media organizations "went along to get along with the warmakers."[25]

He quoted *Washington Post* ombudsman Richard Harwood's reaction to the lawsuit as an example of the cavalier attitude the mainstream media took toward the erosion of First Amendment freedoms: "These highly publicized efforts to transform petty jealousies and minor inconveniences into great issues of constitutional law are absurd. It is difficult to persuade skeptical and not entirely ignorant publics that 48-hour delays in the publication of feature stories on female truck drivers or mess hall crews from Montana threaten the 'people's right to know.'"[26]

Harwood's glib remark glosses over the fact that military control of information may have left reporters with little else to cover than truck drivers and mess hall crews. But it also hints at the second failing of the press in the face of the Pentagon's efforts at controlling its image: They kept their eyes too exclusively on the action at the front (or as near to it as they could get in the pool, with their military escort). Many failed to look elsewhere for ways to report the war.

At the risk of being evicted from the war theater, some reporters ignored Pentagon rules. These became know as unilaterals. *New York Times* reporter Chris Hedges was one such reporter. He said his efforts to get news outside of the pool system were aided by many soldiers and officers who believed in "the role of a free press in a democracy. These men and women violated orders to allow us to do our job." Many were willing to talk to him. Others went so far as to supply him with camouflage uniforms so that he would not be immediately identified as a reporter.[27]

And on the home front, some major stories went virtually unreported. For example, serious, responsible dissenting voices were often not heard. When Henry Gonzales, chairman of the House Banking Committee, introduced in Congress a resolution to impeach President Bush over the issue of the war, it was barely noticed by the media. Consumer advocate Ralph Nader complained that "The media have gone to the point that they don't even cover the bizarre if the bizarre reflects a dissenting ideology."[28] Similarly, Jesse Jackson, who noted that although he spoke in person with Hussein for six hours after Iraq invaded Kuwait, "there was not one serious interview [of Jackson] by a network. A categorical rejection. Now why is there no interest in what we saw, observed?" Jackson asked. "For years now the networks have been busily tossing onto the streets the very researchers, producers, commentators, and staff that could have helped carry out such a role. Instead, we saw the sorry spectacle of network news hiring a squadron of generals to cover the war."[29]

As one critic remarked, "To get at the real story in the Gulf, reporters did not have to travel to the front. They did not even have to travel to Saudi Arabia. Most of the information they needed was available in Washington, but not in Pete Williams's suite. In short, this war needed fewer David Halberstams and more I. F. Stones."[30] Hard-working, independent reporters were needed—those willing to dig into the facts for themselves rather than relying so heavily on the smooth-running Pentagon information office.

NOTES

1. Sissela Bok, *Lying: Moral Choice in Public and Private Life* (New York: Pantheon Books, 1978), ch. 7.
2. Statement by Neil Kinnock, British Labor Candidate, ten-minute video commercial (video transcript).
3. Statement by Joseph Biden, *NBC Today Show,* 17 January 1989 (audio transcript).
4. The authors are indebted to a comprehensive treatment of this case by Professor L. Patrick Devlin, "The Biden Presidential Campaign: A Study in the Ethics of Plagiarism and Puffery," International Communications Association Convention, Dublin, Ireland, June 1990. Write Devlin at the University of Rhode Island, Kingston, Rhode Island 02881-0812.
5. Cf. Marvin Olasky, "Bringing Order Out of Chaos: The Public Relations Theory of Edward Bernays," in Marvin Olasky, *Corporate Public Relations* (Hillsdale, NJ: Erlbaum, 1987), ch. 8, pp. 79-88.
6. "Apples without Alar," *Newsweek,* 30 October 1989, p. 86.
7. Details of this event and the quotations that follow are from Margaret Carlson, "Do You Dare to Eat a Peach?" *Time,* 27 March 1989, pp. 24-30; cf. also "Alar as a Media Event," *Columbia Journalism Review* 28 (March/April 1990): 44-45.
8. "Inquiry: Reporting on Risks," *USA Today,* 15 May 1989, p. 9A.
9. Ibid.
10. William Boot, "The Press Stands Alone," *Columbia Journalism Review* (March/April, 1991): 24.
11. Garth S. Jowett, "Propaganda and the Gulf War," *Critical Studies in Mass Communication* 10 (1993): 287.
12. Charles L. Lewis, "The 'City Editor' of the Persian Gulf Was a Colonel," *ASNE Bulletin* (May/June 1991): 16.
13. Sydney H. Schanberg, "Censoring for Military (Political) Security," *Washington Journalism Review* (March 1991): 23.
14. The background account of the development of military press pools draws on Lewis, "The 'City Editor' of the Persian Gulf War Was a Colonel," pp. 14-21.
15. Bruce W. Sanford, "SPJ Pushing for Pentagon Flexibility," *Quill* (March 1991): 11.
16. John S. Driscoll, "News to Nowhere," *ASNE Bulletin* (May/June 1991): 18.
17. Schanberg, "Censoring for Military (Political) Security," p. 24.
18. Ibid., p. 25.
19. Ibid., p. 24.

20. Ibid., p. 25.
21. Ibid., p. 24.
22. Ibid.
23. Lewis, "The 'City Editor' of the Persian Gulf Was a Colonel," p. 18.
24. Ibid., pp. 18-19.
25. John R. MacArthur, *Second Front: Censorship and Propaganda in the Gulf War* (New York: Hill and Wang, 1992).
26. Cited in Jowett, "Propaganda and the Gulf War," p. 290.
27. Chris Hedges, "The Unilaterals," *Columbia Journalism Review* (May/June 1991): 27.
28. Richard Valeriani, "Talking Back to the Tube," *Columbia Journalism Review* (March/April 1991): 25.
29. John Katz, "Collateral Damage to Network News," *Columbia Journalism Review* (March/April 1991): p. 29.
30. Michael Massing, "Another Front," *Columbia Journalism Review* (May/June 1991): 24.

part **IV**

Entertainment

When the question came up before the Hutchins Commission on Freedom of the Press regarding whether to worry about motion pictures, the first reaction of several of those august scholars was "rubbish." The movies are diversionary, escapist, and silly. What claim can they make to be counted part of the modern press?

Fortunately, a more farsighted view prevailed: However unsophisticated, movies are part of the culture and need to be looked at carefully. The commission invited Will Hays, chief of the Motion Picture Producers and Distributors of America (later the Motion Picture Association of America—MPAA), to present the case for industrial self-regulation, and eventually the Hollywood model of codes and intra-industry regulations was adopted by the commission as the best way of expressing social responsibility in a democratic society.

On the importance of entertainment media and their responsibility to the public, the commission displayed wisdom in its landmark 1947 report. Whereas news and consumer information are vital to democratic life, clearly entertainment occupies most of the broadcast spectrum and cinema screen, and a healthy share of the printed page as well. From these media we receive symbols of who we are, what we should believe, and how we should act. Entertainment, for all its recreational value, does much to educate and socialize us.

Should entertainment programs be subject to ethical reasoning? Robert Redfield, distinguished anthropologist and one of the Hutchins commissioners, urged that the direction of all our social productivity be toward a "new integrity" of idea and institution, a creative order wherein symbols and practices make "coherent sense when we state them and when we comply with them," leading to a "model society that will command the confidence of other free peoples everywhere."[1] Redfield, no dreamy chauvinist, was arguing for the interdependency of social institutions (such as the media) and social beliefs (such as the sanctity of life). Yes, he would argue, the entertainment media must be put to the test of ethical reasoning.

Redfield's intuitions were a preface to ethical theorizing in the 1980s, when narrative discourse and narrative communities became important concepts in the work of Duke University ethicist Stanley Hauerwas. Hauerwas argued that culture is built around stories that distinguish good from evil, hero from villain, success from failure. Because of the importance of story, a community that wants to live responsibly among other communities is obliged to set its compass on truthful narratives, without which a social ethic becomes detached intellectualism.

> The ways the issues of social ethics are identified—the relation of personal and social ethics, the meaning and status of the individual in relation to the community, freedom versus equality, the interrelation of love and justice . . . are crucial categories for the analysis of a community's social ethics. The form and substance of a community is narrative dependent and therefore what counts as "social ethics" is a correlative of the content of that narrative. . . . Good and just societies require a narrative . . . which helps them know the truth about existence and fight the constant temptation to self-deception.[2]

Hauerwas begins his appeal for narrative ethics with a long analysis of the novel *Watership Down,* a rabbit story with a profound political message, a fictional narrative that helps us develop our own. Constructing journalistic narratives, P.R. messages, advertisements, and entertainment programs involves process, hierarchy, imagination, constraint, profits, and power. Our aim is to examine the moral dimension and press toward justified solutions.

George Gerbner underscored the importance of this examination in his lecture at the fortieth anniversary of one of the country's premier communications research institutions: "I think of communications as the great story-telling process that guides our relationships to each other and the world." Later he warned that "children are born into a home in which a handful of distant corporations tell most of the stories to most of the people and their families most of the time."[3] His point was to urge a more careful study of the field, entertainment primarily, and its cultural and moral foundations.

The following chapters raise only a few of the questions and suggest some ways of approaching answers. Violence is a pressing concern; its threat to social order is immediate and dramatic. Nearly 500 people in America die every week from gunshot wounds, many self-inflicted or tragically accidental. Many of these deaths are the result of a momentary act of passion among friends and relatives.

Media violence, some argue, is the same threat one step removed and a hundred times more potent. TV violence sets the stage for social maladjustment, argues Purdue University researcher Glenn Sparks, especially among children.[4] While researchers debate the audience impact, ethicists ask how much media violence is tolerable, even though only one person might be affected, or none.

And what about problems generated by big media's huge financial stake? Fortunes and careers ride on fractions of rating points, and many in the entertainment industry doubt that ethical reasoning has any word to speak at all—money alone counts.[5]

Other problems in entertainment programs are less overt than violence or greed: the stereotyping and typecasting of racial groups, age groups, geographic groups, and communities of faith; or the bias expressed by the omission of substantive narratives about our society's smaller cultures; or the offense created by our no-punches-pulled video explorations of sexual experience, scatological language, profanity, and glorified criminality. It becomes clearer, as we proceed, that every level of the entertainment industry—producer, actor, writer, and viewer—is involved in close encounters with decisions of an ethical kind.

NOTES

1. Robert Redfield, "Race and Human Nature," *Half a Century—Onward* (New York: Foreign Missions Conference of North America, 1944), p. 186.
2. Stanley Hauerwas, *A Community of Character* (Notre Dame, IN: University of Notre Dame Press, 1981), pp. 9–10.
3. George Gerbner, "Telling Stories: The State, Problems, and Tasks of the Art," Fortieth Anniversary Program Highlights, Institute of Communications Research, University of Illinois at Urbana-Champaign.
4. G. G. Sparks, "Developmental Differences in Children's Reports of Fear Induced by the Mass Media," *Child Study Journal* 16 (1986): 55-66.

5. See Clifford Christians and Kim B. Rotzoll, "Ethical Issues in the Film Industry," in *Current Research in Film: Audiences, Economics, and Law,* vol. 2, ed. Bruce A. Austin (Norwood, NJ: Ablex, 1986), pp. 225–237.

chapter 13

Violence

Few issues command as much attention from media reformers as violence on television and in film. Some violence, of course, is inevitable in any drama, or even in comedy and melodrama, as when Fred Flintstone bangs his nose into a doorjamb or Princess Jasmine fights the fiendish Jafar. But the irrepressible increase in real violent crime, much of it perpetrated by juveniles, has been often linked to the rough-and-tumble lives of Dirty Harry, Rambo, the "bloodsport" rascals, and the ever-growing circus of animated superheroes. What a juvenile sees, it is argued, too easily becomes what a juvenile does. Since society cannot endure the anarchy of criminal rule, it must move to eliminate the causes.

Against the censors of violence are combat-hardened libertarians who want all speech protected. Violent programming may or may not breed violent behavior, they contend, but curtailment of speech surely heralds a retreat from democracy into feudalism, a return to the medieval monastery where utterances are controlled and political choices programmed. Such a fate, they claim, is worse than all others, and avoiding it is worth the risk of giving too much latitude.

Much of the current debate over violence in entertainment takes up the arguments of the controversial Meese Commission and its outspoken opponents. Organized in 1985 by Attorney General Edwin Meese, the commission was charged to "determine the nature, extent, and impact on society of pornography in the United States" and to recommend to the attorney general how pornography "can be contained, consistent with constitutional guarantees."[1] The commission's research included content analysis, participant observation, case studies, interviewing, and experimental studies. Its findings supported the cultivation hypothesis advanced by George Gerbner and others, and at points suggested an even more direct link between pornography and the acting out of sex crimes in certain persons. The commission's 1992 recommendations were nearly all in support of tougher enforcement of existing obscenity laws, with even stricter measures against child pornography. The rationale for control and enforcement was a widely shared conclusion that viewing and reading sexually violent material create an incentive for violent sex crimes and develop a socially destructive linkage of sex and violence in the minds of persons who may, under some conditions, act out their new attitudes.

From the first commission hearing, opponents issued charges of comstockery (a pejorative term recalling Anthony Comstock's antiobscenity crusades of the 1880s). The ACLU published a "Summary and Critique" of the commission; entertainment professionals organized to protest the commission's implied call to curtail cinematic art; journalists trailed the commission and reported on the bizarre nature of some of its testimony; and columnists pointed to "dark lunacy" and "potential danger" underlying the commission's report. Much of the opposition can be summarized around five claims:

1. Artistic freedom and aesthetic integrity demand a *laissez-faire* approach. Government has no business policing writers and directors.
2. No direct effects can be documented or proven. Indirect effects are the consequence of living one's life in a world of mediated messages and cannot be made the basis of criminal prosecutions.
3. Violence is a social and historical problem, not the result of violent TV or film. To think otherwise is like blaming John Wayne for the Vietnam War.
4. Much of the worry about media violence is really our fear of changing social institutions. To suppress TV and film is to forcibly maintain traditional notions of family, friendship, and marriage in an era when these social arrangements are undergoing radical change.
5. Boundaries between news and entertainment programming are falling fast. TV news-magazine shows are so hungry for material that anything visual (even if it must be staged for replay) is turned into a major "investigation." All of the free marketplace arguments that traditional news has enjoyed must now be applied equally to entertainment programs. The public has a right to know.

Cases in this chapter raise these questions and struggle with these rejoinders. The first case, "Hear It, Feel It, Do It," brings up the effects argument: Hear violent lyrics, do violent deeds; show a violent program, commit a violent crime. One of the standard industry replies to the effects argument is the movie-rating system, which alerts responsible adults to potentially harmful programs. Who is responsible when ratings and reviews seem to fail? That is the problem in the second case, "Crunchy Terror in T-Rex Park." The third case addresses suffering of the broadest kind. If violence is tragic, a lot of violence is tragic for a long time. Such is our feeling about the Jewish Holocaust, now five decades past. Do we prosecute an injustice to those who suffered if we fail to communicate the depth of the tragedy? Case 63 probes that possibility.

Are all media practitioners oblivious to the violence they contribute to the culture? Hardly. "The Storyteller" explores the problem from inside the industry. In the last case, "Comic Capers," we look at the persistent issue of violence in children's media.

Frustrated by the visual carnage in popular video games like "Mortal Kombat" and "Night Trap," Senator Joseph Lieberman called for Congress to ban them. "We're talking about video games that glorify violence and teach children to enjoy inflicting the most gruesome forms of cruelty imaginable," he said. But in the same breath, Lieberman acknowledged that such games were constitutionally protected.[2] A bill to ban would face a long and politically powerful tradition of artistic liberty for entertainment programmers. Where do we go from there?

61. HEAR IT, FEEL IT, DO IT

Friday evening in October. John McCollum, nineteen years old, is alone in the house. An Ozzy Osbourne fan, he cranks up the family stereo—loud, intense, reverberating. Side one: "Blizzard of Oz." The first song, "I Don't Know," celebrates in the manner of heavy metal the chaos and confusion of human life. The second song, "Crazy Train," points to insanity as the inevitable result of our inability to explain life's contradictions. The third, "Goodbye to Romance," advocates cutting ties to the past as the only way to personal freedom. The last song is "Suicide Solution":

Wine is fine but whiskey's quicker
Suicide is slow with liquor
Take a bottle drown your sorrows
Then it floods away tomorrows
Evil thoughts and evil doings
Cold, alone you hand in ruins
Thought that you'd escape the reaper
You can't escape the Master Keeper
Cause you feel life's unreal
And you're living a lie
Such a shame who's to blame
And you're wondering why
Then you ask from your cask
Is there life after birth
What you sow can mean Hell on this earth
Now you live inside a bottle
The reaper's traveling at full throttle
It's catching you but you don't see
The reaper is you and the reaper is me
Breaking law, knocking doors
But there's no one at home
Made your bed rest your head

> But you lie there and moan
> Where to hide
> Suicide is the only way out
> Don't you know what it's really about.

Masked in a 28-second instrumental break, and heard at one and a half times the normal rate of speech, are the lyrics:

> Ah know people
> You really know where it's at
> You got it
> Why try, why try
> Get the gun and try it
> Shoot, shoot, shoot [repeated]

John McCollum turns off the family stereo, walks to his bedroom, puts another Osbourne album, "Speak of the Devil," on his personal stereo. Volume up, headphones on, he lies on the bed. Nearby, a handgun, .22 caliber. Music. The cool small muzzle against his right temple. Volume up. A muffled pop.

McCollum's body was discovered the next morning. He was still wearing headphones and the stereo's needle was riding around and around the center of the album. He had had problems with alcohol abuse that complicated other serious emotional problems, but in their suit against Osbourne and CBS Records, the McCollum family claimed that these lyrics had a cumulative impact on a susceptible listener; that the impact was antisocial in its emphasis on despair, Satan worship, and suicide; and that the record company had sought to cultivate Osbourne's "mad man" image in press releases and sales promotions and to profit from it. The music was a proximate cause in McCollum's death, the suit alleged, because CBS negligently disseminated Osbourne's albums to the public and thereby "aided, advised or encouraged McCollum to commit suicide." The beat and the words had created in John McCollum "an uncontrollable impulse" to kill himself, a consequence entirely foreseeable and therefore intentional, the suit contended. Death, his family insisted, was brought on by pressures and forces hidden in the grooves and ridges of a plastic disc, made and sold by an industry that does not care.[3]

Can media inspire violent crimes? A celebrated murder case in 1977 confronted the nation with a Florida teenager who shot his neighbor, an eighty-two-year-old woman, took $415 from her home, and went on a spree to Disney World with friends. Ronny Zamora's defense attorney proposed that his client was the victim of "involuntary television intoxication." A person who is drugged or becomes intoxicated without his knowledge is not legally responsible for actions while under the influence. Ronny had seen up to 50,000 television murders in his fifteen years, and he could not determine whether he was on a TV program or committing a crime when he shot the victim, the attorney claimed. A jury saw otherwise, however, and Zamora was convicted. But similar cases keep coming to the courts.

Can violent media inspire self-destruction, and if so, who is responsible? The argument that linked repeated rock album listenings to John McCollum's suicide is similar to the argument in the celebrated "Born Innocent" case that occurred a decade earlier. In September 1974, NBC sent to its affiliates a program starring Linda Blair as a girl whose innocence is shattered through her experience in a girls' reformatory. Because the drama would include violent scenes possibly objectionable to some viewers, NBC ran a warning at the start of the program: "'Born Innocent' deals in a realistic and forthright manner with the confinement of juvenile offenders and its effects on their lives and personalities. We suggest you consider whether the program should be viewed by young people or others in your family who might be disturbed by it." As a portent of the show's later troubles, 15 sponsors withdrew shortly before the broadcast.

"Born Innocent" did, in fact, raise objections from viewers. Hundreds of calls and letters were received by NBC affiliates across the nation, 700 in New York alone. Only a few callers, notably social workers familiar with reformatories, applauded the network for its realistic portrayal of a pervasive problem. Particularly troublesome was one scene in which Blair was raped by four female inmates using a plumber's helper for penetration. The victim was shown naked from the waist up.

The program and its forthright realism would have been largely academic but for a real-life rape three days later. On Baker Beach near San Francisco, nine-year-old Olivia Niemi was attacked by three girls and a boy, ages 9, 12, 13, and 15, who raped her with a beer bottle in a fashion similar to the attack on television. Olivia's mother filed suit for $11 million against NBC and the owners of KRON-TV, charging that NBC was guilty of negligence in broadcasting the program during family viewing hours (8 P.M. on the West Coast). One of the assailants had in fact referred to the television show when she was arrested. The link between dramatic and real violence might not be strictly causal, but the network had not taken adequate precaution against the program's potential effects on young viewers. The case was strengthened by the absence of any similar type of rape on the casebooks of juvenile authorities. If Olivia's attackers had perpetrated a first-of-its-kind rape, their teacher and proximate cause was the television network that had prestaged the event.

NBC declined to argue the facts. Instead, defense attorney Floyd Abrams contended that the First Amendment protected his client from damages from alleged effects of a media program. California Superior Court Judge John Ertola agreed. In September 1976, he ruled in favor of NBC without calling a jury, claiming, "The State of California is not about to begin using negligence as a vehicle to freeze the creative arts."

But the California Court of Appeals overturned the ruling. Niemi had a right to a jury trial on questions of fact, the appellate panel contended.

Before the case was argued, NBC urged the U.S. Supreme Court to quash the trial. At stake, the network claimed, were basic constitutional rights. On behalf of NBC, the American Library Association filed an amicus brief suggesting that the Appeals Court ruling might lead to lawsuits against libraries by victims of crimes suggested in books. The Writers Guild of America wrote of the "chilling effect" on popular drama that a trial on the facts could have. For Niemi, the California Medical Association filed a friend-of-the-court brief. The Supreme Court declined to intervene.

Each side geared up for the coming courtroom battle. NBC would argue that a warning had been given before the drama, that the four attackers had previous juvenile records, and that some testimony suggested none of them had seen the televised rape. Causal explanations for the crime other than the television show rested on stronger psychological evidence. One of the attackers, for example, had been molested by her father. In theory, NBC insisted, the plaintiff's case would shift accountability for criminal acts away from the persons responsible and toward the producers of televised drama.[4]

Niemi's attorney would argue that the rape scene in "Born Innocent" ignored NBC's own production code and the National Association of Broadcasters' Code that at that time proscribed graphic depictions of violence. The rape scene, in fact, had been abridged in telecasts after the first one. No one should be absolved of civil liability because of the First Amendment, the plaintiff said.

Commercial television networks would be hard pressed to justify graphic violence based on Kant's imperative. No reasonable person could will that such portrayals become standard TV fare, since reasonable people do not, by definition, seek to promote gratuitous suffering. There should be little argument here. People who delight in causing or feeling pain are pathologically disturbed or criminally insane. Reasonable people may not choose to avoid all suffering (for example, running into a fire to rescue a child), but suffering without purpose (merely running into a fire, or pushing someone else in) is irrational by any common definition. Likewise, a constant media diet of violence and pain is irrational, assuming even a remote connection between what one views and how one behaves.[5]

Notice how close are Kant (the doer of duty) and Jeremy Bentham (the calculator of pleasure) on this issue. Bentham, the father of modern utilitarianism, wrote: "Nature has placed mankind under the governance of two sovereign masters, pain and pleasure. It is for them alone to point out what we ought to do, as well as to determine what we shall do."[6] Kant's appeal to rational duty would have little prescriptive value if people were unclear about whether to seek pleasure or pain. Let us assume that the history of human civilization is not remiss here: the avoidance of gratuitous violence is the normal response of a rational person.

But "Suicide Solution" is only one song, and "Born Innocent" is only one program, and the rape scene only one sequence in that one program. This is hardly a trend. Certainly not an unrelieved diet of mayhem and bloodletting.

Yet to describe the problem in this way is to miss the point of even the utilitarian response. Hans Jonas, a modern utilitarian, has argued that the consequences of a nuclear holocaust are so incalculable that we must set our goals specifically at eliminating even its possibility.[7] (Notice an underlying Kantian-style commitment to the reasonableness of human survival.) A similar argument warrants eliminating graphic violence on television. If the possibility of increased real violence or loss of sensitivity to violence exists, and the means to avoid the possibility are available and not onerous, then reasonable people will take those means—and ought to, violence being hurtful.

What means are available for avoiding graphic violence on TV? Certainly viewers can choose not to watch, which is the preferred solution of the networks since it imposes no direct obligations on them. Let the buyer beware!

On the other hand, the state could impose limits on TV violence in the same way it regulates cigarette and liquor commercials. (Is there any objection to banning the advertising of unsafe medicines?)

Or again, the television industry—in this case NBC—could set its own limits based on steady evidence that TV violence at least creates a culture of suspicion and fear,[8] and on fidelity to the belief that violence is never inherently justified. But this would require rebuilding Rome, according to syndicated columnist Suzanne Fields. She argues that media violence, unlike the violence in classical literature, occurs in an "ethical vacuum." What's the point of most TV violence? There is none. Even Hansel and Gretel do better than that, Fields claims.[9]

In summer 1993, the nation's four broadcast networks (ABC, CBS, NBC, and Fox) agreed to provide TV viewers with warnings preceding shows that contain violent material. This concession was announced one day before congressional hearings on new technologies to let parents block out violent shows. Perhaps the agreement is a first step toward industry self-regulation and responsibility. Peggy Charren of Action for Children's Television called it a "benign solution, inadequate to the problem."[10]

Important distinctions separate the McCollum case and the "Born Innocent" incident. First, John did not take his handgun onto the street to apply the "solution" to any passersby. Grievous as its consequences were to his family, the harm done was self-inflicted. Second, the message blamed for inspiring McCollum's violence was in an easily repeatable format, unlike the 1974 television show. Whereas Olivia's attackers could have been influenced by a single viewing, McCollum had occasion for a total environment of Osbourne's music, as loud and as often as he chose to listen. Third, the Osbourne persona created by marketers and P.R. writers—with his cooperation—corresponded to his music's destructive themes. Neither Linda Blair nor NBC suffers under a reputation aligned with shower-room violence. Finally, NBC issued a warning as part of its message; CBS Records did not.

Is moral blame less heavy if no one other than the self is directly harmed in a violent act? In quantitative terms, yes. Given the choice of a terrorist blowing up an airliner in the sky or that same person blowing himself or herself up on the ground, we would reasonably opt for the latter. But the McCollum case involves the suicide of a young man who had a history of emotional and behavioral problems. For these individuals we bear obligations to offer aid, not a gun. Self-destruction is no solution to life's turmoils, and promoting self-destruction in music, film, or word is perpetrating a lie. Osbourne did not hand the gun to John McCollum, but his music is distributed in a format that carries no alternative point of view. No voice is heard after "Suicide Solution" arguing that self-destruction is morally wrong. McCollum heard only the most errant element of a many-sided ethical issue.

Is artistic integrity in jeopardy if we attach moral blame to a mere message? Roxanne Bradshaw of the National Education Association, commenting on violence in media, said: "We're not interested in censorship. We're interested in reeducating ourselves and our children about electronic media."[11] No moral theory would excuse media managers and artists from helping in the task Bradshaw describes. The more vulnerable the viewer/listener, the greater the obligation to talk, to help interpret, and to channel responses toward beneficent ends.

California courts excused both CBS and NBC from liability in these two court proceedings; the First Amendment would not tolerate damages sought by aggrieved plaintiffs. But our mutual human responsibility to seek each other's best interests, and to help each other avoid meaningless hurt and harm—a responsibility expressed in both Judeo-Christian and Kantian ethics—knows no constitutional boundaries. NBC need not graphically show the tools and techniques of sexual abuse. CBS Records has no moral right to profit from the genius of an artist who would be foolish and wrong to practice what he preaches. Nonetheless, if the corporation chooses to exercise legal rights to such expression, fair warnings— if not outright disclaimers—would put record buyers on notice. People closest to troubled, vulnerable users of such media could then make more informed choices. In the present case, our objective is to prevent the lie of Osbourne's music from becoming John McCollum's final word.

62. CRUNCHY TERROR IN T-REX PARK

Steven Spielberg's film *Jurassic Park,* based on the novel by Michael Crichton, set all-time box office records for opening weekends when it was released in June 1993. Helping to generate the parade of eager filmgoers was a tie-in with McDonalds restaurants featuring dinosaur-sized portions of familiar food items, and an aggressive television ad campaign during the spring. Little wonder that the Chicago *Sun Times* played this headline over its coverage of the film's opening: "Parents, Kids Jam Local Theaters Despite Film's Violence."

The violence element was a problem, to some at least. A mother who emerged from a Chicago theater with her five-year-old son was in tears: "I thought the movie was too violent for my son. There was too much killing. I would not have taken Teddy to see it if I had known it was this violent. The movie critics didn't tell us how violent the movie was going to be. Then when dinosaurs ate the people, it was sad. I didn't like it."

Despite the film's PG-13 rating, 19 percent of those who saw the film on that first weekend were children under 12, and only 10 percent of them thought the film was too scary for kids, reported Universal Studios exit polls.

The fuzzy stuffed animals that appeared in almost every store in the country might have belied the film's true terror. Most of the dinosaurs in this film were anything but huggable, especially the voracious and vicious raptors. Said one Chicago seven-year-old: "I was really scared when that big dinosaur tried to bite that girl's feet off." Enhanced digital sound effects made the bone-crunching jaws of the T-rex all the more realistic. Eitan D. Schwarz, head of child and adolescent psychiatry at Evanston (Illinois) Hospital wrote:

> Young viewers . . . could experience too vivid and real a terror here. . . . The dialogue that could make the graphic images somewhat comprehensible is too subtle and hard for young children to follow. And there are too few scenes to break the sustained tension . . . and assure young viewers. The end makes an insufficient attempt to restore a sense of safety for young viewers. [This] could be the stuff nightmares are made of.

Children see more death on an average night of prime-time television than they would have seen in *Jurassic Park*. But perhaps they do not feel as much fright. For that is what *Jurassic Park* was all about: the fear of being ripped apart by uncivilized beasts in an environment that suddenly, by the flip of a switch, belongs to them, as it did a long, long time ago.

Only on rare occasions does the viewing public raise a significant voice in the industry-controlled procedure for rating films. One example was the fuss over Spielberg's *Indiana Jones and the Temple of Doom* and *Gremlins*. Both rated PG, the films frightened enough youngsters and angered enough parents that in 1984 the Classification and Rating Administration (CARA) of the MPAA adopted the PG-13 rating: "Parents strongly cautioned. Some material may be inappropriate for children under 13." This was the first change in the rating system in 16 years (apart from the evolution of the M rating becoming GP and then PG). But this additional category only modified the established system; it was not a wholesale renovation.

In the case of *Jurassic Park*, if it could be established that the assigned rating was patently deceptive, we could summarily condemn the MPAA as ethically abhorrent under each of the five criteria described in the Introduction to this book. Such condemnation, however, would be too hasty a gesture in this case.

What happened in the case of *Jurassic Park* may be an example of doing the least to satisfy a moral requirement. Movie producers (represented by the MPAA) do not wish to discourage box office patrons, and neither do theater owners. Ratings are issued in the most inoffensive manner possible: a single letter or two letters with a terse explanation of their meaning (and there are only five categories). It is the least noxious deterrent for a paying customer.

And in many cases, the rating is no deterrent at all. Local theater owners who attempt to enforce the R rating, for example, run afoul of parents' complaints when a child dropped off to see a film is turned away—essentially left without activity or supervision—until the parent shows up again two hours later. R-rated films are so commonly viewed on home-video rentals that the MPAA restriction ("under 17 requires accompanying parent or adult guardian") may be the nation's most widely ignored guideline. The PG-13 rating stops few kids at the theater door and not a lot of adults, either.

What if producers and theater owners were to treat customers as reasonable creatures responsible for the moral tenor of their viewing experiences? Synopses of plots, descriptions of the kinds of scenes in a film, even a more sophisticated set of rating symbols would show good faith toward the viewing public. Some might argue that this information is the bread and butter of movie critics, but most film reviews are little more than re-writes of publicity material. Very few critics study film, and none speak for values other than their own.

In this case, however, we cannot fault the movie industry and entertainment writers entirely. With little investigation beyond noting the film's rating, parents took their children by the thousands to see a movie in which children on screen were terrorized. Was "parental guidance" a sufficiently active element in their decisions? Probably not. The PG-13 rating should have prompted more to ask questions of friends, call the theater manager, or perhaps first see the film themselves.

Proponents of greater liberty in television programming typically emphasize the viewer's right to turn off the set. The wider liberty of the magazine and book publishing industry also presumes that parents will monitor their children's reading material and prevent their exposure to inappropriate material. Surely the same supervisory responsibility must apply to children's selection of motion pictures.

At each point from movie producer to consumer, application of the persons-as-ends principle would help. The movie audience clearly needs more reliable, less laundered information on which to base viewing choices. Yet parents and other adults are responsible also. The chair of CARA has observed, "Our main objective is to provide an early warning signal to parents, who may then exercise their own responsibility to expose their youngsters to more mature film content only as they individually mature."[12] The military analog embedded in this caveat tells an important tale. Parents still control the last, vital link in the movie market system. Exchanging money for tickets is the free act of a consenting buyer who, even in the course of collecting on a purchase, can decide to get up from the seat, go home, and read a book.

63. *"HOLOCAUST" AND TELEVISION'S LIMITS AS A MEDIUM*

Two generations have passed since the terror of Hitler's New Order was unveiled, and survivors of the Holocaust are concerned: When the last of them die, will anyone be able to tell the story in its full tragedy, passion, and horror? Perhaps the task will fall to the media, but that prospect is less than comforting to those most interested in preserving the memory and meaning of their suffering.

In an expensive and serious effort, NBC dedicated nine-and-a-half hours to a docudrama called, simply, "Holocaust," the story of two German families from 1935 to 1945.[13] The Weiss family is Jewish; Josef and Berta Weiss are the parents of a typically close-knit clan that fails to interpret the first signs of Nazi persecution. Their oldest son, Karl, and his Roman Catholic wife, Inge, are sent to Buchenwald and Theresienstadt. Their daughter, Anna, is brutally raped, then killed in a "hospital" for the mentally ill. The middle son, Rudi, escapes the German net and after much hardship takes up arms against the Nazis.

The Dorfs, Erik and Marta, live in Berlin. He is an unemployed lawyer, she an ambitious wife who convinces Erik to join the German SS (Hitler's elite black-shirts). He becomes an aide to "blond beast" Reinhard Heydrich and in that capacity travels the breadth of Europe engineering schemes for ridding the Reich of the Jewish "menace." To add realism to the drama, writer Gerald Green included portrayals of Adolf Eichmann, Heinrich Himmler, and Heydrich.

NBC worked hard to generate an audience for the financially risky miniseries. The network invited prominent Jewish, Catholic, and Protestant leaders to preview the series, and it encouraged the preparation of study guides for school and church discussion on the meaning of the Holocaust and the ways of avoiding another one. Rabbi Irving Greenberg of New York wrote the introduction to the interfaith guide.

Such careful preparation—plus a lot of advertising—worked well. An estimated 120 million Americans saw at least part of the four-night series. The first installment drew a 43 percent share; the third evening drew a 49 percent share (59 in New York City). Ratings were higher in many of the 40 countries that played "Holocaust" in the year following. In the Netherlands, 54 percent watched at least one episode; in Austria, 61 percent.

Reviewers across the country applauded. The *Washington Post* called it "the most powerful drama ever seen on television." Rev. William L. Weiler, executive director of the Office of Christian-Jewish Relations of the National Council of Churches, called the program a "very effective, engaging drama." Rabbi Marc Tannenbaum, director of national interreligious affairs for the American Jewish Committee, who served as a consultant for NBC, remarked: "I have seen it three times and found myself crying each time. The impact of the series is greater than anything I have witnessed since the end of World War II."

Only in one corner of the country a dissenting opinion appeared, and that corner happened to be the most important one—New York City. Two days before the mini-series began, *New York Times* critic John J. O'Connor concluded that the production staff of "Holocaust" had faced "a massive problem and were unable to find satisfactory solutions." The plot was contrived, the actors sterile, and the effect superficial. Perhaps commercial television was simply not the medium capable of telling the terrible story, he mused. To throw Jews and Nazis, fictional or historical, into a second-rate dramatization that will be seen with interruptions for inane commercials is to enter automatically a process of diminishment. Incredible horror is reduced to "effective" on-location settings in Austria and West Berlin. Unprecedented pain is mixed up with the choosing of "correct" costumes. . . . The very barbarity of Nazism is whittled down to an image not dissimilar from the fad for a touch of sadism in lingerie ads. No matter the good intentions of the production staff, the inevitable trivialization is fatal.[14]

Also writing in the *New York Times*, Holocaust survivor Elie Wiesel lashed out at what he saw as stereotyped characters, historical errors, an obsessive theme of Jewish resignation, and errors in the portrayal of Jewish life and liturgy. He called the series "untrue, offensive, cheap: as a TV production, the film is an insult to those who perished and to those who survived. . . . It transforms an ontological event into soap opera. Whatever the intentions, the result is shocking." Wiesel wrote with the passion of one who had seen and survived the Nazi terror:

We see naked women and children entering the gas chambers; we see their faces, we hear their moans as the doors are being shut, then—well, enough: why continue? To use special effects and gimmicks to describe the indescribable is to me morally objectionable. Worse: it is indecent. The last moments of the forgotten victims belong to themselves.[15]

Wiesel had been taken from his home in Sighet, Hungary, in 1944 at age 15 to Auschwitz, where his parents and a sister died, but he survived. "Never shall I forget that night," he recalls in his first book, "which has turned my life into one long night. Never shall I forget that smoke."[16]

On the day after the series concluded, O'Connor followed up his earlier review with a scathing attack on the "shocking insensitivity" of a network's exploiting such serious material for commercial gain. "A monstrous historical fact has been put through the peculiar process that is called commercial television. In its more extreme moments, that processing proved to be almost as obscene as the Holocaust itself."[17]

Letters from viewers poured in. Many were outraged at the commercial interruptions; others were resigned to them. Some abhorred what they perceived as trivialized history; others were gratified that, whatever its shortcomings, the series had raised the consciousness of millions toward the evils of anti-Semitism. In the course of the debate, the network lost one of its most important allies: Rabbi Greenberg. For him the series "lacked the insight and touch of survivors," especially on the question of Jewish resignation. "Holocaust" had portrayed as heroes those Jews who took up arms, as they did in the Warsaw Ghetto. The drama was critical, especially through the character of Inge, of the many who grimly walked in front of the machine guns or into the deadly showers. Why did so many submit? Here was a problem that defied the quick cuts and surface storyline that television requires. Greenberg pointed to the

> overwhelming force and cruelty that made death inescapable and often a relief; the collective responsibility and the way family and children tied the hands of those who would have fought. . . . [Real survivors] realize that just living as a human being, refusing to abandon family or religion or dignity was the true, incredible every-day heroism of millions who died and the few who survived. The absence of this insight may be the gravest flaw of "Holocaust."[18]

Television, by its physical dimensions alone, is a limited medium. It cannot convey the grandeur of vast tracts of landscape; it cannot hope to show finely detailed art.

Is the medium limited, also, in the drama its format can adequately portray? Plots with stereotyped characters and predictable conclusions are obviously television's trump. Intricate plots and extended character development are much more hazardous, especially where continuity must be sacrificed for sponsors' announcements.

A television producer exploring the idea of a mini-series on the Holocaust would have to consider the potential audience, but satisfying the business criterion ought not determine her decision. Does she have writers, actors, and other support personnel to do justice to the script? Even if these resources are available, the decision to produce involves still other considerations.

Once the technical and financial means are in hand, the producer must ask: Is this a story I really want to do? A producer may be drawn to the story (or repelled from it) by hopes for recognition and advancement in the field. She may have a native interest in the story: The plot or theme may strike a creative nerve. Typically, a producer's decision process ends at this point. If the program idea is marketable, if staff and equipment are available, and if she personally wants to produce (for whatever reason), then why not?

Has an important criterion been overlooked? Are there ethically sound reasons why a producer of a mini-series on the Holocaust might choose, in the final analysis, to respect the limitations of her medium, preserving the dignity of those who endured the bitter grief?

This is another form of the question, "To whom is moral duty owed?" In the case of "Holocaust," network producers were admirably sensitive to duties toward their audience. Providing study aids and enlisting the help of concerned agencies could be seen as a public relations ploy, but on the surface it must be applauded as above and beyond the normal concern given a docudrama.

But Rabbi Greenberg, Elie Wiesel, and John O'Connor were raising the matter of duty owed the subject of the drama itself: the victims of the actual Holocaust. Were their concerns given sufficient attention? Perhaps this is a question only victims themselves can answer. At a minimum, Holocaust victims viewing the docudrama must not feel exploited, simplified, or divinized. They must not feel compromised by the inherent limitations of the television medium. Most important, network producers must not be open to the charge that they used the setting of the Holocaust to create just another stock human-interest drama, imposing familiar plot devices onto the Jewish story.

Assistance from survivors at every stage of the process might have produced a more realistic "Holocaust." Turning the project over to creative talent in Jewish heritage agencies might have given a more realistic, less stereotyped rendering. More sensitive allocation of commercials would have shown greater respect to the victims.

Moral duty in this case is also owed the German people. Few Germans today are not repulsed at the heinous human-rights violations of Hitler's Reich. Modern attempts to dramatize the gigantic moral lapse of their fathers and grandfathers must do justice to the economic and political context that made that nation so vulnerable to Hitler's rhetoric. Simple portrayals of Germany in the 1930s to 1940s as brutish and barbaric do injustice to the moral agony of the German people and contribute nothing to the healing of intervening years.

If such moral considerations—based soundly on the persons-as-ends principle— were too costly, too time consuming, or too idiosyncratic, then the network should have faced up to the boundaries of its own universe. Perhaps commercial television, with its time constraints and institutional demands, cannot re-create in dramatic form the intense human feelings and tragedy that after more than a generation still stretch the limits of credibility.

64. "THE STORYTELLER"

In oral cultures, "storyteller" might connote the village historian or tribal sage, the person responsible for interpreting the outside world to kindred with lesser vision, the personal repository of a culture's myth and wisdom. With perhaps the same idea in mind, script writers Richard Levinson and William Link, creators of the police drama *Columbo,* gave the title "The Storyteller" to their introspective drama about the crisis of conscience faced by a television scriptwriter whose work, aired one evening on network television, portrayed several acts of arson. In the story, the show is seen by a youth who immediately after viewing leaves his home to try to burn down his school. The youth dies of smoke inhalation in the fire.[19]

Levinson and Link broke into television writing just as the industry came face to face with questions of the influence of televised violence on the real world. The many studies, essays, and investigations following the Kennedy assassinations, however inconclusive, at least established the intuition that television can be a factor in why real people do some things and not other things. Not that violence was new to popular drama. Levinson and Link grew up on Dashiell Hammett, Zane Grey, and the squeaky door of Dr. Frankenstein's laboratory, and they "survived not only intact but also enriched." But the next decades brought a new fascination with the "actual moment of slaughter," slow-motion carnage, and the chilling spectacle of audiences cheering the cinematic bloodlust. Whose was the moral burden?

The purpose of "The Storyteller" was, in Levinson and Link's words, to "analyze our own feelings and attitudes, not only about the violence issue, but also about the responsibilities, if any, of those of us who enter so many homes and minds each night of the week." To the consternation of some viewers, the drama did not follow predictable television denouement. Instead of taking a point of view and suggesting answers to their dilemma, Levinson and Link were satisfied to "explore the problem . . . to present the audience with the incredible tangle of pros and cons involved." Yet their sense of moral accountability comes through when the mother of the dead boy asks the writer, "You come into people's homes, the homes of people you don't even know. Do you think about that every time you sit down at your typewriter?" The village sage never faced a question like that.

This kind of self-reflection is a big step toward responsible media; it stretches the mind and draws out the issues, even if it reaches no conclusions.

Perhaps it falls to agencies such as the Screen Actors Guild (SAG) to coalesce opinion and reach positions on these matters. Its members and board formally passed an anti-violence resolution in 1974 (and again in 1977) that read, in part:

> While various studies do not lead to absolute conclusions, there is reasonable cause to believe that imitation of violent acts seen on television is a potential danger and examples of this phenomenon are well documented. There is reasonable cause to believe that the excessive violence viewed on television can also increase aggressive behavior patterns and that repetitive viewing of violence leads to greater acceptance of violence as a norm of societal mores. . . . What is disturbing in television programming is the emphasis on violence and the degree of violence portrayed. . . . The extent and degree of violence in television programming is excessive. . . . Degrees of violence can be lowered in entertainment just as we hope to reduce such excess in our society. . . . We challenge those who are responsible for the programs aired to make the effort—and for the sake of all—the sooner the better.[20]

Someone might object to these sentiments, of course. The statement assumes that a reasonable cause connects media violence with real behavior. This, someone might argue, is the same kind of speculative social science that makes up the rhetoric of media watchdog groups.

And another objection: the SAG statement purports to recommend change "for the sake of all," a clear appeal to the utilitarian principle of the greatest good for the greatest number. But that principle can never demonstrate the difference between too much and appropriate violence. Would the SAG statement suggest that violence is appropriate if and only if no one in real life is physically harmed in any way? Unlikely. Everything from eating bacon to brewing moonshine has some inherent risk. And such a prescription would be too late to help the victims anyhow. Would the SAG statement preclude violence that harms a significant number in a significant way? Impossible. Who could calculate such an application? Ergo, the SAG statement and all others like it are mere rhetorical flourishes and soapbox oratory. The only workable principle is to give writers and producers a free hand in the scripts they develop. True art is achieved only in the context of free expression. Artificial or arbitrary constraints will keep television drama forever immature. Even the SAG recognized the whimsy of its statement; since Kathleen Nolan's retirement from leadership, the SAG has not voiced an opinion on violence in drama.

If art requires freedom, is it also morally accountable? Is art good because it is free, or is it good when it captures in poignant and resonant ways a slice of the human search for meaning? The latter principle avoids the facile pairing of art and freedom that excuses so much tripe, and it brings art squarely into the moral domain. Art and ethics are not mutually exclusive categories. It should be possible, then, to conceive a policy for the portrayal of television violence that will remain true to the aspirations of creative talent without violating the genuine moral claims of actors, viewers, and others drawn into the process after major decisions have already been made.

Does the golden mean provide a basis for responsible violence? Appropriate violence must steer away from portraying humans as mere beasts, or as unrealistically angelic. Can specific policies be drawn from such an appeal to principle? Whereas such policy statements often turn into dead letters uniformly ignored, on occasion intelligent manifestoes, conscientiously promoted, have aroused attention and changed opinions.

65. COMIC CAPERS

From the greatest of the old-time crime chasers (Dick Tracy) to bizarre change agents (Incredible Hulk), comic heroes pursue daring and virtue in their own special world of make-believe. Often their denouement involves overpowering some dastardly character, defusing some devastating explosive, or derailing a hunk of heavy machinery—all in the name of protecting the innocent and winning the war against cruelty (see Figure 13.1 on pages 280–281).

But what of the cruelty required of the heroes themselves? Is it possible that the comics' depiction of cruel means to virtuous ends confuses young minds by suggesting that anything is okay if some good is served in the end?

Violence dominates the comics. In 1974, John DiFazio analyzed the comic book treatment of fourteen American values and found that "peaceful resolution of conflict" was one of the values least often portrayed.[21] Our own quick review of a grocery store comic rack revealed plot resolutions involving a woman blowing herself up with a shotgun while trying to save an infant from a monster, the crashing of a boulder on the cranium of a muscle-bound cyclops, and the blinding of a Rebel soldier by a "blue belly" bullet. One can almost hear Frederick Wertham, author of the classic 1954 attack on crime comics, *Seduction of the Innocent*, uttering "I told you so" to the numerous critics who disparaged his work.[22]

Such unrestrained violence was not always the rule in children's literature. Note, for example, the ethic of restraint that characterized the popular Nancy Drew detective series, according to James Lones:

> There was an abundance of violence in the Nancy Drew series, but it was controlled violence. Clubbings, wrecks, assault and battery were common. Attacks fell indiscriminately on many types of characters with Nancy often the target. Despite this violence no one was murdered. Criminals who assaulted their victims did not go beyond beatings. In a decade [the 1930s] when sensational real life kidnappings stirred the population, these fictionalized kidnappings ended happily and no victim of abduction was killed. Guns were used but were either fired as warnings, and not directly at persons, or used as clubs.[23]

Recent commentary on the comic book industry is as troubling as Wertham's case studies. Joe Queenan of the *New York Times Magazine* wrote:

> Over the last decade, comics have forsaken campy repartee and out- landishly byzantine plots for a steady diet of remorseless violence. "Green Arrow" depicts a woman whose eyes have been plucked out by vultures. In "Spider-Man," seven men are ripped to pieces by a wolf. The back pages of "Wolverine" show the hero puffing on a cigarette as blood drips from his lips. . . . "Black Orchid" begins with a woman being tied up and set on fire, then moves on to child abuse, a mutant fed live rats, and a jailed hybrid—half woman, half plant—who avoids rape only because her jailers find her too repulsive.[24]

The comic industry grosses $300 million a year, with DC Comics and Marvel in the distant lead, followed by Archie Comic Publications and then about 200 minor-league hopefuls. One industry distributor explained: "Our readers are teenage boys [with] lots of repressed anger. [They are] going through puberty [and they] like to see characters act out their aggressions."

One concern that ethicists cannot avoid is the question of the effects of the violence on impressionable consumers. And here, as media researchers are well aware, the evidence is both solid and gaseous: advocates line up on both sides. A report from the Group for the Advancement of Psychiatry, concerned about televised violence, found unequivocal negative effects; but the American Academy of Pediatrics could claim with as much gusto that TV teaches beneficial social values. Researchers at Texas Tech in 1980 found no support for the hypothesis that reading violent comics leads to greater aggression among children, but they admitted "it is possible that the effects of comic book reading may be long-term and cumulative."[25]

FIGURE 13.1 Everything the cover promises . . . the inside pages deliver: skull-crushing monsters, prehistoric battles, beatings, and the savagery of war.

The ethicist is faced with puzzling questions: Who is hurt by reading or viewing fictional violence? Would the harm attributed (by some) to media programming come about anyhow, in which case violence in media becomes an insignificant part of the equation? Who should assume moral responsibility for children's media menu: publishers? writers? television directors? sponsors and advertisers? parents?

A reasonable argument could be made that children would read comics and watch cartoons regardless of the style of the conflict and the means of its resolution. Children do not demand violence in media; they are entertained with or without clubs, knives, and pistols. Producers, then, cannot argue that they must provide violence to secure an audience. *Mister Rogers* and *Sesame Street* give muscle to the argument that low-level violence or none at all do not diminish a child's loyalty to the program. Producers would benefit from using the Potter Box technique to face the question of their ultimate loyalties. They cannot reasonably choose concern for their own pocketbooks over service to their juvenile audience. In any case, it seems apparent that production people could move toward more humane conflict resolution without jeopardizing their enterprise.

Ultimate moral duty must fall to those who are most directly involved in the guidance and growth of children. Whereas moral reasoning does not absolve producers and writers, it assumes that the parent/guardian–child relationship is primary for the teaching of values. In Western democracies, the public market-place is kept relatively free, while each family exercises the closer selection of what will become part of its perceptual experience.

At the level of family, the ethic of persons as ends is given most prominent play. Here moral duty is to the child first and foremost, not to the marketplace; each child is the most valued part of the sender-channel-receiver process. Here the concerns of the individual rise to prominence as the values of free and unimpeded media programming recede. Resolving the issue of violence in children's media is chiefly a matter of recovering the notion of family as a moral institution. Only on this intimate level can the ethic of persons as ends truly flourish.

NOTES

1. United States Department of Justice. *Attorney General's Commission on Pornography: Final Report* (1986), p. 1957.
2. Joseph Lieberman quoted in the *Daily Herald,* 2 December 1993, sec. 1, p. 11.
3. *McCollum v. CBS,* 15 Med. L. Rptr. 2001.
4. Material on "Born Innocent" was drawn from "TV Wins a Crucial Case," *Time,* 21 August 1978, p. 85; T. Schwartz et al., "TV on Trial Again," *Newsweek,* 14 August 1978, pp. 41–42; "NBC's First Amendment Rape Case," *Esquire,* 23 May 1978, pp. 12–13; "Back to Court for 'Born Innocent,'" *Broadcasting,* 1 May 1978, pp. 37–38; "Judge Restricts 'Born Innocent' Case to First Amendment Issue," *Broadcasting,* 7 August 1978, pp. 31–32; Karl E. Meyer, "Television's Trying Times," *Saturday Review,* 16 September 1978, pp. 19–20; *New York Times,* 18 September 1978; *Wall Street Journal,* 25 April 1978.

5. If media effects research finally eliminates any connection, and even the possibility of connection, between viewing habits and behavior, then real harm is eliminated as a factor and arguments to curtail media programming for any reason fall away. But the weight of our society's beliefs leans heavily toward a connection, the contours of which are the substance of effects researchers' debates.

6. Jeremy Bentham, *An Introduction to the Principles of Morals and Legislation*, eds. J. H. Burns and H. L. A. Hart (London: Athlone Press, 1970), p. 11.

7. Hans Jonas, *The Imperative of Responsibility* (Chicago: University of Chicago Press, 1984).

8. The many writings of George Gerbner and Larry Gross are just the tip of the iceberg supporting this contention.

9. Suzanne Fields, "The Trouble Is that TV Violence Occurs in a Moral Vacuum," *Daily Herald*, 6 July 1993, sec. 1, p. 8.

10. *Daily Herald*, 30 June 1993, sec. 1, p. 14.

11. *Media and Values* (Fall 1985), p. 9.

12. Richard D. Heffner, "What G, PG, R, and X Really Mean," *TV Guide*, 4 October 1980, p. 39. The quotation by Eitan Schwarz is from a letter to the editor, *Chicago Tribune*, 29 June 1993, sec. 1, p. 14.

13. "Holocaust" was analyzed in the *New York Times*, 14–30 April, 4–7 May, 24 June 1978.

14. John J. O'Connor, "TV Weekend," *New York Times*, 14 April 1978, p. C26.

15. Elie Wiesel, "Trivializing the Holocaust: Semi-Fact and Semi-Fiction," *New York Times*, 16 April 1978, sec. 2, p. 1.

16. Quoted in *Time*, 18 March 1985, p. 79.

17. John J. O'Connor, "TV: NBC 'Holocaust,' Art Versus Mammon," *New York Times*, 20 April 1978, p. C22.

18. Irving Greenberg, Letter to the Editor, *New York Times*, 30 April 1978, sec. 2, p. 30.

19. Richard Levinson and William Link, "A Crisis of Conscience," *TV Guide*, 3 December 1977, p. 6.

20. "SAG Position Re Excessive Violence on TV." Minutes of the Special Meeting of the Executive Committee of the Screen Actors Guild, 29 November 1976, p. 9919.

21. DiFazio's study is cited in Alexis S. Tan and Kermit Joseph Scruggs, "Does Exposure to Comic Book Violence Lead to Aggression in Children?" *Journalism Quarterly* 57 (Winter 1980): 579–583.

22. Frederick Wertham, *Seduction of the Innocent* (New York: Rinehart, 1954).

23. James P. Lones, "Nancy Drew, WASP SuperGirl of the 1930s," *Journal of Popular Culture* 6 (Spring 1973): 712.

24. Joe Queenan, "Drawing on the Dark Side," *New York Times Magazine*, 30 April 1989.

25. Tan and Scruggs, p. 583.

chapter 14

Profits, Wealth, and Public Trust

Entertainment media in America are 90 percent business and 10 percent public service. Or are these figures too weighted toward public service? Only the most unrepentant idealist would argue that public service or social responsibility is a major consideration in most entertainment media decisions. If such social benefits show up in the product, all well and good. But woe the producer, director, editor, or recording executive whose product shows a financial loss, whatever the social gain. The profit motive is the most compelling concern in entertainment industry decisions; some observers would insist it is the only concern.

As prior parts of this volume have indicated, the bottom line of profit and loss affects media of all types; but entertainment media feel the impact most directly. A major survey of executives in the motion picture industry confirmed the intuition that here was a media system operating on essentially amoral criteria. A vice-president of a major production and distribution company commented: "There are no ethical decisions in the movie business. In a word, the profit motive renders ethics irrelevant. The only counterbalance is that certain individuals— and precious few at that—live their personal and professional lives according to some reasonably high standard."[1]

The first case, "Crude Script for Tinsel Town," rehearses a scenario all too common as big media companies assemble their considerable talent and business muscle to guarantee profits in a competitive environment. "The Book that Squeaked" examines the market for confidential personal information and the problem of keeping promises. "The Purpose Is Profit" poses the question: Is the business ethos ever sufficient for a creative media person, however necessary it may be to keep royalty checks coming?

"Deep Trouble for Harry" looks at profits in the pornographic movie industry, with all of its First Amendment complications. Finally, "Super Strip" points to an example of fairness that carries a note of hope for justice apart from legal constraint.

In one sense, it is easy to pick on big league corporate players as having "sold out" to the creative scourge of bottom-line management. Leaders are easy targets, especially leaders who are also conspicuously rich and live around fame. Stereotyping serves no one and solves no problem. We note that the Humanitas Committee has begun to operate seminars for network executives on the issue of human values. The committee head, the Rev. Ellwood Kieser, a Catholic priest, comments: "People creating programming have tremendous moral power. They're aware of the responsibility and sometimes don't have a good conscience about how to use it."[2] In that spirit, the cases below are not moral garbage heaps, the ruins of a corrupted empire, but situations that call for genuine moral reflection and the exertion of moral muscle.

66. CRUDE SCRIPT FOR TINSEL TOWN

Humorist Art Buchwald had already established his national reputation when, inspired by a state visit of the Shah of Iran, he constructed an eight-page motion picture treatment called "It's a Crude, Crude World." In the story, a black African prince loses wealth and throne while in the United States, but discovers love.

Paramount Pictures was interested. Its biggest star, Eddie Murphy, needed new material, and the Buchwald treatment, renamed "King for a Day," looked promising. Paramount optioned the idea and began searching for a screenwriter.

But two years of writing and rewriting finally led to disappointment for Buchwald and his agent, Alain Bernheim. In 1985, Paramount put the project in "turnaround," meaning that Buchwald and Bernheim were free to sell the idea to another studio. Indeed, Warner Brothers picked up the movie idea and began a new round of script preparations for "King Jomo."

But that project, too, was destined for cancellation in early 1988 when Warner executives learned that Paramount was preparing to shoot an Eddie Murphy film called *The Quest*, the story of an African prince who comes to the United States looking for a wife. That film was released in 1988 under the now well-known title "Coming to America," starring Murphy and his pal, Arsenio Hall. It would gather over $130 million from satisfied theatergoers, video renters, and international distributors. Yet Paramount insisted that profits never matched expenses.

That incredible financial assertion lay at the heart of Buchwald's suit against the entertainment giant. He claimed that "Coming to America" was based on his work, and that his contract awarded him a 19 percent share of net profits. Paramount resisted any compromise on its claim of originality for the movie, but contended that even if Buchwald could show that Murphy's movie was "based on" the "Crude World" treatment, there were no profits to distribute. Through a complicated formula devised by film industry accountants, "Coming to America," even with its mega-receipts, was $20 million in the red and would probably never see black. Buchwald, they claimed, held a contract that awarded him nothing.[3]

Whereas the courtroom arguments involved money damages, contract terms, and copyright infringement, the moral issue in this case centers on the power of entertainment corporations to dictate the rules entirely to their advantage. Could a new player hope for fair terms? Not with standard industry contracts that shield profits and accounting procedures that ensure that even a blockbuster hit would show financial loss.

Buchwald had signed a standard contract: money up-front for the idea, plus a percentage if the eventual movie made a profit. In most lines of work, such a contract would function like simple sales commission, providing incentive and fairly sharing the revenue and the risk.

But the long courtroom battle over this treatment finally resulted in a declaration that the standard industry contract was a "contract of adhesion," one in which one party (namely Buchwald) had no room to negotiate, no leverage to adjust terms, no choice but to sign or remain an outsider.

Marketplace competition usually adjusts for such one-sided ventures by offering creative talent an alternative venue, but not in this case. Every major studio had a stake in Paramount's argument for the "standard" contract. Even the Screen Writers Guild, which should have seen the importance for all writers in Buchwald's case, declined to support him. Hollywood production companies circled the wagons against Buchwald, Bernheim, and their lawyers.

The ink never dries on new books and articles describing the worrisome prospects for culture and creativity as big corporations swallow smaller ones and create "media monopoly." Critics of unbridled capitalism have wrung hands over the loss of cottage industries and independent operations in the book trade, the video production business, magazines, and newspapers. Under media monopoly, the pluralism of American voices takes on a scripted sound as subtle cultural imperialism smothers nuance and accent. A closed system in any medium eventually negates the radical vision and moral horizon that animated its founders, whose wealth was often paper-thin but whose courage knew no bounds.

Contracts of adhesion are symbols of centralized power that are prima facie offensive to moral traditions of justice and fairness. Surely no movie executive would dare to sit behind a "veil of ignorance" where the winner takes all. The Rawlsian veil tends to level the playing field, and few industries need such an influence more than American feature films. Buchwald struggled through a civil procedure where a circuit court provided a type of veil, and he came away with an award that amounted to less than a tenth of the cost of litigation.

Paramount made its appeal to a kind of rigorous Kantian ethic: When a person signs a contract, he is obliged to its terms. But contracts are fair instruments when both parties have something to give and take. Too much power on one side forecloses justice, unless moral vision prevails over avarice in the hearts of the powerful. In a tightly controlled system of high risk and huge profit, avarice is often too strong a factor and fairness too feeble.

Creative justice is the film industry's ticket to long-term profitability. Fair dealing in honest negotiation serves the greater interests of all parties, including the consumer of film products, who in this case missed a potentially great comedy for the bawdy showcase that signaled a peak in Murphy's career.

67. *THE BOOK THAT SQUEAKED*

Marcia Chellis and Joan Kennedy had much in common. Both were raised in well-to-do families, both married wealthy and successful men, both were alcoholics. They became acquainted at a meeting of apartment tenants after Chellis's divorce and Kennedy's separation, and they became friends. When Joan joined husband Ted in his bid for the Democratic presidential nomination in 1979, she hired Marcia as an aide and secretary. For three years the two women were virtually inseparable.

By 1982 the Kennedy star had dimmed. Indeed, Democrats around the country were hushed by Ronald Reagan's stunning victory over incumbent Jimmy Carter. The time had come for Marcia Chellis to find other employment.

Chellis terminated her position with Joan Kennedy, and notes taken while she was inside that near-mythic family went with her: notes on Ted's whereabouts, notes on the family's hardships, notes on Kennedy property and their lifestyle, and notes of conversations with her friend and employer, Joan.

Three years later, those notes became the substance of *Living with the Kennedys: The Joan Kennedy Story*, published by Simon and Schuster. The book enjoyed brisk sales, then trailed off, but not before some heated words from the Kennedy family. When the *Chicago Tribune* printed excerpts of the book in its Tempo section, Eunice Shriver (Joan's sister-in-law) wrote to the editor (in part):

> What is the significance of a book that makes a mockery of trust, loyalty, and friendship? What are your readers to gain from the work of a woman who posed as a friend only to make money by peddling gossip and striking at the very foundation of friendship? . . . The values of friendship and trust have been perverted [in this book], and you have played a part in abetting this betrayal.[4]

But author Marcia Chellis saw the problem differently. To *People* magazine she said, "Joan will still see my loyalty in what I chose *not* to include in the book."[5]

At first glance, this case looks as much like an invasion-of-privacy or a reporters-and-sources case as any other dilemma described in this book. But invasion cases nearly always involve outsiders trying to get in (such as photographer Ronald Galella hounding Jacqueline Onassis, before the courts intervened). Chellis was no reporter, not even a book writer, during her travels with the Kennedys. She was simply a confidant.

Perhaps that puts Chellis in the same dilemma as Victor Marchetti or Frank Snepp, who sought to report, entertain, and profit from reminiscences of life inside the CIA.[6] But again the differences are crucial. The former federal agents had agreed, as part of their employment contract, not to divulge information gained on the job. Chellis had apparently made no formal agreements, and her writing posed no arguable compromise to national security interests.

Chellis's *Living with the Kennedys* speaks with clarity to public figures whose stories command a market: Let the famous beware! During her three years of service, Chellis was evidently faithful to her employer, but when official employment ended, the obligations of a confidant also terminated. Now the stories could enter the marketplace, contribute to the Kennedy legend (or detract from it), and almost certainly add a moment of notoriety to a life otherwise on the fringes of fame. Of course, Chellis would not be the last author to open the lives of the Kennedy clan to public view. Richard E. Burke copied nearly the same script with his *The Senator: My Ten Years with Ted Kennedy* in 1992. Starting on Kennedy's mailroom crew, Burke rose to become a top administrative assistant, and to observe firsthand (and participate in) his boss's many extracurriculars and excesses. Eleven years after Burke left his employment with the senator, his book made momentary headlines.

This case requires a close look at the fourth quadrant of the Potter Box, for here questions of a professional's primary loyalties must be confronted. Should Chellis's book have been written? Should a responsible publisher release it? Crucial to any moral resolution is the question: To whom is duty owed?

Marcia Chellis was hired to perform duties that relatively few people need or can afford. She was to be a paid professional friend, companion, coordinator, assistant, sister, spokesperson, secretary, but not a slave. Chellis would take up the cause of the Kennedy campaign, especially Joan's part of it, but not surrender her mind or even ultimately her vote, the ballot box still being secret. From all indications, Chellis performed her duties well. Like most professionals, she invested personal energy and emotion in the job as she became a more intimate part of the private Kennedy circle. When the job ended, she left on good terms, soon to become a different kind of professional—a reporter-author.

A careful look at the duties and loyalties attached to each of these professional roles should have given Chellis pause over the book. In the first role, Chellis stood as a guardian against encroachments by reporters into the Kennedys' private sphere. In the second role, she sought the very information she had been hired to protect, and her search needed go no further than her own diaries and memory. She bore no legal responsibility to remain silent, she had easy access to unique data, and she had a commitment to write, probably encouraged by an attractive publishing contract. But Chellis allowed her advantage in the first role to give her prestige in the second without drawing the distinctions that the fourth Potter quadrant requires.

Surely Joan Kennedy would not have hired Marcia Chellis as a reporter and author. Chellis cannot reasonably argue that she would have been part of the family's inner circle had Joan foreseen that Kennedy privacy would be sold in bookstores or discussed on promotional tours. With respect to the private data that aides have and reporters seek, Chellis should have started her writing career like any other reporter—by hard investigative work—and locked her Kennedy memories in a vault.

Chellis did have a book to write. Her book could have examined the public policy and platform issues that she understood as well as anyone. Former aides need not remain silent about issues that engage positions taken by a former employer. Loyalty does not mean slavery. The mind is free to debate always, and Chellis in her second role was now free to debate publicly. But her "kiss and tell" approach betrayed the loyalty she had pledged. Let her pry into other private lives if she will: the Kennedys should have been a closed book.

Another question emerges from the Potter Box, one that should trouble professional journalists. Should the excerpts have run in the newspaper? The *Tribune*'s Tempo section is usually good entertainment, sometimes helpful in readers' decision making, informative, and, by any measure of community standards, decent. In the case of *Living with the Kennedys*, editors had the chance to exhibit moral insight for Illinois readers and toward a family on the East Coast as well. They missed their chance. A review of the book, even a point-counterpoint interview with Chellis and a spokesperson for the Kennedys, would have served all parties well. Instead they hyped the excerpts in a front-page box, then titled the series "Joan Kennedy: A Confidant's Story" to heighten excitement over "what lies behind the glamour of being a Kennedy wife." The *Tribune* turned a morally objectionable book into a newspaper soap opera. Eunice Shriver's letter, published two weeks after the series concluded, deserves a response from the editors of the (once proclaimed) "World's Greatest Newspaper."

68. THE PURPOSE IS PROFIT

Larry Dowd was in his mid-twenties and already had two million books in print. He held a three-year contract with Argo Publishers that called for eight more books and several cross-country promotional tours.[7]

Dowd's themes came from "sensational" news (political scandals, Hollywood affairs, clergy in sexual trouble) salted with a shrewd instinct for the offbeat twist. One reviewer called his work "very soft-core porn—sex viewed from the soap-suds angle." His books, all mass market paperbacks, were written in a single draft while the author listened to country music or watched television. Dowd told one interviewer, "Yea for TV. I belong to the church of television watchers of America." His editor at Argo said, "Some doctor ought to look at his thyroid to see where he gets all that energy."

Dowd is pleased that his books sell fast even if they die young. "I write stuff I'd like to read, and if it isn't timely any more, I'm really not interested in reading it. I have the attention span of a puppy. Besides, my books are entertainment. They're meant to be read, then exchanged for the next one. Or even thrown away. I'm a very impatient person. I like my books to come out fast. I take a filmic approach to a book. Writing's only part of it; marketing's an important part, too."

Dowd's first novel enjoyed a hefty initial printing of 200,000, and it was still on the shelf when Dowd's fourth book put him over the one-million-sales mark. "I like to work," Dowd told a reporter. "It pays me to work hard. Hardcover reviews would be nice, but meanwhile I like my royalty checks. I look on my career as a business. All I want is to be free and comfortable and not bored."

At one point, his third novel held prospects of a motion picture contract, a possibility that prompted the comment, "I'm going to be in the movies! In pictures! Yea for me!"

The writing and publishing of books has traditionally enjoyed a degree of respectability that places its people and products a notch above most others in the creative arts field, perhaps because books and writing have a long and dignified history, because great books live from generation to generation, and because the manufacture of books is a relatively drawn-out process with several checkpoints. Moreover, the enduring nature of a book makes it all the more subject to reflective criticism. An author or publisher guilty of a non sequitur, for example, would likely endure more prolonged embarrassment than a popular singer whose voice quivers during a live performance.

Authors of books—along with symphonic musicians and composers, painters, and sculptors—have been considered less commercially motivated, less transient and ephemeral than, for instance, writers of pulp magazine tales and illustrators of advertising material. But these stereotypes have shifted with the coming of high-speed offset printing and inexpensive paperback binding. Yet to find a book writer who is thoroughly given to mass-market commercialism still provokes a sense of dissonance, as though a sacrosanct profession has been invaded by a crass profiteer. Perhaps competition for the pop-culture dollar makes commercialism in all media inevitable. But wholesale commercialism? It sounds demeaning, exploitative. On the other hand, a writer oblivious to the audience may starve for lack of sales. Clearly, the business element cannot be ignored.

This line of reasoning is based on the assumption that a creative professional, in addition to owing something to the public, also owes a debt to his profession, to his colleagues, and to the professional tradition from which he profits. A creative talent who turns art into the science of marketing—whose short-term gain is his only measure of success—is unfairly trading on a tradition that he is doing nothing to uphold; rather, his actions, as a Kantian would notice, if copied by enough of his colleagues, would subvert the art side of his business completely.

Ethical egosim, of course, would argue the opposite: Artists have no debt to anyone, save themselves and their creativity. Nothing else counts. Usually egoists justify this radical freedom with arguments that unfettered artists of one era are acclaimed as geniuses in another. This is merely another way of saying that even egoists must answer to higher standards: the ends to which their work may ultimately appeal.

Dowd cannot will that his own standards become the accepted norm. If they were, writers would be public jesters, fools deserving a scornful laugh—but nothing more. Dowd might find his own market significantly smaller. Conceivably, universal application of his standards would do a slow self-destruct to all serious cultural expression. Dowd needs a more mature, more responsible ethic than he currently has. He needs to read a good book before he tries to write one.

69. DEEP TROUBLE FOR HARRY

By most any definition, *Deep Throat* is a pornographic film. Released in 1972 at the crest of the sexual revolution, the film tells the story of a frustrated young woman (played by Linda Lovelace) who cannot "hear bells" during orgasm, no matter who is the partner. She consults a psychiatrist (played by Harry Reems) who diagnoses her problem as freakish: she has a clitoris in her throat. The promiscuous doctor then joins a long line of other bellringers who gratify themselves on, according to the *New York Times*, "virtuoso talent for fellatio."[8]

Neither Reems nor Lovelace had great acting talent, and neither found fortune in this film. Reems had done bit parts in the National Shakespeare Company and other theater when director Jerry Gerard invited him to join the production crew of this new "white coater," a porn genre specializing in portraying flaky doctors. Reems was paid $100 for two scenes, then waived all editing, marketing, and distribution rights to the movie. Two years later Reems was indicted as part of an alleged nationwide conspiracy to profit from the interstate commerce of an obscene movie. He became the first performer to be prosecuted on federal charges for artistic work—a dubious honor. Reems was convicted in Memphis, but on appeal the government declined to retry the case (following the Supreme Court's 1974 Miller decision).

Deep Throat made Lovelace a sex queen. Her starring role helped produce the most successful porn film ever made to that time. The same film typecast her and essentially ended her career, but not before silicone injections enlarged her breasts and tainted blood gave her hepatitis. Wrote Lovelace: "I was a robot who did what I had to do to survive." Her first husband earned $1,250 for Linda's role in *Deep Throat*; she never saw a penny.

Lovelace quit her movie career, remarried, and moved to Long Island, where she began to build a new identity helping at her children's elementary school and giving lectures on the social and personal effects of pornography. She also wore a beeper as she waited for a liver donor—the need for a liver transplant was the result of the silicone injections that helped entertain eight million box office patrons of *Deep Throat*.

Civil libertarians point out that 23 states banned this movie at some point in the ten years after its release. In one important legal battle in Texas, a nuisance abatement strategy was turned back by the federal appeals and U.S. Supreme Court as a dangerous movement toward prior restraint.

Whether the film deserved suppression at all is both a legal and moral problem. In a customs case in Massachusetts concerning the confiscation of a film print, the court heard an expert witness say that *Deep Throat* "puts forth an idea of greater liberation with regard to human sexuality and to the expression of it" that would help "many women" overcome particular sexual fears. Yet to argue that *Deep Throat*'s blatant appeal to lasciviousness has redeeming social benefits that warrant First Amendment protection is really to nullify common definitions of obscenity. Only a First Amendment absolutist can effectively maintain that this film should be freely allowed to find its audience. Only the true believer in *laissez-faire* popular culture would want marketeers of this film to be let loose on the populace at large.

In its much maligned *Final Report,* the Attorney General's Commission on Pornography created five broad categories of material around which to organize its 92 recommendations. The first two categories—sexually violent material and nonviolent materials depicting degradation, domination, subordination, or humiliation—were deemed harmful by most of the commission. Class IV, nudity, was an innocuous category that included both classical art and toddlers bounding around in naked innocence. Class V ("the special horror of child pornography") was so blatantly exploitative that commissioners urged the strongest measures to disrupt and prosecute this market. But the third category (nonviolent and nondegrading materials) was the most controversial.[9] It included portrayals of consensual and equal vaginal intercourse and oral-genital activity or "two couples simultaneously engaging in the same activity." The commission could not cite any film titles that fit this category, so perhaps *Deep Throat* was, in their minds, an example of Class II. Yet many people would claim that *Deep Throat* and other nonviolent pornographic films are mere entertainment that hurt no one (in a demonstrably causal fashion) and attracted no one other than interested, paying customers. As long as unsupervised children are not permitted to rent the video, the market logic goes, let adults choose *Deep Throat* if they wish. And obviously many wish.

But the free-market argument will pass no muster with Linda Lovelace Marchiano. She was the exploited star of the show who now faces medical procedures that will keep her in debt for years, if in fact she survives at all. She is the Agent Orange victim of pornographic profiteering, her body devastated by the chemicals that made her sexy and the trauma that made her desperate.[10]

And the free-market argument must also face the fact that this movie was a financial boon for organized crime. On a $25,000 investment, the Colombo crime family made well over $50 million on *Deep Throat*, with some of the profits being directed to Caribbean drug-smuggling operations.[11]

A principled market cannot exploit (in this case, it was a form of slavery) and abuse its artisans, and it cannot tolerate siphoning wealth into criminal empire building. The porn film business, with *Deep Throat* a shaded example, is too regularly guilty of each count to warrant our waving a free-market flag in its defense. Freedom, Kant argued, is in the pursuit of right reason. Freedom, Niebuhr and his compatriots would urge, is in overcoming greed and prurience through a movement of love guarded by justice. Exploring sexuality in film is inherently a good goal, but this porn film was a heist on humanity. No market potency can justify destroying a life.

A real white coater who sat on the Attorney General's Commission, Park Elliott Dietz of the University of Virginia, stated, as the work concluded:

> As a government body, we studiously avoided making judgments on behalf of the government about the morality of particular sexual acts between consenting adults or their depiction in pornography. This avoidance, however, should not be mistaken for the absence of moral sentiment among the Commissioners. I, for one, have no hesitation in condemning nearly every specimen of pornography that we have examined in the course of our deliberations as tasteless, offensive, lewd, and indecent. . . . It has been nearly two centuries since Phillipe Pinel struck the chains from the mentally ill and more than a century since Abraham Lincoln struck the chains from America's black slaves. With this statement I ask you, America, to strike the chains from America's women and children, to free them from the bond of pornography, to free them from the bonds of sexual abuse, to free them from the bonds of inner torment that entrap the second-class citizen in an otherwise free nation.[12]

70. SUPER STRIP

Jerry Siegel and Joe Shuster were high school students in Cleveland, Ohio, when they came upon the idea of a cartoon figure who, born in a distant galaxy, would escape to earth as a baby, grow up in an orphanage, and, as an adult, impervious to gravity and mightier than a locomotive, would aid the forces of justice in their battle against evil.

Siegel actually conceived the idea. His buddy Shuster liked to draw, so the two fledgling cartoonists set out to sell their story. Five years of pounding on doors finally won them a contract with Detective Comics, and the first "Superman" strip appeared in 1938. Siegel and Shuster were paid $10 a page for their work, about $15 a week per man.[13]

The contract favored the company. The more popular Superman became, the clearer was Siegel and Shuster's loss. Finally, they brought suit against Detective and were awarded some money, but still they had no rights to their hero. When the legal dust settled, Detective fired Siegel and Shuster, and the two creators were left to watch others get rich and famous off their idea. More lawsuits proved futile. Late in 1975, with legal routes exhausted, the men defied the advice of their attorneys and went public with their story.

Their tale was one of sadness and struggle. Neither man had received any money from Superman since 1948, though profits from the Man of Steel were in the multimillions. Shuster now was legally blind, living in Queens with a brother who supported him. Siegel was ill and lived with his wife in a tiny apartment in Los Angeles, where he worked as a government clerk typist for $7,000 a year. The men appealed to Superman's current copyright owner "out of a sense of moral obligation," said Shuster. The National Cartoonists Society and Cartoonists Guild lent their full backing to Siegel and Shuster's moral claim.

The appeal brought results. Warner Communications, which owned movie rights to Superman, claimed "no legal obligation," but "there is a moral obligation on our part." Two days before Christmas, Siegel and Shuster signed a contract with Warner: They would each receive $20,000 yearly for life, and their heirs would also be helped. The creators' names would appear on all Superman productions. At the signing, a Warner executive commended the two cartoonists. The contract, he said, was "in recognition of their past services and out of concern for their present circumstances."

The money awarded Siegel and Shuster presented no threat to the profits of Warner Communications. The sum of $40,000 a year may be less than the company spends in processing receipts from Superman sales. But as a gesture neither required by law nor essential to public relations, it represents an application of the Judeo-Christian ethic of othermindedness.

Consider the dynamics of the award. Siegel and Shuster had sold their idea under the duress of the Depression and at a time in their youth when neither could be expected to negotiate a contract with business savvy. Events had changed dramatically since then. One was now disabled, and the other ill; both were living on a bare-bones income. Exhausted by fruitless legal efforts, they nonetheless persisted in a moral claim for some relief.

Warner could have called their appeal a nuisance. Business is business, after all. Investors who cash in stock certificates, for example, never qualify for ex post facto profits. Farmers who sell a corn crop in November may not appeal for extra payment when the bushel price rises in January. Buyers and sellers each assume part of the risk, and each understands that one could emerge from the deal a clear winner. Because the terms are understood, the bargain is fair.

But contracts are not independent from the economic milieu in which they are made. Were they selling a cartoon character today instead of in 1938, Siegel and Shuster might negotiate for a compensation clause should their idea become a bonanza. Indeed, they could have insisted that direct successors to their character, should Superman ever die (inconceivable until he met his fate in 1992 saving the world from Doomsday), be part of their legacy also. (It seems now that four new Supermen will vie for the honor.) The economic climate of the late 1930s was not ripe for such risk-reducing appendices.

So the recognition awarded Siegel and Shuster was for the cartoonists a humanitarian gesture of life-sustaining aid, whereas to Warner it represented no loss to shareholders and no risk to corporate solvency. Perhaps a thorough application of "others as ourselves" or Rawls's ethic of undifferentiated negotiators would have resulted in larger awards, or royalties for Siegel and Shuster, or a cost-of-living adjustment in their $20,000 annual amount, or life insurance policies to establish an estate for each man. Maybe so. It may be argued that Warner hemmed and hawed until it was expedient for it to make a gesture, quite apart from what was fair for the two penniless cartoonists. But the award, such as it was, points to a residual sense of group solidarity and caring, a dissonant but hopeful interlude in the normally amoral entertainment business.

NOTES

1. See Clifford Christians and Kim B. Rotzoll, "Ethical Issues in the Film Industry," in *Current Research in Film: Audiences, Economics, and Law*, vol. 2, ed. Bruce A. Austin (Norwood, NJ: Ablex, 1986), pp. 225-237.
2. "Whose Values Run Hollywood?" *USA Weekend*, 23-25 October 1992, p. 8.
3. See Pierce O'Donnell and Dennis McDougal, *Fatal Subtraction: The Inside Story of Buchwald v. Paramount* (New York: Doubleday, 1992).
4. *Chicago Tribune*, 5 November 1985, sec. 1, p. 12.
5. *People Weekly*, 23 September 1985, p. 35.
6. Victor Marchetti, *The CIA and the Cult of Intelligence* (New York: Dell, 1980, 1989); Frank Snepp, *Decent Interval: The American Debacle in Vietnam and the Fall of Saigon* (New York: Random House, 1977). Both authors and their books were subjected to national security proceedings.
7. This fictionalized case is based on J. Howard, "Yea for Me!" *New Times*, 2 November 1973, pp. 46-47.
8. Quotation and background material from Edward de Grazia and Roger K. Newman, *Banned Films: Movies, Censors, and the First Amendment* (New York: R. R. Bowker, 1982).
9. United States. Attorney General's Commission on Pornography (1986). The report is summarized in Michael J. McManus, "Introduction" to *Final Report of the Attorney General's Commission on Pornography* (Nashville: Rutledge Hill Press, 1986), pp. xix-xxi.
10. Linda Lovelace has written (with Mike McGrady) on her experience in prostitution and pornography, her victimization, terror, and exploitation in *Ordeal* (New York: Bell Publishing, 1980).
11. McManus, "Introduction" to *Final Report*, p. 295.
12. McManus, "Introduction" to *Final Report*, pp. 491-492.
13. Material in this case is from the *New York Times*, 22 November, 10 and 24 December 1975.

chapter **15**

Media Scope and Depth

For every medium there is a scale; we may call it an aesthetic scale. On one end are the serious artists and producers, careful about the integrity of their craft and insistent that their labors give audiences a better insight into meaningful human life. On the other end are writers and producers who want to provide the most popular product possible. They care little if lofty artistic visions are part of their work; theirs is the task of attracting the largest possible share of the audience—because if they do not, competitors will. Success is measured by bestseller lists and Nielsen ratings.

The pull of the media's commercial base may inevitably lead to television programs, movies, and books that trivialize human dilemmas or escape entirely from them. Perhaps the forces resisting such trends are too weak to mount much of a counterthrust. Yet only the cynic will claim that money is really all that matters in popular culture, and only the most cloudy idealist will assert that money does not matter at all.

Between the demands of art and the marketplace are a host of moral questions that media practitioners face every day: Must art be compromised when it passes from one medium to another? Are stereotyped characters fair to real people? How far should commercial concerns dictate cultural products? What is a fair portrayal of a religious or ethnic character on television?

In the first case, an episode from the civil rights movement serves as storyline for a dramatic film on race and police power. But the small victories for justice won in Mississippi in 1967 and those dramatized in the 1989 film (*Mississippi Burning*) were accomplished by vastly different means. Has fiction become fact for a generation of viewers born after the last lynching? The second case, on the boundary between news and entertainment, questions the moral purposes served by caustic "hate speech" in public debate. "Bigotry as Debate" explores that dilemma.

297

Surely one of our most pernicious habits is entertainment at the expense of moral imagination and personal growth. Are film and TV artists so eager to cut new moral territory that a generation of viewers is growing up without a shred of connection between the values of home and community, and their valueless favorite movies? Do we lose something important and irreplaceable when we scorn long-held values too often? One film critic has "come out" to say just that, and the evidence he presents warrants examination in the third case.

The last case examines media crossover—literature weaving its troubled way into television. Can the nuances of an author's characters survive, especially when that character represents "traditional values"? Or does TV so radically change the creative context that stories written in a book are unrecognizable on screen?

Long before television, Justice Louis Brandeis wrote: "Triviality destroys at once robustness of thought and delicacy of feeling. No enthusiasm can flourish, no generous impulse can survive under its blighting influence."[1] Ought we to wink at mass-mediated entertainment—its romance and simplicity—or is the beast really more fearsome than mad Dr. Frankenstein imagined? These cases raise the question and spotlight the moral issues.

71. HISTORY BURNING

Two days after the U.S. Senate passed the Civil Rights Act of 1964, three civil rights workers heard jail doors close behind them in Philadelphia, Mississippi. The charge was reckless driving, a discretionary offense similar to disturbing the peace: It can mean whatever a law officer wishes on any given day. That year in the rural South, discretionary judgments did not favor Northern whites and activist blacks. Yet this charge seemed to be just a nuisance. Goodman, Chaney, and Schwemer were back in their car just after nightfall, on to the next town, the next rally, the next voter registration. . . .

The federal investigation into their disappearance and deaths took three years, an alleged $30,000 payoff to an informer, and considerable FBI perseverance against local police who were themselves part of the crime. Murder indictments were never brought, though seven of nineteen defendants were convicted of violating federal civil rights statutes. The crime and its aftermath became one tragic chapter in the sad story of resistance to racial justice throughout the 1960s. Against the stories of other martyrs, notably Medgar Evers and Martin Luther King and four children in a Birmingham church, the Neshoba County murders were heinous but not otherwise memorable, unfortunate but not monumental.

Until the motion picture. Titled *Mississippi Burning* and released by Orion Pictures in 1989, the film starred Gene Hackman and Willem Dafoe as FBI agents who cracked the case with dogged zeal and backroom muscle. With odds against them, these warriors from Washington (who frequently warred between themselves) turn Klan-like tactics against the Klan and retrieve for burned-out blacks a moment of righteous vengeance, a small political portion of the deliverance sung about in the black spirituals that introduce and end director Alan Parker's movie.

Not everyone, however, saw restitution and virtue in this fact-based drama. Black columnist Vernon Jarrett complained: "The film treats some of the most heroic people in black history as mere props in a morality play." David Halberstam, who covered the South in 1964 for the *New York Times*, said: "Parker has taken a terribly moving and haunting story and . . . betrayed it . . . into a slapstick between two cops." Civil rights spokesman Julian Bond appeared on the TV program *Nightline* to complain that blacks were not as passive and forlorn as *Burning* suggested, nor were J. Edgar Hoover's agents so inventive. Indeed, everyone admits that the use of a covert agent in *Burning* was pure make-believe and that the characters of the sheriff and his deputy were radically changed to meet dramatic requirements. Critics contended, and filmmakers never denied, that the script "underplays the Klan's impressive organization" and "presents little of the context, much less the content, of the civil rights movement."[2]

Nonetheless, the National Board of Review gave *Burning* its Best Picture award, and the Academy of Motion Picture Arts and Sciences nominated it for seven Oscars, including Best Picture. As for historicity, the film ran the following statement after the long roll of credits: "This film is inspired by actual events which took place in the South during the 1960s. The characters, however, are fictitious and do not depict real people either living or dead."

If documentary film uses footage of actual events to tell a historical story, and dramatic film re-creates a period to provide context for fiction, docudrama roughly combines both. But can it do justice to either?

Los Angeles Times media critic David Shaw remarked that one of the worst examples of the dangers of docudrama was the CBS production of "The Atlanta Child Murders," the story of convicted child killer Wayne Williams (implicated in 23 homicides, convicted of two). The obvious slant of "Child Murders" portrayed Williams as the victim of circumstantial evidence. CBS did precede the two-part show with an advisory that the program "is not a documentary but a drama based on certain facts. . . . Some of the events and characters are fictionalized for dramatic purposes." Viewers were left to their own knowledge of the case to sort out the factual from the fictionalized scenes. Shaw called this kind of television the "bastardization and confusion of fact and fiction."[3]

Professor Gregory Payne was a consultant to NBC during the making of "Kent State," a docudrama of the 4 May 1970 National Guard shootings of four university students. Although he is a proponent of the docudrama genre, Payne has meticulously described the fictionalized interactions of guardsmen and students in "Kent State." For example, the burning of the ROTC building at Kent State on 2 May has never been definitively explained, and only last-minute insistence by consultants and actors kept those ambiguities intact. Payne observes that whatever were NBC's exaggerations (such as building much of the drama around Allison Krause's romance), they were nothing compared with the distortions of James Michener's book *Kent State: What Happened and Why.*

At a conference in Boston, actor Rick Allen, who played guardsman Wesley, noted that his portrayal of being overcome with tear gas and retreating from the line of march was pure fiction intended to humanize the "bad guys" and, in addition, to win a couple of seconds of additional on-camera time (valuable for a young actor). Allen was troubled that history was being written for thousands of viewers on the basis of a director's urging his people to ad-lib.

In 1988 the plight of surrogate mother Mary Beth Whitehead put a spotlight on the womb-for-hire business and its legality. Whose child was Baby M? her natural mother's or William and Elizabeth Stem's, who held the contract? (William was the natural father through artificial insemination.) ABC would help the nation decide with a four-hour, $6 million docudrama. Since neither the Whiteheads nor the Stems would cooperate, ABC used court transcripts, published accounts, and psychiatric evaluations made public with court records. Of course, the obligatory disclaimer preceding the telecast notes that "certain scenes and dialogue are interpretive of this material."[4]

In 1644 John Milton was confident that truth would emerge in a free marketplace of ideas. Though falsehood might grapple for a while, human rationality would eventually make the distinctions since the universe could not end on a lie. In 1985 psychiatrist M. Scott Peck began to forge a new vocabulary based on clinical observations that in some people, deception becomes truth and leads to the grim realities that destroy their lives.[5] Perhaps human rationality is not so powerful as the great liberal democrats believed. And if not, is truthtelling all the more a moral imperative, fragile of understanding as we are?

Is the docudrama genre a powerful vehicle for reviving our culture's important stories, or a cheap distortion based on television's insatiable need for new material?

In favor of docudrama: How many students in the 1990s would know or care about Kent State's Allison, Jeff, Sandy, and Bill were it not for the efforts of NBC, albeit profit-tinged, to give new life to that fateful spring weekend in northeast Ohio? Few, we suspect. How many dry eyes and stoic hearts walked out of theaters after *Mississippi Burning*, unmoved by the suffering and careless about the future of racial justice? None, we believe. Journalist Bill Minor covered the Freedom Summer of 1964 and won the Elijah Lovejoy award for most courageous weekly editor in the nation after his exposure of Klan activity in Mississippi. He defended *Mississippi Burning* as "a powerful portrayal." For viewers who depend on film for stories not experienced firsthand, the movie "got the spirit right."[6]

If a film re-creates the texture of an event such that participants can affirm the veracity of context and struggle, is that not sufficient? History is more than mere facts, and no story corresponds exactly to events. Perhaps the docudrama is our best vehicle for keeping at bay those who claim the Holocaust, in whatever version, never occurred.

The crucial variable is the judgment of the subject. If a docudrama wins the approval of those closest to the real-life drama, viewers are assured that a truthful perspective on events survives the dramatic process. If the subject cannot recognize his or her struggle for all the romantic clichés and garbled characterizations, we rightly worry that rampant revisionism threatens to obscure and distort the meaning of the past. Morally sensitive producers of docudrama will incorporate fictional elements without padding history or violating the pain of those whose stories they tell.

72. BIGOTRY AS DEBATE

"Black Perspectives" was typically a 30-minute talk show produced for distribution on the Public Broadcasting Service (PBS) by WHYY in Philadelphia. The show scheduled for the last week in September, however, was not the ordinary half-hour.

Bring together the head of the American Nazi Party and the Imperial Wizard of the Ku Klux Klan. Cast them with three black interviewers. Result: an expanded 60 minutes of largely uncontrolled, rambling conversation that included several sharply anti-Semitic and racist remarks.

When word of the coming show leaked out, many viewers in Philadelphia were upset that a publicly funded station would produce such a round of diatribes. Three Nazi prison camp survivors living in the city filed suit to prevent the station from putting the show on the air. A local judge ruled in their favor on the day the broadcast was scheduled, and only a reversal from the state's Superior Court kept the 9 P.M. program on schedule. Even then, about 2,000 Jewish, Polish, and black demonstrators protested outside the studio that evening.

The Jewish community was not about to sit by while shades of the Third Reich danced on the screens of the nation's television sets. At WNET in New York, the American Jewish Congress (AJC) accused station management of gross irresponsibility for its plans to air the show.

When the AJC letter was released to the press, WNET perceived it as a claim by the AJC that it had won cancellation of the show. Now the station was in a dilemma. Said one executive: "If we are perceived as yielding to the wishes of one pressure group, we'll be asked to give in to others and there'll be no end to it."

WNET decided to produce its own version of the show, called "The Extremists: American Nazis and the K.K.K." This revised version would include about a half-hour from the original "Black Perspectives" production. "We almost had no choice," said the WNET executive.

Two sides were lined up for battle. The AJC vigorously denied that it had claimed credit for a programming decision at WNET. However, it would not retract its belief that the show was reprehensible and that its cancellation was the only right decision. In Cleveland, the AJC protested: "There is no legal or democratic necessity to publicize falsehood." A *New York Times* critic, pondering the role of the public in media decisions, commented:

> The American Jewish Congress is only one of many groups in this country which knows itself to be in possession of the truth, and if television producers did not resist the constant pressures, the world of television would be an even blander place than it is. One group's falsehood is another's truth.[7]

WHYY felt deserted. Only 105 of the 207 PBS stations aired the program, even when WHYY tacked on a 30-minute follow-up featuring spokespeople from the American Jewish Committee, the National Jewish Community Relations Advisory Council, and the Pennsylvania Human Relations Commission. The president of WHYY criticized PBS affiliates for succumbing to pressure:

> I thought the whole reason for public television was to air public issues that commercial TV wouldn't. . . . Even if our judgment was wrong in this case, the station broadcasts over 5,000 hours of programming a year, and we are not going to allow a few people who object to one program to destroy the whole thing.[8]

The American Civil Liberties Union fully supported the position of WHYY. "The danger of prior censorship by pressure is greater than the danger of irresponsibility by the press," said the ACLU.[9]

In an era when politically correct speech is the law on university campuses and in politics, it is difficult to imagine that program producers would consider staging an event like this one. The "debate" held little prospect of political progress or rapprochement, and much potential for exactly what happened: mudslinging and mindless name-calling. But this program preceded the era of political correctness. If not socially sensitive, the debate was at least robust. And our current worry over "hate speech" does nothing to quiet these voices.

The problem at WHYY is multiplied a thousand times with the coming of public access cable. Herbert Poinsett, based in Tampa, distributes videotape and claims access rights for his message of neo-Nazi bigotry. From Westchester County, New York, the high priest of the Black Israelites, Ta-Har, comes on camera holding a baseball bat and delivers these words: "We're going to be beating the hell out of you white people. . . . We're going to take your little children and dash them against the stones." Other so-called hate shows include productions from the White Aryan Resistance called "Race and Reason" and a series from the Mississippi-based Nationalist Movement called "Airlink."[10] These programs get people angry. No doubt for a tiny few, they also reinforce socially dangerous prejudices.

Yet democratic life holds one value supremely: unpopular speech is most worthy of protection, since it is also most vulnerable to suppression by majority opinion. The ACLU is wrong to minimize the danger of press irresponsibility, but it rightly signals the fundamental danger of suppressing a minority viewpoint. Acts of bigotry are proscribed by law; words of bigotry are protected by constitutional guarantee.

On what moral grounds could the AJC object to the airing of "Black Perspectives" in New York City? Perhaps a closer look at the letter sent from the executive director of the AJC to WNET management will cast a helpful light:

> What is involved here is Channel 13's program judgment—not censorship. Obviously TV and radio stations have the right to decide what shows

they believe are worthy of public viewing. . . . The community . . . has an equal right to question the wisdom of their decisions.

In this instance we believe that any decision by Channel 13 to broadcast a program admittedly racist and anti-Semitic in content, a discussion which has been described by . . . the station which originated it . . . as containing "contradictory and factually inaccurate" statements, would be an act of irresponsible journalism and wretched program judgment.

We do not object to this program because its subject matter is controversial. We do not believe there is anything "controversial" about racial and religious hatred. . . .

We are confident that Channel 13 is not so bankrupt in program ideas that it must give precious air time to a program that projects racial and religious hatred and whose only result can be to inflame interracial and interreligious relations in our city. We recognize your right and authority to decide upon your own programs; we are grateful that in the exercise of that judgment you have understood that carrying this program would be an irresponsible act and a serious abuse of public trust.[11]

The AJC seems to be arguing that the content of the show is so demeaning that it does not deserve the consideration normally accorded to controversial debate. The content is especially demeaning to the AJC and its constituency, of course. Others might find the racial slurs tasteless and stupid, but not intolerable. Indeed, considering the debaters, some harsh language should be expected. Yet the AJC might press its argument that when humans become the subject of racial hatred, speech has passed into the purely destructive zone. One vital need of any culture is survival, and racial hatred never serves that end. Certainly the Judeo-Christian ethic of persons as ends plays a large role in AJC strategy.

But nearly all other ethical foundations can be brought to bear on the AJC's case as well. Applying the golden mean might indicate that vigorous programming should avoid the extreme of inflammatory demagoguery, especially the kind that our century has seen explode so violently and brutally. If we applied utilitarianism, we might see that no one is served by bigotry, and that the aims of groups like the Klan are so contrary to long-term benefits for all that it has, by its own devices, forfeited ordinary rights to the public forum. The categorical imperative could never justify racism as a universal good. If we used the Kantian approach, we might well argue that when public debaters engage, they do so in a format suitable to the topic. Surely a half-hour of heated barbs in a quasi-entertainment format on television solves nothing and sheds no light on important issues dividing cultural camps. In like manner, researcher David Thornburn insists that formal excellence and thematic coherence join in making good television.[12] The veil-of-ignorance approach could be used to equalize the power of a national media network and the relative smallness of a protest group.

WNET's response to the AJC points to the underlying adversarial relationship between media producers and public interest groups. The assumed right of professionals to determine their own standards and set their own agenda is an important and hard-won privilege. But all doctors are accountable to other doctors; no surgeon cuts her own idiosyncratic incision. In this case, it seems, the community of media professionals has strongly questioned WNET'S wisdom, yet WNET continues to assert its "professional" independence. Perhaps with more time to prove its case, WNET could move its colleagues toward a negotiated settlement, but the station can hardly claim that the AJC is encroaching. Public opinion is the business of everyone. Broadcast managers, interest groups, and even First Amendment free-speech advocates should work toward mutually acceptable guidelines that would provide the groundwork for future cooperation, not for the sake of leveling sharpness or even diatribe, but for advancing moral literacy among the distinctive pockets of culture that make up the American nation.

73. "LIFE STINKS"—LET'S FUMIGATE!

In July 1991, the Mel Brooks comedy *Life Stinks* hit the box office. The story concerned a spoiled billionaire who wagers he can live without money for a month. He falls in love with another homeless waif, the beautiful Leslie Ann Warren. Despite somewhat favorable reviews, the box office did not hit back. The movie bombed. When MGM released another version in October, it also bombed.

Media critic Michael Medved cites the Brooks fiasco as one example among many of the "bias for the bizarre" and "preference for the perverse" that permeates the Hollywood film culture. Noting that the film's original title was "Life Sucks," Medved observed that "when an industry attempts to market a comedy with a title that conveys a grim, pessimistic view of human existence, then it's safe to say that industry has lost touch with its public." Evidence for his thesis is as close as the nearest headline. Take for example the Oscar nominations announced in spring 1992 for films released in 1991. Three candidates for Best Actor played murderous psychopaths; one played a homeless psychotic given to delusions; and one played a "good, old-fashioned, manic-depressive neurotic." That same year, a movie called *Silence of the Lambs* swept the Oscars after it won the New York Film Critics Circle award for Best Film, Best Director, Best Actor, and Best Actress; these are impressive credentials indeed for a movie about two "serial killers: one of whom eats, and the other of whom skins, his victims." Medved's conclusion: Hollywood films are at the forefront of a culture war against "traditional values" of long-term marriage, care of fellow human beings, and purposeful life.

Medved has catalogued Hollywood excesses:

- MGM paid $500,000 for the development of a script that includes a graphic scene of the president of the United States having sex with a cow.
- A 1990 release titled *The Cook, the Thief, His Wife, and Her Lover* was reviewed in the *New York Times* as "something profound and

extremely rare." It included "deep kisses and tender embraces administered to a bloody and mutilated cadaver," among other shocking scenes.

- Humans urinate daily, but not often in film. Until recently, that is. In *Doc Hollywood* (1991), Julie Warner interrupts a walk in the woods with her new love to urinate several times in order to throw hunting dogs off the scent of a deer. The camera follows her romp around the woods, then zooms close-up to a shot of leaves dripping with moisture, proof that smart environmentalism saves innocent animals.
- Although human speech is often strong, its strength lies also in the infrequency of certain terms. But the 146 minutes of Martin Scorsese's 1990 film *GoodFellas* contained 246 F-words, 14 S-words, seven A-words, and five references to male genitalia. That was one obscenity every 32.2 seconds of running time.

Medved concluded: "In the final analysis, I worry over the impact of media messages not only on my children but on myself—and on all the rest of us. No matter how sophisticated we believe we are . . . the poisons of the popular culture seep into our very souls."[13]

Medved's book *Hollywood vs. America: Popular Culture and the War on Traditional Values* raised a hornet's nest of protest. *New York Times* book review editor Christopher Lehmann-Haupt called it an "ack-ack attack of a book" filled with superficial analysis, cardboard prose, and a "deep sleep of reason." Julie Salamon in the *Wall Street Journal* called Medved's book a "fundamentalist hell-fire and damnation approach" that "shuts out thoughtful discussion." She wrote: "Mr. Medved fails to prove his provocative argument anywhere in his book." *Spy* called Medved the "mustachioed demagogue."[14]

Much depends, of course, on what constitutes proof and how the framework of reason is conceived. Medved marshals data, but invariably not all the relevant data. Medved advances reasoned arguments, but not everyone will allow his major premise.

Moral guardians have been wary of the motion picture industry ever since John C. Rice administered a prolonged kiss to Mary Irwin in 1896, a dramatic moment that gave the International Reform Bureau initial steam. But the largely Protestant protest lacked central authority and failed to develop a comprehensive moral argument.

When the Catholic Church stepped into a major guardianship role in the 1930s, it suffered no such handicaps. Through the Legion of Decency, the church mustered the most vigorous and popular protest against cinema fare (and media fare in general) of this century. Catholic thinking was at the foundation of the Motion Picture Production Code of 1930 and informed much of the Hays Office's efforts to enforce self-regulation for the industry. For instance, a Catholic layperson was given charge of the Production Code Administration, the industry's own script review and code enforcement bureau.

The Catholic apology for intervention in the nation's entertainment business was delivered most cogently by a Jesuit priest in *Catholic Viewpoint on Censorship*. Harold C. Gardiner placed the Legion's guardianship role in the context of Catholic political philosophy that viewed the state as a natural (meaning God-ordained) institution and therefore one to be respected. Yet custom and tradition are also important social forces, and these are the domain of the many groups that compose the larger nation. Whereas law serves as a final arbiter in civil disputes, the first court of appeal is the informal constraint of group customs and values. This primary arbitrating and civilizing force needs protection.

Given Gardiner's view of the state, individual freedom can never be as simple as doing as one pleases. True freedom is freedom to act as one ought to act. "The fundamental 'oughtness' under which a person can alone act with full freedom is . . . an 'oughtness' that is handed to people by the faculty of reason." The Legion, argued Gardiner, is not a censoring agency able to coerce behavior, but a guide to the reasoned "formulation of public opinion, and whatever suppression of material (films or books) follows as a result of the formed opinion is secondary and accidental to their main purpose." Here is a kind of control, but in the open marketplace apart from legal constraints and dependent on the support of a significant public. Any attempt to suppress the Legion "is an attempt to shut off the channels of free opinion and debate that make for a socially, intellectually, and morally stronger America."[15] The chief means of Catholic protest, the mass boycott of theaters, was a significant brake during the 1930s and 1940s on just the sort of media menu Medved excoriates. But this consensus has all but disappeared.

Though no champion of the church, C. Wright Mills lamented the trend toward mass society and found the decline of the "voluntary association as a genuine instrument of the public" to be one of the most important structural causes of the trend. Social power, he wrote, is in the hands of the "huge corporation, the inaccessible government, the grim military establishment." Mills worried about the absence of "intermediate associations" between the corporation and the family/community, associations which could push big bureaucracy toward public accountability, and nudge family/community into greater civic-mindedness. Without these intermediate associations, we have no arena for responsible public opinion to emerge. Mass media have "helped less to enlarge and animate the discussions of primary publics than to transform them into a set of media markets in mass-like society."[16] Mills's views receive contemporary support from Robert Bellah's *Habits of the Heart* and *The Good Society*.[17] What if a biased film establishment and a blind newspaper establishment each fail to see the social turmoil in modern popular culture?

For those who agree with Medved, what can be done? He argues for the legitimacy of media and consumer-advertiser boycotts. Measuring the impact of boycotts is tricky business at best; sometimes even establishing that a boycott is in effect is difficult. Newsletters like *National Boycott News*[18] show that many groups are protesting: from gay boycotts of Marlboro cigarettes for Philip Morris's donations to Jesse Helms, to the children-led boycott of McDonalds over polystyrene burger boxes. Some of these efforts may move corporate leaders to consider alternatives; others are dismissed as public relations showing corporate social responsibility. If nothing else, modern boycotts give a "public" a greater sense of partnership in the marketplace than the feeling of an individual who merely declines to pay for a theater ticket.

Such strategy seems squarely in line with democratic notions of a vast and divided nation seeking a golden mean through nonviolent market pressure. John Leo, writing in *U.S. News*, said that boycotting "is one of the glories of democracy—direct, principled political action that holds companies and other targets responsible for what they do."[19]

Perhaps film companies need to clean up their acts, make better movies, omit some of the graphic killing and portray some happy and enduring marriages; they need to produce scripts that make a point without constant recourse to shocking language. Perhaps Hollywood film companies are in a race to produce more and more stunning and shocking films, as Medved alleged.[20] But this much seems certain: Opinions in the United States are as polarized as ever between creative libertarians in the major entertainment industries who will accept no intervention from the outside, and disgruntled, disgusted publics who are searching for a means of making their protest effective. The righteous claim First Amendment privilege; protesters cite facile infatuation with gore and sex. As a nation, we lack the scope and depth to make meaningful progress between these two widely separated camps.

74. THE FATHER KNOWS BEST

Professor Ralph McInerny is among the most prolific of modern philosophers, but not only in academic writings. As a hobby, mental exercise, and just for fun, he began writing fiction in 1964. He published his third novel, *Priest*, in 1973. The success of this novel prompted his agent to suggest that he develop a mystery series. Hence Father Roger Dowling entered the literary world.

Father Dowling works at a parish west of Chicago in Fox River, Illinois. But his parishioners and contacts are anything but laid-back hayseed types. Dowling is surrounded by thieves, murderers, conspirators, addicts, corrupted or jaundiced police, ambitious and greedy entrepreneurs, shady Mafia types, and clever attorneys—the stuff of mystery.

In such a setting, one might expect Father Dowling to be an Indiana Jones with a collar—placid in the classroom or church but irrepressible in the field. Instead, Dowling is a rather conservative churchman who worries about trendiness and the loss of piety in the modern world. His mode of solving a crime is to listen with the intensity of a Sherlock Holmes, act with the collegiality of a Barney Fife, and then let those who are not so clever take the credit for the case while he returns to ordinary parish tasks and the responsibilities of his calling.

The Father Dowling Mysteries have sold about 10,000 copies each, many to libraries. They have a loyal following despite modest numbers. That loyalty was enough to attract the interest of NBC in 1988, when its Friday night prime time took the Dowling character (played by Tom Bosley) and gave it a life on the screen. With some changes, of course.

"Roger" might be a nice name for a cowboy or a rabbit, but not for a detective priest. Frank fits better. And a lone priest today would be like a Ranger without Tonto of yesteryear. Add Sister Steve, a streetwise nun who, for all her feminist wisdom, still wears a habit. The Fox River setting is a tad dry, too. Put the good Reverend in Chicago, where he can find some action. Add one murder and one car chase per episode. The result, well. . . .

TV Guide offered a stern review of *Father Dowling* just before NBC called it quits. Merrill Panitt observed that the "long rubber arm of coincidence has never been stretched so far." Somewhere between the book version and the screen, executive producers Fred Silverman and Dean Hargrove "forgot to bless the stories, which follow a set pattern and create an impression of having been turned out by a computer."[21] McInerny himself does not watch television, but from reports he has heard, he wonders whether the TV Dowling reflects anything of the parish calling that characterizes his priest. The network had purchased the name of his gumshoe clergyman, but none of the TV stories followed any of the book plots.

Can television translate the nuances of a fully developed literary narrative in its 30- and 60-minute packages? Notable achievements by Hallmark aside, have prime-time serials or made-for-TV movies fared as well? The popular literary landscape seems littered with writers who saw their narratives so radically altered by TV scripting that questions of integrity and credibility persisted despite the financial windfall. Joseph Wambaugh told one interviewer about his fight to keep "Police Story" honest:

> They pay me a lot of money to use my name and be a consultant and all that business, but they're not listening to me. I'm trying to tell them what a police show should be about, what police life is all about. And so far they are giving me cops-and-robbers stories. What I've gone through with television has been unreal. They brought me in to give them the first true-life television shows about police. Good drama, strong in plot, strong in character, adult shows. And I sit there . . . and they nod their heads and say "Yes, but there's the real world and then there's the real world of television. The folks like lots of shooting and chase scenes." And I keep telling them, that is not what I'm here for. But they can't really free themselves from that misconception yet, and I was terribly naive to think that they could.[22]

Wambaugh's turf was the police department. He had worked on the Los Angeles force. His tape-recorded interviews that formed the basis of successful novels such as *The New Centurions* and *The Blue Knight* were stories of real people he knew. His own honor was at stake in the network version. But police drama was a natural for television. Cops and robbers (and worse) have been ducking TV bullets for years. How could television, with so much experience at it, trivialize a cop story?

McInerny's dilemma was similar, yet for television it was more densely complex. His character was not a *Magnum P.I.* type. "Father Dowdy" might have been an appropriate name for this flatfoot. The Dowling persona is not a progressive; he is not an activist Father Berrigan clone. Rather, Dowling (as written) is religiously sensitive, sympathetic to tradition, mindful of the past, and reluctant—not unwilling—to accommodate cultural trends. He seems to want his people to experience peace of soul as much as restitution of righteousness and proper administration of justice. Can television provide nourishment to such a character?

Some church-based groups readily argue that television stereotyping is never more superficial than in its portrayal of religious life. Donald Wildmon's American Family Association includes that category along with violence, sex, and profanity in its watchdog efforts. Yet Martin Marty of the University of Chicago issued public calls for more religion in prime time. Why? That dimension of life, he claims, has been written out of television.[23] A full picture of life in any community or ethnic enclave needs stories of faith, hope, and love most frequently found in religious faith and institutions.

Given television's track record, Wambaugh had reason to worry about the metamorphosis of his characters, and McInerny had more reason still. Perhaps unwittingly, they each surrendered some loyalty to their readers when they sold rights to TV networks. Perhaps McInerny should have written a tougher bargain and retained a share of control. Yet Wambaugh illustrates how difficult that can be even for a streetwise negotiator.

Finally, the issue must revolve around the purpose of the creative material. If McInerny writes simply to sell books and build royalties, then the more lucrative the television contract, the better the deal. Among those who stress personal happiness, such a monetary approach to the creative arts could be justified provided no unnecessary harm is done to others. But McInerny does not situate his own goals in these terms, nor his sense of purpose as a writer. Indeed, we contend that writers owe primary loyalty to the art, the craft, the expression of human mind and spirit that generates our mythology and narrative. Fidelity to characterization, with all the nuances of behavior and belief that make Father Dowling a rare crime fighter, becomes a necessary condition to the opening of new markets and media channels. Television purchased rights to the Dowling persona but used the last name and vocation only, essentially creating a new character. Fidelity to the craft, we contend, should suggest a completely new name as a more honest move by the small-screen artists.

Good literary writers also need to become good readers of the fine print of television contracts. Selling rights for reasonable profits should not become a game in which wealthy media companies overrule cultural distinctions and determine mythological agendas. Writers have an obligation to keep their characters honest, in any medium.

NOTES

1. Louis Brandeis, with Samuel Warren, "The Right to Privacy," *Harvard Law Review* 4, 15 December 1890, p. 196.
2. *Time*, 9 January 1989, pp. 57-59. See also William Swislow's review in *Quill* (March 1989): 21.
3. *TV Guide*, 20 April 1985, p. 5.
4. Tom Shales reported on and reviewed "Baby M." His column appeared in the *DuPage Daily Journal*, 20 May 1988.
5. M. Scott Peck, *People of the Lie* (New York: Simon and Shuster, 1985).
6. *Quill* (March 1989): 24-26.
7. Walter Goodman, letter to editor, *New York Times,* 25 December 1977, sec. 2, p. 35.
8. James Karayn quoted in Walter Goodman, "How Should Public TV Handle the Inflammatory?" *New York Times,* 11 December 1977, sec. 2, p. 39.
9. Les Brown, "7 PBS Stations Reject Klansman and Nazi Interview," *New York Times,* 1 October 1977, p. 48.
10. Richard Zoglin, "All You Need Is Hate," *Time,* 21 June 1993, p. 63.
11. Undated press release issued by the American Jewish Congress, headed: "New York's Public TV Station Won't Share Panel Discussion with Nazi, Ku Klux Klansman."
12. David Thornburn, "Interpretation and Judgment," *Critical Studies in Mass Communication* 10 (June 1993): 113-127.
13. Michael Medved, *Hollywood vs. America: Popular Culture and the War on Traditional Values* (New York: HarperCollins/Zondervan, 1992), pp. 18, 24, 25, 29, 344.
14. Christopher Lehmann-Haupt, *New York Times,* 5 October 1992, C17. Julie Salamon, *Wall Street Journal,* 2 November 1992, A14. *Spy* (August 1993), cited in the Chicago *Sun-Times,* 7 July 1993, p. 47.
15. Harold C. Gardiner, *Catholic Viewpoint on Censorship* (New York: Hanover House, 1958), pp. 106-107.
16. C. Wright Mills, *The Power Elite* (New York: Oxford University Press, 1956; Galaxy Books, 1959), pp. 306-311.
17. Robert N. Bellah et al., *Habits of the Heart* (Berkeley: University of California Press, 1985), and Bellah et al., *The Good Society* (New York: Knopf, 1991).
18. *National Boycott News* is published by the Institute for Consumer Responsibility, 6506 28th Ave NE, Seattle, WA 98115.
19. John Leo, "When in Doubt, Boycott," *U.S. News & World Report,* 21 December 1992, p. 35.
20. Medved's contentions regarding stereotyping and values are supported by recent television research. See "Women and Minorities on Television: A Study in Casting and Fate," a Report to the Screen Actors Guild and the American Federation of Radio and Television Artists, June 1993, by George Gerbner.
21. Merrill Panitt, "Father Dowling Mysteries," *TV Guide,* 1-7 April 1989, p. 39. The production company for the Dowling mysteries, Viacom, succeeded in selling 11 new episodes to ABC after the NBC cancellation. Those episodes were aired in the first quarter of 1990. Ralph McInerny said in an interview with the authors that he is as

distant from the ABC series as he was from the NBC one, and in fact only the network changed, not the storyline, cast, or conception.

22. Quoted in Steven V. Roberts, "Cop of the Year," *Esquire* (December 1973): 153.

23. Martin Marty, "We Need More Religion in Our Sit-coms," *TV Guide*, 24 December 1983, pp. 2-8.

chapter **16**

Censorship

"Censorship," one of the ugly words of the English language, speaks of the repression that democratic beliefs officially and inexorably condemn. It warns of the consequences of state tyranny, church tyranny, union tyranny, corporation tyranny—the strong hand of any institution silencing the dissenting voice. "Liberty," on the other hand, provokes cherished feelings that resonate with our deepest human longings—an elusive goal, perhaps, but eminently worth the sacrifice required for each step in its advance.

So by our ideals we set the stage for the great paradox of democratic theory: liberty can never be absolute, censorship can never be absent. Liberty requires constraints at every level—speech, sex, movement, health care, business, religious practice—in order for people to create an ordered society. That which we prize most must be taken in measured portions.

Few of our essential constraints partake of the spirit of Star Chamber repression in seventeenth-century England. The jailing and hanging of writers no longer occurs at the whim of a monarch. Yet many contemporary restrictions are nonetheless called censorship. One of our fundamental questions, then, is where to draw the lines. This is the question of ethics.

At the end of World War II, the Hutchins Commission on Freedom of the Press struggled over this question as it deliberated toward a theory of press freedom that would promote social responsibility as a new and important concept in media studies. All of the commission members were ardent democrats; some might even be called dreamy-eyed in their praise of democratic virtues. True liberals in the historic sense, they held free inquiry to be paramount. Yet they wrestled with the question of censorship. The chief philosopher of the commission, William Ernest Hocking of Harvard, captured the dilemma poignantly in an essay written as plans for the commission were being laid:

Are . . . thoughts all equally worthy of protection? Are there no ideas unfit for expression, insane, obscene, destructive? Are all hypotheses on the same level, each one, however vile or silly, to be taken with the same mock reverence because some academic jackass brings it forth? Is non-censorship so great a virtue that it can denounce all censorship as lacking in human liberality?[1]

The cases in this section attempt to point out a few of the dimensions of those questions. The first case, "Ice-T on Ice," wonders whether lyrics that advocate murder are mitigated by the artist's pronouncements of selective violence and inner struggle. The second case, "Cruising on Instinct," approaches the problem of censorship from the viewpoint of a group that feels directly threatened by prevalent media stereotypes.

The third case, "Cable TV and Sex," points to our increasing technical ability to channel programs to specific markets. Assuming the consent of the buyer, should choices abound?

The last case, "*Show Me*," moves the debate from television to books, and from home and theater into a public institution where neighborhood service has been a slogan, now under fire.

While the reader puzzles with us over these democratic conundrums, we may be encouraged in the knowledge that to do so—to read this book and think about these questions—is testimony that we are at least on the way to answers. In too many societies, the range of permissible media is tightly defined by a power elite. At least we can claim the advantage of a bias toward latitude: censorship must be justified. In these cases, we ask whether modern censors have demonstrated their case for building dikes against the flow.

75. ICE-T ON ICE

I got my twelve gauge sawed off.
I got my headlights turned off.
I'm 'bout to bust some shots off.
I'm 'bout to dust some cops off. . . .
Chorus:
COP KILLER, it's better you than me.
COP KILLER, fuck police brutality!
COP KILLER, I know your family's grievin'
(FUCK 'EM!)
COP KILLER, but tonight we get even.
I got my brain on hype.
Tonight'll be your night.
I got this long-assed knife
and your neck looks just right. . . .
Chorus:
DIE, DIE, DIE PIG, DIE!
FUCK THE POLICE! [repeat]

Seldom have song lyrics generated the controversy that followed the release of Ice-T's "Cop Killer." Law enforcement groups in Texas and New York state called for a boycott of products from Time Warner Inc., owner of the record company that released the album. The Los Angeles City Council urged Time Warner and retailers to halt sales of *Body Count,* the rap-metal album that included the song. Sixty members of Congress blasted the lyrics as "despicable" and "vile" and expressed their "deep sense of outrage" that the company was continuing to distribute the album. Even President Bush and Vice President Quayle spoke against the recording. Three record-store chains stopped selling the album in response to the protests.[2]

Opponents of the recording argued that it was socially irresponsible because it encouraged violence against police. In their letter to Time Warner Vice President Jeanette Lerman, the members of Congress wrote: "It appears you have chosen potential profit over any reasonable sense of public responsibility." And the Los Angeles City Council voiced its concern about the "lack of social responsibility that promotion of this recording indicated in the wake of the riots in Los Angeles."

Ice-T said his critics misunderstood the song, which he called fiction. "At no point do I go out and say, 'Let's do it,'" he said. "I'm singing in the first person as a character who is fed up with police brutality." And before the controversy arose, Ice-T had been telling audiences the song was directed against those police who abused their power.

The album, he argued, "has a brain—this album's mentality is a progressive mentality against racism. It's hate against hate, you know. It's anger." Irrational white fears were fueling police opposition, Ice-T said. At the same time, he said the song should make police feel nervous. "I think cops should feel threatened," he said. "I feel threatened. I grew up threatened. They should know that they can't take a life without retaliation." The record was meant as a check on police power. It was "an editorial"—voicing a point of view already expressed in other art forms such as paintings and theater.

Ice-T said Time Warner gave him the creative freedom he needed to express his point of view, knowing that he was not just making recordings for shock value. And Time Warner rose to his defense. Amid the protests, Time Warner said the company stood by its "commitment to the free expression of ideas for all our authors, journalists, recording artists, screenwriters, actors and directors" and said that banning the song "will not make violence and rage disappear." In another statement, the company reiterated a commitment to free expression, saying, "It is not a matter of profits, but principle." The company's president, Gerald Levin, writing in the *Wall Street Journal*, said Time Warner "won't retreat in the face of threats of boycotts or political grandstanding. . . . Cutting and running . . . would be a destructive precedent." Levin said that "Cop Killer" does not advocate an assault on police and "doesn't incite or glorify violence"; it is "the artist's rap on how a person in the street feels. . . . It's a shout of pain and protest" and is "raw with rage and resentment." At a shareholders meeting, the company pressed its defense of the recording over the protests of more than 20 people, including two wounded policemen and actor Charlton Heston, who read sexually explicit lyrics from another song on *Body Count.*

Then, only two weeks after Time Warner's vigorous defense before shareholders, Ice-T and Warner Brothers Records announced that "Cop Killer" would be dropped from the *Body Count* album at the performer's request because the record distributor had received death threats. Although Time Warner's board was reportedly growing uncomfortable with the controversy, Warner Vice President Bob Merlis said the record company had not pressured Ice-T to drop the song; it had simply met with him and described reports about the controversy.

The intensity of protests on both sides suggests that cogent arguments can be made in this case from diametrically opposed perspectives. Those who protested the lyrics know that open advocacy of violence as a means of expressing anger can add kerosene to burning embers and lead to a social bonfire. Democracy is committed to peaceful change as the first order of business. Anger can take many forms, but the lyrics of this song allow for little nuance or subtlety. "Dust some cops off" is a major linguistic leap from "We are angry with social injustice"—which was apparently Ice-T's reason for making the music.

On the other hand, Ice-T reasons, subtleties and metaphors have not brought change. So, he argues, let me open my mind to you. Look what's inside. Feel for a moment—through music—what I feel. Forget about being nice. The world isn't nice. Here's my head in language that resonates with my people. Hear what we're saying!

It appears to be a moral confrontation without middle ground. Even police groups were divided in their opinion of the song: Two African-American police organizations opposed actions against the album and the company, citing the right to free speech. The National Black Police Association said Ice-T "is entitled to voice his anger and frustration with the conditions facing oppressed people."

Rawls's veil of ignorance offers a starting point for discussion. If the key parties involved—Ice-T, urban police, poor urban African-Americans, listeners and the public, and Time Warner—enter the veil of ignorance, the parties that reenter as the most vulnerable are urban blacks and white police, the first on Ice-T's authority and the second because of Ice-T's lyrics.

If you are a big-city cop, you protest the song; you argue that even without legal prohibition, no responsible writer will produce a song so directly calling for violence against police. But if you are a young black person in the inner city, you say an injustice must be expressed; in fact, the songwriter has a moral obligation to speak—and the right to express even an inflammatory opinion.

How can we weigh these competing claims? Behind the veil, we might argue that since the death of one party forecloses discussion, both parties, for all their disagreements, must affirm the right of survival for all. That would require that survival rights include the moral responsibility to refrain from inflaming others to violence.

Beyond that is, perhaps, stalemate. Promises by city authorities to try harder for fair treatment of citizens of all colors are an old stanza. Ice-T is tired of that song. To muffle his own lyrics is to say that what is in his head is too socially destructive to legitimately be there: If he cannot sing his mind, perhaps he should change his mind. Ice-T would be forced to admit to moral blame.

The agape principle (persons as ends) could get the discussion started again. It says that weighing claims is not the issue; both parties' interests must be considered because they are persons. Moreover, the assumption is that they are persons whose primary interest is each others' welfare. Agape dictates "You first"—unconditionally. It asks: How can your best interests be advanced? Under agape, the artist treats all parties, but especially the most vulnerable ones, as he would want to be treated. He must consider the effects of his actions on others, not just act to advance his self-interest. Likewise, the protesters must consider the feelings of the artist. Anger is real and deep, and cannot be dismissed with do-gooder promises.

Is the loving thing—the course most in keeping with agape—for Ice-T to express the anger of urban blacks who feel the sting of police brutality or know others who have? If Ice-T's motivation is to voice this anger with the goal of bringing about constructive change, not just further destruction, this course can be morally justified. But love would also dictate that Ice-T consider the potential effect of his song on police—not because he is legally obligated, but because they, too, are part of the larger community of human beings. "Hate against hate" only further severs the tenuous ties between contending groups and points to a complete breakdown of community. Hate denies the humanity of the other. Hate as an antidote to injustice always leads to violence, and so the "war of all against all" is engaged. Agape (other-minded care and devotion) is against such a war. Moral life requires forgiveness, reconciliation, and strong mutual regard. Hate walks down a different road completely.

Ice-T himself pointed the way to a more ethically justifiable course. He told an interviewer after the controversy that he was working with an organization that would take inner-city children to activities like skiing or golfing that would let them break their "mental chains." And his album that followed *Body Count, Home Invasion,* included the song "Gotta Lotta Love," in which he urged Los Angeles gangs to keep their cease-fire. Actions like these reflect an ethic that promotes healing rather than destruction.

But the only way, under agape, to salvage the lyrics of "Cop Killer" is to place them in such a context that no listener is led to believe that Ice-T would sponsor or act on the belligerence he feels. He made a start by telling concert audiences that the song was aimed at abusive police, not all police. But his spoken introduction on the recording can be interpreted as an endorsement of violence against the Los Angeles Police Department just as much as an effort to limit it. The song should carry a clear disclaimer, an admission of frustration and excess. The performer then appears less the leader of anarchy and more the heartbeat of troubled urban youth.

A generation ago, leaders crying against injustice firmly renounced the "hate against hate" approach to change. Their words and experiences carry lessons for both sides in this controversy.

76. CRUISING ON INSTINCT

It seemed like *déjà vu*. During the summer of 1979, film director William Friedkin brought a crew to Manhattan's gay district to do location shots for a film about a sadomasochistic homicide. Titled *Cruising*, the film starred Al Pacino as an undercover detective out to find the killer. While investigating, Pacino's character becomes confused about his own sexual identity and finally, maybe, commits a murder in the same bloody mode used by the man he had been stalking. Scenes from the film show torture, mutilated genitals, men urinating on other men for erotic pleasure, and several murders of gays by gays.

Soon after Friedkin arrived, a *Village Voice* writer published the story of the movie, and homosexuals in New York took to the streets. Several hundred protested nightly. Gay bars that had agreed to cooperate with Friedkin for location shots were damaged. Friedkin and his staff were the targets of cans and bottles, and they were pressured to abandon the project. Gays claimed that the film was dangerous to them; it would provoke brutality from oppressive straights; it would legitimize violence against gays.

New York Mayor Ed Koch refused to cancel Friedkin's license. "To do otherwise would involve censorship," he said. "It is the business of the City to encourage the return of filmmaking to New York. Whether it is a group that seeks to make the gay life exciting or to make it negative, it's not our job to look into that."

Then, eleven years later, director Paul Verhoeven began work in San Francisco on a script by writer Joe Eszterhas for the film *Basic Instinct*. Michael Douglas was cast as a reckless detective out to find an ice-pick killer.

Protests came quickly from the National Organization for Women and gay activist groups like Queer Nation and Act-Up. Crowds chanted slogans and blew whistles to interrupt filming. The complaint: the only women in the script were lesbians or bisexual murderers. "The good guy, as always, is the straight white male," said one protester. "There is a complete inability to give any sort of balance here."

After a meeting with the gay groups, Eszterhas revised about a dozen pages of script, but director Verhoeven felt the changes weakened the plot and rejected all of them. He said in a written statement: The movie "is a psychological thriller about a police detective investigating a series of brutal, baffling murders. It is not a negative depiction of lesbians and bisexuals."[3]

The ethicist's task is to evaluate the moral claims advanced by the gay rights groups (which held the welfare of their public uppermost), the mayors of New York and San Francisco (who must make political decisions based on the interests of the city as a whole), and the filmmakers (interested in creative and artistic integrity).

Gays could hardly object to *Cruising* merely because it exposed a distasteful, violent side of one of their fringe subcultures. Initially, the gay community felt that Friedkin was creating a sensationalized version of truth, but eventually these objections were waived. Indeed, a public examination of any culture—whether the deviant brutishness of sadomasochism or the redemptive idealism of Boys' Town—is fair game for the movie industry. Dramatization of cultures should be true to the spirit of the group under examination, and if the film is critical, the criticism should be fair, not based on wild exaggerations or naive stereotypes.

New York's mayor seemed to base his argument on the utilitarian principle. A healthy city budget serves the interests of all the people, and film licenses contribute to that end. The moral content of the film is not the city's concern. Whereas the prospect of a city official censoring a filmmaker's work is ominous and unacceptable, the mayor's confusion of means and ends cannot stand up to ethical scrutiny. A healthy city budget is indeed laudable, but not at the expense of common decency. For example, a city would be condemned for importing and selling slaves in order to raise revenue. No calculus of benefit justifies slavery today. Sadomasochism per se, though it involves supposedly consenting adults, involves the same kind of moral condemnation and should not be a means of public revenue-making. Can films about S-M barbarity claim immunity from the same moral charges?

In the case of *Basic Instinct*, the problem centered on fairness and balance. Why should a film portray women as evil and men as good, or women as lesbian and men as straight, or women as killers and men as saviors? What would such images mean as they circulated throughout the culture? Said one protester: "We have never told studios to never make gay and lesbian villains. But why can't they have a person who is gay who is also a cop and who is obviously not sick?"

A case similar in issue, if not in setting, arose when director Peter Weir took a movie production crew to Lancaster County, Pennsylvania, to shoot the murder mystery *Witness*. In the film, Philadelphia detective John Book (played by Harrison Ford) seeks refuge on an Amish farm and falls in love with a young widow (played by Kelly McGillis). The Pennsylvania Bureau of Motion Pictures has been among the nation's most aggressive promotional units, and its success in attracting Weir and Paramount was the result of hard work. But the Amish were not happy. Their problem was not the likelihood of minor misrepresentations or even the prospect of increased tourism disturbing their lifestyle. Their complaints were fundamental to a world view that regards mediated reality as an objectification of culture that leads to alienation. Drama is wrong, their bishops argued, because it obscures appearance and reality; it deceives. Violence is also wrong, and to watch dramatic violence is irrational. They also resented the intrusion of Paramount on fairness grounds. "We have done nothing against these people [Paramount]. How would they like for us to come and invade their privacy and expose their way of living to the whole world?"[4]

The filmmaker's concern for integrity and freedom is a social value that needs jealous guarding. Artistic freedom has been a long time in coming, and its legal status today is reasonably secure. Its moral status is more difficult to evaluate, simply because it enjoys legal sanction. At a minimum, one could argue that the purpose of art is to explore the meaning of humanness, its qualities and ambiguities, in such a way as to move the quest for meaning toward an ethically justifiable goal. This restriction excludes art for the sake of exploiting an audience; it even argues against art for the sole end of profit-making. Friedkin and Verhoeven may quarrel with the "in such a way" clause, but an ethicist would insist that all creative effort is goal directed. Hollywood filmmakers and city administrators should make their true goals a part of the conversation.

77. CABLE TV AND SEX

Academy Cablevision began service in a Midwestern city of a half million in the mid-1980s. Nearly a decade later it began to offer "Telecinema." For a monthly fee of $7.95, customers could get a converter box with a key enabling them to pick up four extra channels: one a children's channel; two offering neighborhood cinematic fare; and Channel F, described by Academy's program director as its "X-rated service." Debra MacDonald reviews and purchases movies for Channel F. She explained:

> Nudity, innuendoes, and a little blood—nothing more. Our policy is to show no graphic or oral sex, no penetration, and no male frontal nudity or erections. Those are the guidelines our lawyers advised, and the city goes along with it. Sure, they monitor us. And if the city doesn't like a movie, we pull it.
>
> Our typical titles are things like *Campus Playmates* and *Swinging Playmates*, the stuff you might see at a drive-in. We definitely stay away from the movies shown in art theaters, although several of our customers actually wanted more males and more explicit sex. I remember a letter from a 65-year-old woman who said that she and her husband enjoyed the adult movies, but they would like to see more male frontal nudity. So we have all kinds of people watching, but many of them wouldn't be caught dead walking into an adult movie house.

Because Telecinema uses a converter box with a key, parents can control family viewing. Children cannot inadvertently (or purposefully) tune in adult movies. But the main reason for the box and key is not protection of children, said MacDonald. It is the protection of the customer's monthly bill. "Our subscribers don't want a babysitter coming over and rolling up a twenty-dollar bill on Telecinema," she explained. If parents really want to protect children, they have the option of getting a filter on the box that would eliminate Channel F altogether. But no one has ever requested that, said MacDonald. She added:

> We're all kind of glad that Madonna's video—the "Justify My Love" thing—never made it on MTV. It takes the pressure off when someone else up the line makes the decision. We would have carried it, sure, but people would have complained. They would have said that MTV was offering better stuff than Channel F.[5]

An ethicist might initially ask whether the viewing of such programs by informed adults constitutes a genuine dilemma at all. If Channel F is properly controlled and the viewer sufficiently informed, there should be no unconsenting viewers.

Control and information become two key elements in the ethicist's approach to the question. Unlike a movie house, cable television has no brightly colored marquees alerting every passerby to the promiscuity of the product. Cable is more intrusive than a movie theater, more accessible, less ritualistic; watching cable requires less of a commitment from its viewers than going to a theater. And consumers have control of the product so only those who want it get it (after certain other minimal conditions such as age or parental supervision are met).

An ethicist might also argue that a cable company issue a specific policy regarding its adult channel. How much sex is allowed? A stated policy would alert viewers to the product and allow them the freedom of informed choice.

No ethical framework except hedonism would advocate that the values portrayed in most sex thrillers become the social norm. And hedonism, because it focuses on greed and denies the individual's responsibility to the social whole, is not a moral option. Under any moral framework, control and information become minimum conditions for sexual content on the television screen.

Debra MacDonald was delighted to avoid the decision over Madonna's controversial music video. "Justify My Love" was a sexual escapade, a stream-of-consciousness experience on tape, a let-your-imagination-go video that some acclaimed as art and others called pornography. By now Justice Potter Stewart's famous line about obscenity, "I know it when I see it," seems to apply—the judgment of moral culpability is in the eye of the beholder. Yet Debra knew that her own cable company would be the first line of attack if viewers considered Madonna too experimental. Surely there is a place for art that reaches far beyond a Clark Gable love story, but even here, such art should be identified and its access controlled.

Although a viewer's personal ethics may argue rigorously against sexual brutishness, imposing a sexual ethic on the public raises other concerns. Our society regulates gambling, a business venture that makes no claim to moral foundations. To permit gambling operations the same freedom of enterprise we give to ice cream shops would be to expose ourselves to dangerous and destructive impulses. If we control a casino cruise ship, can we not by the same logic sanction sexual fare on the television, assuming there is sufficient control and information to protect the unsuspecting viewer?

Perhaps the greatest good for the greatest number is a principle that would allow us this option. If viewers are consenting and informed adults, and if nonviewers are not being intimidated, let the buyer beware. Applying the golden mean, we may also argue on behalf of a sexually stimulating movie, after safeguards are observed. Some might argue that scintillating movies that are rated R are a reasonable compromise between the truly obscene and the altogether sexless.

Television is less adept, perhaps even negligent, at developing sexually mature drama that respects the persons-as-ends principle. Here is where the ultimate test is rendered. Movies without a responsible sex ethic may pose little public menace, but the viewer is the loser; the one who feeds an appetite for brutality and greed is the tragic victim. The persons-as-ends principle, or "do unto others," assumes that the self is also well cared for. The principle cannot condone self-injury, even if the self wills it and no one other than the self is intimidated.

78. SHOW ME *AND PRESSURES ON LIBRARIES*

Folks in Oak Lawn, a south Chicago suburb, were incensed. The book *Show Me* was now available in the local public libraries, and—worse—it was being read by children.

Show Me is a picture book.[6] Full-page photos of teenagers in various sexual acts—masturbation, oral sex, and so forth—are used to teach reproduction and anatomy. Younger children explore each other's genitals. Photos of erections and insertions teach the joys of sexual exploration. A commentary by Dr. Helga Fleischhauer-Hardt explained that parents should use the book with children as part of the process of teaching kids about their sexuality. "In no way can looking at the pictures damage a child, even if he or she does not yet understand them," she wrote.

According to protesting parents, the actual use being made of the book by its mostly younger readers had little to do with academic physiology. Children were observed giggling over its contents, perhaps enjoying a salacious moment not intended by the author. Indeed, when librarian James O'Brien responded to the first wave of protests, he discovered that both copies were "absent from the library without benefit of check-out."

But the books' disappearance did not quiet the protest. State Representative Jane Barnes joined a group of concerned Oak Lawn residents who claimed *Show Me* was obscene and pornographic. O'Brien was ordered by the Village Library Board to investigate the allegations.

During the weeks that followed, the media turned out for board meetings as never before. So did townspeople. Security guards and the fire marshal got involved in crowd control, and a referendum to increase the library's tax base was soundly defeated.

Finally, the Oak Lawn Library agreed to place *Show Me* in the office of the children's librarian and to lend it only to adults and parents. Nonetheless, Representative Barnes pushed a bill through an Illinois House committee that would have held librarians liable for criminal prosecution under obscenity laws, while State Senator Jeremiah Joyce did the same in the Illinois Senate. Neither bill passed.

Response from professional librarians and others concerned about censorship was understandably strong. Judith Krug, executive director of the American Library Association's Office of Intellectual Freedom, claimed that the bill would have a "chilling effect" on librarians' rights. The *Chicago Sun-Times* called Joyce's effort a "stupid bill . . . insidious. . . . It lets book-banners bare their fangs and it could intimidate librarians and library boards into censoring good literature."[7]

The issues surrounding book censorship have a long and complicated history. The liberal reaction in seventeenth-century England was against book censorship primarily. Limiting the reproduction and distribution of heretical books was, long before that, the domain of established religious bodies. Many contemporary political regimes exercise a censorship over books that is more vicious and complete than medieval monasteries ever dreamed. So the battle still rages between an unrestrained freedom of expression, full-fledged censorship, and a middle ground wherein freedom is given wide berth but restricted for reasons that appear to be in a community's public interest.

Pragmatists would ask about the value of Fleischhauer-Hardt's thesis, but research, typically, disputes any claims to value or makes such claims ambiguous. A national survey conducted by the Family Research Council showed higher teenage pregnancy rates among those who participated in programs at family planning clinics, linking information to unwanted pregnancies. In a different study on AIDS-related information programs, researchers found that use of condoms by teens actually diminished after exposure to information. Of the teens who did change behavior, only one in five altered behavior to reduce the chance of exposure to HIV. Summarizing several tests of the efficacy of sex education, researchers reported in *American Psychologist* that neither positive nor negative effects, such as measurable behavioral change, have been demonstrated.[8] Should controls on sex information therefore be stronger, lighter, or unchanged?

When professional librarians are asked for an opinion, the debate often turns acrimonious. Feelings are strong and accusations are not always helpful in moving toward principled answers. An article in the *Library Journal*, for example, uses *ad hominem* tactics to explain the rationale of those who would keep certain books from general circulation. The article suggests that a censor is a person with "some suppressed impulses which he often wishes others to suppress also."[9] Modern censors keep alive the spirit of Puritan New England, with its oppressive tangle of dark, subliminal, masochistic drives, according to the article.

The American Library Association (ALA) has been extremely cautious over the influence of groups like Citizens United for Responsible Education and the National Congress for Academic Excellence. The ALA has characterized such public interest groups as right-wing do-gooders who seek to encroach on librarians' professional domain. Said the ALA:

> The crucial point is that these educational pressure groups, like other right-of-center pressure groups, view "the others"—be they professional educators, students, women—as unable to reason, unable to choose from the bewildering array of often contradictory material on a given issue. They seem to see themselves as the guardians and proponents of the correct idea.[10]

Public pressure groups hold that professionals have imported liberal values not indigenous to the communities they serve. To return control of educational and library facilities to parents and communities seems to them a reasonable demand, however threatening it may be to the outside professional.

A socially responsible public library system cannot be oblivious to the tastes and sensitivities of its community of patrons. To claim that professional privilege or expertise should dominate library policy decisions is to circumvent Rawls's rule that justice is approached only in negotiations that have excluded the social differences factor. That principle might be implemented by asking a third party to negotiate between competing value groups. Such third parties could well be professional persons such as teachers, social workers, clergy, or library and publishing scholars. Third-party groups might be more successful in finding ways to offer reading material that challenges traditional ideas without subverting deeply held values.

Certainly books on sexual practice for adults are considered legitimate for most community libraries. However, youngsters receiving first training in the meaning of sexuality need to inherit values that many parents still make it their goal to provide. Public libraries should not write their mission so broadly as to compete against the value systems of families in this delicate matter. *Show Me* cannot provide the moral framework for sexual instruction that a family can. The book, like sex itself, should not be a matter of idle and superficial curiosity, available to any youngster who knows of its presence. The persons-as-ends principle is not upheld when the sexual imagination turns exploitative, and no reasonable person could wish that all youngsters learn to imitate the apparent freedom of the models used in *Show Me*.

NOTES

1. William Ernest Hocking, "The Meaning of Liberalism: An Essay in Definition," in *Liberal Theology: An Appraisal*, eds. David E. Roberts and Henry P. Van Dusen (New York: Charles Scribner's Sons, 1942), pp. 54-55.
2. Details of this case are described in *Los Angeles Times*, 19 June 1992, F1; 24 June 1992, B3; *New York Times* 19 June 1992, C24; 20 June 1992, sec. 1, p. 9; 30 June 1992, A21; 30 July 1992, C13; *Washington Post*, 25 June 1992, C1; *Rolling Stone,* 20 August 1992, pp. 29-32; *Chicago Tribune*, 4 April 1993, sec. 13, p. 4.
3. Quotations are taken from *New York Times*, 26 July 1979, B7; *New York Times*, 4 May 1991, "Arts," p. 11; *Washington Post*, 4 June 1991, B1.
4. John Hostetler and Donald Kraybill, "Hollywood Markets the Amish," in *Image Ethics*, eds. Larry Gross et al. (New York: Oxford University Press, 1988), pp. 226-235.
5. This case is based on an interview with a cable company director who wished to remain unidentified, along with her company. Names used here are fictitious.
6. *Show Me! A Picture Book of Sex for Children and Parents,* photography by Will McBride, text by Helga Fleischhauer-Hardt (New York: St. Martin's Press, 1975).
7. Material for this case was drawn from a paper by James M. O'Brien, head librarian, Oak Lawn Public Library, "A Chronological History of a Censorship Challenge"; *Chicago Sun-Times,* 3 December 1980, p. 16; and 5 December 1980, p. 51.
8. Joseph A. Olsen and Stan E. Weed, "Effects of Family Planning Programs for Teenagers on Adolescent Birth and Pregnancy Rates," *Family Perspective* 20 (Fall 1986): 153-195.

See also June A. Flora and Carl E. Thoresen, "Reducing the Risk of AIDS in Adolescents," *American Psychologist* 43 (November 1988): 965; and Jeanne Brooks-Gunn and Frank F. Furstenberg, Jr., "Adolescent Sexual Behavior," *American Psychologist* 44 (February 1989): 249.

9. Eli M. Oboler, "Paternalistic Morality and Censorship," *Library Journal*, 1 September 1973, p. 2397.

10. American Library Association statement, quoted in Susan Wagner, "Right-of-Center Censorship Increasing, ALA Finds," *Publishers Weekly*, 13 February 1978, p. 58.

Epilogue

Questions of social ethics have always been the subtext of news stories, advertising messages, and entertainment programs, but the last generation of newspaper readers and television viewers has come to discover that ethics of the media is a big news story too. A financial reporter is nabbed for passing corporate secrets to eager investors, and news columns wonder about other press perks. A network news host asks two young adults—one a convicted rapist and the other his former accuser—if they care to embrace, and the nation groans in disdain. Automobile ads, mum on quality, tout image adventure. The stories go on.

The approach to media ethics argued in the cases and commentaries in this book links itself strongly to a notion concerning media and public life called *social responsibility theory*. Social responsibility has been an important theme in the life of peoples and nations since the Greek peripatetics. A century ago it was used in England to call for prison and legal reform. Robert Hutchins and his Commission on Freedom of the Press used it prominently in their report, *A Free and Responsible Press* (1947). The term captures the two sides of a classic democratic dilemma: A press free of all constraints could easily run amok in its own drive for power and profit; a press too constrained by the power of the state would fail to achieve its lofty mission—informing citizens—and would turn the clock back to the dreaded Star Chamber. But free of state control and responsible to the public for essential democratic services, the press could flourish and the people's delicate experiment in democracy could mature. "Social responsibility" became an appeal to the ethics of telling the truth over making profits, telling all the truth over exposing special interests, and practicing truthtelling with the flinty eye of fairness that recognizes how hard it is to hit the truth dead center.

For all its potential, the social responsibility theory of the media has had a stadium of detractors for every player on the field. The press itself was scornful of Hutchins's work. (The commission's benefactor, Henry Luce, graded its output "a gentleman's 'C' and no better.") Academics have challenged its misty appeal to broad coverage and public involvement. One astute critic argued that the theory "reaffirms the existing social order while at the same time providing the cloak of moral rectitude for those who claim to follow the doctrine."[1] To be powerful, an idea cannot be merely a garment.

A socially responsible press is a medium in tension, conscious of its obligations to enlighten readers and viewers and all too aware of its deadlines and competitors. No real news event follows a textbook case study. Each time a reporter goes out or an ad agent begins selling a campaign, something new is happening. In this frenzied world, how can "obligation to truth" or "comprehensive coverage of minority groups" hope to hold its own against "get the quote" and "shoot the tear-jerking photo"? How can truthtelling be allowed to give a competitor an advertising edge? How can respect for minorities be written into television comedy? Somewhere in the sorting out of these media imperatives, a practitioner must begin to assign priorities—and then live by them. That process is called *moral reasoning.* We contend that journalists, advertising executives, public relations practitioners, and entertainment programmers should be among the best-trained moral thinkers in the land.

In an address to journalism educators on terrorism and the media, Fred W. Friendly argued that clever investigative techniques are not enough: "We need to make journalists *think.*" The thrill of the craft—"getting the goods on the bad guys"—must be linked to the satisfaction of achieving a professional's "insight and discipline."[2] Friendly was echoing the concerns of a print media colleague, Charles Seib, former *Washington Post* ombudsman, who urged less emphasis on such skills as copy editing, editorial writing, even newswriting, and "more emphasis on more basic matters, personal integrity, the making of ethical judgment. . . . Ethical quandaries are much more significant aspects of the journalist's real world . . . and much more difficult matters" than journalism schools have realized.[3]

The media serve a broad purpose in democratic life. As our technological society becomes increasingly complex, we expect the press to inform us fully on all issues. We need accounts of our common public life, enlightened consumer information, and entertainment programs with redeeming value. Newspapers, videotext, magazines, interactive cable, network television, and the now ubiquitous personal computer together form a paramount social institution, so deeply embedded that we label our present era, for better or worse, "the information age." In order to measure and critique this social enterprise meaningfully, we have operated in this volume from the perspective of social ethics. With the Potter Box as a springboard, we have advocated a wide-angled type of moral reasoning compatible with the media's informational and entertainment missions.

Increasing interest in professional ethics—ethical reasoning concerning job-related questions—has not always led to a deepening of ethical reflection and a broadening of moral concern. Some conversations about sources, truthtelling, and privacy are short indeed. It is important to understand why journalists and professionals in persuasion and entertainment alternately care about and resist turning the moral spotlight on their work.

Nobody likes to be told what to do or think, least of all the press. But that objection aside, the following are some common responses to questions of professional conduct, elaborated in terms of what those responses mean to many people in communications industries.

1. If I don't hurt anyone, I've done okay.

Meaning: I have an important job to perform that demands skill with words, shapes, colors, graphics, and continuity. I want to do the best I can as an artist, and as long as nobody is deliberately harmed by what I do, the moral element is satisfied. All other considerations are questions of aesthetics.

Comment: The moral quest that seeks to bring no harm to people is honorable but insufficient. Although it avoids adding to the considerable weight of human suffering in the world, it is less aggressive in identifying and resolving problems already there. Morality requires beneficence—that we do certain things and not merely avoid the hurtful. Morality also requires that we look at motivations and intentions, which are not always expressed in behaviors. The minimalist appeal to "cause no harm" is often blind to what sociologist Robert Bellah calls the "habits of the heart."

Journalists who use this approach to ethical reasoning usually mean something different than do advertising, public relations, and entertainment professionals. Most journalists understand that many of their stories will hurt someone in some way, so in the minds of journalists, this inclination to cause no harm is qualified to mean: cause no harm unnecessary to the public's need to know what is happening. This is an important qualification, but it still falls short of stipulating media's positive duties. And it does not indicate when harm may be necessary. This qualified statement also assumes a lot about the phenomenon called "the public," and we need to know more about why public information is deemed so important.

2. If I do what I feel is right, that's all a person can be expected to do.

Meaning: The world is full of competing moral systems and contradictory assertions about what is right and wrong. Arguing over these competing claims only leads to frustration. The point of morality is that each person has to do what he or she believes is right. Beyond that, you are imposing your answers on someone else, and that is wrong.

Comment: No moral system would suggest that people violate conscience. In that sense, doing what feels right is an important and probably universal moral guide. But it is not enough. First of all, our feelings can experience wild fluctuations not always within our control. During periods of disappointment, feelings toward the self vary widely. Or we may be brainwashed or drunk; feelings at those times would be disastrous guides for moral action. More important, the appeal to feelings isolates each person into an autonomous, self-enclosed moral system. Whereas some visions of the human person may point to this kind of individualism, this book insists that humans are accountable to each other, interdependent and not isolated selves. To lodge our ultimate moral appeal inside ourselves is to risk deception and isolation.

3. The Code of Ethics sits on my desk and hangs on the wall. I go strictly by the book.

Meaning: Test my conduct against an objective standard, and I'll smell like a rose. If the Code doesn't outlaw it, don't bother me. I respect the profession I'm in, but I don't have patience with introspective moral gnat-chasers who want all my internal vibrations to resonate with the angels. Let me do my job, and judge me by the standards of the profession.

Comment: Taking professional codes seriously is a much-needed antidote to moral individualism. Adjusting to commonly held standards generates an ethos of accountability that overcomes the deficits of egoism and holds open the possibility of ethical debate from a base of community norms. But a simple appeal to codes on desktops may be a shield against tough moral inquiry from outside the profession. Doctors alone do not create standards for doctors, nor lawyers for lawyers, and, thankfully, neither do politicians alone create moral standards for politicians. Professions need dialogue with each other, with citizens, and with wider communities of concern in order to inhibit a professional privilege that begins to detach itself from all other jurisdictions. In worst-case situations, the appeal to codes can be a ruse for business as usual. The mere fact that Shaka could command the immediate execution of any of his subjects, a social code commonly understood, does not make ancient Zulu law necessarily moral. Organizations are too prone to self-interest for us to accept the notion that all codes are genuinely inspired by disinterested ethical concerns.

4. Honesty demands that we cease all this hype about ethics and get to the heart of the matter: You get the story as best you can, write as fast as you can, and the rest is history. We have a job to do.

Meaning: My career is top priority.

Comment: Honest careerism may be a more virtuous path than feigning concern over the moral imagination but neglecting the duties that such reflection imposes. Careerism is not to be quickly despised, since it does have the benefit of directing a titanic wave of energy into a profession that cannot be satiated. As an alternative to lethargy or corruption, careerism has many attractive pluses, not the least of which are the personal rewards of meeting important goals and receiving acclaim for one's talents. Many professionals would find this fourth statement closest to their own disposition.

Yet we come back to the inadequacy of conducting one's life as though only the self and its needs mattered. In formal ethical theory, such an approach is called *hedonism.* Although the word suggests images of wild extravagance, it means simply that in a calculus of pleasure, only elements that promote the self's happiness get counted. Such an approach, if widely shared, would likely spell the end of responsible media practice and revive the era of hucksterism.

Perhaps this response points with keenest hindsight to the strategic problem of grounding our moral inquiry in norms. Apart from norms, ethics is a guess, a majority vote, or a personal choice. Norms give ethics a foundation and make moral claims obligatory. Norms eliminate the "every person for herself" modality as quickly as they question the professionalization motif that seeks autonomy from outsiders. Norms become the bedrock of ethical behavior and thinking, the sounding board and center point of dispute resolution. Norms also make claims on us that cannot be dismissed, only submerged or suppressed.

Our use of the Potter Box in the preceding cases involves grappling with norms. In the southeast quadrant, below loyalties and adjacent to professional and cultural values, rest norms. Why should the demands of social justice overrule some institutional concerns for profit? Norms become the substance of our appeal. Why should librarians exercise caution over displaying controversial books? Ultimately norms become the center of the argument.

Norms concern our picture of what reality is like—how everything got here and what the meaning of our lives is. If existence has mostly instrumental meaning, then norms concerning one's right to life, to medical or educational enhancements, will be based on one's productivity—that is, on one's instrumental value to others. If existence has intrinsic meaning, norms would carry different obligations and be based on different foundations.

Of course, not everyone agrees on how reality is constituted—thus, we also disagree on what norms reflect the reality in which we live. Because we want belief to be voluntarily adopted (not coerced), we hold freedom of speech and conscience to be a guiding social norm. But even this statement requires that we explain why beliefs ought not be forced on everyone. Some cultures obviously believe they should be.

In a pluralistic culture, many opinions and world views compete for public attention; sheer numbers sometimes discourage us from considering any of them. Intellectual detachment is said to provide the distance a communicator needs in order to see the world and its complexities objectively. In fact, all of us need some detachment in order to develop critical knowledge about our own intellectual commitments. On the other hand, living in perpetual detachment is impossible, for choices must be made and the grounds for making choices must be acknowledged. So our many harmonies coexist, competing for expression in public policy and appealing as best they can to the needs and aspirations of both true believers and skeptics. Pluralism, if you will, is God's gift to heretics.

In the Introduction, we selected five normative proposals with profound impact on our common civilization. In the cases, we suggested how those ethical norms might effect a morally justified conclusion to a genuine dilemma. For some cases, we worked with more than one norm. For others, we found common ground between two norms. At times we merely pointed to the normative dimension but were not explicit and did not flesh them out. Our intention was to coax readers into applying the ethical norms.

Journalism is a profession in search of norms. Advertising, public relations, and entertainment professionals are right there with news reporters in the hunt for foundations to moral claims. The search is complicated by the reality that most public communication projects need to respect a variety of responsible visions of truth and even to represent them to some degree in their pages or through airtime. Yet without norms, media ethics languishes. Is there a moral recipe that a film company or ad agency can adopt to provide normative grounding and pluralistic freedom?

We believe that helpful directions lie in the fuller notion of the human person as a communal being. Enlightened rationalism was a triumphal notion in the era of divine-right monarchy, but its emphasis on individual autonomy has tended to obscure the social and communal nature of the human person. One cannot read far into the writings of Hutchins commissioners like Hocking, Niebuhr, Shuster, or Hutchins himself without finding explicit reference to persons in community as a core element, an irreducible essential. Human beings are not, in fact, autonomous and isolated. Neither do bonds of community submerge the person in the soup of statism or tribalism, disallowing moral choice and replacing conscience with Leviathan. Rather, "persons in community" reflects the essential social bonds that define human life and acknowledges that persons are truly moral agents. The five normative principles woven through this book are, in a sense, alternative explanations of the person-community connection, with varying implications for how that connection ought to be expressed in the professions of culture formation.

Are these implications crystal clear and airtight? Any professional will describe the dangers. Looming from one side is the threat of prudery and its consequence: programming that portrays a false sense of innocence about human affairs. On the other side is moral anarchy, the abandonment of all moral principle except that of absolute freedom. Responsible media can ill afford the danger of either. Society is not served by the mindless dumping of its moral traditions; nor do we explore the moral life intelligently through casuistry or naiveté.

Our cases, therefore, present one of the most perplexing issues for a pluralistic culture: how to achieve moral continuity and, at the same time, moral exploration. If "culture" means anything, it means a common ground of moral understanding ordering the lives of diverse people. Media should both respect and challenge that common ground.

Especially in convoluted and stressful times, a continuing stream of questions and debates will catch news, advertising, public relations, and entertainment in its wake. As long as law-bending, stereotyping, and violence subvert our democratic experiment, media will find themselves in the storm center. Understanding communication ethics may be hard work with few direct incentives and no immediate material gains, but the media professional whose career includes its probing is serving the audience well: doing the good work of building a socially responsible press. On that premise this book is offered. Toward that end this book is only a short installment.

NOTES

1. Herbert Altschull, *Agents of Power* (White Plains, NY: Longman, 1984), p. 304.
2. From a speech at the Association for Education in Journalism and Mass Communication (AEJMC) annual meetings, Memphis, Tennessee, August 1985.
3. Speech to the Association for Education in Journalism, East Lansing, Michigan, 11 August 1981.

Recommended Reading

INTRODUCTION

Bayles, Michael. 1989. *Professional Ethics,* 2d ed. Belmont, CA: Wadsworth.
An overview, for upper-level undergraduates, of ethical issues faced by professionals as a group. Bayles examines the meaning of professional obligation and challenges the traditional norms that usually go unquestioned.

Betsworth, Roger G. 1990. *Social Ethics: An Examination of American Moral Traditions.* Louisville, KY: Westminster, John Knox Press.
Four cultural narratives are used to teach ethical thinking: the biblical story; the gospel of success; well-being and psychotherapy; and America's manifest destiny. Although theorists and concepts are not taught directly, these narratives emphasize ethical vision and a deep self-understanding as crucial to morality.

Bonevac, Daniel, William Boon, and Stephen Phillips, eds. 1992. *Beyond the Western Tradition: Readings in Moral and Political Philosophy.* Mountain View, CA: Mayfield.
Ancient (e.g., Confucius and Maimonides) and contemporary writings on ethical wisdom, virtuous character, and the good life. Divided into four major sections: African, West Asian and Southern Mediterranean, South Asian, and East Asian.

Bowie, Norman E. 1985. *Making Ethical Decisions.* New York: McGraw-Hill.
An anthology of classical and contemporary writers, organized around such important issues as relativism, respect for principles, morality, rights, virtue and justice, and equality. An effective companion text for courses in media ethics.

Callahan, Daniel, and Sissela Bok. 1980. *Ethics Teaching in Higher Education.* New York: Plenum.
Essays prepared for the Hastings Center Project on the Teaching of Ethics. Includes important chapters on the goals of ethics instruction, whistle-blowing, and the history of ethics in university curricula.

Carman, John, and Mark Juergensmeyer, eds. 1991. *Bibliography of Comparative Religious Ethics*. New York: Cambridge University Press.
Annotated entries are organized by religious tradition and cover each religion's central concepts. Includes both primary and secondary references.

Christians, Clifford G. 1991. "Communication Ethics," *Communication Research Trends* 11, 4:1–34.
Work in forty countries is cited in order to map out the current state-of-the-art in media ethics.

Dyck, Arthur, J. 1977. *On Human Care: An Introduction to Ethics*. Nashville, TN: Abingdon.
Uses the Potter Box to introduce ethical questions regarding world populations and the environment. In the process of dealing with issues in the medical profession, readers are confronted with the basic problems in ethical theory.

Gert, Bernard. 1989. *Morality: A New Justification of the Moral Rules*. New York: Oxford University Press.
Addressed primarily to the ordinary reader, Gert nonetheless develops a sophisticated theory of moral obligation. The book gives a set of ten moral rules that can be justified for all rational persons, rules such as don't kill, don't deceive, don't deprive of pleasure, and so forth.

Goldman, Alan H. 1980. *The Moral Foundations of Professional Ethics*. Totowa, NJ: Rowman & Littlefield.
Intelligent and careful defense of a rights-based theory of professional ethics in the liberal tradition. Focuses on the key issue—whether professions are governed by special moral principles that differ from our common moral framework.

Holmes, Robert L. 1993. *Basic Moral Philosophy*. Belmont, CA: Wadsworth.
Designed for students with no previous background in ethics. Introduces the main issues, concepts, and theories of Western moral philosophy. Includes excellent summaries of divine command theory, Kantianism, consequentialism, and the ethics of virtue.

Jaksa, James A., and Michael S. Pritchard. 1994. *Communication Ethics: Methods of Analysis*, 2d ed. Belmont, CA: Wadsworth.
A variety of case studies are included in each chapter, ranging from interpersonal to organizational communication. The central issue is the current crisis of confidence in spoken and written words as it affects the professions, public figures, and institutions.

Johannesen, Richard L. 1990. *Ethics in Human Communication*, 3d ed. Prospect Heights, IL: Waveland Press.
Places ethical responsibility in the context of political philosophy and communication theory. Includes cases and analysis of ethics codes.

Kultgen, John. 1988. *Ethics and Professionalism*. Philadelphia: University of Pennsylvania Press.
From a pragmatist perspective, examines institutional practices and rules in such areas as confidentiality, professional paternalism, social action, and the workplace.

Lebacqz, Karen. 1985. *Professional Ethics: Power and Paradox*. Nashville, TN: Abingdon.
A skillful blend of theory and practice examining rule morality, virtue and character, and professional structures.

MacIntyre, Alasdair. 1966. *A Short History of Ethics*. New York: Macmillan.
Outlines in a readable manner the history of moral philosophy in the Western tradition, from Homer in ancient Greece to twentieth-century ethicists.

Paterson, Philip, and Lee Wilkins. 1994. *Media Ethics: Issues and Cases,* 2d ed. Dubuque, IA: William C. Brown.
Thoughtful case studies and analyses from several media ethicists.

Rogers, Jack B., and Forrest E. Baird. 1981. *Introduction to Philosophy: A Case Method Approach.* San Francisco: Harper and Row.
A textbook introducing 12 major philosophers from Socrates to Wittgenstein through simulated cases, role-playing, questions, and a contemporary response.

Taylor, Paul W. 1975. *Principles of Ethics: An Introduction.* Encino, CA: Dickensen.
Well-written chapters for beginners. Provides excellent definitions of ethics, morals, and values. A good overview of utilitarian and Kantian ethics.

Tong, Rosemarie. 1993. *Feminine and Feminist Ethics.* Belmont, CA: Wadsworth.
Introductory chapters on the ways in which feminist ethics compares to traditional ethics. Excellent summaries of Gilligan's Ethics of Care, Noddings's Relational Ethics, Ruddick's maternal ethics, and other feminine and feminist approaches.

NEWS

Black, Jay, Ralph Barney, and Robert Steele. 1992. *SPJ Ethics Handbook.* SPJ National Headquarters, PO Box 77, Greencastle, IN 46135.
Handbook for working journalists and students that combines practical advice with codes of ethics and guiding principles. Case studies are included and readers instructed to work through them by asking ten questions and applying the principles.

Christians, Clifford G., and Catherine L. Covert. 1980. *Teaching Ethics in Journalism Education.* New York: Hastings Center Monograph.
Survey of ethics teaching and substantive issues in journalism ethics today. Outlines four instructional objectives.

Christians, Clifford G., John P. Ferré, and P. Mark Fackler. 1993. *Good News: Social Ethics and the Press.* New York: Oxford University Press.
This book develops a communitarian model for the press's context and structure. It is designed as a theoretical alternative to the individualistic approaches to media ethics that have dominated under the Enlightenment's influence.

Cooper, Thomas W. 1989. *Communication Ethics and Global Change.* New York: Longman.
Essays from 16 countries on important issues in media ethics. Overview chapters on the important international issues are included in sections I and III. Codes of Ethics included in the Appendix.

Elliott, Deni T., ed. 1986. *Responsible Journalism.* Beverly Hills, CA: Sage.
Nine essays by academics, examining issues in press theory and social responsibility.

Goodwin, H. Eugene, and Ron F. Smith. 1994. *Groping for Ethics in Journalism,* 3d ed. Ames: Iowa State University Press.
Explores a variety of issues: conflicts of interest, deception, misrepresentation, privacy, sources, and incompetence. Based on interviews with a wide-ranging sample of professionals and academics, and a review of the media codes and literature.

Hulteng, John L. 1985. *The Messenger's Motives: Ethical Problems of the News Media,* 2d ed. Englewood Cliffs, NJ: Prentice-Hall.
Built on a series of cases and illustrations that show how the media operate. Questions how successfully they live up to contemporary codes of ethics.

Klaidman, Stephen, and Tom L. Beauchamp. 1987. *The Virtuous Journalist.* New York: Oxford University Press.
Built around real-life cases, this volume describes the character traits and professional virtues needed for fair, truthful, and competent journalism.

Knowlton, Steven R., and Patrick R. Parsons, eds. 1994. *The Journalist's Moral Compass: Basic Principles.* Westport, CT: Praeger.
An anthology of 24 readings, from John Milton to John Merrill. Together they seek to describe the basic principles that govern contemporary American journalism. These common principles (many of them embodied in the SPJ Code of Ethics) are set against the major issues that challenge them.

Lambeth, Edmund B. 1991. *Committed Journalism: An Ethic for the Profession,* 2d ed. Bloomington: Indiana University Press.
Outlines a framework for ethical journalism from the codes, ideals, and best practice in the field.

Merrill, John C. 1989. *The Dialectic in Journalism: Toward a Responsible Use of Press Freedom.* Baton Rouge: Louisiana State University Press.
Examines the tension between responsible action and freedom in the context of the Western intellectual tradition.

Pippert, Wesley G. 1989. *An Ethics of News: A Reporter's Search for Truth.* Washington, DC: Georgetown University Press.
Analysis of ethical issues in news, based on author's personal experiences. Focuses on the issue of truthtelling.

Rivers, William L., Wilbur Schramm, and Clifford Christians. 1980. *Responsibility in Mass Communication,* 3d ed. New York: Harper and Row.
A classic text on media ethics that argues for the social responsibility option.

PERSUASION AND ADVERTISING

Baum, Robert J., Norman E. Bowie, and Deborah G. Johnson, eds. 1984. *Business and Professional Ethics Journal* 3, Spring/Summer.
Special double issue in which advertising professionals, educators, and philosophers discuss important topics: manipulative advertising, professional advertising content, and children as consumers.

Beauchamp, Thomas L., and Norman E. Bowie. 1983. "Ethical Issues in Advertising." In *Ethical Theory and Business,* 2d ed. Englewood Cliffs, NJ: Prentice-Hall.
Case studies, legal opinions, and essays on such ethical issues as deception and creating consumer demand.

Capitman, William. 1971. "Morality in Advertising—A Public Imperative," *MSU Business Topics,* Spring.
A Reply to Theodore Levitt.

Chonko, Lawrence B., Shelby D. Hunt, and Roy D. Howell. 1987. "Ethics and the American Advertising Federation Principles," *International Journal of Advertising,* October, pp. 255–274.
An important study examining the effectiveness of recent American Advertising Federation principles.

Cone, Fairfax. 1969. *With All Its Faults.* Boston: Little, Brown & Co.

A sensitive practitioner looks at his business from the vantage point of 40 years experience.

Gossage, Howard. 1986. *Is Advertising Worth Saving?* Urbana: University of Illinois Press.
A renowned practitioner and perceptive critic examines the philosophies and practices of his business and finds them wanting.

Jugenheimer, Donald W., Dean M. Krugman, Vincent P. Norris, and Kim B. Rotzoll. 1982. *Working Papers on Advertising and Ethics.* Papers presented at the AAAA Convention, University of Illinois at Urbana.
Suggests principles to guide advertising ethics and applies them to advertising organizations, the audience, and teaching.

Kottman, E. John. 1977. "The Parity Product—Advertising's Achilles Heel," *Journal of Advertising* 6:4, 34–39.
An examination of one of advertising's enduring ethical areas.

Levitt, Theodore. 1970. "The Morality (?) of Advertising," *Harvard Business Review*, July–August.
A provocative position on advertising as a form of "alleviating imagery."

Mander, Jerry. 1979. "Four Arguments for the Elimination of Advertising." In *Advertising and the Public,* ed. Kim Rotzoll. Urbana: University of Illinois Department of Advertising.
A major attack on four presumably inherent dimensions of the advertising process.

Modic, Stanley J. 1987. "Forget Ethics—And Succeed?" *Industry Week,* October 19, pp. 17–18.
A 1987 survey among *Industry Week* readers reveals that many felt business ethics were lower than two years earlier.

Ogilvy, David. 1963. *Confessions of an Advertising Man.* New York: Atheneum.
A literate statement of how advertising should be practiced, by a most influential modern practitioner.

Palmer, Edward, and Aimee Dorr, eds. 1980. *Children and the Faces of Television.* New York: Academic Press (especially chapters 15–21).
Seven authors examine the behavioral, political, and ethical dimensions of advertising to children.

Rotfeld, Herbert J., and Patrick R. Parsons. 1989. "Self Regulation and Magazine Advertising," *Journal of Advertising* 4, 33–41.
A major survey of magazines examines their acceptance policies.

Rotzoll, Kim, and Clifford Christians. 1980. "Advertising Agency Practitioners' Perceptions of Ethical Decisions," *Journalism Quarterly* 57, Autumn, 425–431.
On the basis of their research, the authors examine key ethical dimensions of advertising agency practice, as seen by the practitioners.

Rotzoll, Kim, James Haefner, and Charles Sandage. 1990. *Advertising in Contemporary Society,* 2d ed. Cincinnati: South-Western Publishing (especially chapters 1–4).
An explanation of advertising's roots in the market and the world view of classical liberalism; visions of advertising as an institution; the strains on advertising under the neo-liberal world view.

Terkel, Studs. 1975. *Working.* New York: Avon Books, pp. 112–147.
Among others Terkel interviews are six people involved in the advertising business.

Zanot, Eric. 1985. "Unseen but Effective Advertising Regulation: The Clearance Process," *Journal of Advertising* 4, 44–51.
Traces clearance procedures normally followed by major advertisers, agencies, and media.

Codes, Guidelines

The advertising business involves a wide array of guidelines, codes, and standards dealing with the legal and ethical dimensions of the process. These are some of the more important sources:

Council of Better Business Bureaus
845 Third Avenue
New York, NY 10022

American Advertising Federation, Inc.
1225 Connecticut Ave., NW
Washington, DC 20036

National Association of Broadcasters
1771 N Street, NW
Washington, DC 20036

Association of National Advertisers
155 East 44th Street
New York, NY 10017

PERSUASION AND PUBLIC RELATIONS

Baker, Lee W. 1993. *The Credibility Factor: Putting Ethics to Work in Public Relations.* Homewood, IL: Business One Irwin.
The major theme is that ethics—ethics codes, individual conscience, company guidelines, careful decision making—are the foundation for achieving credibility. Several examples of companies that prospered by taking ethics seriously. Filled with practical advice and a wide range of cases and illustrations.

Bernays, Edward L. 1923. *Crystallizing Public Opinion.* New York: Boni and Live Right.
———. 1965. *Biography of an Idea: Memoirs of Public Relations Council Edward L. Bernays.* New York: Simon and Schuster.
Bernays makes it clear how much the world depends on the proper formation of public attitudes.

Bivins, Thomas H. 1987. "Applying Ethical Theory to Public Relations," *Journal of Business Ethics* 6, 195-200.
———. 1988. "Professional Advocacy in Public Relations," *Business and Professional Ethics Journal* 6:1, 82-91.
———. 1989. "Ethical Implications of the Relationship of Purpose to Role and Function in Public Relations," *Journal of Business Ethics* 8, 65-73.
Examines public relations as a professional domain, and connects those features of its social role to the relevant ethical theories.

Creedon, Pamela J. 1989. *Women in Mass Communication: Challenging Gender Values.* Beverly Hills, CA: Sage Publications.
A book accounting for the increased number of women in mass media occupations, with several chapters contributed by public relations scholars.

Culbertson, Hugh M., Dennis Jeffers, Donna Stone, and Martin Terrell. 1993. *Social, Political, and Economic Contexts in Public Relations: Theory and Cases.* Hillsdale, NJ: Lawrence Erlbaum.

Attempts to explain public relations theory and practice in terms of the social sciences. Includes six detailed case studies, carefully chosen across a range of situations from police-communications relations to osteopathic medicine.

Ellul, Jacques. 1973. *Propaganda*. New York: Vintage.
Always innovative, Ellul explores public attitude formation as part of the larger social issue surrounding *la technique*.

Ferré, John P., and Shirley C. Willihnganz. 1991. *Public Relations and Ethics: A Bibliography*. Boston, MA: G. K. Hall and Co.
A comprehensive, annotated bibliography of 285 English-language sources on public relations and ethics.

Grunig, Larissa A. Forthcoming. "Toward the Philosophy of Public Relations." In *Rhetorical and Critical Approaches to Public Relations*, eds. Elizabeth Lance Toth and Robert L. Heath. Hillsdale, NJ: Lawrence Erlbaum.
First major attempt to construct a conceptual framework for studying public relations ethics. Influenced by a feminist perspective; argues that public relations involves not persuasion but an exchange of information.

Hiebert, Roy Eldon. 1966. *Courtier to the Crowd: The Story of Ivy Lee and the Development of Public Relations*. Ames, IA: State University Press.
The story of one of the founding geniuses in public relations.

Kruckeberg, Dean, and Kenneth Starck. 1988. *Public Relations and Community: A Reconstructed Theory*. New York: Praeger.
Explores the social responsibility of public relations practitioners in contemporary American society.

Lippmann, Walter. 1922. *Public Opinion*. New York: Macmillan.
This book sets the agenda for much of twentieth-century thinking on media in general and public relations in particular.

Olasky, Marvin N. 1987. *Corporate Public Relations: A New Historical Perspective*. Hillsdale, NJ: Lawrence Erlbaum.
Tells how public relations has contributed to our understanding of industry, from railroads to the movie business.

Sinclair, Upton. 1920. *The Brass Check*. Pasadena: CA.
No advocate of the profession of public relations, Sinclair was one of the first to tell us why we should be watchful.

ENTERTAINMENT

Alley, Robert S. 1977. *Television: Ethics for Hire?* Nashville TN: Abingdon.
Interviews with Norman Lear, Alan Alda, Earl Hamner, and others give insight into the aims and ethics of industry pace setters.

Cooper, Thomas W. 1988. *Television and Ethics: A Bibliography*. Boston: G. K. Hall and Co.
This volume cites 1,170 sources, many of them annotated, on all aspects of television and ethics.

DeLong, Thomas A. 1991. *Quiz Craze: America's Infatuation with Game Shows*. New York: Praeger.
History of radio and TV game shows from 1930 to the present. Lots of information about the personalities behind the programs.

Denzin, Norman. 1991. *Hollywood Shot by Shot: Alcoholism in American Cinema.* New York: Aldin de Gruyter.
A cultural studies approach to six eras of Hollywood stories about alcoholism. Denzin helps us understand how we came to regard alcoholism as a sickness.

Does Television Change History? 1987. Proceedings of the Second National Conference on Television and Ethics, 6 March, Emerson College, Boston, MA.
Attempts to distinguish documentary and docudrama, and evaluates the issues involved in ethically producing the latter.

Final Report of the Attorney General's Commission on Pornography. 1986. Nashville, TN: Rutledge Hill Press.
An attempt by experts summoned during the Reagan administration to speak definitively on the dangers of pornography.

Gross, Larry, John Stuart Katz, and Jay Ruby, eds. 1988. *Image Ethics: The Moral Rights of Subjects in Photographs, Film, and Television.* New York: Oxford University Press.
Original essays on the ethics of representation viewing moral questions in terms of the subject rather than the rights of producers and filmmakers.

Holbrook, Morris B. 1993. *Daytime Television Gameshows and the Celebration of Merchandise: "The Price is Right."* Bowling Green, OH: Popular Press.
American consumerism reflected in a popular show, by a marketing scholar who frankly does not like what he sees.

Jhally, Sut, and Justin Lewis. 1992. *Enlightened Racism: The Cosby Show, Audiences, and the Myth of the American Dream.* Boulder, CO: Westview.
How prime-time television presents race and class images. This case study examines the popular show starring Bill Cosby and Felicia Rashad.

Mander, Jerry. 1978. *Four Arguments for the Elimination of Television.* New York: Morrow.
Some ideas are harmed by their treatment on television, says the author. Four provocative chapters and a radical conclusion.

Newcomb, Horace, and Robert Alley. 1983. *The Producer's Medium: Conversations with Creators of American TV.* New York: Oxford University Press.
Interviews with notable producers (e.g., Norman Lear, Richard Levinson, William Link, and Garry Marshall) about the values they express as artists.

Phelan, John M. 1980. *Disenchantment: Meaning and Morality in the Media.* New York: Hastings House.
Proposing that a public philosophy arises from the humanities, Phelan addresses the problems of new technology and cultural freedom.

Robinson, Deanna Campbell, Elizabeth B. Buck, Marlene Cuthbert, and the International Communication and Youth Consortium. 1991. *Music at the Margins: Popular Music and Global Cultural Diversity.* Newberg Park, CA: Sage.
Forty scholars from twenty countries analyze the social construction of popular music meanings, and the industrial structure that produces and distributes the product.

Thayer, Lee, ed. 1980. *Ethics, Morality, and the Media.* New York: Hastings House.
Twenty-seven essays and speeches—most by practitioners on the current status of media ethics, with a long introduction ("Notes on American Culture") by the editor.

Index

About the Authors

Clifford G. Christians is a professor of communications at the University of Illinois, Urbana-Champaign, where he directs the doctoral program in communications and heads the media studies unit. He has a B.A. in classics, a B.D. and Th.M. in theology, an M.A. in sociolinguistics from Southern California, and a Ph.D. in communications from Illinois. He has been a visiting scholar in philosophical ethics at Princeton University and in social ethics at the University of Chicago. He has published essays on various aspects of mass communication (including ethics) in *Journalism Monographs, Journal of Broadcasting, Journalism History, Journal of Communication, Journal of Mass Media Ethics, Communication,* and *International Journal of Mass Communication Research.* He has coauthored a third edition of Rivers and Schramm's *Responsibility in Mass Communication;* has coauthored *Jacques Ellul: Interpretive Essays* with Jay Van Hook; and has written *Teaching Ethics in Journalism Education* with Catherine Covert. He contributed the article "Media Ethics" to the *International Encyclopedia of Communications.* He is coauthor of *Good News: Social Ethics and the Press* (Oxford, 1993).

Mark Fackler is associate professor of communications at Wheaton (Illinois) College. He holds an A.B. in philosophy, an M.A. in communications, an M.A. in theology, and a Ph.D. in communications from the University of Illinois. His professional experience includes writing for magazines and radio, and public relations. He has been guest lecturer at the Poynter Institute for Media Studies. He is coauthor of *Good News: Social Ethics and the Press* (Oxford, 1993).

Kim B. Rotzoll is dean of the College of Communications and professor of advertising at the University of Illinois, Urbana-Champaign. He holds a B.A. in advertising, an M.A. in journalism, and a Ph.D. in sociology from Pennsylvania

349

State University. He is the senior author of *Advertising in Contemporary Society* and an author of *Advertising Theory and Practice*. He has published articles in *Journal of Advertising*, *Journal of Advertising Research*, *Journal of Consumer Affairs*, *Journalism Quarterly*, *Christian Century*, *Journalism Educator*, *Journal of Advertising History*, and several anthologies. His teaching and speaking interests concern advertising as a social and economic institution, and advertising ethics as well as advertising history. He has been a guest lecturer in China, Denmark, and Bahrain.